Special Offer from MKS

MKS has earned a reputation for providing high-quality, user friendly software tools to the computing environment. As part of our commitment to provide leading-edge software technology, MKS is pleased to offer owners of "Learning UNIX - Second Edition" **a 20% discount off the suggested retail price of all MKS products.**

Take your new understanding of the powerful world of UNIX one step further with MKS Toolkit. MKS Toolkit is a powerful set of software tools designed to make computing tasks quick and easy on your PC. MKS Toolkit gives you:

- more than 190 software development tools including the KornShell, awk, awkc, grep and vi
- MKS UUCP communications utility and nr news reader
- Visual differencing

So take advantage of this special offer from MKS and call today for your own copy of MKS Toolkit. Join the thousands of users around the world and pack more power in your PC.

Other fine products from MKS include:

MKS RCS — revision control/configuration management software with Visual Differencer and MKS Make

MKS LEX & YACC — compiler construction tools

MKS Data Express — DOS and Windows based communications utilities

For more information on MKS products and services, or for multi-user pricing, call **1-800-265-2797 (US & Canada) or 519-884-2251.**

This certificate entitles the purchaser of
"Learning UNIX"
to a 20% savings off the retail price
of any MKS product,
when purchased directly from
MKS using Visa, MasterCard or American Express.

This offer does not apply to upgrade products and
cannot be used in conjunction with any other
special offer from MKS.

Take advantage of this savings today by calling MKS at
1-800-265-2797 (continental US & Canada) or
519-884-2251.

For more information on MKS products and services contact:

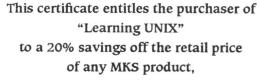

35 King Street North
Waterloo, ONT N2J 2W9
Phone (519) 884-2251
FAX (519) 884-8861

Fax: (519) 884-8861
Internet: inquiry@mks.com
CompuServe User ID: 73260,1043
BIX User Name: MKS
BBS: (519) 884-2861

LEARNING UNIX®

Second Edition

LEARNING UNIX®

Second Edition

James Gardner

A Division of Prentice Hall Computer Publishing
201 West 103rd Street, Indianapolis, Indiana 46290

Dedicated to
all the folks at MKS.
Keep up the good
work!

Publisher
Richard K. Swadley

Acquisitions Manager
Jordan Gold

Development Editor
Phillip W. Paxton

Production Editor
Katherine Stuart Ewing

Formatters
Pat Whitmer and Holly Paxton

Editorial Assistant
Lynnette Quinn

Technical Editor
Rich Jones

Marketing Manager
Greg Wiegand

Cover Designer
Dan Armstrong

Book Designer
Michele Laseau

**Director of Production
and Manufacturing**
Jeff Valler

Imprint Manager
Kelli Widdifield

Production Analyst
Mary Beth Wakefield

Proofreading/Indexing Coordinator
Joelynn Gifford

Graphics Image Specialists
Tim Montgomery
Dennis Sheehan
Sue VandeWalle

Production
Nick Anderson
Ayrika Bryant
Rich Evers
Kim Hannel
Srephanie J. McComb
Juli Pavey
Linda Quigley
Kim Scott
Susan Springer
Suzanne Tully
Dennis Wesner

Indexers
John Sleeva
Suzanne Snyder

OVERVIEW

C O N T E N T S

Second Edition

PREFACE TO THE FIRST EDITION

Learning something new can start out being exciting, but it can become tedious if there is no way to experiment, investigate, practice, and eventually use the new information. With the superb combination of text and software that is available in this book, you have the best of all affordable and portable environments to learn and to enjoy UNIX. *Learning UNIX*; this book couldn't have a better title.

I have been cheering the development of this book since the beginning of the project. Why? Because I love the UNIX world and have the greatest respect for the work of Mortice Kern Systems (MKS—the developer of the UNIX tools for MS-DOS that are included with this book). Whenever I have to use a DOS system for any extended period, I install the MKS Toolkit, at least to maintain my sanity, if not for the convenience. It isn't just the MKS software that I like; it is the excellent documentation as well, much of which is the work of Jim Gardner. Now, in this book, we see that Mr. Gardner is good at writing more than man pages (the standardized format of the online UNIX reference manual); he has brought a clarity to UNIX utilities that comes only from an intimate familiarity and a style that is appealing to anyone.

This book not only complements the many fine UNIX books published by Sams Publishing, but stands on its own with honor.

Unlike MS-DOS, UNIX is more than a program loader. The UNIX utilities are what have made UNIX so popular. Because the utilities are written so that they can be tied together to perform complex tasks, the UNIX environment is synergistic; it is more than the sum of its parts. The best way to reach a level of competence with these tools is to use them separately and together to solve as many problems as you can. Once you become familiar with the UNIX KornShell, you will never want to see an MS-DOS prompt again. Once you begin solving your data and text input, output, and translation problems by using the UNIX utilities rather than writing programs in C (of some other programming language), you will begin to appreciate UNIX as I do.

Read this book; use these tools; and enjoy the flexible, configurable, extensible and practical world of UNIX.

Ben Smith
Editor of *BYTE Magazine* and author of *UNIX Step-by-Step*
Peterborough, NH, 1991

INTRODUCTION

Learning UNIX guides you through a series of hands-on explorations that are geared toward helping you learn to use the UNIX operating system productively...but you don't need a UNIX machine to do the work. This book includes a software package that simulates UNIX software but runs on DOS or PC DOS on an ordinary IBM PC or IBM-compatible computer.

This book provides everything you need to make your DOS machine look and feel like UNIX. There are several benefits to this approach.

> If you are curious about UNIX, you can "test the waters" without having to spend time or money to get a UNIX machine.

> Sites that are planning to migrate to UNIX in whole or in part can prepare people for the transition using their current DOS systems.

> You can mix UNIX work with DOS work. For example, you can use your normal DOS applications in the usual way, but if you have a task that is easier to do with UNIX commands, you can use the UNIX-simulation software to get the job done.

In short, this book's approach gives you the power of UNIX with the availability and familiarity of DOS.

DOS and UNIX Comparisons

If you're already a DOS user, you'll be pleased with this book's constant cross-references between DOS and UNIX. This book shows you how UNIX ideas compare to DOS ideas: where the two systems are similar and where they are different.

The differences can be considerable or they can be subtle. This book will explain new concepts carefully and completely so that you'll have no trouble with the large-scale differences between the systems...and it will guide you around the booby traps that lie in wait for DOS users who are unaware of technical subtleties.

A Level Playing Field

One of the greatest strengths of UNIX is its potential for customization. There are many different ways you can tailor the system to your needs and preferences. When you start using an existing UNIX system, it probably won't work exactly the way that the manuals describe because someone else may have adjusted the system to his or her tastes. This can bewilder newcomers.

You don't have to worry about such complications if you use the software that comes with this book. You won't have to cope with someone else's UNIX customizations, because you'll be on DOS. The software that comes with this book starts everyone with the same initial setup. I will certainly talk about customization and show how you can fine-tune the software to work the way you want; but that comes in later chapters, after you've gained some experience with the system. In this way, you can start your UNIX education on solid ground: a level playing field for everyone.

What This Book Deals With

Learning UNIX looks at the software that the majority of UNIX users work with on a daily basis. Unfortunately, there are important UNIX applications that are outside the scope of this book. For example, I don't discuss standard UNIX compilers or the wealth of other programming tools available on the system. Such software is an important part of UNIX, but only for a limited segment of the user population. This book concentrates on the features of UNIX that everyone can use.

The book therefore begins with several chapters discussing such basics as

How to log on and start working with UNIX

How UNIX files are organized and used

Popular commands for examining and manipulating files

The many ways to combine simple commands to perform complex operations

The vi screen editor, probably the most widely used text editor available under UNIX

The KornShell

After dealing with the fundamentals, you will be ready for the main event: several chapters discussing the *KornShell.* UNIX shells are programs that run other programs. To a large extent, your shell determines the "face" that UNIX presents to you. The shell is responsible for the system's look and feel.

Most UNIX systems provide several different shells, and therefore several different "faces." With a collection of shells to choose from, users can pick the one that best fits their needs and tastes. Because of limited time and space, this book looks at only one shell: the KornShell.

The KornShell is comparatively new, but its popularity is growing rapidly. It is a descendant of the Bourne Shell, one of the first UNIX shells and one that is still a favorite for many people. The chapters on the KornShell will show you the power and versatility of the shell, and suggest ways you can use it to best effect. The KornShell is your key to productivity with UNIX, and this book will make sure that you understand its vast potential.

Through Darkest UNIX, Armed Only with Manual Pages

I've said that the purpose of this book is to guide you through a series of hands-on explorations. Exploring lets you determine how UNIX software can help you in your work. Therefore, the first two parts of this book lead you on a series of walks to show you the general lay of the land. The third part of the book provides you with the information you need to strike out on your own and truly explore.

This book provides the information in the form of reference manual pages, known in the UNIX world as *man pages.* The man pages tell you everything you need to know about the commands supplied with this package. They go far beyond the scope of the tutorial work in the first part of the book. Typically, the tutorial discusses the most useful or important features of commands, while the man pages give complete details on every feature.

Think of it this way: the tutorial is the guidebook, describing interesting things to investigate on your travels. The man pages are the detailed map, giving directions on how to get exactly where you want to go.

Man pages aren't intended for casual reading. They're intended to provide quick answers to urgent questions. Most give the facts as tersely as possible; the fewer words you have to read, the faster you can find out what you want to know. You may find this terseness intimidating at first, but you'll soon appreciate it. Nothing is more annoying to experienced users than fumbling through pages of verbiage in search of the one fact they need. Since you'll be an experienced user after you've worked through this book, I've written the man pages in a form that's well-suited to your future needs.

The Role of the MKS Tools

The software supplied with *Learning UNIX* was prepared by Mortice Kern Systems (MKS) for use with this book. This software package is called the *MKS Tools.*

The MKS Tools are derived from MKS Toolkit, a package of UNIX-like commands and utilities available for DOS, OS/2, and Windows NT. Most of the MKS Tools work exactly like their counterparts in MKS Toolkit. A few of the tools have been altered slightly so that they are appropriate in the educational context of this book but are less useful for real applications.

Installing the MKS Tools

Appendix G, "Installing the MKS Tools Package," and the installation page at the end of this book give full instructions for installing the MKS Tools on your DOS system. Please read the appendix and instruction page, before starting the main body of this book, and install the software in the manner described.

Typographical Conventions

When the text says that you should enter Ctrl-A, hold down the Ctrl key and press the A key. The same applies for entering any other Ctrl sequence.

When the text says that you should enter Alt-A, hold down the Alt key and press the A key (while holding down Alt). The same applies for entering any other Alt sequence.

UNIX software often uses the notation ^A for Ctrl-A. The same applies for other sequences using the caret (^) sequence. For example, the vi screen editor displays ^L for the Ctrl-L character (the ASCII formfeed).

This book often contrasts UNIX commands with DOS commands that do the same sort of thing. To distinguish the two, DOS commands are written in uppercase, but UNIX commands are written in lowercase and a special typeface. For example, I talk about the DOS MORE command and the UNIX more command. This is more than just a convention with UNIX commands; almost all UNIX commands must be entered in lowercase. (Of course, DOS lets you enter commands in both upper- and lowercase.)

How to Use This Book

To get the most out of the tutorial part of this book, you should be seated at a DOS system terminal, have MKS Tools installed, and try the examples as the book discusses them. As an active participant, you'll find you grasp topics more quickly and more thoroughly. Learning by doing is the most effective form of learning.

I particularly encourage you to experiment with the commands this book discusses. If you have a question about how the software behaves, try it out. Some of your best sessions may resemble two-way discussions with the system: you ask a question by trying something out, and the system gives an answer by providing the results of your experiment.

Of course if you're going to experiment, you have to use a bit of caution. Here are some tips:

Don't experiment with files that you care about. Make copies first, then work with the copies.

If you want to try a new command, read the man page first...and be sure to read the whole man page, not just the first little bit.

UNIX commands are usually stingy with output. For example, most don't display any messages if they do what you ask them to do successfully; they only issue messages if something goes wrong. As a result, you shouldn't worry if you type a command and the command displays no output. This usually means that the command worked the way you wanted it to work.

Doing the Exercises

Throughout the book I offer exercises for you to try. You must do some of these exercises at a terminal; others you can think about anytime.

Why are there exercises that aren't directly related to entering commands on a computer? Because UNIX is more than just a collection of useful software. It's a way of doing work, and a way of putting simple pieces together to form a sophisticated whole.

I want to teach you how to see problems the UNIX way. When you've developed this ability, you'll find your productivity with UNIX increases enormously. It may take you a little time to get on the same wavelength as UNIX, but when you do, I think you'll reap the benefits.

A Personal Word

No computing system is perfect, and UNIX has its share of exasperating idiosyncrasies. When I was first exposed to UNIX ten years ago, I complained about its perverseness to anyone who would listen. UNIX software didn't make sense to me, it wasn't like anything I was familiar with, and it was full of cryptic features that seemed to be far more trouble than they could possibly be worth.

I got over the initial hurdles and reached a point where I could do what I wanted to do on the system; but I still grumbled. Sometimes it seemed like the designers of UNIX had intentionally gone out of their way to make the software obscure.

My work took me to other computing systems. Once in a while I would be attacking a major problem when it occurred to me, "This would be a lot easier to do on UNIX." I found I was searching through system documentation looking for commands that did the same jobs as UNIX commands; and if I couldn't find them, I'd feel cheated. What kind of a computer didn't have software like the grep, diff, or find commands of UNIX? How could anyone use such a system?

The more I worked with other systems, the more fondness I felt for UNIX.

Now I do most of my work on DOS, but I use MKS Toolkit because I want and need features that only UNIX offers. I don't have the patience to work without UNIX tools at my fingertips. Without them, I waste time on trivial details that just slow me down.

No one likes to be slowed down when there's a better way available. Despite its warts and wrinkles, I think UNIX is that better way. By the end of this book, I hope you'll agree with me.

Part

I

FINDING
YOUR WAY
AROUND
UNIX

Chapter

1

OPERATING SYSTEMS

This chapter discusses what an operating system is and what it does for you.

In particular, this chapter looks at the Disk Operating System (DOS) as an operating system, and then compares it with UNIX. The intention is to clarify some general points about operating systems and to address misconceptions that often interfere with understanding what an operating system does and doesn't do.

After talking about operating systems in general, I zero in on UNIX. Like any other system in active use, UNIX is evolving to keep pace with the computing industry. I provide some background on the history of UNIX and look at directions for its future. In particular, I discuss the Portable Operating System Interface (POSIX) and other efforts to standardize the behavior of UNIX-like systems. Finally, the chapter looks at the UNIX philosophy and some of the principles that guided the design of UNIX.

What Is an Operating System?

An *operating system* is software that supervises the ways you can use the resources of a computer. With some computers, the operating system is a single program; with others, it is a collection of programs that interact with each other in a variety of ways.

The operating system is part butler and part security guard. The sections that follow describe both of these roles.

The Operating System as a Butler

As a butler, an operating system performs services that would be too complicated or dangerous for other programs to do for themselves. For example, when a program "wants" to write output to a file on disk, the program prepares the output, and then calls on the operating system to perform the actual write operation. In this way, the operating system looks after all the complications of choosing an area on the disk that can hold the output, transmitting the data, keeping the disk organized, and so on. The program instructs, "Write this," and the operating system does the rest of the work.

Here are a few other services that operating systems typically provide.

Executing a program: When you type a command that you want to execute (like the command to sort the contents of a file), it's the operating system that does all the work of loading the program into memory and starting the program.

Keeping track of the time and date: Some types of hardware have a built-in clock, but even in these cases, the operating system sets the clock and reads it when a program wants to know the time.

Performing most operations related to input, output, and disk organization, including maintaining the organization of files on disks, receiving input from a keyboard, and writing output to a display screen.

The Operating System as a Security Guard

As a security guard, the operating system protects the users and their data. For example, I just mentioned that the operating system performs all the actual write operations. In doing so, the operating system makes sure that data written to one file doesn't get written on top of data belonging to another file. The operating system keeps files from interfering with each other.

If several people can use the computer simultaneously, the operating system also keeps those users from interfering with each other. For example, it makes sure that they can't read or write to each other's files unless they have permission. It also allocates to users their fair share of the computer's resources; each gets a share of the memory, a share of the disk space, a share of the available processing time, and a share of any other facilities the computer has to offer. Some operating systems can deny certain users access to certain facilities. For example, a user may be allowed only to run a small collection of programs.

Operating systems often restrict computer access to authorized users. If you try to communicate with such a system, it prompts you to identify yourself with a name and a password. If you aren't an authorized user, the operating system won't allow you to work on it.

The Layers of an Operating System

Conceptually, an operating system can be divided into three components.

- The utilities
- The shells
- The kernel

I'll discuss each of these in the sections that follow, but first I should warn you that the division between these components may not be clear-cut. Many systems are constructed in ways that hide the distinctions between these components; UNIX stands out as one of the few systems that uses these distinctions to give users more flexibility.

Utilities

The *utilities* of an operating system are the standard commands and programs associated with the operating system. For example, the utilities of DOS are the commands that you expect to find on every DOS system: CHKDSK, DISKCOPY, BACKUP, and so on.

Utilities are the most visible part of the operating system. If you're a typical computer user, you use utilities many times a day—for copying or deleting files, for backing up your system, and for many other routine chores. The utilities are responsible for much of a system's look and feel.

At the same time, the utilities are the most changeable components of the operating system. Utilities are just programs. You can easily write or buy different programs that provide similar services. For example, a computer bulletin board in my town offers nine replacement programs for the standard DOS SORT utility. The bulletin board advertises these programs as faster, more versatile, or easier to use than the SORT command that comes with the operating system. People who want to use one of these alternate SORT commands can get rid of the old SORT (or rename it) and put a new SORT in its place.

Shells

A shell is a program that runs other programs. On DOS, such a program is usually called a *command interpreter.* You're probably familiar with the standard DOS command interpreter COMMAND.COM.

To understand what a shell does, consider all the things that COMMAND.COM does on DOS when you type a simple command like FORMAT A:

The process of executing this command involves the following steps:

1. The shell prompts you to input a command (frequently with the notation C>).

2. As you type the command, you can correct typing mistakes by backspacing and by using other methods.

3. After the Enter key is pressed, the shell analyzes the line to "figure out" that you want to execute the FORMAT command.

4. The DOS shell executes the FORMAT command by finding the file named FORMAT.COM and using the contents of that file as the FORMAT program.

5. After FORMAT is finished, the shell prompts you to enter a new command.

The shell "talks" with you on behalf of the operating system. It reads the command lines that you type, determines what they mean, and does whatever is necessary to carry out those commands.

Often shells offer additional, more sophisticated facilities. For example, some shells have features you can use to reduce the amount of typing you do.

Some shells may enable you to set up short forms for longer commands.

Shells may keep a record of all the commands you've entered recently so that you can edit or re-execute those commands in some simple way.

Shells may enable you to execute a collection of commands that have been stored in a file. In this way, you can set up a file containing any sequence of commands, and then execute all the commands in the file with a single command line.

Some operating systems only recognize one shell. On such systems, only one piece of software has the capability of running other programs; you can't use anything else. Operating systems like DOS and UNIX, however, do not tie you down to one shell. They make it possible for you to write or buy a different shell and to use that shell in place of the standard one. On the bulletin board I mentioned before, four shells are offered as alternatives to the standard DOS shell.

The standard DOS shell is called COMMAND.COM, and I'll refer to it a lot in the chapters to come. There are several popular shells in wide use on UNIX systems, including the Bourne Shell, the C Shell, and the KornShell. This book concentrates on the KornShell because it's the standard shell for UNIX System V (pronounced *system five*) Release 4.2, and because I believe it's the most suitable shell for learning and using UNIX.

Built-In Commands

Usually when you execute a program, the shell has to find the file that contains that program, load the program into memory, and then start executing the program. This can take a significant amount of time, especially on older computers with slow processors and disks.

To save time, some shells have *built-in commands*, commands they can execute immediately without finding and reading an appropriate file. The commands used most often are frequently built into the shell to reduce the amount of delay in execution. For example, the familiar DIR, DEL, and TYPE commands of DOS are built into DOS's COMMAND.COM so that they can be executed as quickly as possible.

The Kernel

The *kernel* is the collection of software that provides the basic capabilities of the operating system. Programs rely on the kernel for services and security. For example, if a program wants to write output, it can perform a lot of operations to format the output and prepare it for delivery to the output device. When this work has been done, the program must call the kernel to do the actual job of taking data from memory and making it appear on the monitor screen or in a disk file.

Most users have no direct contact with the kernel; its operations are as invisible as the wires that run through a wall to feed power to an electric outlet. However, the nature of the kernel affects everything you do with your computer. The capabilities of the kernel are probably the most significant factor in determining what programs can and can't do.

The Kernel and the Shell

Kernel suggests the heart of a seed or nut, just as the kernel is the heart of an operating system.

Shell suggests the part of a nut that surrounds and hides the kernel. The shell is all you can see until you crack open the nut. In the same way, a shell in an operating system stands between the kernel and the user; it's the part you can see.

Comparing UNIX and DOS

Now that I've discussed the basic components of operating systems in general, I've laid the groundwork for comparing UNIX and DOS. At this point, I make the comparisons in general terms. Later chapters provide more specific details.

A brief look at the history of the two systems and the factors that influenced their developments should help you understand the differences between the current versions of UNIX and DOS.

Brief History: UNIX

The first UNIX system was developed by AT&T Bell Laboratories of Murray Hill, New Jersey, in the late 1960s. It was a research system, constructed to try new concepts of operating system design and to provide a handful of expert computer scientists with a highly productive programming environment. It wasn't intended to be commercial, nor was it intended to be used outside Bell Labs. UNIX contrasted with operating systems of that day in several ways.

> It was intended for use by only a small number of people, unlike large commercial systems that sometimes allowed hundreds of people to work simultaneously on the same machine.
>
> The programmers assumed all UNIX's users were experienced professionals.
>
> UNIX had few security provisions because all its users were friends working for the same research group.
>
> It was intended as a system for developing new programs, unlike most other systems of the day that were designed to run large-scale business programs day in and day out.

These factors made UNIX a programmer's dream. As a result, university computer science departments became interested in the system, and AT&T made UNIX available to educational institutions for a nominal fee. Throughout the 1970s, UNIX use spread slowly. It proved to be popular in colleges and universities, where students and teachers appreciated the programming power and flexibility it gave them. UNIX became the operating system of choice for many of the most enterprising programmers of that time. Graduates fresh out of school wanted to work on UNIX, and programmers with adventurous ideas found they could produce programs more easily on UNIX than on other systems. As a result, many ambitious programs started life on UNIX and only later were transported to more mainstream operating systems.

During this time, AT&T upgraded the system often. For example, as more and more people began to use UNIX, security became a more important issue. Consequently, AT&T introduced new security features that brought UNIX more in line with what was available on other systems.

At the time, AT&T owned the rights to the UNIX name, but nothing prevented other companies from producing systems that looked and acted like UNIX. UNIX look-alikes began to appear in the late 1970s. The rise of personal computers in the early 1980s accelerated this trend; it was a boom time for tiny companies started by recent computer science graduates, and often UNIX was the system they wanted.

The majority of UNIX look-alikes were derived directly from versions of AT&T's UNIX code. Manufacturers licensed the code from AT&T, converted it to run on their own machines, and often added extra features to make the products more attractive. Because AT&T retained ownership of the UNIX name, other manufacturers gave their UNIX look-alikes other names—XENIX, AIX, UCOS, and HP/UA to name a few. There was a steady growth in the number of machines for which a UNIX-like operating system was available—some supported directly by AT&T and some supported by other vendors, usually based on AT&T's code. (A few UNIX look-alikes were written from scratch without using AT&T code as a starting point, either because the designers didn't want to pay AT&T licensing fees or because they thought starting from scratch would produce a better product.)

The machines on which UNIX originated were minicomputers, much more powerful than the microcomputers of the same era. Over the years, however, microcomputers have grown in speed and power. The current-generation micros are comparable to the original machines that ran UNIX. Thus, UNIX and UNIX look-alikes are quite at home on the microcomputers of today.

AT&T sold its UNIX System Laboratories (USL) to Novell in 1993. Later that year, the ownership of the UNIX trademark was transferred from Novell to X/Open, so today X/Open owns the UNIX trademark, although Novell holds the source code license.

Brief History: DOS

MS-DOS and PC DOS arrived on the scene in the early 1980s. Because DOS was constructed much later than UNIX, its programmers could build on existing experience with UNIX and borrow many UNIX features. DOS systems also owe much to CP/M, an operating system that ran on some of the earliest microcomputers. (Version 1.0 of DOS was based on CP/M; later versions incorporate more UNIX-like concepts.)

DOS was designed specifically for IBM personal computers. Originally, these computers might have as little as 64K of memory. As a result, DOS had to be small because size was a major constraint. The designers had to economize, so they couldn't incorporate many desirable UNIX features they might have borrowed.

Over the years, PCs grew more powerful, with more memory and speed. Versions of DOS for such systems could be more comprehensive because they weren't as limited by memory and speed considerations. Thus, DOS grew up to take advantage of new, more powerful machines.

Even so, DOS hasn't advanced to the current state of UNIX. UNIX began on machines comparable to modern micros; DOS began on much smaller machines. Those limited origins still have their effect on DOS's behavior. In my opinion, UNIX is much better equipped, especially in its multiuser and multitasking capabilities, to cope with today's powerful PCs than DOS is.

The Multiuser System Versus the Single-User System

UNIX is a *multiuser* system. The designers of UNIX anticipated that several people would use the system and that each person would have personal files he or she didn't want to share with the other users. You can picture a multiuser system as an office where users have their own separate desks but also have access to some resources held in common, such as the photocopier and the water cooler. In a multiuser system, common resources might include certain directories and the line printer.

DOS, on the other hand, is a *single-user* system. If you start a standard DOS system, you are automatically given access to every file on the system. (DOS *hidden files* and *read-only* files are a little harder to access than normal files, but only a little. Making a file hidden or read-only can prevent accidents, but it doesn't prevent you from accessing those files if you really want to.)

File security is only one difference between multiuser systems and single-user systems. If you want to start using a multiuser system, you have to identify yourself so that the system knows which user you are. Thus, UNIX users go through a *log-in* procedure during which they tell the system their names and enter passwords to prove they are who they claim to be. With standard DOS, you simply turn on the machine and start working; you don't have to identify yourself because DOS has no facilities to distinguish among different people who may use the same machine.

Both DOS and UNIX provide facilities you can use to customize the system to your personal needs. With standard DOS, however, the customizations affect everything you do with the machine. With UNIX, customizations made by one user need not affect other users. Typically, when you log in to a UNIX system, the system identifies who you are, and then looks to see whether you've asked to have any personal customizations in effect while you're using the computer. Those customizations stay in effect as long as you're working. If you *log out* and another user logs in, the system cleans away your customizations and checks for any customizations desired by the new user. Each user starts with a completely clean slate, unaffected by others who might use the system.

A multiuser system lets users set up their work sessions according to their tastes, without interfering with other users who share the same machine. A multiuser system makes it possible for you to set up private files that no one else can access, as well as public files that are available to all.

Multitasking Versus Single-Tasking

In the description of multiuser systems, I spoke as if one person uses the machine for a while, and then that person leaves and another one logs on. With a UNIX system, several people can use the same system simultaneously. This process is called *multitasking* because the system seems to perform several tasks at the same time.

DOS, on the other hand, is a *single-tasking* system. It can do only one thing at a time. A few special arrangements can make it look like DOS is doing several jobs simultaneously (for example, with the print queue, you can start printing something, and then do other work while the printer prints), but these few special arrangements don't approach the versatility of true multitasking.

Software such as Microsoft Windows introduces a form of true multitasking to DOS. In essence, Windows and similar programs act as small operating systems working within DOS itself. They supervise the multitasking process using the technique described in the box titled **How Multitasking Works**.

UNIX's multitasking facilities are versatile. Not only can several different users work with the system simultaneously, but a single user can actually run several different programs at the same time. A UNIX user often can start a long job running and work on a shorter job while waiting for the long job to finish. This is one reason why you can be more productive with UNIX than with a single-tasking system; you can do several things at once.

How Multitasking Works

Some types of hardware can do several things at once because they contain multiple processors. The majority of computers, however, has only a single processor and can really only do one thing at a time.

Computers like this can still perform multitasking, because the processor is much faster than the many devices attached to the computer. For example, if a program is waiting for you to type input, the processor is (mostly) idle.

Even if you are typing quickly, the processor is still idle most of the time. It can handle each input character in such a small fraction of a second that it spends much time waiting for you to enter the next character. The same is true when the computer is reading or writing to a disk. Writing and reading a disk is thousands of times faster than a typist types, but it is still much slower than the processor, so the processor has a lot of idle time.

In a multitasking system, the processor doesn't waste this idle time. If the system is waiting for you to type a character, it switches to work for someone else for a moment. After it has done some work for that person, it comes back to you to see whether you've entered something yet. In other words, the operating system tries to keep the processor as busy as possible by doing a bit of work for one user, a bit for another, and so on. In many cases, the processor is so fast that you can't tell that it is working in this fragmented way.

Note that the operating system "tells" the processor to switch from one program to another. The processor doesn't do so on its own. In the case of Microsoft Windows and other DOS products that simulate multitasking, Windows tells the processor to switch from one program to another. DOS doesn't run more than one program. It runs the single program Windows, which then goes on to run all the other programs.

Why You Should Investigate UNIX

Now that I've discussed a few of the features of UNIX and how they differ from those of DOS, it should be clearer why UNIX is worth investigating. Here's a quick checklist:

UNIX makes it possible for you to share a system with other people without interfering with each other.

Multitasking enables you to do several things at once. If you start a long job, you aren't forced to wait until it is finished; you can work on something else in the meantime.

UNIX is a *mature* system. It has been in use for 30 years, and it's gone through a thorough shakedown period. UNIX programmers have had a lot of time to eliminate bugs and deficiencies. UNIX has also benefited from the

rise of UNIX look-alikes; the pressure of competition has forced continuing improvements.

A great deal of popular software is available on UNIX. Before and after the rise of personal computers, UNIX stood out as the favorite system for the development of leading-edge programs.

Many commercial systems are particularly good at one class of jobs but poor at others. Because UNIX is extremely customizable, you can streamline it to do the work you do the most.

You can find UNIX (or a UNIX look-alike) for almost any type of hardware. This makes it possible for you to use the same utilities on a wide variety of machines. Most other operating systems are *proprietary* and only run on machines that come from a single manufacturer. DOS runs on clones as well as true IBM PCs, but it doesn't run on larger machines or on computers that don't use one of the family of microprocessing chips used in PCs.

With all these advantages, UNIX has become a dominant force in the computing industry. Companies want to hire people with UNIX expertise. Software developers strive to offer their products on UNIX. Certainly, DOS is still more widely used than UNIX, but even DOS is under pressure to become more like UNIX and to offer the same powerful facilities that UNIX does. For all these reasons, I strongly believe that it's worth an investment of your time to see what UNIX can do for you.

The Different "Flavors" of UNIX

I've already mentioned that the market offers many products with the look and feel of UNIX. To help you distinguish among them, the sections that follow give encapsulated descriptions of some prominent UNIX-like products in use today as well as in the past.

AT&T System V

In the past, UNIX System V from AT&T was the preeminent UNIX system. As I noted earlier, AT&T owned the UNIX name, and therefore its product was the only one that could actually use the name. UNIX System V was available on many types of hardware and went through several revisions since the first System V release (in the mid-1980s).

In 1993, AT&T sold its UNIX System Laboratories (USL) to Novell. Later that year, the ownership of the UNIX trademark was transferred from Novell to X/Open. Today, the UNIX trademark is owned by X/Open, although Novell remains the holder of the source code license.

Berkeley BSD

Berkeley UNIX, *Berkeley Software Distribution* (*BSD*), is an interesting anomaly. In the mid-1970s, the University of California at Berkeley used AT&T's UNIX extensively, but felt that they could improve on it. With AT&T's permission, they brought out a set of modifications to the AT&T UNIX system, which Berkeley then sold to interested parties (especially colleges and universities).

AT&T's UNIX continued to evolve, and so did Berkeley's modifications, often in completely different directions. The systems were still recognizably UNIX, but they differed in utilities, in shells, and especially in the kernel. Many heated backroom arguments arose over which was "better," AT&T's UNIX or Berkeley's.

Others

Many other vendors offer versions of UNIX (based on some release of AT&T UNIX) or versions of UNIX-like software. These go by such names as AIX (IBM), HP/UX (Hewlett Packard), OSF/1 (DEC), SCO UNIX (SCO), Solaris (SUN), and UNIXWare (Novell).

Most vendors attempt to provide compatibility with true UNIX, plus additional features that make their products more attractive.

The Promise of Standards

Many operating systems are based on UNIX. Although these packages have strong similarities, they also have substantial differences. In recent years, various organizations have worked to establish *standards* for all UNIX-like systems and to ensure a level of uniformity among all the look-alikes. In the sections that follow, you will see the standards that are being written, why they're being written, and how they may affect the future of UNIX.

POSIX

POSIX is the umbrella name for a family of standards being developed under the auspices of the *Institute of Electrical and Electronics Engineers* (*IEEE*). The following list describes the most important members of this family:

POSIX.1 dictates the services to be provided by the kernel.

POSIX.2 describes the utilities and the features that must be offered by any shell.

POSIX.3 describes facilities for testing POSIX systems.

POSIX.4 specifies the *real-time* computing services that the kernel can offer. (Normally, programs don't need to keep track of time; they just run as fast as possible. However, programs that control moving objects in the real world—robots and other machines—must be able to keep track of time and synchronize their actions with the objects they control. This process can be difficult and requires a variety of special services from the operational system.)

POSIX.7 defines common facilities for system administration.

There are other standards in the family, each describing a separate aspect of the operating system and related software. At the time of this writing, POSIX.1 through POSIX.4 have been finalized and are official standards. Other standards in the family are still under development and will take a few more years before they are finished.

The IEEE POSIX standards also are being ratified as international standards by the Organization for International Standardization (ISO). There is close coordination between the IEEE and ISO working groups to ensure that the standards developed fulfill both needs.

The POSIX.1 standard has been endorsed by the United States Federal Government, as Federal Information Processing Standard (FIPS) Standard 151-2. The computing purchases of all branches of government must conform to this standard. If any federal agency wants to buy a different type of system, it needs special congressional approval.

In all likelihood, the other POSIX standards will also become FIPS standards as they are finalized. At the time of this writing, a FIPS for POSIX.2 is awaiting endorsement by the United States Federal Government. Traditionally, many other governments and corporations follow the U.S. government's lead. Thus, with the backing of the U.S. government and a large number of companies throughout the computing industry, POSIX will have a dominant effect on the shape of UNIX in years to come.

System V Interface Definition (SVID)

POSIX standards reflect their UNIX heritage, but are being implemented on other operating systems that are unrelated to UNIX. One of the base documents that was used as input to the POSIX process was the definitive UNIX specification from AT&T, called the *System V Interface Definition* (*SVID*).

The SVID predates the POSIX standards and covers a broader spectrum of services. Where there are differences, AT&T is committed to moving toward the POSIX definition of an interface, as parts of POSIX become full-use standards.

X/OPEN

X/Open began as an organization of European UNIX system manufacturers committed to providing systems that implemented a single common interface to operating system services. That definition was written down in the X/Open Portability Guide (XPG).

XPG defers to POSIX where there is a POSIX interface definition and otherwise incorporates a SVID definition. Additionally, X/Open has been instrumental internationalizing UNIX-like software by introducing features to accommodate differences in languages and other local conventions. Internationalization affects such things as

The standard character set used in text files—different languages use different alphabets and punctuation characters.

The order in which characters are sorted—"alphabetical order" varies from country to country.

The language in which the operating system displays diagnostic messages.

The way the system writes numeric values—for example, some cultures use a period as a decimal point (as in 3.14159); others use a comma (3,14159)

The way monetary values are displayed.

The formats of dates and times.

X/OPEN is very active in the POSIX community.

> ### Which Is the "Standard" Standard?
>
> If you're confused by having at least three different documents vying to be the "standard" standard for UNIX, you're not the only one. Several large groups are jostling for position in the UNIX market at present, and who gets to write the standard is one issue of contention. In the long run, I believe POSIX will become the UNIX standard, but because POSIX is still under development, these groups are trying to use their own standards to affect the way that POSIX unfolds. The balance of power seems to shift from week to week, providing much amusement for the computing industry, even in the off-season for baseball.

Portability

You might wonder why it's so valuable to create a standard for UNIX-like systems. One of the most important reasons is that standards ensure portability.

Porting is the process of taking a program that runs on one type of computer and getting it to work on another type. This can be a difficult job, especially if the computers have different hardware and different operating systems. On the other hand, if the computers are running the same operating system (or similar operating systems) and the program does not rely on idiosyncrasies of the hardware, porting can be easy.

Standardizing the behavior of UNIX-like operating systems is the first step in simplifying the job of porting. If programmers know that all UNIX-like systems offer a standard set of features, programmers can use those features (and only those features) in the applications they write. By restricting themselves to the features guaranteed to be available on all UNIX look-alikes, applications become easier to port.

Portability is important for several reasons.

> If you upgrade to a new computer, you usually want to move all your favorite programs to the new machine. This is particularly important for companies that have a lot of programs set up to do their bookkeeping, billing, production, and so on. The companies don't want to rewrite all their software just because they bought a new machine. Programs should last longer than hardware.

Many companies use many different types of computers. For example, big jobs may run on a large computer, and other work is done on PCs. Ideally, you'd like to be able to use the same programs on each computer you own so that you don't have to learn a lot of different programs and so that you don't get confused as you switch from system to system.

Any company that writes and sells programs is pleased when it can sell the same program to people on a wide variety of systems.

Porting also applies to data: you can ship data from one machine to another. This process is easy if the systems use the same data formats. Standards can ensure that different systems keep the same kind of data in the same formats so that you don't have to reformat when data goes from one computer to another.

Familiarity

Familiarity is another benefit of standardization. Learn one UNIX-like system, and you'll be familiar with all such systems. There may still be some variations; almost every software manufacturer adds features to its package, to make the package a better buy than its competitor's package. For the most part, though, familiarity with one UNIX-like system carries over to the other UNIX-like systems.

An Introduction to the UNIX Philosophy

As I discussed how different UNIX look-alikes can be, you might have wondered how they can all be recognized as UNIX-like systems. The common thread that draws them all together is the UNIX *philosophy:* the design principles that dictated the original form of UNIX and have continued to influence UNIX-like systems through the years. The sections that follow look at some of these design principles and how they are reflected in UNIX-like systems.

Reducing User Effort

UNIX software goes to great lengths to reduce the effort a user expends to do work. For example, UNIX utilities have been streamlined in many ways to reduce the number of keystrokes you're required to type on the command line.

Command names are as short as possible. For example, the UNIX command for copying files is cp, not COPY (as in DOS), and the UNIX command for

moving files is mv, not MOVE. (Dropping the vowels from a command name is a favorite UNIX trick.)

Most command-line options are only a single character.

Short forms can be used in many parts of the command line. For example, with UNIX, you represent a large collection of filenames with a single symbol. I'll talk about this feature in the section *Glob Constructs* in Chapter 4, "Basic Tools: Five Ways to List a Directory."

UNIX commands are as terse as possible, and therefore they can be hard to understand at first glance. The commands often look like just a snarl of characters. Don't be intimidated by this. Reading the commands can be difficult, but when you have learned what the commands do, using them is easy.

The underlying rationale is that you only have to learn a command once, but you have to use it frequently over a long period of time. UNIX commands may take longer to learn, but they're much faster to use after you've done so; it's a short-term sacrifice for a long-term gain. You probably won't find UNIX user-friendly when you first start using it. Like most friendships, your esteem for UNIX has to build with time.

Combining Small Tools into Larger Ones

Life would be simple if there were a specific utility for every job you could possibly want to do. If that were true, you would only have to execute one command for any given job. However, there's a practical limit to how many utilities an operating system can provide, not to mention the limit on the number of utilities that a person can learn to use.

The number of utilities an operating system can reasonably provide is therefore relatively small—a few hundred commands at most. Those commands, however, must cover the complete spectrum of jobs that people want to do with their computer. Any operating system's designers therefore must choose a set of utilities that is small but can do all necessary jobs.

The UNIX approach is to make utilities that are basic and simple but can be combined to do more complex jobs. As you'll see in later chapters, UNIX offers a multitude of ways commands can be combined.

In *pipelines,* where the output of one command is input to the next.

With *command substitution,* where the output of one command is used to construct a new command line.

With *command programming constructs,* which enable you to write "programs" with statements that are operating system commands.

All of these combination methods (and more) will be thoroughly covered in later chapters.

Customizing

I've already mentioned several times that UNIX enables you to customize the system and your work sessions with the system, but why is customizing really an advantage?

To give you an idea of the benefits of customization, look at a job that many people do frequently: backing up their hard disk on diskettes. If you use the UNIX-like MKS Tools commands on DOS, the command line

```
find c:/ -mtime -7 ¦ tar -cvf a:archive -
```

finds all the files on disk C: that you have changed in the past week and backs them up to the disk in drive A:. You probably think the line would be difficult to remember, but the beauty of UNIX customization is that you don't have to remember it. Instead, you might set up the name backup to be a synonym or *alias* for the command. After you've done that, you can just type the command

```
backup
```

and the system runs the complicated command line for you.

You might be asking why the system doesn't just supply a standard backup command instead of forcing you to set up an alias. The answer is that different people can choose to back up their system in different ways. The preceding command backs up anything that has changed in the last week. You might want to back up on a daily basis instead of on a weekly basis, or you may want only to back up certain files. If the system enables you to define your own backup command, you can customize it to suit your work habits. If you have to use some standard backup command, you have less flexibility.

Pipes

In the last section I discussed the command line

```
find c:/ -mtime -7 ¦ tar -cvf a:archive -
```

This line is actually a combination of two commands: the `find` command locates files that have a certain property, and the `tar` command writes out a set of files to drive A:. The two commands are joined by the *pipe* symbol (¦), also called the *or-bar, stick,* or *vertical bar*). The pipe symbol takes the normal output of one command and submits it as input to another command. In the preceding example, it takes the list of files that `find` writes and submits that list as input to `tar`. The `tar` command then backs up all the files in the list. This is a typical example of using pipes to combine commands, a very frequent operation on UNIX.

You may already be familiar with *pipes,* because they're also available in DOS. This is an example of the influence that UNIX had on the design of DOS. From experience with UNIX, the DOS designers knew that pipes were useful, so they implemented pipes under DOS.

Chapter Review

An operating system is software that supervises the ways you can use the resources of a computer. It provides services and enforces security. Operating systems have the following three layers:

- The utilities: a set of commands and programs that can perform standard tasks like printing or copying files

- The shells: programs that let you invoke other programs

- The kernel: the underlying software that supports all the other software that the computer runs

The UNIX operating system was developed for use on minicomputers by AT&T in the late 1960s. It spread slowly, primarily through colleges and universities. Because modern microcomputers are comparable to those old minicomputers, UNIX is well suited to the current generation of micros. DOS, by contrast, started on much smaller machines and hasn't caught up with recent hardware enhancements.

UNIX is a multiuser system, designed to accommodate the needs of many people using the same machine. It is also a multitasking system so that several people can use the same machine simultaneously.

Many UNIX look-alikes are on the market today, with names like AIX, HP/UX, OSF/1, SCO, Solaris, and UNIXWare. The POSIX family of standards and other standards (SVID, X/Open) ensure that these different products stay in step with each other, which will in turn ensure portability of software and data.

UNIX was designed in accordance with several philosophical principles including

> Giving high priority to reducing user effort

> Providing a collection of simple commands, plus a variety of ways to combine those commands to perform more complex tasks (for example pipes, which take the output from one command and send it as input to another command)

> Allowing users to customize their dealings with the system

Exercises

1. Make a list of the ten most common command lines you type in the course of a day. Analyze this list. Are any of these command lines particularly difficult to type? Are there any sequences of commands that you frequently type in a row?

2. Are there any commands that you find you have to look up in the manual almost every time you use them? If so, what is it about the command that you have to look up?

3. What are the five most time-consuming jobs you have to do with the computer on a regular basis? With any of these jobs, is there anywhere that you could save time by substituting a single command for a commonly used sequence of commands?

4. What are the five most common typing mistakes you make when you're typing a command line? Can you think of a way that operating system software could reduce the probability of your making those mistakes?

Chapter

2

GETTING STARTED: HELLO, WORLD

This chapter shows you how to start up the MKS Tools software that comes with this book and how to enter a few simple commands (assuming that you've already installed the software by following the instructions in Appendix G, "Installing the MKS Tools Package" and at the end of this book). The goal is to make you feel at home with the software and to discuss several basic principles about UNIX software.

Manual Pages: The First Step

In UNIX parlance, the reference manual descriptions for commands are called *man pages* (short for *manual pages*). For example, the description of the cp command is usually called the cp man page, even if this documentation is actually several pages long.

Part III of this book provides man pages for each of the MKS Tools commands in the *Learning UNIX* software package. These man pages are the key to developing a full appreciation of UNIX. They tell you everything you need to know about the commands and how to use them.

Man pages are not light reading. UNIX documentation is usually written as tersely as possible; the fewer words you have to read, the faster you can find answers to your questions. As a UNIX novice, you may find the man pages intimidating at first. Ultimately, however, you'll have to tackle the man pages to find out more about the commands you want to use. Here's a strategy for familiarizing yourself with the man pages, with a minimum of confusion and aggravation:

1. Read the introduction to Part III, titled *How to Read a Man Page.* You can read this any time you want (for example, right now).

2. As you work through the book, keep track of the commands it discusses. (The chapter review at the end of each chapter summarizes the commands that the chapter has discussed.) Find the man page for each of these commands and read it.

3. Don't worry if the man page overwhelms you the first time you read it. The man page may be dealing with concepts that haven't yet been covered by the book. By the time you finish everything else, however, you should be able to work through the man pages with a fuller understanding.

4. As you read a man page, write down any questions you may have about what you read. If you can't find answers to your questions in the man page (or in other parts of this book), experiment with the commands to find out what you want to know. If you don't mind writing in books, write down what you find out on the man page itself, so the answer will be there if you want to look it up again.

Logging In

The first step to using a UNIX system is to *log in* to the system. As mentioned in Chapter 1, "Operating Systems," there are two steps to the log-in process.

1. Telling the computer who you are

2. Proving your identity by entering your personal password

I'll walk you through this process now. You should be seated at a PC, following along as I discuss each step in order to get practice with the software. Remember, you should already have the software installed on your machine; if not, turn now to Appendix G, "Installing the MKS Tools Package," and the installation page at the end of this book and follow the installation procedure described there.

Interrogate the System

As you work through UNIX sessions in this chapter and the ones to follow, don't just follow the steps mechanically. Think about what you're doing and "interrogate" the system. You should ask questions that occur to you as you go along. Ask why UNIX requires you to do some things but not others. Ask why the designers chose a particular approach to a problem. Write down these questions and try to find answers, either from this book, from experienced UNIX users, or by experimenting with the software. I promise that you'll learn faster and more comprehensively with this approach (and you'll be less likely to fall asleep at the keyboard).

You can start the MKS Tools either from the DOS C> prompt, or from within Microsoft Windows.

To start the MKS Tools from the DOS C> prompt, enter the following commands:

```
cd \lu
lu
```

The first command goes to the directory that holds the UNIX simulation software. The second command starts the MKS Tools.

To start the MKS Tools from within Microsoft Windows, open the Learning UNIX Program Group and double-click the Learning UNIX (with MKS Tools) icon.

The MKS Tools program issues the message

```
login:
```

This is what you will see when you begin work on a normal UNIX system. In response to this message, enter your *log-in name* (also known as your *userid*). The installation process asked you to choose a log-in name. Type that name now and press Enter when you're finished.

In a typical log-in procedure, the system would next display

```
Password:
```

asking you to enter your password. But you're a new user, so you don't have a password yet. You'll see how to create a password for yourself later in this chapter.

This is all you have to do to log in to a UNIX system. In a moment, you'll see the system display a $ to prompt you to enter your first command.

What Are You Talking To?

I said that "the system" prompts you to enter your first command. In fact, it's the shell that does the prompting. The log-in procedure automatically starts the shell program to interact with you: to read the commands you enter, to find the programs that will carry out those commands, and to start those programs running.

Entering a Command

Now that you've logged in successfully, it's time to enter your first UNIX command. Type the following:

echo Hello

and press Enter. (Make sure that echo is in lowercase.) You'll see that the system types back

```
Hello
```

on the display screen.

This is all that the UNIX `echo` command does: it displays everything else that appears on the command line. As another example, try

echo Hello there!

You'll see that the system displays

Hello there!

`echo` is a simple command, so simple that you may think it's useless. However, future chapters will show that `echo` has many different uses; you'll be seeing it a lot.

Correcting Typing Mistakes

Before I discuss `echo` in more detail, I should tell you how to correct any typing mistakes you make as you enter commands to the KornShell.

Backspacing

As you might expect, pressing the Backspace key erases the character immediately before the cursor. Try it by typing

echox

then backspacing to erase the x.

Every time you press the Backspace key, another character is erased. You can backspace all the way to the beginning of the current line if you want, but you can't backspace any farther.

Erasing an Entire Line

Pressing the Esc key erases the entire line . . . sort of. To see what I mean, type some nonsense like

xxx

and then press Esc (don't press Enter first). You'll see the display change to

xxx\

and then the cursor jumps down to the next line on the screen. What does this mean? It means that the line with the \ on the end of it no longer counts. In effect, it's been erased, even though it still appears on the screen. If you now type a command like

```
echo hi
```

and press Enter, you'll see

```
hi
```

appear on the screen. The KornShell discards the xxx that you typed first, and executes the echo command that you typed afterward.

You might wonder why the shell doesn't make the xxx line disappear on the screen when you erase it with Esc. There are some technical reasons for this related to the origins of UNIX. In those old days, some terminals weren't able to delete lines, particularly typewriter terminals that displayed everything on paper. However, there's also a philosophical reason for not making the line disappear. Suppose you go to a lot of trouble to enter a complicated command line, but decide to delete the line when you're near the end. You'll find it useful to be able to see the original line so that you can remember what you did right and correct what you did wrong. The shell leaves the original line on the screen so that you don't have to reconstruct it again from memory.

Editing Modes

In Chapter 9, "Customizing," you'll see how editing modes can change the behavior of the Esc key. For the time being, however, Esc is the line-erase key.

Making Errors

What would have happened if you had tried to execute the original

xxx

line? Try it and see. Type the line and press Enter. You'll see that the shell displays the following message:

```
xxx: not found
```

This means that the shell could not find any appropriate program named xxx. Because the shell couldn't find the program, it couldn't execute the command.

The Importance of Lowercase

The first time you typed the `echo` command, I told you to make sure that `echo` was in lowercase. The reason is that UNIX systems are *case-sensitive:* they pay attention to the case of all letters in all command lines, whether the letters are used in the command name itself or in other parts of the command line. Try entering

ECHO Hello

You'll get the message

`ECHO: not found`

because `ECHO` is not the same as `echo`.

MKS Tools Are Forgiving

Because you are working with the MKS Tools rather than a true UNIX system, you can get away with typing some commands in uppercase. However, there's no reason to do this; lowercase is the natural alphabet for UNIX, and you should get used to it now.

More About *echo*

Now that I've covered the basics of entering UNIX commands, let's go back to the command I started with: `echo`. As you saw, the command consists of the word `echo`, followed by the words you want `echo` to display. These words are called the *arguments* of the command. For example, in

echo Hello there!

the arguments are `Hello` and `there!`.

In most UNIX commands, arguments are separated by *whitespace.* Whitespace is made up of any number of blank characters or tab characters. For example, see what happens if you put extra blank characters between arguments, as in

```
echo   Hello      there!
```

You'll see that `echo` displays

```
Hello there!
```

the same way it did before. When the shell executes `echo`, it puts exactly one blank space between each pair of arguments, no matter how much whitespace the original command line contained. This is typical of all UNIX commands: the amount of whitespace you use to separate arguments doesn't affect the behavior of the command.

But you might be saying, what happens if you really want to put a lot of whitespace between your arguments? You can get this by using double quotation marks, as in

```
echo "Hello      there!"
```

The output of this command is

```
Hello      there!
```

By using double quotation marks, you make one big argument that has a lot of blanks in the middle. When `echo` displays this argument, it displays the blanks as part of the argument.

You can also use single quotation marks (apostrophes) as in

```
echo 'Hello      there!'
```

The effect is the same in this case. Try it.

`echo` (and many other UNIX commands) can accept a huge number of arguments. In MKS Tools, the command line for `echo` can be up to 8,192 characters long. For reasons that you'll see later, it's important for UNIX commands to be able to accept very long command lines. In contrast, DOS usually imposes a maximum of 127 characters on any command line.

The DOS ECHO Command

You may be aware that DOS has an `ECHO` command of its own. (Remember that I'm writing DOS commands in uppercase and UNIX ones in lowercase, so `ECHO` is the DOS command and `echo` is the UNIX one.) `ECHO` can display

---

output in the same way that `echo` does, because DOS borrowed its `ECHO` command from UNIX. However, there are some differences between the two commands. For example, the DOS version preserves the number of blanks between arguments. The output of

```
ECHO Hello     there!
```

is

```
Hello     there!
```

You'll see other differences between the two commands as you examine more sophisticated features of UNIX.

Choosing Your Password

Now that you've gained some familiarity with entering commands, there's an important administrative job that you should do while you're still at the terminal: you should choose your password.

When you signed on at the beginning of this chapter, you had no password. In the interest of security, you should choose a password as soon as possible so that other people can't sign on under your name. (Even if you aren't concerned about security right now, thinking about it is a worthwhile exercise. If and when you begin working on a real UNIX system, you owe it to yourself and other users to take sensible precautions.)

What sort of password should you choose? Here are a few guidelines:

A UNIX log-in password can consist of any sequence of zero or more characters. It can contain blanks, punctuation characters, and other characters you might think of as unusual. Uppercase letters aren't the same as lowercase ones, so `HELLO` and `hello` are different passwords.

Don't choose a normal English word. It's easy to find an online dictionary, and it's easy for someone to write a program that runs through the dictionary, trying each word until it finds the one you've chosen as your password.

Don't choose any piece of personal information that someone else might be able to guess. Names of family members or their birthdates are too obvious.

Don't choose some entirely arbitrary collection of characters. If a password is too difficult to remember, you'll be tempted to write it down somewhere close to your computer, and when a password is written down, it becomes vulnerable to prying eyes.

If your password has less than six characters, it's relatively easy to guess. It's not hard to write a program that tries every single character, every two-character combination, and so on. However, the longer your password, the longer it takes for a program to try all the combinations. With more than six characters, the process is usually too time-consuming to be worthwhile.

Try some sort of variation on a simple word or phrase. For example, instead of `hello there`, you could write it backwards (`ereht olleh`) or better, put in punctuation characters, as in `h,el,lo-th,ere` or `he.ll;o#there!`. This sort of thing is usually easy for you to remember, but very difficult for a person or program to guess.

The *passwd* Command

When you've decided on a suitable password, you can use the UNIX `passwd` command to set your chosen password. The `passwd` command also lets you change passwords, so I'll look at both setting a new password and changing an old one.

Start by typing the command

```
passwd
```

and then press Enter.

Usually, the `passwd` command begins by asking you to enter your old password to prove who you are. This prevents someone from sneaking up to your desk and changing your password while you're not there. However, you don't have a password yet, so `passwd` doesn't ask for your old password.

`passwd` now asks you to enter the new password you've chosen. Do so and press Enter. You'll notice that the new password doesn't appear on the screen as you type it. This is a security precaution; even if people are watching you as you type, they won't see what your password is.

Because the new password didn't appear on the screen when you entered it, you might have made a typing mistake without knowing it. To avoid confusion, `passwd` asks you to enter the new password a second time. Do so and press Enter. If you typed the new password the same both times, passwd records that as your new password; if there was some difference between the first time you typed the new password and the second, passwd assumes that you made a typing mistake. Of course, passwd can't tell which time you made the mistake. As a result, it displays the message

```
Passwords do not match. Try again.
```

and asks you to enter the new password again (two times).

Your New Password

The next time you log in, you'll have to type your new password when the log-in procedure asks `Password:`. When you enter the password, you won't see it appear on the screen. Once again, this is a security precaution so that people looking over your shoulder can't see your password on the screen.

Logging Out

When you have changed your password, you might decide that you're finished for the time being. To end your session with UNIX, you must *log out,* also called *signing off.*

The steps you have to take in order to log out depend on the shell you are using. With the KornShell of the MKS Tools package, you sign off by typing

exit

and then pressing Enter.

With different shells and different versions of UNIX, the exit command may not work. The following list gives some alternate ways of signing off a UNIX system; these don't work with the MKS Tools, but you can try them on other systems if exit doesn't work.

You can try entering one of the following commands:

```
logout
logoff
log
bye
```

You can try entering the Ctrl-D character. On many UNIX systems, this stands for *end of file* or *end of input*, and tells the shell that you are finished entering commands. (Because Ctrl-Z often stands for *end of file* on DOS, you can log out from the MKS Tools package by pressing Ctrl-Z and then Enter.)

Chapter Review

Man pages describe UNIX commands in full. Part III of this book provides man pages for every command in the MKS Tools package.

To start working with a UNIX system, you must log in. During the log-in procedure, you tell the system your name and enter a password to prove that you are who you say you are.

The echo command simply displays its arguments on the display screen. echo puts a single blank character between each argument. If you want additional whitespace, put the arguments (including the whitespace) in single or double quotation marks.

With the KornShell, you can delete single characters by pressing the Backspace key. You can delete the whole line by pressing Esc.

Almost all UNIX commands must be entered in lowercase. If you enter them in uppercase, the system will not recognize the command names.

The passwd command lets you change your password. You must enter your old password, then enter your new password two times.

To end a session with UNIX, you must log out, also called *signing off*. With the KornShell, you can log out by entering exit.

Exercises

1. Read the man page for the banner command. Log in and use banner to display the word Hello.

2. Use banner to display Hi there with one word per line. Then use banner to display Hi there with the words all on one line. What happens if you use banner to display a string with more than 12 characters? Try it.

3. Log out and log in again. When you log in, intentionally enter a nonsense user name (a name that isn't the name of anyone authorized to use the system). What happens? Why do you think UNIX takes this approach?

# Chapter 3

THE UNIX FILE SYSTEM: GO CLIMB A TREE

The DOS method of organizing and handling files was strongly influenced by the example of UNIX. Because of this, the two have much in common. This chapter begins by looking at the things you do most often with files: read them, copy them, move them, and get rid of them.

After discussing the nature of files, this chapter examines the way UNIX organizes files. Like DOS, UNIX organizes files into *directories*. If computer files are similar to the paper file folders you might find in an office, directories are similar to the filing cabinets that hold such file folders.

Files are contained in directories, but these directories might be contained in larger directories, which are contained in even larger directories, and so on. If you want to work with a particular file, the system has to know which sequence of directories it must search in order to find the file you want. A *pathname* is a way of specifying a file by giving a sequence of directories and the file's name. UNIX and DOS pathnames often look very similar; the most obvious difference is that DOS separates the parts of a pathname with backslash (\) characters, while UNIX uses slash (/) characters.

Full pathnames aren't the only way to refer to files. UNIX also lets you cd to a directory (just as in DOS) and then refer to files under that directory with *relative* pathnames. This chapter will examine the concept of *current directories* on DOS and UNIX, and I'll show how they can save you some typing.

The discussion of directories shows how to create directories with mkdir and how to get rid of them with rmdir (similar to the DOS MKDIR and RMDIR commands). The chapter also discusses principles of copying files to directories and moving files in and out of directories.

UNIX users have established well-used conventions for naming certain files and directories. For example, various types of information files are usually stored under a directory named /etc. I'll give an overview of these conventions, as a "map" for most of the UNIX file systems you're likely to encounter.

After I have shown how similar the UNIX and DOS file systems are, this chapter will look at some of the ways in which they differ. One of the most important differences is the concept of *file permissions,* restricting the ways people can use files. The chmod utility is the basic UNIX command for changing the permissions associated with a file; chmod is similar to the DOS ATTRIB command, but chmod has a wider range of uses.

Another important difference between UNIX and DOS is the way they handle multiple devices. On DOS, you're probably familiar with the concept of disk drives labeled A:, B:, C:, and so on. UNIX doesn't have special device names like this. Instead, UNIX devices have names that look exactly like the names of disk files.

For example, a DOS system might refer to a line printer with a special device name like PRN or LPT1. A UNIX system might create a *special file* for a line printer named /dev/lp. This looks like a normal disk file, but if you write data to the /dev/lp file, it has the effect of writing output to the printer. UNIX systems use a similar approach for floppy disk drives, tape drives, and so on. All of this will be explained in more detail later in this chapter.

Working with Files

The installation procedure that created your `userid` also created some sample files for you to work with. In this chapter, you'll be working with the following files:

`sonnet`	Contains Shakespeare's Sonnet 18
`nursery`	Contains various nursery rhymes

These two files are *text files,* containing lines of ordinary text. In Chapter 6, "Text Files—Veni, Vidi, *vi,*" I'll show you how to create text files of your own using the `vi` text editor.

Look Ma, No Suffixes!

If you're familiar with DOS, you'll notice that the files `sonnet` and `nursery` don't have suffixes (also called *filename extensions* on DOS). This is an important distinction between DOS and UNIX. On DOS, most files have suffixes; on UNIX, suffixes are much less common. You can create UNIX filenames with suffixes; for example, the files could have been called `sonnet.txt` and `nursery.txt` to show they contain text, or `sonnet.pm` and `nursery.pm` to show they contain poems. However, most UNIX users believe in minimizing their typing, so they avoid suffixes unless there is a strong reason to use them.

The other type of file used on UNIX (and DOS) is the *binary file.* On UNIX, any file that isn't a text file is a binary file. Binary files can contain any kind of data, not just text. For example, software packages commonly use binary files to hold such information as:

Spreadsheets and graphics
Databases
Executable programs
Numeric data

Of course, it's not absolutely necessary to use binary files to hold such information. You could, for example, store numeric data as strings of digits held in a text file. However, numbers stored in binary form almost always take up less disk space than numbers stored as text digits, so binary files are usually more efficient.

Files created by word processors are usually binary files. These files contain text, but they also contain other types of data describing how the text should be formatted (type font, paragraphing, margin settings, and so on). Because of these special formatting *control characters,* most word processor programs find it more practical to use binary files than text files.

File Formats on Other Operating Systems

Some other operating systems have many other file formats besides binary and text. For example, an operating system might have one file format for executable programs, several formats for databases, several different types of text files, and so on. The operating system itself provides services that read and write these different file formats.

In UNIX, the operating system only provides services for binary and text formats. A program that wants to write to a database, for example, does all the formatting first and then calls the binary input/output routines to write the database as a binary file.

In other words, the UNIX operating system doesn't do any special formatting; programs that want special formatting have to do it themselves. On other systems, the operating system (instead of the programs) may do the formatting. This reduces the amount of work that programs have to do, but it also reduces the amount of control they can exercise over their data. Programs don't have a choice; they must use the "official" formats recognized by the operating system.

Reading Files: The *more* Command

You're ready to start working with files, so you should log in to the MKS Tools software, following the procedures described in the previous chapter. When you're logged in, enter the following command:

```
more sonnet
```

You'll see that this displays a sonnet on your screen, as shown in Listing 3.1. What you see are the contents of the text file sonnet.

Listing 3.1. Contents of **sonnet**.

```
                    Sonnet XVIII
                 William Shakespeare
Shall I compare thee to a summer's day?
Thou art more lovely and more temperate.
Rough winds do shake the darling buds of May,
And summer's lease hath all too short a date.
Sometime too hot the eye of heaven shines,
And often is his gold complexion dimmed;
And every fair from fair sometime declines,
By chance, or nature's changing course, untrimmed:
But thy eternal summer shall not fade
Nor lose possession of that fair thou ow'st,
Nor shall Death brag thou wand'rest in his shade
When in eternal lines to time thou grow'st.
   So long as men can breathe or eyes can see,
   So long lives this, and this gives life to thee.
```

After the last line of sonnet, you'll see the message

```
[sonnet](EOF)
```

This is an example of a more message. You can press Enter or the Spacebar to tell more to quit. This will return you to the shell's $ prompt. Please see the next section, *Displaying Long Files,* for information on more messages.

The UNIX more command is comparable to the DOS TYPE command. They both display the contents of a file on the terminal screen. In general, a command of the form

```
more filename
```

displays the contents of any text file named filename.

The Word *Print*

If you're a DOS user, the word *print* may suggest the action of producing output on paper. However, UNIX software often uses the word *print* to describe the process of displaying text on the terminal screen. For example, it would be normal to say that more prints the contents of a file. Most UNIX systems have facilities for producing hard copy output, but UNIX is geared toward helping people work productively without paper.

In deference to DOS users, this book normally uses the word *display* to describe the action of making text appear on the terminal screen. However, we'll use *print* now and then, just to remind you of the UNIX terminology.

Displaying Long Files

Now enter the command

```
more nursery
```

This displays the contents of the text file called nursery. This file is quite long. Unless you have a huge monitor, the file is too long to fit on the screen.

You'll see that more displays the first 24 lines of the file on your screen and then displays the message

```
[nursery](56%)
```

at the bottom of the screen. On most monitors, more highlights this message in some way, usually displaying it in *reverse video* (dark letters on a light background).

After more has displayed the [nursery](56%) message, it waits for you to read what is displayed on-screen. When you are ready to see more, you have the following choices.

- ■ If you press Enter, more displays the next line of the file. Pressing Enter repeatedly displays the file line by line.

- ■ If you press the Spacebar, more displays the next 24 lines in the file. Pressing the Spacebar after each screen displays the file screen by screen.

- ■ If you enter q, more quits. You can do this if you've already read enough of the file to find out what you want. If you don't press q, more quits after it displays the last line in the file, indicated with the [EOF] message.

You can mix the preceding approaches if you like. For example, you can use the Spacebar to read through the file screen by screen until you find text in which you're particularly interested. You can then use Enter to read through this text line by line. When you reach the end of the text you wanted to see, you can use q to quit.

> ## The DOS MORE Command
>
> DOS users may be familiar with the DOS MORE command. It's similar to the UNIX version, except that you use it in conjunction with TYPE, as in
>
> ```
> TYPE FILE ¦ MORE
> ```
>
> or with the < construct, as in
>
> ```
> MORE <FILE
> ```
>
> Both the DOS and UNIX versions of the command can display output in a screen-by-screen fashion. One difference is that the UNIX more lets you quit with q and lets you display all or part of the file line by line by pressing Enter.

Multiple Files

You can also use more to display several files in a row. For example, enter the command

more sonnet nursery

more displays the contents of sonnet first, then pauses and displays the message

```
[sonnet](EOF)(Next file nursery)
```

This indicates that it's ready to display the next file, and that the name of the file is nursery. You can use the space bar to display the first screenful of nursery or q to quit.

Now try displaying the files in the opposite order, by entering the command

more nursery sonnet

When more pauses at the end of the first screenful of nursery, type :n, and then press Enter. This stands for *next* and tells more to skip ahead to the next file. You'll see that more displays the first screenful of sonnet.

You can use more to display the contents of any number of files. Using :n, you can skip from one file to the next whenever you choose. You can skip backward, too, by typing :p (for *previous*) and pressing Enter. more goes back and displays the previous file. You can use numbers to go back and forth inside a file. For example, 10b goes back ten lines, whereas 5f skips forward five lines.

The *cat* Command

The more command is the most convenient method for reading a file, because it pauses after each screenful of text. It's similar to the DOS MORE command. But UNIX has a less sophisticated command named cat.

cat simply writes the contents of one or more files to the screen, without pausing when the screen fills up. Enter the command

cat nursery sonnet

and you'll see the contents of both files zip past on the screen. (This is similar to the behavior of the DOS TYPE command.)

cat has its uses, as you'll see in later chapters. However, if you just want to see what's in a text file, you'll find that more is the most suitable command for that purpose.

Finding Out What Files You Have

On a DOS system, you'd use the DIR command to display a list of files in a directory. On UNIX, the comparable command is ls, short for *list*. Enter the command

ls

and you'll see a list of names, sorted down columns in alphabetical order:

```
browse.v    data    edit.v    profile.ksh  sh_histo  source
comics.lst  doc.v   nursery   program.v    sonnet
```

These are the names of the sample files that were created when you created your userid. Among them you should see the sonnet and nursery files that you've worked with in this chapter.

You've probably noticed that the output of ls is substantially different from the output of DIR, even though the two commands do approximately the same thing. The following list examines the differences:

> The output of ls is in lowercase, while the output of DIR is mostly in uppercase. I've mentioned before that lowercase is the preferred UNIX style.

> The output of ls is sorted in alphabetical order, while the output of DIR is not.

> DIR displays information on its entries, including the size of files, and their creation date and time. ls only displays the names. However, I'll show you later in this chapter how to use options with the ls command to obtain all the information shown by DIR.

Copying Files

DOS users are familiar with the DOS COPY command for copying files. The comparable UNIX command is named cp (in keeping with the UNIX tendency to drop vowels and put all names in lowercase). In most respects, cp works much like COPY. For example, try the command

`cp nursery poems`

This copies the existing nursery file into a new file named poems. You can display the contents of the new file with

`more poems`

The old nursery file is still around, as you can see if you try the command

`more nursery`

cp doesn't delete the old file. It just makes a new one.

Silent Running

When the DOS COPY command copies a file, it usually displays a message of the form 1 File(s) copied. When cp copies a file, you'll notice it prints no output. This is in keeping with the UNIX philosophy of keeping output to a minimum. Many UNIX utilities only print messages if something goes wrong; if they're successful in doing what they intend to do, they see no need to brag.

You can also use cp to copy into an existing file. Enter the following command:

`cp sonnet poems`

If you now try

`more poems`

you will see that poems has the same contents as the sonnet file. The cp command *overwrites* the previous contents of the poems file with the contents of sonnet.

Removing Files

You don't really need the `poems` file that you created in a previous section; it's just a copy of one of your other files. On DOS, you get rid of files using the DEL command (short for *delete*); on UNIX, you use `rm`, short for *remove*. For example, enter the command

```
rm poems
```

This gets rid of the `poems` file. To see that the file is gone, enter the command

```
more poems
```

You'll see that the `more` command prints a message saying that it can't *open* the input file poems. This means that it can't find the file: you just removed it using `rm`. You can also use the `ls` command to see that the `poems` file is gone.

`rm` can remove several files at a time. To see how this works, enter the following commands:

```
cp sonnet junk1
cp sonnet junk2
```

These `cp` commands create files named `junk1` and `junk2`. Don't worry about these files; you're going to remove them right away. Enter the `rm` command

```
rm junk1 junk2
```

and both files disappear. (You can use `ls` to see that they're actually gone.)

Contrast the behavior of `rm` with the DOS DEL command. On older versions of DOS, DEL ignores everything but the first argument, so a command such as

```
DEL junk1 junk2
```

deletes `junk1` but not `junk2`, something that certainly confused me the first time I encountered it. On newer versions of DOS, the same command displays the message

```
Parse Error 1
```

and doesn't delete either file.

Moving Files

The UNIX `mv` command *moves* a file. In one respect, this is similar to the DOS RENAME command. For example, enter the command

```
mv sonnet sonnet18
```

This moves the file sonnet to the new name sonnet18. Enter

```
more sonnet
```

and more will tell you that sonnet can no longer be found. Enter

```
more sonnet18
```

and you'll see that sonnet18 now has the contents of the old sonnet file. In effect, you've renamed the file. To put things back the way they were, enter

```
mv sonnet18 sonnet
```

which changes the file's name back to sonnet.

A little later on, I'll show that mv can do more tricks than just renaming files. However, I can't discuss these tricks until I talk about directories later in this chapter.

Rules for UNIX Filenames

According to the POSIX standard, a UNIX filename can contain any of the characters in the following list. This is called the *portable character set* for filenames. Many UNIX-like systems let you use other characters too, but the characters in the table are the only ones you can be sure are accepted by every UNIX system.

```
abcdefghijklmnopqrstuvwxyz
ABCDEFGHIJKLMNOPQRSTUVWXYZ
0123456789
. (dot)
_ (underscore)
- (dash)
```

There are no restrictions on the way these characters can be used. For example, DOS only lets you have one dot (.) in a filename, but UNIX lets you use several. DOS does not let you have names that begin with a dot, but this is perfectly valid on UNIX. For example, the following names are valid in UNIX, but not on DOS:

```
.profile   ellipsis...   please.read.me
```

The POSIX standard allows names to be up to 14 characters long. (DOS allows a maximum of eight characters, plus a three-character suffix.) Many UNIX-like systems allow names to be much longer than 14 characters, but 14 is the maximum if you want your filename to be valid on every UNIX system.

In filenames the uppercase characters are different from the lowercase characters. For example, FILE is not the same name as file. They are two distinct files, with no connection to one another. Of course, having two names that are so similar is bound to be confusing, so it's a good idea to avoid names that only differ in the case of their letters. Most people stick to lowercase letters most of the time.

MKS Tools Note

The DOS file system does not distinguish between upper- and lowercase letters in filenames. Therefore, the MKS Tools software cannot make the distinction either. This is one of the few ways in which the package differs from a real UNIX system.

More About File Suffixes

Earlier, I mentioned that you can use suffixes on UNIX filenames if you want. However, there are differences in the ways that DOS and UNIX handle suffixes.

The DOS file system treats a suffix as a special part of the name, and makes sure that the suffix has three characters at most. In the output of DIR, the suffix is shown as a separate part of the name. Internally, DOS stores the suffix and the rest of the name as separate parts of the filename.

On UNIX, the suffix is usually not special, and the dot is just another character in a name. You can use suffixes if they help you organize and identify your files, but that's up to you. The file system doesn't treat suffixes specially. For example, there's no limit to the length of a suffix. You can also have several things that look like suffixes, as in report.doc.1. Some utilities give special treatment to filenames that begin with a dot; but that's a feature of particular programs, not the operating system itself.

DOS treats the dot as a special character that separates the first part of a filename from the suffix. On UNIX, the dot is just another character, with no special meaning or treatment.

Files and Directories

If you're a DOS user, you are almost certainly familiar with the concept of *directories*. In both DOS and UNIX, a directory contains files in the same way that an office filing cabinet contains file folders. Directories let you organize your files: you can use directories to group together files that have similar types or purposes, making it faster and easier to find the files you want. Directories give *structure* to a file system, in the same way that a chain of command gives structure to an organization.

When a file system uses directories, the structure of the file system is usually compared to a *tree*. The files of the system are like the leaves, and the directories are like the branches. Each leaf attaches to a single branch; each branch can support several leaves, and can also support several smaller branches.

In the same way, every file in a UNIX file system belongs to some directory. Each directory can contain several files, and can also contain several other directories, called *subdirectories*. Subdirectories can have subdirectories of their own, in the same way that branches can have branches of their own. Figure 3.1 shows a simple tree-like file structure on a UNIX system.

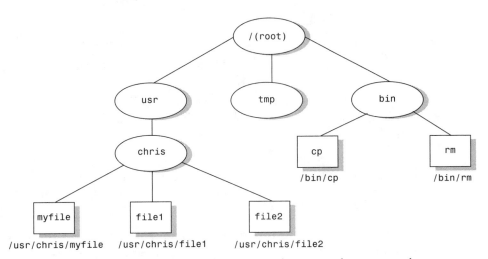

Figure 3.1. *This is a simple UNIX file structure. Ovals represent directories, and squares represent files. The pathname of each file is given below the square that represents the file.*

The Root Directory

At the top of Figure 3.1 there is a directory with the simple name / (the slash character). This directory is called the *root directory,* and it is present in every UNIX file system. As the name suggests, the root directory is the base of the file system tree. Every file in the file system is either contained in the root directory or in some subdirectory of the root.

Pathnames

Figure 3.1 also shows the pathnames of the files it depicts. A pathname is a way to specify a file that you want to work with. A full pathname describes a path through the file system tree, beginning at the root and ending at the file you want. For example, consider the full pathname

```
/usr/chris/myfile
```

This full pathname consists of several *components,* as follows:

> The first component is the / at the beginning of the name. This indicates that the path should begin at the root.
>
> The second component is usr. The system looks for usr in the root directory and finds that usr is a directory. The path therefore leads to the usr directory.
>
> The next component is chris. (The / between usr and chris is there to separate the components.) The system looks for chris in the usr directory and finds that chris is also a directory. The path therefore leads to the chris directory.
>
> The final component is myfile. (Again, the / between chris and myfile is just a separator.) The system looks for myfile in the chris directory. This is the end of the path.

As you can see, a pathname is like a map that takes you through a series of directories until you reach the directory or file you want.

> **Terminology Note**
>
> Except for the root, every directory is a subdirectory of some other directory. Therefore, it's superfluous to use the word *subdirectory*, and in most cases you simply call everything a directory. I only use the word subdirectory when I want to stress the relationship between a subdirectory and the directory that contains it.

The last component of a pathname is often called the *basename*. For example, the basename of

```
/usr/chris/myfile
```

is `myfile`. The basename of

```
/usr/chris
```

is `chris`.

The collection of components that precede the basename is often called the *dirname*. For example, the dirname of

```
/usr/chris/myfile
```

is `/usr/chris`, and the dirname of

```
/usr/chris
```

is just `/usr`. UNIX documentation frequently uses the terms *basename* and *dirname*.

Slash Versus Backslash

UNIX uses the slash (`/`) character to separate the components of a pathname. If you're a DOS user, you're probably aware that DOS uses the backslash (`\`) for the same purpose. Make sure that you don't get the two mixed up. You can't use the backslash as a separator on UNIX, because UNIX uses the backslash for other purposes. You're almost certain to get confusing results if you use the backslash to separate pathname components on a UNIX system.

The Current Directory

Enter the command

```
ls
```

As you've already seen, the ls command lists the contents of a directory...but which directory? It lists the contents of the *current directory,* also called your *working directory.*

If you're familiar with DOS, you probably know what a current directory is, but in case you don't, I'll explain the concept from the start.

Figure 3.1 showed how you could specify files with pathnames, giving a "map" of the path from the root to the desired file. But this can mean a lot of typing. For example, suppose that you're working with a collection of files under the directory /usr/chris.

```
/usr/chris/file1
/usr/chris/file2
/usr/chris/file3
    ...
```

It's a lot of extra work to type /usr/chris in front of every filename. Ideally, you'd like to tell the operating system, "Every file I mention is going to be under /usr/chris unless I say otherwise." That way you can simply type the names

```
file1
file2
file3
 ...
```

For this reason, both UNIX and DOS use the concept of a current directory. You can specify any directory in the file system as your current directory; then if you give a filename without telling what directory the file is in, the system looks for the file in the current directory.

You've already used this concept without thinking about it. When I talked about the cp command at the beginning of the chapter, you used the command

```
cp sonnet poems
```

In this command, sonnet and poems are filenames, but not full pathnames. The system therefore assumes that sonnet and poems are in your current directory.

Determining Your Current Directory

How can you tell what your current directory is? The pwd (print working directory) command displays the name of your current directory. Enter the command

pwd

and you'll see that the system displays a directory name, such as

```
c:/lu/usr/jim
```

Of course, you'll see your own login name instead of jim. On a true UNIX system, you wouldn't see C: because this kind of device name comes from DOS, not UNIX. This directory name has several components. The last component (the basename) should be your userid. The other components (the dirname) are determined by the way you installed the MKS Tools software on your system.

When you log in, the system automatically sets your current directory to this directory, called your *home directory*. Your home directory is your personal directory. Typically, people use the home directory to keep personal files of various sorts. In Chapter 9, "Customizing," I'll show how you can use files in your home directory to customize the behavior of the system. Right now, the only files in your home directory are the sample files that were set up when you created your userid during installation.

The *cd* Command

The cd command lets you change your current directory. It is almost exactly like the DOS CD command. For example, enter the command

cd /

Entering this command sets your current directory to /, the root of the file system. If you now enter

ls

the command lists the contents of the root directory. Now enter

cd lu
ls

The cd lu line sets your current directory to a directory named lu under the root directory. This is where the MKS Tools software is stored if you use the standard installation as described in Appendix G, "Installing the MKS Tools Package," and

the installation page at the end of this book. The `ls` command displays the contents of the `/lu` directory. The output will be

```
bin     etc     lu.bat  tmp     usr
```

Enter

cd etc

and you go to a directory named `etc` under `lu`. Typing

ls

now shows you the contents of `/lu/etc`, a set of information files used for system administration and other jobs. You will see

```
issue       large.fnt   passwd      utmp
italic.fnt  lib.b       small.fnt
```

You can get back to your home directory simply by typing

```
cd
```

A `cd` command without any argument sets your current directory to your home directory. Enter

pwd

and the system shows you that you're back in your home directory.

Here's one more useful trick when using `cd`. Enter

cd
cd /

to set your current directory to the root, then enter

cd -

(the final character is a dash or minus sign). You'll see that the system displays the name of your home directory, showing that you're back in that directory again. The reason is that `cd -` goes back to the previous current directory. Enter

cd -

again, and you'll see that you've gone back to the root. Enter

cd -

one last time, and you'll see that you're back in your home directory. `cd -` can switch back and forth between directories, a helpful thing to remember if you happen to be doing a job that deals with files in two directories.

> **Note**
>
> The cd - command only works when you're using the KornShell as your shell. If you're using some other shell, cd - may not work.

> **DOS CD Versus UNIX cd**
>
> The biggest difference between the DOS CD and the UNIX cd is that
>
> cd
>
> goes to your home directory on UNIX, while
>
> CD
>
> displays the name of your current directory on DOS. This means that CD without arguments on DOS is like pwd on UNIX.

The . and .. Notations

On UNIX (and on DOS), the notation . (just a dot character) stands for the current directory, and the notation .. stands for the directory that contains the current directory. For example, enter

```
cd
pwd
cd ..
pwd
```

You'll see that the first cd command moves you to your home directory, and the second cd command moves you from your home directory to the directory that contains your home directory (probably a directory named /lu/usr). Now enter the commands

```
cd .
pwd
```

You'll see that you're still in the same directory. The command

```
cd .
```

has no effect; it changes the current directory to `.`, which stands for the current directory.

The `..` directory is often called the *parent directory* of the current directory. The parent directory contains the current directory.

Use `cd` to return to your home directory, and then enter

cd ../..

Ask yourself what directory you should be in now. Use

pwd

to see whether you were right. Finally, enter

cd

to return to your home directory.

Working with Directories

Now that I've discussed the basics of directories, let's look at a few operations that you can perform on directories.

Listing the Contents of a Directory

You've already seen that the `ls` command can list the contents of your current directory. You can also list the contents of a different directory, just by specifying the directory name. For example,

ls /

lists the contents of the root directory.

ls /lu

lists the contents of `lu` under the root directory.

Creating Directories

The `mkdir` command creates new directories. It is comparable to the DOS MKDIR (or MD) command. For example, enter

cd

to make sure you're in your home directory, then enter the command

mkdir newdir

This creates a directory named newdir under your home directory. If you enter the command

ls

you'll see that newdir is now listed in the contents of the current directory.

Enter the command

ls newdir

to list the contents of the new directory. You'll see that ls simply returns without printing anything. The newdir directory doesn't contain anything yet, so there are no names for ls to display.

Distinguishing Files and Directories

You'll notice that directory names can look a lot like filenames; for example, there's no visual difference between a filename like sonnet and a directory name like newdir. In fact, you could create a directory named sonnet if there wasn't already a file with that name. (If you try to create a directory named sonnet, the system will tell you that the current directory already contains something named sonnet.)

So how can you tell whether a particular name is a file or a directory? One solution is to use ls -p instead of just ls. -p is an option that tells ls to mark each directory name with a / character. You'll learn more about options for ls in Chapter 4, "Basic Tools: Five Ways to List a Directory."

Copying and Moving into Directories

To put something into the newdir directory, enter

cd

to go to your home directory, use the command

cp nursery newdir

This copies the `nursery` file into `newdir`. If you now enter

ls newdir

you'll see that the output is

nursery

The general rule is that if the last argument in a `cp` command is the name of a directory, the other arguments should be files to be copied into that directory. `cp` will then make copies of those files and store them in that directory, using the same basenames as the original files.

The same principle applies to moving files. Enter the command

mv sonnet newdir

This moves the `sonnet` file into `newdir`. Enter the commands

ls
ls newdir

and you'll see that `sonnet` is no longer in your home directory. `mv` moved it into `newdir`.

Relative Pathnames

You've moved `sonnet` into `newdir`. Now you'll want to move it back. Do this with the command

mv newdir/sonnet .

How does this work?

> First, look at the name `newdir/sonnet`. This is similar to the pathnames you've seen, but it doesn't have the / at the beginning. It's a *relative pathname,* telling where a file is relative to the current directory. In this case, the file is in `newdir` under the current directory, and the file's name is `sonnet`.

> The second argument is the dot character (`.`). As mentioned previously, this is shorthand for the name of the current directory.

As a result, the preceding command moves `sonnet` out of `newdir` and into the current directory. Use the commands

ls
ls newdir

to see that `sonnet` is back in your home directory and no longer in `newdir`.

As another example, ask yourself what command you'd need to display the contents of the `nursery` file in the `newdir` directory. The answer is

`more newdir/nursery`

Try this command to see that it works.

Finally, ask yourself what command you'd need to remove the copy of `nursery` from `newdir`. Enter this command, then use the `ls` command to verify that you were right.

Relative Pathnames Versus Absolute Pathnames

The general rule is this: if a pathname starts with a slash (`/`), it is an absolute pathname, beginning at the root. If it does not start with a slash, it is a relative pathname, beginning at the current directory.

Removing Directories

The `rmdir` command removes a directory. The `rmdir` command is comparable to the DOS `RMDIR` command. For example, enter

`rmdir newdir`

This should remove the `newdir` directory.

If you didn't get rid of the `newdir/nursery` file as I suggested in the last section, you will find that `rmdir` doesn't work on this directory. Before you can remove a directory with `rmdir`, you have to remove all the files and subdirectories under that directory. Remove the `newdir/nursery` file and try again.

You Can't Saw Off a Branch When You're Sitting on It

You cannot use `rmdir` to remove a directory if you have used `cd` to make that directory your current directory. You must use `cd` to switch to a different directory first, then you can use `rmdir`.

Common Directories

Over the years, UNIX users have developed *conventions* for the use of directories on UNIX systems. You can think of these conventions as rules of thumb that people have found useful in the past; they aren't mandatory, but they're almost universally observed. You might compare them to the map-making convention of putting North at the top of the map; you can do things differently if you want, but it's likely to lead to confusion.

Most UNIX systems have the following directories under the root directory:

/bin   Holds many of the utilities and other programs that can be executed on the system. bin stands for *binary,* and utilities are almost always binary files.

/dev   Holds *device files* (discussed later in this chapter).

/etc   Holds various information files that are used for system administration and other purposes. For example, the file /etc/passwd typically holds the names of all authorized users, their passwords (encrypted so that no one can read them), and other kinds of personal information.

/tmp   Can hold *temporary* files for people or programs. For example, the UNIX sort program for sorting the contents of files sometimes needs disk space to hold the partly sorted contents of a file temporarily. If so, sort creates a file under /tmp and uses this file to hold partly sorted data. When sort has finished its work, it removes the working file from /tmp. As another example, suppose you're about to start working on an important data file and are afraid you'll make a mistake. You could use the command

```
cp data /tmp/just_in_case
```

to save a copy of the file in /tmp with the name just_in_case. Then if you do make a mistake that ruins the file, you can copy back the original from /tmp. After you've made your changes successfully, you can get rid of the copy under /tmp. Many large UNIX sites automatically clean out /tmp on a regular basis by deleting any file that's been in /tmp for more than a day.

/u   Holds the home directories of system users. For technical reasons, there's a limit to the number of files and directories that can be stored under one directory. Therefore on UNIX systems with a large number of users, it's possible that the home directories won't all fit under /u and additional directories will be necessary. You might also see directories named /usr, /u1, /u2, and so on containing the home directories of additional users. (The convention of using /u for user directories is not universal. Some sites prefer different names.)

Organization of the MKS Tools

The MKS Tools package associated with this book uses an organization that is similar to that of a UNIX system. If you followed the standard installation procedure from the installation page at the end of this book and Appendix G, "Installing the MKS Tools Package," everything associated with this package is stored in the directory /lu under the root directory on your hard disk. The /lu directory has subdirectories /lu/bin to hold the software, /lu/etc to hold information files, /lu/tmp for temporary files, and /lu/usr to hold the home directories of system users.

Organizing Your Home Directory

Many people find it convenient to organize their home directories in a way that parallels the root directory. They use mkdir to create the following subdirectories under their home directory:

bin	Holds the user's own executable programs
etc	Holds various information files
tmp	Holds temporary working files

You will also find it convenient to create a directory for every project (or group of projects) you work on. For example, suppose you prepare quarterly reports for your company, and each report consists of a financial analysis and personnel ratings. You might create a directory structure like the one shown in Figure 3.2.

In this structure, you make a new directory for each quarter. The directory for a quarter has two subdirectories, finance and personnel. The finance directory might contain separate subdirectories for

Spreadsheets
Analysis documents
Charts

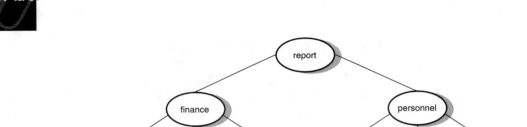

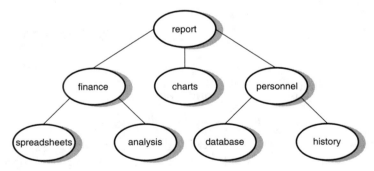

Figure 3.2. *One possible structure for a directory containing all the information for a quarterly report.*

The `personnel` directory might contain separate subdirectories for

    Personnel databases
    Personnel history documents
    Charts

This isn't the only possible method of organization. For example, instead of having one directory for finance charts and another for personnel charts, you may find it useful to have a single directory for charts, as shown in Figure 3.3.

Figure 3.3. *Another possible structure for a directory containing all the information for a quarterly report. Both financial and personnel reports make use of the charts in the charts directory.*

There is no definitive way you can use directories to organize your files. The most important principle is to make sure that you do use directories. Without directories, you get what is called a *flat filing system,* comparable to spreading all your file folders out on a desk rather than putting them in some kind of order inside a filing cabinet. Directories make it easier to find files and to show the interrelationships between files.

File Characteristics

The UNIX file system records various kinds of information about each file, called the *characteristics* of the file. File characteristics include the following:

- The size of the file
- The date and time that the contents of the file were last changed
- Who is permitted to use the file, and how they are permitted to use it

The sections that follow explore these characteristics in more detail.

File Permissions

Because DOS was designed as a single-user system, it has a simplistic approach toward file permissions as follows:

> You can *hide* a file so that it doesn't appear in the output of DIR. This makes it a little harder for other users to find the file, but it doesn't prevent them from reading or writing the file when they find it. (A skilled user can easily write a program to find hidden files.)

> In later versions of DOS, you can mark a file as *read-only* using the ATTRIB command so that you can read the file but not write to it. This prevents you from overwriting the file by accident, but it doesn't provide any security against other users. Anyone else using the system can use ATTRIB to make the file writable again, then overwrite the contents.

UNIX, on the other hand, was designed as a multiuser system and therefore has a broader approach to file permissions. Its approach is not as comprehensive as many other commercial systems; remember that UNIX was originally constructed for use by a handful of professionals all working for the same company, so they did not devote themselves to building in an extensive security system. Still, the UNIX file permission system is quite adequate to meet the needs of most computing sites.

A UNIX file has three sets of permissions: those that apply to the file's *owner*, those that apply to the file's *group*, and those that apply to everyone else on the system.

> **The Limitations of DOS**
>
> The sections to come will examine the file permissions available on UNIX. Unfortunately, these cannot be simulated well on a DOS system because of DOS's limited permission capabilities. Thus the MKS Tools software cannot let you try out the full range of UNIX permissions. I will discuss the software's limitations after I give some background about UNIX permissions.

The Owner of a File

Every user on a UNIX system has an assigned identification number, called a `userid` number. This is automatically assigned when you are authorized to use the s ystem. When you create a file, UNIX records your `userid` as one of the file's characteristics. From that point on, you are considered the file's *owner.* There are ways you can transfer ownership to someone else, and there are special cases in which you can create a file without becoming the owner, but in general, you are the owner of every file you create.

The *owner permissions* of a file apply to the owner only. For example, you can set the permissions of a file you own so that you are the only one who can read the file or write to it. I'll show how to do this in a later section.

UNIX Groups

The system administrator of a UNIX system can create *groups* on the system. A group is a collection of users who are affiliated in some way. For example, the administrator might create a separate group for each project that uses the machine, or a group for each department in the company.

One person can belong to several groups. One of these is considered your *primary group;* the rest are *secondary groups.* The system administrator decides which groups you can belong to and which one is your primary group.

When you create a file, UNIX records your primary group as one of the file's characteristics. From that point on, the file belongs to your primary group. There are ways to change which group a file belongs to, but this book won't look at those.

The *group permissions* of a file apply to everyone belonging to the same group (whether the group is their primary group or one of their secondary ones). For example, you can set up a file so that everyone in the group can read it but outsiders can't. I'll show how to do this in a later section.

Other Permissions

The *other permissions* of a file apply to everybody on the system who is not the file's owner or in the file's group (in other words, the outsiders). For example, you can set up a file so that everyone on the system can read it. I'll show how to do this after you look at the types of permissions that you can put on a file.

Types of File Permissions

There are three types of file permissions. Each is represented by a code letter.

r   Lets you read the file.

w   Lets you write to the file.

x   Lets you execute the file; for example, if a file contains an executable program, you need x permission to be able to execute the program.

These types of permissions can be separately assigned (or not assigned) to the file's owner, to its group, and to all others. They are always written in this order: rwx.

For example, suppose you are working on a file that will be part of a larger project. As the owner of the file, you might give yourself read and write permission on the file, and give read permission to other workers in your group and to everyone else on the system. You would write this set-up as

rw-r--r--

The first three characters rw- stand for the owner's permissions: read and write, but not execute. (It is traditional to put a dash (-) in place of permissions that have not been given.) The next three characters stand for group permissions: r-- means read permission but not permission to write or execute. The final three characters stand for other permissions: again, r-- means read permission but not write or execute permission.

As another example, consider

rwxrwxr--

In this case, both the owner and the owner's primary group have rwx permission (read, write, and execute), while others only have r-- permission (read only).

```
rwxr-x--x
```

says that the owner has full permissions, the group has permission to read and execute, and others only have permission to execute.

```
r--------
```

says that only the owner has permission to read (but not to write or execute), and no one else can use the file for any purpose.

Types of Directory Permissions

A similar system of permissions applies to directories. You use the same codes, but they have slightly different meanings.

r	Lets you read the names of files and subdirectories contained by the directory. You can only read their names; to read the contents of a file, you need read permission on the file itself.
w	Lets you create new files and subdirectories under the directory.
x	Lets you search through the directory. This is a weaker permission than r; it only lets you determine if a particular file or subdirectory exists. If you have x but not r, you can try to access a file or subdirectory if you know its name, but you can't browse through the directory to find what names the directory contains.

Listing File Characteristics

A form of the ls command can list the characteristics of a file or directory. For example, enter the command

```
ls -l sonnet
```

(where -l is a dash character followed by the lowercase letter l). The command displays output of the form

```
-rwxrwxrwa 1 jim      0        707 Feb 17 15:52 sonnet
```

The output you see won't be exactly like the previous line. In place of jim, you'll see your login name, and in place of Feb 17 15:52, you'll see the date and time that you last changed the sonnet file, but the rest should be similar. Examine this output piece by piece.

-	The first character is a dash for files, or the letter d for directories.
rwxrwxrwx	Permissions for the file; in this case, the owner, the group, and all others have full permissions on the file. (See the sidebar for possible differences in this part of the output.)
1	Stands for the number of *links* to the file. The concept of links is beyond the scope of this book. On DOS, this number will always be 1.
jim	Stands for the userid of the file's owner. This is taken from a file of information that UNIX stores under the /etc directory. With MKS Tools, this file is /lu/etc/passwd, and the first person named in that file is assumed to own every file on the system.
0	Stands for the file's group. This too is taken from a file of information that UNIX stores under the /etc directory. The MKS Tools just use 0 for this, because DOS doesn't have groups.
707	Stands for the size of the file, expressed as a numbe~ bytes. (One byte equals one character in a text f~
Feb 17 15:52	For a file, this is the date and time that th~ changed; for a directory, it's the date a~ directory was created.
sonnet	The name of the file or direct~

In other words, ls -1 tells you exactly the same ~
DIR command does.

You don't have to specify the name of a fi~

```
ls -1
```

you'll get the same sort of informati~
current directory.

As another example, enter the ~

```
mkdir junkdir
ls -1
```

67

This creates a directory named junkdir, then uses ls -1 to display the characteristics of the current directory again. You'll see that everything is the same as before, except that there is now a line for junkdir. This line begins with d to show that it is describing a directory. Get rid of junkdir with

rmdir junkdir

before you go on to the next section.

DOS Variations in Permissions

The version of ls that comes with the MKS Tools software is based on ls from MKS Toolkit. Because DOS does not have the concept of group or other permissions, this ls uses the permissions part of its output to display information on DOS file characteristics. In particular, you may see the letter a somewhere, standing for the DOS *archive bit;* this bit is on if the file has changed since the last time it was backed up. You may also see the letter h, indicating a hidden file, or the letter s, indicating a system file.

None of these letters appears on a true UNIX system. UNIX does not have such concepts. They are only present because this version of ls tries to give DOS information in the UNIX format.

The *chmod* Command

The ~hmod command sets the permissions for a file or directory. The general form of ~and is

~ame

~tes the permissions that you want and name is the name of the file ~rmissions you want to set.

~ke many forms, but the most useful form is this:

!ling which permissions you want to set. You can ~p, o for other, or a for all.

~ions on or a - if you want to turn permis-

3. Use one or more letters telling which permissions you want to turn on or off. The standard letters are r, w, and x.

As an example, enter the following command:

```
chmod a-w sonnet
```

This changes the permissions for the sonnet file. In a-w, here's what each part means:

a	Says that you want to change permissions for all users: the owner, the group, and others.
-	Says you want to turn permissions off.
w	Says that you want to turn off write permissions.

Enter the following

```
ls -l sonnet
```

and you'll see that the permissions are now

```
r-xr-xr-x
```

Write permission has been turned off for each type of user. Remember that you m¹
see an a somewhere in the permissions because of the DOS archive bit, and t¹
first character on the line will be - because sonnet is an ordinary file.

Now enter

```
chmod a+w sonnet
ls -l sonnet
```

and you'll see that write permission has been turned bac¹
user. The + turns permissions on, while the - turns th¹

Next is a list of some more examples. As noted befo¹
permissions properly, so you shouldn't try to
just provide more illustrations of how chmo

```
chmod o-rwx file     # UNIX only --
```

turns off all permissions for other us¹

```
chmod ug+x file     # UNIX on¹
```

turns on

69

turns off all permissions for all users, then turns on full permissions for the owner and read permission for the group. As a result, outsiders cannot do anything with the file, the group can only read it, and the owner has full permissions.

Device Files: All the World's a File

On DOS, there are two ways to refer to specific devices.

Disk drives are typically referred to by letters, followed by colons, as in A:, B:, C:, and so on.

Devices attached to *communications ports* are typically referred to by names. For example, the printer can be referred to by the name PRN. (DOS communication ports are plug-in connections, typically found on the back of the machine where you can connect printers, modems, and other devices.)

On UNIX, however, all devices are referred to as if they were files in the file system. Typically, special devices are set up as if they are files under the directory /dev (a directory dev for devices under the root). For example, /dev/lp might represent a line printer. Copying a file to this, as in cp file /dev/lp, has the effect of printing the file on the line printer. Other files and directories under /dev might represent tape drives, terminals, or other devices attached to the UNIX system.

Devices with the MKS Tools

Because it simulates UNIX on DOS, the MKS Tools software finds it venient to use DOS's lettered disk drive system rather than using /dev. ou may refer to different disk drives by letter. For example, A:/file file named file, under the root directory of disk A:.

/dev are set up by the system administrator as part of the ystem. Different types of UNIX and UNIX look-alikes tting up these files. This process can be very compli- e a UNIX or UNIX look-alike system, you must

Device Drivers

When you perform I/O (input and/or output) on a file under /dev, the operating system sees that you want to work with a special device and does whatever work is necessary to make it possible to read or write to that device. As much as possible, the system tries to make it look like the device is just another file in the file system. To do this, the system makes use of a *device driver,* software that handles actual I/O with the device. Different devices require different device driver programs; writing device driver programs is far beyond the scope of this book.

The Null Device

Many UNIX systems contain a special file under /dev called /dev/null. This is not present with MKS Tools, but it is common enough on UNIX that it should be discussed.

Any data written to /dev/null simply disappears forever. You may wonder why you would ever find this desirable. The answer is that some programs produce output that you want to disregard; in such instances, you can simply send the output to /dev/null. When /dev/null is used this way, it is sometimes called a *bit bucket* or *sink*. Similarly, if you try to read from /dev/null, you are immediately told that you've reached the end of the file. Thus, /dev/null is called a *null file* or *empty file*.

The /dev/null file is sometimes called a *bit bucket* or a *sink*. Data that comes in never comes out. In future chapters, I'll show examples where /dev/null comes in handy.

Chapter Review

A text file contains only readable text. You can read the contents of a text file one screen at a time by using the more command. more lets you read several files in a row, and go back and forth between different files.

A binary file can contain any kind of data. I have not yet discussed commands for reading the contents of binary files.

Files on UNIX have an owner and a group. A set of owner permissions, group permissions, and other permissions is associated with each file. r permission lets someone read a file; w lets someone write to the file; and x lets someone execute the file. You can change permissions with the chmod command.

The `cp` command can copy files into other files, as in

cp file1 file2

or it can copy several files into a directory, as in

cp file1 file2 file3 dir

You can use the `mv` command in similar ways to move a file to a new name or to move several files into another directory.

The `rm` command can get rid of one or more files.

The `cd` command changes your current directory and the `pwd` command displays the name of your current directory. The notation . stands for the current directory, while .. stands for the directory containing the current directory.

The `ls` command can list the contents of a directory. If you do not specify a directory name, `ls` lists the contents of the current directory. When used in the form `ls -l`, the command lists additional information about the files and subdirectories of a directory including

> Permissions
> Owner and group
> The size of a file, expressed as several bytes
> The date and time a file was last changed or a directory was created

The root directory is the base of the UNIX file system. Absolute pathnames refer to a file or directory by describing a path through a sequence of directories, from the root to the file or directory desired. Relative pathnames describe the same sort of path, but begin at the current directory instead of the root. An absolute pathname begins with the / character, while a relative pathname does not. You can use an absolute pathname anywhere that a relative pathname is valid, and vice versa.

By convention, UNIX systems use the directory /etc to hold various kinds of information files, /dev to hold device files, /bin to hold standard executable programs, /tmp to hold temporary working files, and /u to hold the home directories of users. Many people find it helpful to use the same sort of organization for their home directories.

Special devices such as printers or tape drives are represented as files in the UNIX file system, usually under the /dev directory. Reading or writing to a device file has the effect of reading or writing to the device. /dev/null is a special device, called a null device; data written to /dev/null simply disappears.

Table 3.1 summarizes several UNIX commands, what they do, and their DOS counterparts.

Table 3.1. UNIX commands and their DOS counterparts.

UNIX	DOS	Purpose
cat	TYPE	Display file contents
cd	CD	Change current directory
chmod	ATTRIB	Change file characteristics
cp	COPY	Copy files
ls	DIR	List directory contents
mkdir	MKDIR	Create directories
more	MORE	Display file contents, with pagination
mv	RENAME	Rename (move) files
pwd	CD	Print working directory name
rm	DEL	Get rid of files
rmdir	RMDIR	Get rid of directories

Exercises

1. Use the pg command to display the contents of the sonnet and nursery files. What differences do you see between the way that pg works and the way that more does?

2. What are the advantages of having three commands that display the contents of a file (more, cat, pg)? Are there any disadvantages? If so, what are they?

3. cd to the /lu directory. Using an absolute pathname with the ls command, list the contents of your home directory. Do the same thing again, only this time use a relative pathname. cd back to your home directory when you're done.

4. Suppose a new user named Chris wants to use your system. Create a new home directory for chris under the /lu/usr directory. (If your system already has a user named chris, pick a different name.) Copy the sonnet and nursery files into the new directory for chris.

5. Set up the following subdirectories under the chris directory: bin, tmp, stuff. Move the sonnet and nursery files from the chris home directory to the stuff subdirectory.

6. Now suppose that Chris is leaving to live in Tahiti. Get rid of the chris directory created in the previous exercises.

7. Under your home directory, copy the nursery file into a new file named no_read. Use the chmod command to make this file read-only.

8. Using rm, try to delete no_read. What happens? Can you still delete the file? Read the rm man page if you need help.

9. Read about the -i option of the rm command in the rm man page. Enter the commands

```
cp sonnet nursery /lu/tmp
rm -i /lu/tmp/sonnet /lu/tmp/nursery
```

and reply to rm's questions so that you delete /lu/tmp/sonnet but not /lu/tmp/nursery.

Chapter

4

BASIC TOOLS: FIVE WAYS TO LIST A DIRECTORY

Chapter 3, "The UNIX File System: Go Climb a Tree," showed how the ls command can list the contents of a directory, and how ls -l lists additional information about files and directories.

This chapter examines five different ways to do the same sort of job. This might sound odd or redundant, but there are several reasons why it makes sense.

It shows there are several ways to do the same task. There is no uniquely "right" answer.

Each approach uses a different format for displaying the information. Each of these formats has its strengths and weaknesses. When you know how to produce information in a variety of formats, you have more freedom to choose within a particular context.

Most importantly, the different approaches illustrate several ways you can combine UNIX commands to produce results.

The first technique you'll look at is the use of *command options*. As you probably know from working with DOS, options modify the behavior of commands. In particular, you'll look at various options that you can use with the `ls` command, to change the information that `ls` outputs and the format of that output.

The second technique uses *glob constructs,* also called *wildcard constructs* or *filename generation constructs.* UNIX lets you use simple character strings to stand for a collection of filenames, in much the same way that some DOS commands use *.* to stand for every file under a directory. The UNIX facilities for filename representation are more extensive than the DOS facilities, and they're carried out in a different way. The way glob constructs are handled has repercussions that I'll discuss in detail.

The third technique uses the UNIX `find` command. This command searches through a directory to identify files and subdirectories that meet certain criteria. For example, you can use `find` to display all the files under a directory that have changed in the last week.

The fourth technique uses *redirection* to divert the output of a command like `ls` into a file. This is convenient when you want to keep the information for later use. Otherwise, the information just sweeps past on the screen and disappears forever.

The fifth technique uses *pipes* in a variety of ways. A pipe takes the output from one command and feeds it as input to another command. Using pipes you can link together several commands into a *pipeline* that performs a complex task with simple components. DOS has pipes too, but DOS utilities don't exploit pipes as effectively as UNIX utilities do.

ls Revisited

I've discussed several forms of the `ls` command.

```
ls
```

displays the names of the files and subdirectories in the current directory;

```
ls dirname
```

displays the names of the files and subdirectories in the directory given by `dirname`; and

```
ls -l dirname
```

provides detailed information about the files and subdirectories of `dirname`, including the size of the files, their permissions, and the date and time the files were last modified.

The Form of UNIX Options

The `-l` in the last `ls` form in the previous section is an example of a UNIX *option*. Most UNIX options take the form of a dash (`-`) (the minus sign) followed by a single letter or digit. Contrast this with DOS, where command options usually begin with a slash (`/`) instead of a dash. The option `-l` is usually pronounced *dash-ell*.

In UNIX commands, it matters whether option letters are uppercase or lowercase. For example, the `ls` command has both an `r` and an `-R` option, with completely unrelated effects.

Options must come immediately after the command name, before any other arguments on the command line. For example, you must write

```
ls -l dirname
```

If you switch the position of `-l` and `dirname`, you'll get incorrect results. Try it and see.

Options of *ls*

Now it's time to examine several of the more useful options of the `ls` command. Sign on to the MKS Tools software and follow along as I discuss each example.

Changing the Columns

First, enter the command

```
cd /lu/bin
```

to make `/lu/bin` your current directory. This directory contains a lot of files, and that will make it easier to see what I'm talking about.

Enter the command

`ls`

As always, `ls` displays the basenames of the files and directories under `/lu/bin`, arranged in columns with names sorted in alphabetical order down the columns. Now try

`ls -x`

(with a lowercase x). This gives you the same kind of output, except that names are sorted in alphabetical order across the columns instead of down the columns.

You can use this option to display the contents of any directory. For example, enter

`ls -x /`

This displays the contents of the root directory in the new form.

Now enter

`cd`

to return to your home directory.

Across or Down?

In some versions of UNIX, the default is for `ls` to sort names down columns, as we've shown. In others, the default is for `ls` to sort names across columns even if you don't specify `-x`. If the default is to sort names across columns, specifying the `-C` (uppercase C) option will sort down columns.

Size Information

Enter the command

`ls -s /lu`

This command displays the size of each file and subdirectory under the `/lu` directory. Sizes are given *blocks,* where each block is 512 bytes long. You'll find that measuring file sizes in terms of blocks is more convenient than in the byte counts that DOS uses. The numbers are smaller, so they're easier to compare and understand, just as it's simpler to measure long distances in miles rather than inches.

> ### How Big Is a Block?
> With the MKS Tools `ls` command, a block is 512 bytes, or half a kilobyte. On some other systems, blocks are 1,024 bytes, or a full kilobyte.

You'll see that subdirectories are shown with a size of zero. This is one way that you can distinguish files from the subdirectories on DOS. Unfortunately, subdirectories don't necessarily have a size of zero on UNIX, so you can't distinguish files from directories using this technique on a true UNIX system.

The first line of output gives the total of the file and subdirectory sizes for the directory. This is just the sum of the other numbers shown. For example, the output of `ls -s /lu` is

```
total 1
    0 bin        0 etc        1 lu.bat        0 tmp        0 usr
```

Combining Options

You can specify several options in the same command. For example, enter

```
ls -s -x
```

This displays file and subdirectory sizes in the column format discussed previously.

```
ls -s -x /
```

does the same thing for the root directory.

When you specify several options for a command, UNIX lets you use a short form to save typing. Simply enter the dash followed by all the letters and digits for the options you want. For example, enter

```
ls -sx
```

and you'll see that the output is the same as for

```
ls -s -x
```

When you specify several options, the order of the options usually doesn't matter. For example, all of the following are equivalent:

```
ls -s -x
ls -x -s
ls -xs
ls -sx
```

There are a few commands in which the order of the options does matter, but these are special cases. I'll note them as you encounter them.

Sometimes options can conflict with each other. For example, the -x option asks for a column form of output, while the -1 option asks for full information, including permissions, file sizes, and so on. What happens when you use both options? Try it.

```
ls -1x
```

The output is the same as if you had just entered

```
ls -1
```

With -1, ls is obliged to provide full information on files and subdirectories. Because there's too much information to put into multiple columns, ls just ignores the -x.

If two options conflict with each other, a command often chooses one option as the important one and ignores the other. You might think that UNIX commands should give an error message instead of simply ignoring an option, but that would be at odds with the UNIX philosophy. UNIX presumes that users would rather see some kind of output than receive an error message.

File Types

Enter the command

```
ls -p /
```

You'll see that ls puts a slash (/) on the end of each subdirectory name, although it prints each filename without the slash. This is another way that you can use ls to distinguish between files and directories.

The -F option is related to -p. Enter

```
ls -F /
```

and you'll see that the output is similar to the output of ls -p. Directory names end in /. You'll also see that some files have a * at the end of their names. These are files that are *executable.*

On a true UNIX system, files are executable when you have x permission on them. Under DOS, all files are considered executable, so all files are marked with an *.

Information About a Directory

The `-d` option tells `ls` that you want information about a directory rather than its contents. For example, enter

```
ls -l /lu/etc
```

and you'll see the usual `-l` information on the contents of `/lu/etc`. Enter

```
ls -ld /lu/etc
```

and you'll see the usual `-l` information on `/lu/etc` itself.

Information About Subdirectories

The `-R` (uppercase) option tells `ls` to *walk* through the file system tree, listing the contents of each directory and subdirectory it encounters. (This is comparable to the DOS TREE command.) To see how this works, begin with the commands

```
cd
mkdir testdir
cp sonnet nursery testdir
```

to create a subdirectory named `testdir` under your home directory and to make copies of the `sonnet` and `nursery` files under `testdir`. Next, enter the command

```
ls -R
```

You'll see that `ls` first displays

```
.:
```

and lists the names of the files under the current directory. (Remember that . stands for the current directory.) `ls` then prints a blank line followed by

```
./testdir:
```

and the names of the file under `testdir`. If `testdir` contained a subdirectory of its own, `ls` would continue to list the contents of that subdirectory, and so on through the tree of files and subdirectories under your current directory.

You can, of course, combine the `-R` option with other `ls` options. For example, enter

```
ls -Rl
```

This combines the `-R` and `-l` options to print full information on the files under the current directory, then under subdirectories of the current directory, and so on.

Other *ls* Options

The `ls` command accepts many other options. I won't discuss them in this part of the book. Although the other options are useful in specialized cases, most people will never need them. For full details, see the `ls` man page later in this book.

Note that many of the options described in the man page are only useful on a true UNIX system. For example, the `-u` option tells `ls` to display files in the order in which they were last accessed for either reading or writing. DOS does not keep track of the time of last access, so there's no way that the MKS Tools version of `ls` can implement `-u` correctly.

Filenames That Begin with a Dot and Hidden Files

By default, most UNIX versions of `ls` do not list files or directories with names that begin with the dot character. Such names are used for *initialization files* and other work files, as I'll discuss in later chapters. By specifying the `-a` option, you can tell `ls` to list these initialization files along with the ones it usually lists.

On DOS, although filenames cannot begin with a dot, they can have an attribute associated with them that makes them *hidden* files. These files aren't listed when you run the DOS DIR command.

The difference between `ls` and `ls -a` on DOS is that `ls -a` displays hidden files, displays . (standing for the current directory) and displays .. (standing for the parent directory of the current directory), as well as all the other files and directories.

Glob Constructs

If you're like most DOS users, you've probably used commands like

```
COPY A:*.* C:
```

to copy everything from diskette A: to your hard disk C:. The construct `A:*.*` stands for all the files on A:. This kind of short form enables you to work with a group of files without having to type the names of all the files.

Like many features of DOS, `*.*` and similar constructs originated on UNIX. UNIX calls these constructs *glob constructs, wildcard constructs,* or *filename generation constructs.* You can use these constructs in place of pathnames, or as part of pathnames, to reduce the amount of typing you have to do.

What Does Glob Mean?

At one time, there was a UNIX program named `glob` that converted glob constructs into filenames. I've heard a few speculations as to why people called it `glob`, but none of them sounds convincing. Unearthing the truth of this UNIX legend is a job for a better historian than I.

The *?* Glob Construct

The simplest UNIX glob construct is the question mark (?). This stands for any single character that can appear in a filename, except the slash (/) separating pathname components. For example, enter the command

```
more ?onnet
```

When the shell sees the ? glob character, it tries to *expand* the argument that contains the character. This means that the shell makes a list of the names of all existing files with names that look like a character followed by `onnet`. In this case, there is only one such file: `sonnet`. Therefore, the shell changes the previous command into

```
more sonnet
```

then executes the command.

Now, let's make the situation a little more complex. Enter the command

```
cp nursery bonnet
```

to make a new copy of the `nursery` file called `bonnet`. Now see what happens if you enter the command

```
more ?onnet
```

Again, the shell expands `?onnet` into a list of all filenames that have the appropriate form. Now that you have two files with names that are in the right form, the preceding command becomes

```
more bonnet sonnet
```

When the `?onnet` construct has been replaced with the list of filenames, the shell executes the command. (The list is always sorted in alphabetical order.)

As another example of the same thing, enter the command

`echo ?onnet`

You'll see that the output is

`bonnet sonnet`

Once again, the shell expanded the `?onnet` construct into a list of filenames, changing the original command into

`echo bonnet sonnet`

Thus, `echo`'s output gives the list of names.

Here are a few more examples of the use of `?` as a glob construct:

`more ??????`

displays the contents of all files in the current directory with names that have exactly six characters.

`ls -l ???????`

lists file information on all files with names that have exactly seven characters.

`echo /lu/etc/??????`

displays the names of all files under `/lu/etc` with names that have exactly six characters.

As a final example, enter the command

`echo ?`

When the shell sees the `?` argument, it tries to expand that argument into a list of matching filenames. But the argument stands for a file with a name that is only one character long, and if you've been following this tutorial as you've gone along, your current directory won't contain any such files. This means that the `?` can't be expanded into an appropriate filename list. As a result, the argument just stays as `?` and `echo` displays

`?`

If an argument can't be expanded into an appropriate list of filenames, the shell leaves that argument as it is.

> ## When Glob Expansion Happens
> Under UNIX, the shell expands any arguments that contain glob constructs
> and then executes the expanded command line. Under DOS, glob constructs
> are expanded by each individual program rather than by the shell. Some
> programs have not been written to deal with glob constructs, so the usual
> glob constructs don't work. As a result, glob constructs work with any
> UNIX command or program, because they're expanded by the shell before
> the command or program is executed. On DOS, glob constructs only work
> with specially written commands.

The * Glob Construct

The asterisk (*) is a glob construct that expands to any string of zero or more characters. For example, issue the command

```
echo *t
```

When the shell sees the * in the argument *t, it expands the argument into a list of all files in the current directory with names consisting of any string of characters, followed by a t. In other words, the above echo command displays the names of all files in the current directory with names ending in t. Similarly,

```
echo s*
```

displays the names of all files whose names begin with s.

The * is commonly pronounced *star* when it is used in glob constructs. For example, *t is usually pronounced *star-tee*.

Enter the commands

```
cp sonnet sonnet18
echo sonnet*
```

You'll see that the output is

```
sonnet sonnet18
```

The * matches zero or more characters; thus, sonnet* matches both sonnet and sonnet18.

You'll recall that this chapter is devoted to different things you can do with a directory listing. You've probably guessed how glob constructs let you do this. Enter the command

```
echo *
```

Because the * can stand for any string of characters, the shell expands * into a list of all the files in the directory. Similarly,

```
echo /lu/etc/*
```

displays the names of all files in the /lu/etc directory.

Note the difference between this kind of list and the kind produced by the ls command (without options). The list produced by echo consists of all the filenames on a single line, with a single space between each name. The list produced by ls is arranged into columns.

As a final example of the use of *, enter the command

```
cp * testdir
```

which copies all the files under the current directory into the testdir directory you created a few sections ago. The shell replaces the * with a list of all the appropriate names in the directory. Note that testdir will be one of these names, because * expands to names of both files and directories. When cp tries to copy testdir into itself, it will output an error message, but don't worry about it.

To get rid of everything under testdir, enter the command

```
rm testdir/*
```

This removes every file under testdir. You should be able to figure out how the command works.

Differences Between * and ? in UNIX and DOS

The * character means almost the same thing in DOS as it does in UNIX; it stands for an arbitrary string of characters. In DOS, however, * does not match the dot character. Thus, the DOS command to copy everything in the current directory into testdir would be

```
COPY *.* TESTDIR
```

> while it would be only
>
> ```
> cp * testdir
> ```
>
> under UNIX. You need to write `*.*` on DOS because of the difference in the way the two treat the dot character. Similarly, a DOS command like `DIR *T.*` will not list all the filenames that end in `T` because the `.*` stands for zero or more characters in the suffix after the `T`.
>
> The same principles apply with the `?` character. On DOS, `?` never matches the dot character.

The *[]* Constructs

The `?` and `*` glob constructs are recognized by both DOS and UNIX. UNIX, however, has additional glob constructs that DOS does not recognize.

Matching a Set of Characters

The first glob construct that is unique to UNIX is written as a set of characters inside square brackets, as in

```
[abc]
```

This construct can match any one of the characters inside the brackets. For example,

```
[abc]def
```

could be expanded to any or all of

```
adef      bdef      cdef
```

It will not match names like `abdef` or `bcdef` because `[abc]` only matches a single character.

Remember that the shell only expands glob constructs to produce filenames of existing files. Enter the command

```
echo [abc]onnet
```

and you'll see that the output is only

```
bonnet
```

The argument `[abc]onnet` could also be expanded to `aonnet` or `connet`, but your current directory doesn't contain anything that has these names. The only appropriate file is `bonnet`, so this is the only name created by the expansion. Enter the commands

```
cp sonnet connet
echo [abc]onnet
```

and you'll see that the output is now

```
bonnet connet
```

All glob constructs are expanded by checking for existing files with names of the appropriate form.

You can put *ranges* of characters inside the square brackets by specifying the first character in the range, a dash (-), and the last character in the range. For example,

```
[a-z]
```

stands for all the lowercase characters. Enter the command

```
echo [a-z]onnet
```

and you'll see that the output is

```
bonnet connet sonnet
```

This is the set of all files with names that have the appropriate form. Note that `[a-z]onnet` is not the same as `*onnet`. `*onnet` also includes files that start with a digit, with uppercase letters, and with other characters valid in filenames (- and .).

The square brackets can contain several ranges. For example,

```
[a-zA-Z0-9]
```

stands for the lowercase letters, the uppercase letters, and the digits. (Remember that UNIX filenames can contain both upper- and lowercase letters.)

A Special Case

If you want a dash (-) sign in the list of characters inside square brackets, you have to put it at the beginning or the end of the list. For example, `[-az]` matches a dash, the letter a or the letter z. You would not get the same effect if you wrote `[a-z]`, because the construct looks like a range of characters.

Matching Anything Not in a Set of Characters

If the first character inside the square brackets is an exclamation point (!), the construct matches any single character that is not inside the brackets. For example,

```
[!abc]
```

matches any character except a, b, or c. Enter the command

```
echo [!abc]onnet
```

and you'll see that the output is

```
sonnet
```

The construct [!abc]onnet expands to a list of all filenames ending in onnet, except those that begin with a, b, or c. Similarly, enter

```
echo [!n-z]onnet
```

and you'll see that the output is

```
bonnet connet
```

The [!n-z] stands for any character outside the range n through z.

Combining Glob Constructs

You can combine glob constructs if you like. For example, enter the command

```
echo [n-z]*
```

The output is the list of all names that begin with any character from n through z.

Quotation Marks and Glob Constructs

Enter the following command:

```
echo You are my lucky *
```

You'll see that the final * is expanded into a list of the files and directories under your current directory. This probably doesn't surprise you, but it does raise the question of how you would output an actual * character using the echo command.

The answer is to enclose the character in single or double quotation marks. For example, you can enter any of

```
echo "You are my lucky *"
echo 'You are my lucky *'
echo You are my lucky "*"
echo "You are" 'my lucky *'
```

and get the output

```
You are my lucky *
```

As long as the * is inside an argument that is quoted, the shell doesn't try to expand it into a file list.

The same goes for other glob constructs, of course. For example, enter

```
echo Put on your old grey ?onnet
echo "Put on your old grey ?onnet"
```

and you'll see that expansion happens in the first command but not the second.

Unbalanced Quotation Marks

If you're putting arguments into quotation marks, there's a chance that you might leave off a quotation mark by mistake. For example, enter

```
echo 'Hello
```

without putting in the closing single quotation mark. When you press Enter, you'll see

```
>
```

appear on the screen. Here's what is happening. You didn't put in a single quotation mark to close off the string, so the shell is still gathering input for the string. It prompts you with > rather than the usual command prompt to show you that it expects a continuation of the previous line. Enter a single quotation mark (') to finish off the string, then press Enter. You'll see that echo displays the string Hello, plus a blank line. The blank line shows that the argument for echo went to another line. If the shell prompts you for input with >, remember that this means the shell is looking for a continuation of the previous line. This frequently means that you forgot a quotation mark in the previous line.

The Backslash and Glob Constructs

Quotation marks around an argument tell the shell to ignore any special meaning that a glob construct has. You can do the same thing by putting a backslash (\) in front of the construct's special characters. For example, enter

```
echo \*
```

and you'll see that the command simply displays

```
*
```

In UNIX, the backslash is called the *escape character*. When you put it in front of any special character, it turns off the special meaning of that character.

The backslash only turns off the special meaning of the character immediately following it. For example, enter

```
echo \* *
```

The output is a * followed by the names of everything in your current directory. Because of the backslash, the shell does not expand the first *; however, the second * has no backslash, so it is expanded normally.

The *find* Command

Continuing with the discussion of different ways to display the contents of a directory listing, I'm going to turn to a UNIX utility I haven't yet discussed: the find command. This has no relationship to the DOS FIND command. The UNIX find command has some features in common with the DOS TREE command, but it is more versatile than TREE.

The UNIX find command finds the names of files and directories that meet a specified set of criteria. To get an idea of find's output, enter the command

```
find /lu -print
```

This displays the names of all files and directories under the /lu directory, including those in subdirectories, sub-subdirectories, and so on. Names are grouped by directory and subdirectory. The first name in the list is /lu, the name of the directory itself.

The general form of a simple find command is

```
find dir -print
```

where dir is the name of the directory containing the files and subdirectories you want to list. For example, enter

```
find . -print
```

and you'll see the contents of the current directory (.).

Enter the command

```
ls
```

and contrast the output of ls with the output of find. The ls command only displays the basenames of files and directories; find displays absolute pathnames (if the directory is given with an absolute pathname, as in /lu) or relative pathnames (if the directory is given with a relative pathname, as in ., the current directory). Thus

```
ls /lu
```

displays

```
bin etc lu.bat tmp usr
```

but

```
find /lu -print
```

displays

```
/lu
/lu/bin
/lu/bin/banner.exe
```

and a list of all the other files and directories under /lu.

Complex UNIX Options

The examples of find commands that you've looked at so far all end with -print. This argument looks like a UNIX option because it starts with a dash (-). However, it is longer than other options discussed so far. As you've seen, the options of most UNIX commands are only one character long (not counting the dash).

-print is an example of a more complex kind of UNIX command option. Like other options, it starts with a dash, but the option name itself can be longer than one character.

The find command has many examples of complex UNIX options. In the subsections to follow, you'll see some of the options of find and how you can use them productively.

> ### The `-print` Option
>
> The `-print` option tells `find` to display the names that it finds under the given directory. With some versions of UNIX, you have to remember to specify `-print`; otherwise, `find` won't display anything. With MKS Tools, `find` automatically displays its results, whether you specify `-print` or not. I'll always include the `-print` option in the examples to remind you that it is necessary with some versions of UNIX; however, if you want to save some typing, you can omit it for the purposes of these exercises.

The Type of Files

The `-type` option tells `find` what kind of thing you want it to find. (Note that this option has no connection with the DOS TYPE command.) For example, enter the command

```
find . -type d -print
```

`find` displays the names of all directories under your current directory, but does not display the names of any files. Enter

```
find . -type f -print
```

and `find` displays the names of all files, but not directories. Contrast this with

```
find . -print
```

which displays all the filenames plus the names of the directories `.` and `testdir`. The `-type` option tells `find` to select only certain types of names to print.

Notice the form of the options.

```
-type d
-type f
```

This is one of several standard forms for complex UNIX options: the option name (`-type`), followed by whitespace, followed by another argument. The argument `d` stands for directories and `f` stands for files.

Whitespace Separation

With most versions of UNIX, you can put one or more whitespace characters between a complex option like `-type` and the value that follows it.
However, a few older versions require exactly one space as separation.

You'll see many other options with a similar form.

```
-name value
```

where `name` is the name of the option itself, and `value` is some value that provides
additional information. You'll see another example of this in the next section.

Interrupting Commands

Some of the `find` examples suggested in this section and those that follow
can take a good deal of time to execute. The time required depends on
factors such as the type of machine you have and the number of files on your
hard disk.

If you discover that a particular example takes longer to finish than you want
to wait, you can interrupt the command by pressing Ctrl-C. This is one
standard technique for interrupting programs on UNIX systems. The Del
(or Delete) key is also widely used as an interrupt on UNIX systems, but that
won't work on DOS.

If you interrupt a command with Ctrl-C, the command might not stop right
away. Several commands are designed to ignore interruptions until they
reach a convenient time to quit.

You shouldn't interrupt a command if the output of the command is
important for subsequent exercises. However, if the output is just being
displayed on the screen, you can usually skip looking at the output without
missing much.

Change Times

The `-ctime` option tells `find` to display the names of files that have been changed in a certain number of days. For example, enter

```
find . -ctime 1 -print
```

`find` displays the names of all files under your current directory that were changed one day ago but haven't been changed since (in other words, those files that were changed yesterday). Because `find` looks at arbitrary 24 hour periods and not actual calendar days, this will probably include files such as `bonnet` and `connet` (which you just created recently), but will not include files that you haven't touched recently.

Now enter

```
find . -ctime 2 -print
```

This displays the names of all files under your current directory that were changed two days ago but haven't been changed since. (Of course, there would not be any such files if you didn't touch any files yesterday, and if you're scrupulous about setting the date and time on your system to reflect the real date and time.) Similarly,

```
find . -ctime 3 -print
```

displays the names of all files under your current directory that were changed three days ago but haven't been changed since. In general, the option

```
-ctime n
```

tells `find` to look for files that were changed n days ago but haven't been changed since.

A file is considered to have changed if its contents have been changed. If you just read the file, without changing the contents, the file itself does not change. For example, a command like

```
cp bonnet connet
```

does not change `bonnet`, because it just reads the contents of the file; however, it does change `connet` because it copies data into the file.

Now suppose you want to find the names of all the files that have been changed in the past week (because you want to back them up). Consider (but don't enter) the command

```
find / -ctime 7 -print
```

(You can enter the command if you want, but it might take a long time to finish.) The command looks under the root directory for all files that were changed exactly seven days ago. The option `-ctime 7` does not, for example, display files that were changed today.

To get around this problem, you need some way to specify change times of seven days or less. Do this with the option

```
-ctime -7
```

The `-7` stands for *seven days or less,* which is the same as *within the past week.* Thus if you enter

```
find / -ctime -7 -print
```

the command displays the name of every file that has changed in the past week. You can enter this command now to see how it works, but be warned that it will search your entire hard disk. The process might take several minutes, depending on how fast your machine is and how many files you have. You might prefer to try a faster command like

```
find . -ctime -7 -print
```

which only searches your current directory rather than the entire disk.

You can also use an option of the form `-ctime +n` to find files that last changed more than n days ago. For example,

```
find . -ctime +7 -print
```

finds files that were changed more than a week ago.

Other Time Options

The `-atime` option works in the same way as `-ctime`, but it looks at *access times* rather than change times. A file is accessed whenever you try to read or write it. DOS doesn't keep track of access times, so the MKS Tools version of `find` treats `-atime` and `-ctime` as equivalent.

The `-mtime` option works in the same way, but it looks at *modification times* rather than change times. A file is modified whenever you change its characteristics (in other words, its permissions). Again, DOS doesn't keep track of modification times, so the MKS Tools version of `find` treats `-mtime` and `-ctime` as equivalent.

Comparing Change Times

The `-newer` option can serve much the same purpose as `-ctime`. The option has the form

```
-newer file
```

where `file` is the name of a file (an absolute or relative pathname). This option tells `find` to compare all the files in a directory to the given `file` and to display those files that are newer (those with contents that have been changed more recently than the contents of `file`). For example, enter the command

```
find . -newer nursery -print
```

This displays all the files in the current directory with contents that have been changed more recently than the contents of the `nursery` file. The list should include all the files you've created while working through this chapter.

Name Forms

The `-name` option lets you use `find` to display a collection of file and directory names that have a given form. The option has the format

```
-name "form"
```

where `form` describes the form of a name using glob constructs. For example, enter the commands

```
cp sonnet testdir
find . -name "?onnet" -print
```

`find` tells you all the files and directories under the current directory with names of the given form. This includes the copy of `sonnet` that the `cp` command puts into `testdir`.

Note that the `form` must be put inside double or single quotation marks. You should be able to figure out why. If you entered the command

```
find . -name ?onnet -print
```

the shell would immediately expand `?onnet` into a list of matching names. (Remember that the shell expands any argument that contains a glob construct, unless the argument is enclosed in single or double quotation marks.) The expansion would create

```
find . -name bonnet connet sonnet -print
```

which is not a valid form for `find`.

If you put quotation marks around `form`, the shell doesn't expand the glob constructs. The whole `form` is passed without change to the `find` command, and `find` can use that `form` to identify matching filenames. If you omit the quotation marks, the shell expands the glob constructs immediately, before invoking `find`; the `find` command itself never sees the glob constructs.

Here are a few more examples of the `-name` option that you might find useful:

```
find / -name "*.bak" -print
```

searches the entire file system for files and directories with names that end with the suffix `.bak`. Files with this suffix are created by some programs as back-up copies of other files.

```
find / -name "*.tmp" -print
```

searches the entire file system for files and directories with names ending with the suffix `.tmp`. Files with this suffix are often temporary working files that can be deleted.

```
find . -name "*.doc" -print
```

searches the current directory for files and directories with names ending with the suffix `.doc`. Files with this suffix often contain documents produced by a word processing program.

Negating an Option

You can reverse the meaning of any `find` option by putting an exclamation mark (!) in front of it. For example,

```
find . ! -name "?onnet" -print
```

displays the names of all files and directories with names that do not end with `onnet`.

```
find / ! -ctime -365 -print
```

displays the names of all files and directories that have not changed in the last 365 days. You might use this command to identify files that are no longer in active use and that might be candidates for deletion.

```
find . ! -newer connet -print
```

displays the names of all files and directories under the current directory that are not newer than `connet`.

Combining Options

A `find` command can contain several options. In this case, `find` only displays the names of files and directories that satisfy all the criteria. For example,

```
find . -type d -newer sonnet -print
```

displays the names of all directories that are newer than the `sonnet` file.

Redirection

Commands like `ls` and `find` can produce a great deal of output, especially when you turn them loose on large directories. You might already have had the experience of watching the output from one of these commands disappear off the top of the screen before you could read it.

This section looks at a way to save a directory listing so that you can read it later. The approach does not use new commands, but it uses old commands in a slightly different way.

I/O Streams

UNIX programs perform input and output on *streams.* You might picture a stream as a door between the program and the kernel of the operating system. If the program wants to read input, it asks the kernel to deliver some input through the door; if the program wants to write output, it sends data out the door and the operating system does whatever else is necessary to deliver that data to its intended destination.

The streams used by a program are numbered. In effect, each door has its own number. These numbers are called *file descriptors.* File descriptors help the program distinguish between one door and another. For example, a command like

```
cp sonnet new
```

would have one stream (door) for the sonnet file and another for the new file. The cp program would tell the kernel to bring in data through the sonnet door and send out the same data through the new door. cp would use file descriptor numbers to tell the kernel which door was which.

In order to use a stream, the program has to *open* the stream; this is like opening a door. More precisely, the program must ask the kernel to open the stream, just as you might get a butler or a security guard to open a door for you. The kernel opens the stream and assigns a file descriptor number to the stream; this is like painting a number on the door so that you have a way to refer to the door and distinguish it from all others.

To see how this works, let's go back to the cp command shown previously. cp says to the kernel, "Open a stream that lets me read from the file sonnet," and "Open a stream that lets me write to the file new." The kernel does whatever work is necessary to create the two streams, and gives cp a file descriptor number for each door. The file descriptor numbers let cp identify the two doors later on when it starts reading and writing.

Notice that cp tells the kernel whether it wants to read or write on a stream. This lets the kernel check whether you have appropriate read or write permissions on the associated file. It also offers a bit of insurance against programming errors; if a program says it only wants to read a particular stream but later tries to write on that stream, the program might have an error and the kernel might have to kill the program to prevent trouble.

Standard Streams

When you ask the shell to execute a program, the shell automatically opens the following three streams for the program:

- The *standard input* stream, which always has the file descriptor number 0. This is set up so that the program can only read from the stream, not write to it.

- The *standard output* stream, which always has file descriptor 1. This is set up so that the program can only write to the stream, not read from it.

- The *standard error* stream, which always has file descriptor 2. This is set up so that the program can only write to the stream, not read from it.

The program can use these streams as soon as it starts executing. If it wants to use another stream, it has to ask the kernel to open a new stream and wait until the kernel has set up the stream appropriately.

Standard Output

Normally, when the shell sets up a standard output stream for a program, the stream is attached to the monitor screen. As a result, if the program writes data to the standard output, the data shows up on the monitor screen. Commands like `ls`, `echo`, and `find` display their information by writing to the standard output.

You can tell the shell to attach the standard output stream to a file rather than the terminal screen. For example, enter the command

```
ls >info
```

You won't see any output on the screen from this command. The `>info` notation is an instruction to the shell. DOS users will be familiar with this redirection construct, because you can use the same notation on DOS. The notation says that you want the shell to attach the standard output of this `ls` command to a file named `info` instead of to the monitor screen. When `ls` produces its information, it just sends the information out the standard output door as usual; however, the kernel delivers the information to a new file called `info` instead of to the monitor. Enter

```
more info
```

to display the contents of `info`, and you'll see that it contains the output that `ls` usually displays on the screen.

This gives you a new way to display the contents of a directory: save the output of `ls` or `find` in a file, then display the file with `more`. For example, enter

```
find . -type f -print >out
more out
```

In the first instruction, you *redirect* the standard output of `find` into a file named `out`. In the second instruction, you read the contents of `out` with `more`. Note that this technique avoids the problem of information disappearing from the screen faster than you can read it. All the information is saved in a file, and then you can read the file bit by bit, using `more`.

Redirection Order

A redirection argument can appear anywhere on the command line. For example, the following are equivalent:

```
find . -type f -print >out
find . -type f >out -print
find . -type >out f -print
find . >out -type f -print
find >out . -type f -print
>out find . -type f -print
```

In most cases, however, you'll find that it's a good policy to put the redirection at the end of the command; it makes the command easier to read.

Appending to the Standard Output

Now enter these commands:

```
ls -l >out
more out
```

This saves the output of ls in the out file you just created, then uses more to read the file.

With the >out notation, the output of ls *overwrites* (replaces) the previous contents of out. Sometimes, however, you want output to add to what is already in a file rather than overwriting the current contents. To do this, use >> rather than >. For example, enter

```
find . -type f -print >>out
more out
```

The >>out construct *appends* the output of find to the existing contents of out. The more command will show you that out contains the output of the previous ls command, followed by the output of the find command.

Here's a practical example of redirection in action. Suppose you want a list of all files in the file system with names ending with the .bak or .tmp suffixes. You can get this list with the commands

```
find / -name "*.bak" -print >out
find / -name "*.tmp" -print >>out
more out
```

The first `find` command uses >out, so it overwrites the current contents of out. The second `find` command uses >>out, so it appends new data to the current contents of out. Finally, `more` displays the result.

You can use this kind of redirection as a way to put text into a file. Enter the commands

```
echo "Mary had a little lamb" >out
echo "Its fleece was white as snow" >>out
echo "And everywhere that Mary went" >>out
echo "The lamb was sure to go." >>out
more out
```

and you'll see that the contents of out are

```
Mary had a little lamb
Its fleece was white as snow
And everywhere that Mary went
The lamb was sure to go.
```

The first `echo` command uses >out to overwrite the previous contents of out. The subsequent commands use >>out to add to the contents.

Redirection Is Handled by the Shell

It's important to remember that redirection is handled by the shell, not by the command itself. The shell sets up the standard output, standard input, and standard error streams for a command, then starts the command running. If the command line contains any redirection constructs like >out, the shell uses them to set up the standard streams, then throws the constructs away. The command itself doesn't know that it's been redirected.

For example, if you enter

```
find . -type f -print >out
```

the shell sets up the standard output for the command to go to out, then executes the command as if it were

```
find . -type f -print
```

The command itself doesn't know that its output has been redirected.

Standard Input

The standard input stream is usually associated with the keyboard. As it happens, you haven't examined many commands that take input from the keyboard, but there is one: the cat command discussed in Chapter 3, "The UNIX File System: Go Climb a Tree," reads from the standard input if you don't give it an input file. For example, enter

```
cat >out
This is an example of input.
It goes into the "out" file.
^Z
```

where ^Z is the Ctrl-Z character (not a ^ followed by z). On DOS, Ctrl-Z stands for *end of file,* or in this case, *end of input.* UNIX uses the Ctrl-D character for the same purpose, but because MKS Tools is a simulation of UNIX on DOS, you have to use the DOS Ctrl-Z.

The previous cat command reads the standard input and writes to the standard output; because the standard output is redirected to out, the text you typed is copied to out. You can see this for yourself by entering

```
more out
```

which displays

```
This is an example of input.
It goes into the "out" file.
```

As an example of redirecting the standard input, enter the command

```
cat <out
```

The <out construct tells the shell that cat's standard input should be the out file. Because the command line doesn't redirect the standard output, the output goes to the screen. In other words, the preceding command displays the contents of out.

more is another command that reads the standard input if you don't specify an input file. For example, enter

```
more <nursery
```

and you'll see that more uses the nursery file as its input. The preceding command has exactly the same effect as

```
more nursery
```

but the different forms are processed differently. In the first form, the shell sets up nursery as the standard input for more; it then invokes more without any arguments. Because more doesn't have any arguments, it reads from the standard input, which is the nursery file. In the second form, the name nursery is passed as an argument to more and more reads that file.

You'll see more examples of redirecting the standard input in future chapters, after I've discussed other commands that make use of input.

Standard Error

Programs use the standard error stream when they want to write out a diagnostic message. By default, the shell associates the standard error stream with the terminal screen.

You might wonder why UNIX separates the standard output from the standard error. They're both output streams, and (by default) they both display information on the screen. To see why it's a good idea to separate the two, enter the command

```
find testdi -type f -print >out
```

Notice that I asked you to type testdi, not testdir. This is a simple typing error, the sort of mistake that's easy to make. You'll see that find displays a message saying that it can't find testdi.

find displayed this message on the standard error, and the message appeared on your screen. If find had written the message on the standard output, the message would have gone into out, because the standard output was redirected to out. As a result, you wouldn't see the error message; if you didn't notice the typing mistake, you might think that the find command did its job properly, even though an error took place. By writing important messages on the standard error rather than the standard output, a program can make sure that you see the message, even if the standard output has been redirected.

There is a way to redirect the standard error if you really want to. For example, if you're a programmer, you know that you frequently get a lot of errors the first time you compile some new source code. In this case, you might want to redirect those error messages into a file so that you can read them at your leisure, rather than have them flash by on the screen. You can redirect the standard error with a construct of the form

```
2>file
```

where `file` is the name of the file where you want the program to write the errors. Remember that 2 is the file descriptor number for the standard error, so `2>file` redirects the standard error. For example, enter

```
find testdi -type f -print >out 2>errout
```

This command contains the typing error you made before. The command redirects the standard output into `out` and redirects the standard error into a file called `errout`. Enter the command

```
more errout
```

and you'll see that it contains the error message produced by `find`.

Pipes

In the last section, you looked at a way of saving a directory listing in a file. By displaying that file, you can display the directory contents (or more precisely, what the contents were at the time that the listing was obtained).

One advantage of saving directory listings in files is that long listings don't disappear off the top of the screen. In this final section, you'll look at another way to get around this problem: pipes.

Pipelines

A *pipe* connects the standard output of one command with the standard input of another command. In other words, the output of one command is *piped into* another command as input.

To connect two commands with this kind of pipe, just put the or-bar character (¦) between the two commands. For example,

```
find . -type f -print ¦ more
```

tells the shell to create a pipe between the two commands

```
find . -type f -print
more
```

You'll recall that if `more` is called without arguments, it reads its input from the standard input. This means that the information produced by `find` is piped as input into `more`, and then `more` displays that information. By piping information into `more`, you don't have to worry about lines disappearing off the top of the screen before you have a chance to see them.

You can use the same approach with `ls`. For example, enter

```
ls -l ¦ more
```

This pipes the output of `ls  -l` into `more` to make the output easier to read.

Machines and Bins

In order to understand the distinction between pipes and redirection, some people find it helpful to picture commands as machines that take input and produce output, and to picture files as bins that can feed input into a machine or take output from a machine. Using output redirection in a set of commands such as

```
find . -type f -print > out
```

```
more out
```

is like saving the output of the `find` machine in a bin named `out`, then wheeling the bin over to a new machine named `more` and running the contents of the `out` bin through the `more` machine. In contrast, using pipes such as

```
find . -type f -print ¦ more out
```

is like hooking up the `find` machine to the `more` machine so that whatever comes out of `find` immediately goes into `more`.

Thus, output redirection with > always sends the output to a file (a bin), and piping with ¦ always sends the output to another command (a machine).

A sequence of commands linked together by pipes is called a *pipeline*. You can put any number of commands into a pipeline, and you'll see some examples of this in later chapters. For now, the most important use of pipes is using `more` to paginate the output of other commands.

DOS Pipes Versus UNIX Pipes

As experienced DOS users probably know, DOS also lets you create pipe-lines. However, there is a difference between the ways that DOS and UNIX handle pipes.

On DOS, the system executes the first command in the pipeline and saves its output in a temporary file. After the first command is finished, the system executes the next command in the pipeline, passing the temporary file as input, and saving its output in another temporary file. After this second command is finished, the next command in the pipeline is executed, and so on until all the commands are finished. The temporary files created during this process are deleted when they are no longer needed. With this approach, the system only executes one command at a time.

On UNIX, the system executes all the commands simultaneously. Data is not stored in temporary holding files; it is piped directly from the memory of one executing command into the memory of another. This means that you can get faster results because you don't have to wait for one command to finish before the next command starts working.

Chapter Review

Table 4.1 shows the ls command options discussed in this chapter. For a complete option list, see the ls man page.

Table 4.1. Options for the ls command.

Option	Meaning
-a	List all files, including names starting with dot
-C	Multicolumn output, sorted down columns
-d	Give information only on directory itself
-F	Mark directories with /, executables with *

Option	Meaning
-l	Give complete information
-p	Mark directories with /
-R	List information on directories, subdirectories, sub-subdirectories, and so on
-s	Display size in blocks
-x	Multicolumn output, sorted across rows

Table 4.2 shows the glob constructs that can be used in arguments for UNIX commands. If an argument contains a glob construct, the shell expands the argument by checking for any appropriate file or directory names with a form that matches the form of the argument. If there are matching names, the shell replaces the argument with a list of all matching names, sorted in alphabetical order. If there are no matching names, the shell leaves the argument alone. The shell does not perform filename expansion on arguments enclosed in single or double quotation marks, and it ignores the special meaning of any character preceded by a backslash (\).

Table 4.2. UNIX glob constructs.

Construct	Meaning
?	Match any single character
*	Match any sequence of zero or more characters
[...]	Match any single character inside the brackets
[!...]	Match any single character not inside the brackets

The find command displays the names of all files and subdirectories under a directory that meet specified criteria. The criteria are specified by complex options. Options for find include those given in Table 4.3.

Table 4.3. Options for `find`.

Option	Meaning
`-print`	Display results
`-atime` *n*	Find files accessed *n* days ago
`-ctime` *n*	Find files changed *n* days ago
`-ctime` *-n*	Find files changed within the past *n* days
`-mtime` *n*	Find files with characteristics that were modified *n* days ago
`-name` *form*	Find files with names matching *form*
`-newer` *file*	Find files newer than *file*
`-type d`	Display only directories
`-type f`	Display only files

UNIX programs perform I/O using streams. A stream is like a door through which a program can obtain input or send output. Each stream has an associated file descriptor number to distinguish it from other streams.

When the shell invokes a program, it sets up three streams.

The standard input (file descriptor 0)

The standard output (file descriptor 1)

The standard error (file descriptor 2)

By putting redirection constructs on a command line, you can tell the shell to redirect one or more of a program's standard streams so that the stream is associated with a file instead of the keyboard or the monitor screen. Table 4.4 shows the possible redirection constructs. These constructs can appear anywhere on the command line; however, a command line is usually easier to read if you put redirection constructs at the end.

Table 4.4. Redirection constructs.

Construct	Meaning
`>file`	Send standard output to `file`, overwriting current contents
`>>file`	Append standard output to `file`
`<file`	Read from `file` as standard input
`2>file`	Send standard error to `file`

If you are entering input from the keyboard, you enter a special character to indicate the end of the input. On DOS and on MKS Tools, the character is Ctrl-Z; on UNIX, the character is usually Ctrl-D, but this can be changed by customization.

A pipe takes the standard output of one command and feeds it in as the standard input of another command. Pipes are indicated by putting the or-bar (¦) between commands. A sequence of commands joined by pipes is called a pipeline. The more command is very popular as the last command in a pipeline, because it makes it easier to read large amounts of output.

Exercises

1. Read the man page for the `ls` command. Use the appropriate option of `ls` to display the contents of your home directory in reverse alphabetical order.

2. Read the man page for the `head` command. Use `head` to display the first five lines of `sonnet`. Then use `head` to display the first ten lines of `nursery`. Why is `head` useful when UNIX already offers so many other ways to display the contents of a file?

3. The `ls -s` command tells you file sizes in terms of blocks. The `du` command does much the same thing. Read the man page for `du` and find out the sizes of your home directory and the `/lu` directory.

4. The `df` command determines the amount of free space on a device. Read the man page for `df` and find the amount of free space on your hard drive.

5. Use `banner` to display big-letter versions of all filenames ending in `onnet` under your current directory.

6. Enter the command

   ```
   echo "It's time!"
   ```

   This shows that you can put a single quotation mark (used as an apostrophe in this example) inside double quotation marks. Use `banner` to display the words DON'T PANIC in large, friendly letters (one word per line).

7. The KornShell lets you enter two separate commands on the same line by separating them with a semicolon (;). For example,

   ```
   ls ; ls /lu
   ```

   has two `ls` commands, one displaying the current directory and one displaying /lu. Use `echo` to display the string Faster; ever faster. (Hint: you'll need quotation marks to overcome the special meaning of the ;.)

8. Find the names of all files under /lu that have the .exe suffix. What do these files hold?

9. Create a file containing the names of all the files under your home directory.

10. The `cal` command creates a calendar; see the `cal` man page. Using `cal`, create a file that contains calendars of the next three months.

11. `cd` to the /lu/bin directory. Using `ls` and `banner`, display the filenames in this directory with large letters.

12. Using `find` and `banner`, display the filenames in the /lu/bin directory with large letters. What's the difference between this and the output of the previous exercise?

Chapter

5

POPULAR TOOLS

This chapter examines a few of the most popular commands in UNIX. You'll find that the commands are straightforward and simple to use. However, you can combine them with other commands, through pipes and redirection, to perform very sophisticated operations.

The grep command scans one or more text files to see if they contain specified strings. At its simplest, you specify a string like abc, and grep displays all lines that contain the string. However, grep also has a sophisticated pattern-matching ability that lets you specify more complex searching jobs. For example, you can ask grep to look for lines that begin with the letter A and end with the letter Z. You'll see just how useful this can be in the examples, and in later chapters of this book.

The diff command compares two text files and displays the differences between the two. This is particularly useful when you have two closely related files to compare,

such as two different versions of the same report. `diff` can quickly summarize how the two versions differ.

The `wc` command displays the number of lines, words, and characters in a text file.

The `sort` command lets you sort the contents of text files according to selected criteria. In some respects, it is similar to the DOS SORT command, but the UNIX `sort` is more versatile.

The `tar` command is one of several commands that can be used to back up and restore files in a UNIX system. The facilities of `tar` are also convenient when you are shipping files from one system to another.

The `lp` command can print hard copy versions of text files. Some UNIX and UNIX look-alike systems call this command `lpr`.

Searching for Strings: *grep*

The `grep` command searches through one or more files and displays lines that contain matches for a specified string. For example, enter

```
grep Mary nursery
```

This searches through `nursery` and displays all the lines that contain the string `Mary`. It is important to enter the arguments in the right order.

```
grep string file
```

The `string` you want to find must be given before the `file` you want to search.

The Origin of the Name `grep`

As you'll see shortly, `grep` can display lines that match *regular expressions.* Thus the command could be called Global Regular Expression Print, or `grep` for short.

To be technically correct, the name actually comes from a command from a UNIX text editor, which is written `g/re/p`, where g stands for *global,* `re` is a regular expression, and p stands for *print.* However, the effect is the same.

You can use `grep` to search through several files. For example, enter

```
grep the sonnet nursery
```

This searches through `sonnet` and `nursery` and displays all the lines that contain the string `the`. Notice that the string might be part of longer words like `thee` or `breathe`.

You may find that the output of the last `grep` command is too large to fit on the screen. To avoid losing information off the top of the screen, you can always pipe the output through `more`. To do this, enter the line

```
grep the sonnet nursery ¦ more
```

This pipes the output of `grep` through the `more` command so that you can read through the output screen by screen.

You can use `grep` to search for strings that contain blanks. However, you must enclose the search string in quotation marks. For example, enter

```
grep "The lamb" nursery
```

and `grep` displays all lines in `nursery` that contain `The lamb`.

Clarifying with Quotation Marks

`grep` command lines can be confusing to look at because it's difficult to distinguish the string argument from the files. Some people make it a policy to enclose the string argument in quotation marks, even when it's not necessary. For example, in the command

```
grep "the" sonnet nursery
```

the quotation marks around the string `the` make it stand out from the filenames that follow it.

Case Sensitivity

Normally, `grep` pays attention to the case of letters when it looks for strings. For example, enter

```
grep "the" sonnet nursery
grep "The" sonnet nursery
```

You'll notice that the two commands display different collections of lines. The first looks for the (entirely in lowercase), while the second looks for The (with the first letter in uppercase).

From time to time, you may want grep to ignore the case of letters. To do this, specify the option -i before the string argument. For example, enter

```
grep -i "the" sonnet nursery ¦ more
```

In this case, grep displays lines that contain either the or The, as well as any other combination of upper- and lowercase letters.

Remember that the option -i comes before the string argument. In UNIX commands, options come before arguments.

Regular Expressions

grep searches for strings that meet specified criteria. So far, you've only used it to look for strings that exactly match the string given on the command line. However, you can specify more sophisticated searching criteria by using *regular expressions.*

A regular expression is a string that describes a pattern of characters. Regular expressions can contain special characters, sometimes called *metacharacters.* Regular expressions can also contain normal characters, in other words, letters and digits. The next sections discuss the most common metacharacters and how you can use them in grep commands.

Note

This chapter describes a collection of the most useful regular expressions. However, there are many others that I don't touch on here. For a complete description of all recognized regular expressions, see Appendix C, "Summary of Filename Generation with Glob Constructs."

The Beginning of a Line

The caret (^) is a metacharacter that stands for the beginning of a line. For example, enter

```
grep "^Mary" nursery
```

The argument in quotation marks is a regular expression made up of the metacharacter ^ (the beginning of the line) followed by the normal characters Mary. The regular expression therefore tells grep to look for lines where Mary occurs at the beginning of the line. Enter

```
grep "Mary" nursery
```

to see the contrast. If you omit the ^, grep displays lines that contain Mary anywhere in the line.

As another example, enter the two commands

```
ls -l >out
grep "^d" out
```

The ls command obtains information about the current directory and redirects that information into out. Then the grep command looks for all lines that begin with the letter d. Lines that begin with d provide information about directories. As a result, the grep command extracts only the information about directories and displays that information on the screen. You can use the same principle to obtain information on ordinary files only. Enter

```
grep "^-" out
```

and the grep command only displays the lines that begin with -. These lines describe files.

Regular Expressions Never Match More Than One Line

grep always searches one line at a time. You cannot tell grep to find a string that starts on one line and ends on another.

The End of a Line

The dollar sign ($) is a metacharacter that stands for the end of a line. For example, enter

```
grep "lamb$" nursery
```

to display all lines that contain lamb, followed by the end of the line. grep therefore displays all lines that end in lamb.

Enter

```
grep "lamb" nursery
```

to see the contrast. This displays lines that contain lamb anywhere in the line.

Metacharacters Aren't Always Special

The $ has its special meaning only when it appears at the end of a regular expression. For example, consider $1.00 as a regular expression. Here, it's clear that $ can't stand for the end of the line; you can't follow the end of a line with additional characters. As a result, grep knows that you're looking for a real dollar sign followed by a string that matches 1.00.

The same principle holds for ^. If you want it to stand for the beginning of the line, it has to appear in an appropriate place in the regular expression (usually at the beginning). Otherwise, grep assumes that you're looking for a real caret character.

Matching an Arbitrary Character

The dot (.) is a metacharacter that will match any other character. For example, enter

```
grep ".he" nursery
```

This searches through nursery for lines that contain any character followed by he. You'll see lines that contain words like the, The, She, and so on. With some lines, you may have to look closely to see where the matching string is. For example, in the line

```
And everywhere that Mary went
```

the matching string is whe inside everywhere. In the line

```
And sat down beside her
```

the matching string is ' he' (the space and the he at the beginning of her).

118

. (Dot) and ?

Because . can stand for any character, it serves the same purpose as the ? glob construct. However, it can be misleading to draw too many comparisons between regular expressions and glob constructs. Regular expressions are used when you want to locate strings in text files; glob constructs are used when you want to generate a list of filenames in a command line.

It is often useful to combine the dot metacharacter with other metacharacters. For example, enter

```
grep "^.he" nursery
```

This displays all lines that have a string matching .he at the beginning of the line. These lines begin with The, There, and She.

Be careful to remember the special meaning for the dot. For example, consider the command

```
grep ".$" nursery
```

At first glance, you might think that this displays all lines ending in a period. However, enter the command, and you'll see this isn't so. The regular expression .$ stands for any character followed by the end of the line; in other words, it stands for the last character on the line. As a result, grep finds a match on every line of the file, except for lines that don't contain any characters at all.

You'll learn how to display all lines that end in a period later in this chapter.

Character Repetitions

The asterisk (*) is a metacharacter that stands for zero or more repetitions of the preceding character. For example, enter

```
grep "uf*e" nursery
```

You'll see that the output is

```
Little boy blue
Little Miss Muffet
Sat on a tuffet
And frightened Miss Muffet away.
```

The regular expression uf*e stands for a u, followed by zero or more f characters, followed by an e. In

```
Little boy blue
```

there are zero f characters between the u and the e. In the other lines, there are two.

---

* : Glob Versus Regular Expressions

In regular expressions, * always refers to the preceding character. For example, a* matches a, aa, aaa, and so on. as well as a zero number of as.

In glob constructs, * stands for any string of zero or more characters and has nothing to do with the preceding character. For example, a* as a glob construct expands to all files whose names start with a, including files named abc, apple, aardvark.doc, and so on. The glob construct * is most similar to the regular expression .*.

The * is most often used in the .* construct, which stands for any string of zero or more characters. For example, enter

```
grep "W.*e" nursery
```

This looks for any line that contains a W followed by any number of characters, followed by an e. In the output, you'll see the lines

```
Wee Willie Winkie
Who could travel much faster than light
Who ate a bad apple and died
```

The .* always matches the longest possible string of characters. For example, in

```
Wee Willie Winkie
```

the W.*e expression matches the whole line, even though We, Wee, Willie, Wee Willie, and so on, are strings that start with *W* and end in *e.* Matching the whole line doesn't make any difference when you're using regular grep, because grep always prints the whole line anyway. It can make a difference when you use regular expressions with other UNIX software (for example, the vi text editor, which is discussed in Chapter 6, "Text Files—Veni, Vidi, *vi*").

As another example of `.*`, enter

```
grep "^A.*r$" nursery
```

This regular expression may look cryptic at first, but you should find it simple if you take it apart piece by piece:

`^A`	An uppercase letter A at the beginning of the line
`.*`	followed by any sequence of zero or more characters
`r$`	and having a lowercase r at the end of the line

The regular expression therefore stands for any line that begins with A, ends with r, and has zero or more characters in between. This matches the lines

```
Along came a spider
And sat down beside her
```

Character Sets

In the last chapter, you saw that you could make a glob construct that stood for a set of characters by enclosing the characters in square brackets. The same trick works in regular expressions. Enter

```
grep "[Tt]he" nursery
```

and you'll see all lines that contain either The or the. Enter

```
grep "[TS]he" nursery
```

and you'll see all lines that contain either The or She.

When you use character sets like this, it's important to enclose the regular expression in single or double quotation marks. Otherwise, the shell will assume that the character set is a glob construct and expand it.

Character sets in regular expressions can contain ranges, just like the ranges in the corresponding glob construct. For example, enter

```
grep "[a-z]he" nursery
```

This displays lines that contain any lowercase character followed by he.

If the first character after the opening bracket is a caret (^), the construct stands for any character that is not inside the character set. For example, enter

```
grep "[^a-z]he" nursery
```

This displays lines that contain any character that is not a lowercase letter, followed by he. These lines include such matches as The, She, and ' he' (where he follows a blank character). Note that ^ doesn't mean *the beginning of a line* when it appears inside brackets in this way.

! Versus ^

[!a-z] is the glob construct that matches any character that is not a lower-case letter. [^a-z] is the regular expression that does the same thing. Notice that the glob construct uses the exclamation mark (!), while the regular expression uses ^. (I've never heard a good explanation for the two being different. It's just one of those UNIX idiosyncrasies you have to get used to.)

Metacharacters and the Backslash

How would you display all the lines that end in a period? I've already mentioned that

```
grep ".$" nursery
```

doesn't work, because the dot is a metacharacter.

The answer is to use the backslash (\) character. You've already seen that you can tell the shell to ignore the special meaning of a glob character by putting a backslash in front of the character. The same trick works for metacharacters in regular expressions. Enter

```
grep "\.$" nursery
```

and grep displays only the lines that end with a period.

Summary of Regular Expressions

Table 5.1 shows the regular expressions that we've discussed so far, and Table 5.2 reviews the glob constructs. These tables should help you compare and contrast the two.

Table 5.1. Regular expressions.

Construct	Meaning
^	Beginning of a line
$	End of a line
.	Matches any character
*	Zero or more repetitions of the previous regular expression
[...]	Matches any character listed inside the brackets
[^...]	Matches any character not listed inside the brackets

Table 5.2. Glob constructs.

Construct	Meaning
?	Matches any character
*	Matches any string of zero or more characters
[...]	Matches any character listed inside the brackets
[!...]	Matches any character not listed inside the brackets

Using *grep* in Pipes

If you don't specify a file for grep to search, grep searches the standard input. This makes it possible to use grep in pipes, to extract information from other commands. For example, enter the command

```
ls -l | grep "^d"
```

This executes ls -l to obtain information about the current directory, then pipes that information through grep. grep displays all the lines that begin with d, the ones that provide information about directories. Similarly,

```
ls -l | grep "^-"
```

only displays information about the files under the current directory.

You'll recall that the -p option of ls marks directories by putting a slash (/) at the end of their names. Enter

```
ls -p / ¦ grep "/$"
```

This executes ls -p on the root directory, then pipes the result through a grep command that only displays lines that end with a slash. As a result, the preceding command displays the names of all the directories under your root directory. If the list is too long to fit on your display screen, you could enter

```
ls -p / ¦ grep "/$" ¦ more
```

to pipe the information through more. Remember that there is no limit to the number of commands you can connect in a pipeline.

With a bit of imagination, you should be able to figure out many ways you can use grep in a pipeline to select only the information you want to see. For example, how would you obtain a list of all the files under the root directory that were changed in the month of April? You can use ls -l to obtain the change dates of all the files under the directory, and then use grep to display all the output lines that contain the string Apr.

```
ls -l / ¦ grep "Apr"
```

You can, of course, use a similar command for any other month of the year. (Note: the preceding grep command just displays any line that contains the string Apr. Remember that the output of ls -l displays many other pieces of information besides the change date. If any of these other pieces of information contains the string Apr, grep displays the line, even if the file didn't actually change in April. Such coincidences happen only rarely, but you should be aware of the possibility.)

Extended Regular Expressions

According to the POSIX.2 standard, grep also accepts *extended regular expressions* in addition to the basic regular expressions discussed in previous sections. Extended regular expressions make it possible for you to make more sophisticated searches; for example, with an extended regular expression, you can search for several different strings at once.

The *-E* Option

If you want to use an extended regular expression with grep, you must specify the -E option. This tells grep that you are going to use an extended regular expression rather than a basic one.

The `-E` option for `grep` is a feature of the POSIX.2 standard; it is not currently recognized by SVID or older versions of UNIX. Those older versions of UNIX used a separate command named `egrep` to search using extended regular expressions. For example, where POSIX.2 would say

```
grep -E "regexp" file
```

older versions of UNIX would say

```
egrep "regexp" file
```

AT&T is committed to conforming to POSIX at some time in the future. Be warned, however, that if you use an older version of UNIX, you may need to use `egrep` instead of `grep -E`.

Multiple Choice

In extended regular expressions, the or-bar (¦) is a metacharacter that separates several possible choices. For example, enter

```
grep -E "Little¦Wee" nursery
```

The `-E` tells `grep` that you're using an extended regular expression. The expression `Little¦Wee` matches either `Little` or `Wee`. You'll see that the output is

```
Little boy blue
Little Miss Muffet
Little Jack Horner
Wee Willie Winkie
```

The or-bar indicates a multiple choice: either/or. In this context, it has nothing to do with pipes. In fact, you need to enclose the regular expression in single or double quotation marks to ensure that the or-bar isn't interpreted as a pipe symbol.

You can write several alternatives separated with or-bars. For example, enter

```
grep -E "sheep¦cow¦lamb" nursery
```

and `grep` displays lines that contain any of the three specified animals.

The Beginning and End of a Word

In extended regular expressions, the construct `\<` (a backslash followed by an opening angle bracket) stands for the beginning of a word. For example, enter

```
grep -E "\<he" nursery
```

and `grep` displays all lines from the `nursery` file containing words that begin with `he` (such as the word `her`).

Similarly, the construct \> (a backslash followed by a closing angle bracket) stands for the end of a word. For example, enter

```
grep -E "he\>" nursery
```

and grep displays all lines from the nursery file containing words that end with he (such as the word the).

Of course, you can combine the two. "\<he\>" matches he if and only if he is a complete word. For example, enter the command

```
grep -E "\<he\>" nursery
```

The command searches through nursery to see if there are any lines that contain the word he (in lowercase). There are no such lines, so grep does not display output. Now enter,

```
grep -E -i "\<he\>" nursery
```

The -i option tells grep to ignore the case of the letters, so grep looks for the words he, He, HE, and hE. This time grep finds the line

```
He stuck in his thumb
```

Remember that you can combine options if you like, so you can write

```
grep -Ei "\<he\>" nursery
```

if you want to save yourself some typing.

Why Do You Need the Backslash?

You might be wondering why grep wants you to enter \> and \< instead of just > and <. The answer should be clear if you look at an example. If you just wrote

```
grep -E <he nursery
```

the <he looks like a redirection construct. Even if you put it inside quotation marks, as in

```
grep -E "<he" nursery
```

there's still the possibility of confusion. By using a backslash, you turn off the meaning of < and > as redirection constructs. If you omit the backslash, grep looks for the characters themselves. For example, <he stands for a < character followed by he.

Fast Searches

Earlier, we mentioned the `egrep` command and how earlier versions of UNIX used this separate command for extended regular expression searches. Such systems also had a third command named `fgrep`, which worked like `grep` and `egrep` but didn't use regular expressions. For example,

```
fgrep "^abc" file
```

looks for the ^ character followed by abc; it wouldn't recognize ^ as a special character meaning the beginning of a line. Because `fgrep` didn't need to worry about the meanings for special characters, it usually worked faster than either `grep` or `egrep`.

To get the same effect, POSIX.2 supplies a `-F` option for `grep`. For example, enter

```
grep -F "^Mary" nursery
```

to search for a ^ character followed by `Mary`. The nursery file doesn't contain that string of characters, so `grep` doesn't display output.

Fast searches with `grep` `-F` are good if you don't want to use any metacharacters or if you just want to search for a string without doing anything fancy. Remember that if you use an older UNIX system, you'll have to use `fgrep` instead of `grep` `-F`.

Backwards Compatibility

To keep old-timers happy, POSIX.2 actually has `fgrep` and `egrep` commands that work like `grep` `-F` and `grep` `-E`.

Comparing Files: *diff*

The `diff` command compares two text files to see how they differ. In order to understand how `diff` works, you need to do a little setup by executing the following commands:

```
echo "Roses are red" >2line
echo "Violets are blue" >>2line
cp 2line 3line
echo "Some poems rhyme, but this one doesn't." >>3line
```

Notice that the second and third `echo` commands use >> to append text to existing files. To see what you've created, enter the commands

```
more 2line
more 3line
```

Notice that `2line` contains

```
Roses are red
Violets are blue
```

and `3line` contains

```
Roses are red
Violets are blue
Some poems rhyme, but this one doesn't.
```

Comparing the Two Files

You're now ready to use `diff` to compare the two files you've just created. Enter the command

```
diff 2line 3line
```

and you'll get the output

```
2a3
> Some poems rhyme, but this one doesn't.
```

In essence, the output of `diff` tells what you would need to do if you wanted to change the first file into the second file; in this case, it tells how to change `2line` into `3line`. The output

```
2a3
```

says that after line 2 of `2line`, you'd have to *append* line 3 of `3line`. (The a in `2a3` stands for *append*.) The output also shows you what line 3 of `3line` is.

```
> Some poems rhyme, but this one doesn't.
```

Notice that this line begins with a > character. In `diff` output, lines from the first file (in this case `2line`) are always marked with <, and lines from the second file (in this case `3line`) are always marked with >.

To summarize the output of the command, `diff` tells you that you'd have to add a line, and it shows you what line you'd have to add.

Deleted Lines

Now try the command in reverse. Enter

```
diff 3line 2line
```

You'll get the output

```
3d2
< Some poems rhyme, but this one doesn't
```

Again, `diff` tells what you would need to do to change the first file into the second file. In this case, it tells what you'd have to do to change `3line` into `2line`. The `3d2` says that you would need to delete line 3 from the first file (the `d` stands for *delete*); the 2 in `3d2` says that line 2 in `2line` is the last line before the one deleted.

Notice that the line from `3line` (`Some poems...`) is marked with a `<` character. As mentioned earlier, `diff` always uses `<` to mark lines from the first file being compared (in this case, `3line`) and uses `>` to mark lines from the second file (in this case `2line`).

> `diff` reported that you had to delete lines from 3line to get 2line.
>
> Many people find it helpful to adopt the policy of always comparing files in the order
>
> `diff old new`
>
> where `old` is the older file of the two and `new` is the newer. By being consistent, you can save yourself a great deal of confusion. However, this is just a useful policy, not a hard and fast rule.

Changed Lines

Now let's make a change in 2line and try the comparison again. First, enter the command

```
echo "Peonies are pink" >>2line
```

Make sure you use >> in the above command. This adds another line to 2line so that 2line now contains

```
Roses are red
Violets are blue
Peonies are pink
```

Now enter the command

```
diff 2line 3line
```

You'll see that the output is

```
3c3
< Peonies are pink
---
> Some poems rhyme, but this one doesn't.
```

This time the output starts with the line 3c3. `diff` is saying that if you want to change the first file (2line) into the second file (3line), you need to change line 3 of 2line into line 3 of 3line. The c in 3c3 stands for *change*. As the above output shows, `diff` also tells you how the lines are different: the line marked with < is what was in the first file (2line), and the line marked with > is what was in the second file (3line). `diff` uses --- to separate the line from 2line from the line from 3line.

Now, try one more experiment. Enter the following commands

```
cp 2line 4line
echo "THE END" >>4line
```

Be sure to use >> so that the line is appended to 4line. After executing the above command, the contents of 4line will be

```
Roses are red
Violets are blue
Peonies are pink
THE END
```

Now enter the command

```
diff 3line 4line
```

This time the output is

```
3c3,4
< Some poems rhyme, but this one doesn't
---
> Peonies are pink
> THE END
```

The first line says that line 3 in 3line changes into a range of lines in 4line. The range is written 3,4, which stands for lines 3 through 4. (As another example, a range of the form 5,10 stands for lines 5 through 10, inclusive.) Again, diff shows you what lines were in the first file (marked with <) and what lines were in the comparable position in the second file (marked with >); the two groups of lines are separated with ---.

Now, try one more experiment. Enter the commands

```
cat 3line 3line >6line
cat 4line 4line >8line
```

The first cat command creates a new file named 6line which contains two copies of 3line; the second cat command creates a new file named 8line that contains two copies of 4line. The contents of 6line are given in Listing 5.1, and the contents of 8line are given in Listing 5.2.

 Listing 5.1. Contents of 6line.

```
Roses are red
Violets are blue
Some poems rhyme, but this one doesn't
Roses are red
Violets are blue
Some poems rhyme, but this one doesn't
```

Listing 5.2. Contents of **8line**.

```
Roses are red
Violets are blue
Peonies are pink
THE END
Roses are red
Violets are blue
Peonies are pink
THE END
```

Now enter the following command

```
diff 6line 8line
```

to compare the two files. The output is given in Listing 5.3.

 Listing 5.3. Results of Comparing **6line** and **8line**.

```
3c3,4
< Some poems rhyme, but this one doesn't
- - -
> Peonies are pink
> THE END
6c7,8
< Some poems rhyme, but this one doesn't
- - -
> Peonies are pink
> THE END
```

You'll notice that this output reports two changes. The first begins with the heading 3c3,4. This says that to change 6line into 8line, you have to change line 3 from 6line into lines 3 and 4 from 8line; the output from diff also shows the lines in question. After that comes another set of changes, beginning with the heading 6c7,8. This says that to change 6line into 8line, you also have to change line 6 from 6line into lines 7 and 8 from 8line. Again, the output shows the lines in question.

This example demonstrates that diff may report several groups of differences between the same two files. Each group begins with a heading that tells whether the difference is an addition, a deletion, or a change.

132

Summary of *diff* Output

To review what I've discussed, suppose you enter the command

```
diff old new
```

to compare two files named `old` and `new`. The output of `diff` will divide into separate pieces. Pieces can have one of three forms.

```
XaY,Z
> new lines
```

says that `new` contains lines that are not in `old`. The number X gives a line number in `old`; the new lines were added after this line. The new lines are numbers Y through Z in `new`. The new lines are marked with the > character. If there is only one new line, you'll only see XaY.

```
X,YdZ
< old lines
```

says that `old` contains lines that are not in `new`. Lines numbered X through Y in `old` were deleted in order to get `new`. Line Z in `new` is the last line before the ones that were deleted. The old lines are marked with the < character. If there is only one old line, you'll see only XdZ.

```
W,XcY,Z
< old lines
---
> new lines
```

says that `old` contains lines W through X in the same location where `new` contains lines Y through Z. The old lines are marked with < while the new lines are marked with >. If there is only one old line, you'll only see one line number before the c. Similarly, if there is only one new line, you'll only see one line number after the c.

If there are no differences between the files being compared, `diff` issues no output. It simply returns, without displaying anything. To see this, enter the commands

```
cp 4line fourline
diff 4line fourline
```

There are no differences between `4line` and `fourline`, so you will see no output. As is often the case with UNIX commands, `diff` only displays output if there is something significant to say.

> **Cleaning Up**
>
> In order to clean up unneeded files, I recommend that you enter the command
>
> ```
> rm [23468]line fourline
> ```
>
> This removes all files created during this discussion of diff.

The Size of Text Files

The wc command offers a quick way to determine the size of a text file. Enter the command

```
wc sonnet
```

You'll see that the command displays the following.

```
17    118    690    sonnet
```

The first number is the number of lines in the file, the second is the number of words, and the third is the number of bytes (characters). The name of the file is given at the end of the line.

You can use wc on a list of files, as in

```
wc sonnet nursery
```

For each file, wc displays a count of lines, words, and bytes, in that order.

If you do not specify any files, wc displays information about the standard input. For example, enter

```
wc <sonnet
```

This displays a count of lines, words, and bytes in sonnet. You'll notice that it doesn't display the name of the file. Because the shell takes care of redirection before calling wc, wc doesn't know the name of the file it is examining. wc only knows that it is reading the standard input.

The -l option tells wc to display only a line count. For example,

```
wc -l nursery
```

only displays the number of lines in nursery. This feature is particularly useful in pipelines. For example, enter

```
find . -type f -print ¦ wc -l
```

The find command produces a list of all files under the current directory, and the wc command displays the number of lines in this list. As a result, the preceding command displays the number of files under the current directory.

The -w option tells wc to display only a word count, and the -c option tells wc to display only a byte (character) count. For more information, see the wc man page.

Sorting Text Files

The sort command lets you sort the contents of a text file. sort offers you the choice of sorting according to several different criteria: alphabetical order, numeric order, time/date order, and so on.

Throughout this section, you'll use a file named comics.1st, located under your home directory. This file was created at the time you installed your userid. The file contains information about a collection of comic books. Listing 5.4 shows a few representative records. Currently the records are in random order. You'll be sorting this information in several ways as you go along.

 Listing 5.4. Contents of the `comics.1st` file.

```
Detective Comics:572:Mar:1987:$1.75
Demon:2:Feb:1987:$1.00
Ex-Mutants:1:Sep:1986:$2.60
Justice League of America:259:Feb:1987:$1.00
```

Sorting Prerequisites

In order for the sort command to sort a file properly, the file must meet the following conditions:

- The file must be a text file.

- The file must contain one *record* per line. This means that each line of the file must be a separate record; you can't have records that extend over several lines, and you can't put several records on the same line.

■ Each record must be made up of zero or more *fields*. A field is just a piece of information. The different fields of the record must all be separated by the same character. For example, you can separate fields with blanks, with commas, with colons, or with any other suitable character.

Looking at the `comics.1st` file, you can see that the file satisfies these criteria. The file is a text file, and each line describes a different comic book. Each line contains several pieces of information (fields), and the fields are separated from each other with colon (`:`) characters.

Simple Sorting

The simplest `sort` command is just

```
sort comics.1st
```

Enter this command. You'll see that `sort` displays the sorted result on the standard output; Listing 5.5 shows the beginning of this output.

 Listing 5.5. Beginning of sorted comics list.

```
Batman:566:Sep:1986:$1.00
Border Worlds:1:Jul:1986:$2.80
Boris the Bear:1:Sep:1986:$1.50
Boris the Bear:3:Dec:1986:$2.30
```

The `sort` command does not change the contents of the input file. If you use `more` to display `comics.1st`, you'll see that the file is still in random order.

You can write the sorted result into a file with normal redirection. For example, enter

```
sort comics.1st >out
more out
```

You'll see that `out` contains the same data as `comics.1st`, only it is sorted. When you use `sort` in this way, the output file must not be the same as the input file. For example, you could not use `>comics.1st` to write the sorted output back into the original file. If you want to overwrite a file with its sorted contents, use the `-o` option; this option is described in the `sort` man page.

By default, `sort` sorts according to all the information in the record, analyzed character by character. If two records begin with the same character, `sort` looks at the second character to see which character should come first; if the second characters are also the same, `sort` looks at the third characters, and so on.

Merging Files

The `sort` command lets you *merge* the contents of several sorted or unsorted files. The result is sorted, and it contains all the records from all the input files. For example,

```
sort sonnet nursery >out
```

merges the contents of the given files, sorts everything, and writes the combined result into out. (The preceding command isn't very useful; who wants to sort lines of poetry? However, the command does demonstrate the principle.)

Sorting Keys

Suppose now that you want to sort according to some different piece of information in the record. For example, suppose that you want to sort according to date of publication. You do this using *sorting keys* (frequently shortened to *sort keys*).

A sorting key tells `sort` to look at one or more specific fields in a record, instead of looking at each record as a whole. A sorting key also tells what kind of information is stored in a particular field (such as a word, a number, or a month) and how that information should be sorted (in ascending or descending order).

A sorting key can refer to one or more fields. Fields are specified by number. The first field in a record is field 1, the field after the first separator character is field 2, and so on. In the comic book list, the name is field 1, the issue number is field 2, the month is field 3, the year is field 4, and the price is field 5.

A single `sort` command can have several sorting keys. The most important sorting key is given first; less important sorting keys follow. As an example, you'll sort by year, then by month within the year. Therefore the first sorting key should refer to the year field, and the second to the month field.

A sorting key has two halves. The first half tells the number of the field where the key begins. For the first sorting key (referring to the year), you will start with 4 (because the year is field 4). After the number comes a letter indicating the type of data in the field and how the data should be sorted. Possible letters include

<CR>d   The field contains upper- and/or lowercase letters, and/or digits. The field should be sorted in *dictionary* order, ignoring all other characters (except whitespace characters). Uppercase letters will always precede lowercase ones; thus ZITHER will precede apple because uppercase letters come first.

<CR>f   When sorting the field, upper- and lowercase versions of the same letter should be considered equivalent.

<CR>M   The field contains the name of a month. With this method of comparison, sort only looks at the first three characters of the month and ignores the case of letters. Thus, January, JAN, and jan are all equal.

<CR>n   The field contains an *integer* (a positive or negative number that doesn't have a fractional part or an exponent). Some versions of sort may allow fractions, but not MKS Tools.

Putting an r after any of these letters tells sort to sort in reverse order, from highest to lowest rather than from lowest to highest. For example, Mr means to sort in the order December, November, October, and so on.

For the sorting key based on the year, you use n. Thus, the first half of the sorting key is 4n.

The second half of a sorting key tells where the sorting field ends. It consists of the number of the last field in the sorting key. In the example, this is 4, because the year field is field 4. If you omit the second half of a sorting key, sort assumes that the key extends to the end of the record.

The two halves of the sorting key are separated with a comma, and the whole key is preceded by -k to indicate that it is a sorting key. Thus the full sorting key for the year field is

-k   4n,4

-k is POSIX.2

The -k format for a sorting key is dictated by the POSIX.2 standard. There are older forms in which you can specify sorting keys, but these are deprecated by POSIX and may become obsolete at some point in the future.

The M code is an extension to the POSIX.2 standard, but it is found in most UNIX and UNIX look-alike versions of sort.

The second sorting key refers to the month field. This key will have the form

```
-k  3M,3
```

because the month field is field 3.

The Separator Character

A `sort` command that uses sorting keys needs to know which character is used to separate fields within a record. You give `sort` this information by specifying the option `-t` followed by the character used to separate fields. For the `comics.1st` file, the option is `-t:`.

Putting the sort keys and the `-t` option together, you get the command

```
sort -t: -k  4n,4 -k  3M,3 comics.1st >out
```

Notice that the name of the file you want to sort comes after all the other options, including the sorting keys. The beginning of the resulting out file is shown in Listing 5.6.

 Listing 5.6. Beginning of comics lists sorted by year and month.

```
Howard the Duck:29:Jan:1979:$0.35
Moonshadow:2:May:1985:$1.75
Moonshadow:3:Jul:1985:$1.75
Bozz Chronicles:2:Feb:1986:$1.75
```

As an exercise in the use of sorting keys, try to sort the comics list according to price. Then try to sort the comics list in reverse order according to date of publication.

Archiving Tools: *tar*

The `tar` command is often used for *backing up* disk files to tapes or diskettes. More precisely, tar can create and manipulate *archives*. An archive is a single file that contains the complete contents of a set of other files. An archive can contain whole directories; it keeps a record of the directory structure (that is, which file belongs to which subdirectory) so that you can use tar to restore the directories just as they were at the time they were backed up. The name tar was derived from tape archive, but you can store archives on any medium, including hard drives and floppy disks.

Creating Archives

The most common command form for creating an archive file is

```
tar -cvf outfile directory
```

where `outfile` is the name you want to give to the archive file and `directory` is the name of a directory with the contents you want to back up. For example, put a formatted blank diskette in drive A: and enter the command

```
tar -cvf a:archive .
```

In this case, the command backs up the current directory (.) and stores the resulting archive in a file named `archive` on the diskette in A:. The archive will contain all the information needed to recreate everything in your current directory, including everything in all subdirectories. The archive also records file and directory characteristics (in other words, permissions) so that you can restore characteristics if and when you restore the directory contents.

The preceding command line contains several options. Look at each of these in turn:

`<CL>-c`	Tells `tar` to *create* an archive.
`<CL>-v`	Tells `tar` to be *verbose*. This option isn't necessary, but when you use it, `tar` displays information about everything it is doing as it creates the archive. This lets you keep track of `tar`'s progress.
`<CL>-f a:archive`	Gives the name of the archive file. If you put a dash (-) in place of the archive filename, the archive is written to the standard output.

The preceding options are the only ones that you'll normally need when you create the archive file.

In some cases, you may only want to back up specific files, rather than an entire directory. You can do this in several ways. The most straightforward way is to list the files on the command line, as in

```
tar -cvf a:archive file file file ...
```

Notice that the name of the archive file must come immediately after the `-f` option. The files that you want to back up come afterward. Of course, you can use glob constructs to generate the list of filenames. For example

```
tar -cvf a:archive *.doc
```

backs up every file with the `.doc` suffix.

`tar` can also read the list of files you want to back up from the standard input. If you want to do this, put a dash (-) in place of the directory name. I'll give some examples of this next, but they're simply for you to think about; don't try to enter them.

```
tar -cvf a:archive -
```

says that you want to type the filenames from the standard input. When you have issued this command, you can begin typing the names (because the standard input is associated with the keyboard). You must type each filename on a separate line. To indicate the end of the list of names, enter a line that consists only of the character Ctrl-Z (then press Enter).

The technique of reading names from the standard input lends itself to use with redirection and pipes. For example, consider the following:

```
find / -ctime -7 >weeklist
tar -cvf a:archive - <weeklist
```

This uses `find` to identify any files that have changed in the last seven days. The output of `find` is redirected into a file named `weeklist`. The `tar` command has the correct format to read the list of files from the standard input, but because of redirection, `weeklist` is used as the standard input. As a result, `tar` backs up all the files that have changed in the last seven days. You can use this approach for weekly backups. You can combine the two previous commands into a single command line using pipes, as in

```
find / -ctime -7 ¦ tar -cvf a:archive -
```

This is similar to the previous example, but it uses a pipe to connect the `find` and `tar` commands. The standard output of `find` is the list of names; the pipe feeds this list of names to `tar` as its standard input. You may think this example is complicated, but it's exactly like the previous one, except that it doesn't use `weeklist` as an intermediary holding file for the list of names.

Backup Drives and UNIX

With a true UNIX or UNIX look-alike system, you would normally *mount* a tape or diskette drive to do a backup. The mount operation lets you associate a directory in the normal file system with the contents of a tape or diskette, by making use of a special device file for the tape or diskette drive. Such procedures vary from system to system and are outside the scope of this book.

> The examples in this section avoid such complications by using standard
> DOS notation (drive A:, drive B:, and so on). This notation works with the
> MKS Tools and illustrates most of the points you'll see on a true UNIX or
> UNIX look-alike system.

Examining Archives

Another form of the `tar` command lets you read the contents of an existing archive
file. Enter the command

```
tar -tf a:archive
```

This produces a list of all the files currently contained in the archive. With large archives, you may want to use

```
tar -tf a:archive ¦ more
```

By piping the output through `more`, you can read the output screen by screen.

You'll notice that this form of the command has two options.

`<CL>-t`	Tells `tar` you want to see a *table of contents*.
`<CL>-f a:archive`	States the name of the archive file, as in the previous form of the command.

To obtain more details on the contents of the archive, enter

```
tar -tvf a:archive
```

The addition of the `-v` option produces more verbose output. In this case, each line
of output is similar to the information produced by `ls -l`.

Extracting from Archives

Another form of the `tar` command lets you extract files from an archive file. Put the
disk containing your `tar` archive into disk A: and enter the commands

```
rm sonnet
tar -xvf a:archive ./sonnet
```

This gets rid of the existing copy of sonnet, then extracts the backed up copy from the archive. The -x option stands for *extract*. As before, -v asks tar to display what it is doing, and -f a:archive gives the name of the archive. The name at the end of the line tells which file you want to extract.

You can extract several files at a time. The general form would be

```
tar -xvf a:archive file file file ...
```

where the file arguments name the files that you want to extract. As you might expect, you can use glob constructs in the usual way to generate the list of files. If you do not put any filenames on the end of the command, tar extracts everything from the archive.

Files extracted from an archive normally overwrite any files of the same name that already exist. For example, tar -xvf a:archive sonnet will overwrite sonnet if it already exists. If you want to control this process, you can add the -w option to the command line. For example, enter

```
tar -xvwf a:archive ./sonnet ./nursery
```

You'll see that tar checks with you before extracting each file. Enter a y if you want tar to go ahead with the operation and an n if you want tar to skip the operation. At the moment, it doesn't matter whether you answer yes or no, because the archived versions of the files are the same as the ones in the current directory. You have to be more careful if the archived versions are different from the existing ones; then you must decide whether you want to keep the existing ones as they are or restore the archived versions (thereby overwriting the previous contents of the existing files).

Other Backup Software

There are several other commands found in UNIX and UNIX look-alikes that can be used for backup and restore operations. The best known of these is cpio, found in MKS Toolkit and on all AT&T UNIX systems after Version 7. The POSIX.2 standard offers pax, an archiver utility that can work with tar archives and cpio files.

The principles underlying cpio and pax are similar to those of tar, although the command line options are different.

Printing Hard Copy

According to the POSIX.2 standard, UNIX systems should offer an `lp` command that sends text output to the printer. The simplest form of this command is

```
lp file
```

where `file` is a text file. Due to space limitations on the disks, this command is not part of the MKS Tools that come with this book.

Many UNIX and UNIX look-alike systems do not have an `lp` command. The most common alternative is named `lpr`. You can use `lpr` to print files with a command line of the form

```
lpr file
```

You might wonder what the difference is between `lp` and `lpr`. Different versions of the commands take different options; they may also work differently internally. To see how the commands work with any particular UNIX or UNIX look-alike system, read the manuals that come with that system.

Both `lp` and `lpr` print the standard input if there is no `file` specified. This means that you can use them at the end of a pipeline, as in

```
ls -l ¦ lp
```

This pipes the output of the `ls` command into `lp`, which then prints the output on a line printer (or some other hard copy device). Remember that you can't use this technique with the MKS Tools, because there is no `lp` command.

Printing with MKS Tools

There are (at least) two ways you can print the files that you create with MKS Tools commands. First, you can quit your MKS Tools session and print the file with the normal DOS PRINT command (or whatever command you normally use to print DOS text files). Second, you can use the command

```
cat file >PRN
```

inside an MKS Tools session. `cat` copies the contents of the text `file` to the DOS PRN device. Copying data to PRN has the effect of sending the data to the printer, if you have a printer attached directly to your system.

Note that the cat approach only sends the text of the file. If your printer requires special control characters as well as normal text, you may not get the sort of output you expect. For example, most laser printers require formatting instructions as well as the text you want to print; if you simply send the output of cat (sometimes called *catting a file*) into PRN, you may not get any output.

Chapter Review

The grep command can search through a set of files and display all lines that match a given string. The general form of the command is

```
grep options string file file file ...
```

Possible options are given in Table 5.3. It is a good idea to enclose string in single or double quotation marks. If there are no files given on the command line, grep examines the standard input.

Table 5.3. Options for grep.

Option	Meaning
-E	Use extended regular expressions
-F	Do not use regular expressions
-i	Ignore the case of letters when comparing

The string argument for grep can be a regular expression. A regular expression is a string used to match a pattern of characters in a file. Regular expressions can contain metacharacters, which give special criteria for pattern matching. Table 5.4 summarizes the metacharacters discussed in this chapter; those marked with [Ext] are extended regular expressions and are only special when you specify the -E option for grep. Appendix C, "Summary of Filename Generation with Glob Constructs," gives a complete description of all recognized metacharacters.

Table 5.4. Regular expression metacharacters.

Construct	Meaning
^	Beginning of a line
$	End of a line
.	Matches any character
*	Zero or more repetitions of the previous regular expression
[...]	Matches any character listed inside the brackets
[^...]	Matches any character not listed inside the brackets
¦	Separates multiple choices [Ext]
\<	The beginning of a word [Ext]
\>	The end of a word [Ext]

The fgrep command searches for strings inside files, but does not recognize regular expressions. The egrep command searches for strings inside files, but always uses extended regular expressions.

The diff command compares two files to see how they differ. The format of the command is typically

```
diff old new
```

The output shows the changes necessary to change the old file into new. Output may show that lines were appended, deleted, or changed.

The wc command counts the number of lines, words, and bytes (characters) in a text file. Table 5.5 shows possible options for wc. You can use wc in pipelines to count such things as the number of files under a directory.

Table 5.5. Options for wc.

Option	Meaning
-l	Show line count only
-w	Show word count only
-c	Show byte (character) count only

The sort command can sort the contents of a text file according to a variety of criteria. The file must consist of one record per line, and each record must be divided into fields with a specified separator character. The general format of a sort command line is

```
sort options file file file ...
```

Output is written to the standard output; you can use redirection to save the sorted output in a file. The -t option tells what character you are using to separate fields.

Sorting keys (or sort keys) indicate which field(s) should be considered for the purpose of sorting. They also tell what the fields contain. A sorting key has the general form

```
-k start,end
```

where start is the number of the field where the sorting key begins and end is the number of the field where the sorting key ends. The start number can be followed by characters from Table 5.6.

Table 5.6. Codes that can be used in sorting keys.

Code	Meaning
d	Sort in dictionary order
M	Sort in month order
n	Sort in numerical order
r	Sort in reverse order

The tar command can be used to back up and restore files. tar manipulates archives, files that can contain the contents of many files and directories. To create an archive, use

```
tar -cvf archive name name ...
```

where archive is the name of the archive file you want to create and the names are names of files or directories with contents you want to save in the archive. If you specify _ in place of the list of names, tar will read names from the standard input; you can use redirection to supply this list of names from a file, or use pipes to supply the list of names from another command's output. To list the contents of an existing archive, use

```
tar -tf archive
```

To extract files from an archive, use

```
tar -xvf archive name name ...
```

The `lp` command is a POSIX.2 command for producing hard copy output. Many UNIX and UNIX look-alike systems have an `lpr` command to perform the same function.

Exercises

1. Search all the files under your current directory and find all occurrences of the string `ex`. (Hint: use a glob construct to generate the list of filenames.)

2. Search all the files under your current directory and find all occurrences of the string `ex` at the beginning of a line.

3. The level of a directory X is the number of directories between X and the root. For example, a directory `/u/chris/dir` has a level of 2, because `/u` and `/chris` come between `/dir` and the root. Display the names of all directories on your hard drive with a level greater than 2. (Hint: pipe the output of `find / -type d` through `grep`.)

4. Enter the following commands:

   ```
   du >out1
   du >out2
   diff out1 out2
   ```

   Explain the `diff` output. (Note: `du` was discussed in the Exercises for Chapter 4.)

5. Use a single command line to count the number of files in the `/lu` directory. (Hint: use `find` and `wc`, with pipes.)

6. Use a single command line to produce a file that contains a sorted list of all the files in your home directory and its subdirectories.

7. Sort the `comics.lst` file according to title and price. Pipe the output through `more` so that you can read it.

8. Read the man page for the `pr` command. This command can format text files in a nice, readable form for printing on a line printer. Format the `sonnet` file into a file named `nice` and examine the results with `more`.

9. Repeat the previous exercise, but use pipes instead of using `nice` to hold the formatted version of `sonnet`.

10. Skim through the man page for `bc`. `bc` is a desk calculator program that lets you perform extensive arithmetic operations. Use `bc` to find the average of the numbers 34, 82, and 192. (Although this exercise seems quite arbitrary, it will actually require you to learn many of the fundamentals of using the `bc` program.)

TEXT FILES—VENI, VIDI, *vi*

This chapter deals with the vi text editor, a program for creating and editing text files. The vi text editor lets you enter text, change text in a variety of ways, and save that text in files.

The *vi* Text Editor

There are many text editors available on UNIX and UNIX look-alike systems, but the most popular is almost certainly vi. vi is a screen editor; this means that when you start editing a file, the display screen shows the current contents of the file. As you enter editing commands, the commands usually do not appear on the screen; instead, the text displayed on the screen changes to reflect the changes you have made.

This contrasts sharply with *line editors* like the EDLIN editor of DOS. With a line editor, you do not see the text of your file unless you explicitly enter a command asking to see it. For the most part, the display screen shows the commands that you type, not the text.

vi was one of the earliest screen editors created; at the time vi was designed, line editors were far more common. Now, the balance has shifted in the other direction, and today, most widely used editors (such as WordPerfect and Microsoft Word) are screen editors.

> ### How to Pronounce vi
>
> Many UNIX purists claim that the proper pronunciation of vi is *vee-eye* (pronouncing each letter separately). Others claim that UNIX purists should have better things to do with their time, and pronounce it *veye* or *vie* (a single syllable). In keeping with the UNIX philosophy, I suggest you customize the pronunciation to suit your own tastes.

Contrasting *vi* with Word Processors

If you're a DOS user, you're probably familiar with one or more of the popular DOS word processors (such as WordPerfect or Microsoft Word). Before I discuss how vi actually works, it's worthwhile to take a moment to contrast the text editor vi with word processors.

The most popular word processors are primarily concerned with the production of documents. They are designed to work with different types of printers, and to give you the ability to use special typefaces, font sizes, and other tricks of the printing trade.

vi is primarily concerned with creating text files, especially text files that will be used by other programs. For example, vi has several features aimed at helping programmers prepare source code files that can be run through compilers to produce executable programs. It is seldom used to produce documents directly. On UNIX systems, vi is often used to create text files that can be run through the troff text-formatting program to produce actual documents.

If you're expecting vi to be similar to word processors, you'll be disappointed. vi is missing several features offered by most word processors, particularly the features aimed at producing hard-copy documents. But by the same token, word processors often have difficulty doing the things that vi does well. You'll find, for example, that word processors typically put special characters (characters aimed at formatting the files for output to a printer) into files. Such characters aren't useful in straight text files; most of the time the characters are just gobbledygook that confuses other programs that try to read the files.

The proper approach is to recognize the strengths of both types of programs. Use a word processor when you want to produce a document. Use vi when you want to produce a text file for use by another UNIX program.

Online Files for Learning *vi*

Much of the rest of this chapter works through files that you'll find under your home directory. Each of these files is designed as an online exercise for using vi. You use vi to read through the files, and as you go, the files suggest exercises you can do while using vi.

Quitting vi

As you work through the exercises, you can quit at any time by pressing Esc and then typing

```
:q!
```

This tells vi to quit immediately, without saving any changes to the exercise file. If you were using vi to edit a file, you would almost never use this command; you would normally save your work before quitting. However, these are just exercises and there's no benefit to saving the work.

---

browse.v—Browsing Through Text

The first vi exercise file is named browse.v. In order to work through the exercises in the file, enter the command

```
vi browse.v
```

The file tells how to read files using vi. I recommend that you enter the preceding command now and work through the exercise file. The rest of this section essentially repeats what you will see in the file; if you don't want to work through the file, you can read the book instead. However, I think you'll learn about vi faster if you actively work through the file rather than passively reading the book. (Of course, having the text of the exercise files in the book is useful for reference and for study when you aren't at your computer.)

```
This file is the vi Browser's Guide.  In it, we will describe
how to move backward and forward through a file while using vi.


*****************************************************************
*******          Part I: Moving Around in a File     *******
*****************************************************************

When reading files with vi, you must keep track of the
position of the cursor.  The cursor is a small line or box that
indicates a particular position on the display screen.  On some
systems, the cursor blinks; on others, it does not.

Because you have just started using vi, the cursor marks the
first nonblank character on the first line of the screen.  When
you start a vi session by reading in a file, the cursor always
appears at the first nonblank character of the file.

Now press the Enter key.  You will see that the cursor moves
down to the first nonblank character of the next line.  Keep
pressing Enter.  See where it puts the cursor on each line.
When you get to the bottom of the screen, keep pressing Enter.
New lines will appear one at a time.  Keep pressing Enter until
this line is the top one on the screen.  Then stop and read some
more.

Press the - (the minus sign) key.  You will see that the
cursor moves up to the first nonblank character of the previous
line.  In other words, entering a minus is the opposite of
pressing Enter.

Keep pressing - until the cursor gets to the top line of the
screen, then press it once more.  You will see the whole screen
move down to make room for an old line at the top.  Thus, Enter
and - let you go backward and forward through the file.  Just
those two keys will let you read everything in this file.  If
you ever find that you've read everything on the screen and have
no other instructions, just keep pressing Enter to read more of
the file.  If you want to review something that is no longer on
the screen, back up with -.
```

Positioning the Cursor on the Screen:

If you just use Enter and - to move the cursor, you move very
slowly. Here are three commands for moving the cursor faster:

(a) Typing **L** (for Low) moves the cursor to the bottom line of
the screen.

(b) Typing **H** (for High) moves the cursor to the top line of
the screen.

(c) Typing **M** (for Middle) moves the cursor to the middle line
of the screen.

Try all of these. It's important that you use uppercase for
L, **H**, and **M**. The case of letters is important in **vi**.

Moving the Cursor Up and Down:

Now, hold down the Ctrl key and press the D key (this is called
pressing Ctrl-D, sometimes shortened to ^D). You will see several
new lines appear at the bottom of the screen. Ctrl-D moves Down
half a screen.

Press Ctrl-D once more, and then press Ctrl-U (hold down Ctrl and
press U). You will see that Ctrl-D moves the cursor down half a
screen, and Ctrl-U moves it up. Using Ctrl-D and Ctrl-U to move
forward and backward through a file is less work than using
Enter and -; you don't need to press as many keystrokes.

Ctrl-D and Ctrl-U move quickly, moving half a screen at a time.
Ctrl-F (for *forward*) and Ctrl-B (for *backward*) move almost a
full screen at a time. Right now, press Ctrl-F, and then Ctrl-B.

Ctrl-F (probably) took you forward off this screen and Ctrl-B
brought you back. Ctrl-F and Ctrl-B are good for moving very
quickly through files. They aren't particularly good for going
through this **vi** file, however — they move too far in one jump
and you'll lose what is on the screen. But remember them for
later work.

For practice, use Ctrl-U or Ctrl-B to go back to the beginning
of the file, then use Ctrl-D or Ctrl-F to come back to this
point in the file. You shouldn't have trouble finding this spot
again, because it comes right before the Part II heading.

```
********************************************************************
*******      Part II: Horizontal Cursor Movement      *******
********************************************************************
```

In the last section, you moved the cursor up and down. In this
section, you'll move the cursor back and forth on the line.
Just keep pressing Enter or Ctrl-D to see new material.

The cursor is likely to be on the first nonblank character of
some line. Press the **l** (lowercase ell). The cursor will move
one character to the right.

Pressing **l** repeatedly keeps moving the cursor to the right,
until you get to the end of the line. Then it stops because it
can't go any farther.

Now press **h**. You should see the cursor move to the left. By
pressing **h** repeatedly, you can move the cursor to the left
margin.

Vertical Line Movement:

Between **h** and **l** on a standard keyboard are **j** and **k**.
Pressing **j** moves the cursor down one line. Pressing **k** moves
the cursor up one line.

k and **j** move up and down like - and Enter. However, when
you press **j** or **k**, the cursor stays in the same column on the
screen; when you press - or Enter, the cursor goes to the
first nonblank character of the line. Check this out for
yourself.

Moving to the Start or End of the Line:

Moving the cursor back and forth on a line can take a long time
if you are using **h** and **l**. Try this instead. Move the
cursor to the beginning of a line and enter the **$** character.
You will see the cursor jump to the end of the same line.

Press the **0** (zero) key, and the cursor jumps to the beginning
of the line. Thus **$** and **0** give you a quick way to jump to
the end or the beginning of a line.

Word Movement:

Now move the cursor to the beginning of this very line, and type
w (lowercase). You will see that the cursor jumps from the
N in **Now** to the **m** of **move**. **w** stands for **word**, and
the **w** command jumps to the start of the next word...more or
less.

Keep typing **w** and you will see that the cursor usually jumps
from one word to the next, but occasionally stops at things
normally not thought of as words. For example, it will stop at
the comma after **line**. This is because **vi** defines a **word**
as a sequence of alphabetic/numeric characters or a sequence of
nonalphabetic/numeric characters (not including blanks). As a
result, **vi** regards punctuation characters as **words**. You'll
get used to this quickly.

Keep pressing **w**, and you'll see the cursor jump from the last
word on one line to the first word of the next. Pressing **w**
sends the cursor to the beginning of the next word, even if that
means going to the next line.

Now press **b** (lowercase). You will see that the cursor jumps
backward to the beginning of a word. If the cursor is already
at the beginning of a word, it will jump back to the start of
the previous word. However, if you use the arrow keys to move
the cursor to the middle of a word, pressing **b** goes to the
start of the word that contains the cursor. Try it.

```
****************************************************************
*******              Part III: Searching            ******
****************************************************************
```

You now know how to move the cursor up and down on the screen
and back and forth on the line. In this part of the guide, I'll
discuss another way to move through text: searching.

When you begin looking at a file, **vi** puts the cursor at the
file's first line, but often what you want to look at is in the
middle of the file. You can use Ctrl-D to work your way down
through the file...but this can take time. If you know what
sort of material you are looking for, it is often faster to use
the search facility. The search facility tells **vi** to search
through the file from the current cursor position to the next
occurrence of a particular word or phrase.

Searching Forward:

To see how it works, start by pressing Ctrl-D or Enter until this entire paragraph is on the screen. Move the cursor to the beginning of this line and type a slash (/). Be careful not to confuse this with the backslash (\).

When you type the slash, you will see the cursor move down to the bottom of the screen. Now type the word **hello**, then press Enter. You will see the cursor jump to the beginning of the word **hello** above. When you type a word or phrase after a slash, **vi** searches forward for the next occurrence of that string of characters. The cursor is placed on the first character of the string that is found.

Now, move the cursor to the beginning of this line and type a slash followed by Enter. You will see that **vi** finds this occurrence of **hello**. If you just type a slash without anything after it, **vi** looks for the most recent word or phrase you searched for.

Searching Backward:

Move the cursor to this line and type a question mark (?) followed by the word **hello**, then press Enter. You will see that **vi** moves the cursor backward to the previous occurrence of **hello**. When you type a word or phrase after a question mark, **vi** searches backward for that string of characters. As you might guess, if you just type a question mark followed by Enter, **vi** searches backward for the most recent thing you searched for. Try it.

Case Sensitivity:

When you type characters after a slash or question mark, you should make sure you enter them in the correct case. For example, ask **vi** to search for **hello**, but type the word in uppercase. You will see that **vi** prints the message **Pattern not found** at the bottom of the screen. As it turns out, this file does not contain the word **hello** in uppercase, although it has the word many times in lowercase.

Patterns and Regular Expressions

In a vi command, anything after a slash or question mark is called a pattern. The patterns of vi are the same as the regular expressions used by grep.

Regular Expressions in vi:

In order to make searching more useful, **vi** lets you use
regular expressions, just like the ones used by **grep**. For
example, the caret character (^) stands for the beginning of a
line. Move the cursor to this line and type

/^**line**

vi will look for the word **line** occurring at the beginning of a
line (which is this one).

The end of a line is represented by the dollar sign ($). Move
the cursor to this line and type

/**line$**

You will see that **vi** will search forward for a line
that ends in the word **line** (the previous line).

Inside patterns, the dot (.) stands for any character. For
example, move the cursor to the beginning of this line and type

/**t.e**

You will see that the cursor moves to the word the. Type /
over and over, and the cursor will keep jumping forward to any
sequence of three letters that starts with **t** and ends in **e**.
Were you surprised that the cursor jumped into the middle of the
word **letters**? **vi** finds character strings, even when they
are in the middle of larger words.

Whenever you enter a pattern, remember that the dot has a
special meaning. It may look like the end of a sentence, but
don't be fooled. For example, move the cursor to the beginning
of this paragraph and type

/**end of a sentence.**

The cursor moves to the string **end of a sentence**, in the
previous paragraph. The dot in the pattern matches the comma in
the actual string. This is a mistake that beginners frequently
make.

Inside patterns, a dot followed by a star (*) stands for any
sequence of zero or more characters. For example, move the
cursor to this line and type

/^**Y.*s$**

You will find the next line that begins with the letter **Y**, ends
with the letter **s**, and has any number of characters in between.

Wrap-Around Searches:

```
By default, all searches in vi wrap around from the bottom of
the file to the top.  For example, consider a string consisting
of two percent signs (%%).  This line is the only place in this
file where that string occurs.  Now move the cursor to this line
and search forward for the two percent signs.  The search starts
by going down to the bottom of the file.  Because vi won't
find the string by then, vi goes back to the top of the file
and keeps searching, eventually finding the string on the
preceding line.

Similarly, if you use question marks to search backward through
a file, the search will wrap around from the top of the file to
the bottom, if necessary.


*****************************************************************
*******          Part IV: Moving to a Line          *******
*****************************************************************


I had to save this last part until the end because it tells you
a quick way to go to the end of a file.  Just type G
(uppercase), and the cursor goes to the last line of the file.
If you type a number before the G, the cursor moves to that
line in the file.  For example, 1G goes to the first line of
the file.  Try going to the first line of the file, then coming
back here to the end.

Remember, to quit vi now, type :q! and press Enter.
```

edit.v—Editing Text

The second vi exercise file is named edit.v. In order to work through the exercises in the file, enter the commands

```
cp edit.v myedit.v
vi myedit.v
```

This makes a copy of the edit.v file, then uses vi to read the copy. I suggest looking at the copy rather than the real thing, just in case you make mistakes or someone else wants to try.

The exercise file tells how to create and edit files using vi. As in the last section, I recommend that you enter the preceding command now and work through the exercise file. The rest of this section essentially repeats what you will see in the file.

The browse.v file explained how to read through a file using
vi. Unless the text suggests a different way to move through
the file, just read through this file by pressing Enter or
Ctrl-D.

```
****************************************************************
*******              Part I: Entering Text              *******
****************************************************************
```

The most commonly used command for entering text is **a**
(standing for append or add). The steps for using **a** are
simple.

1. Determine where you want to add text and move the cursor to
the character immediately before that point.

2. Type the letter **a**. This switches you to Insert Mode,
where anything you type is added to the text showing on the
screen.

3. Type your text (as many lines as you want).

4. Press the Esc key. This tells **vi** that you are finished
entering text at this location. In other words, you leave
Insert Mode and enter Command Mode. Anything you type now
will be regarded as a command. For example, Ctrl-D
is regarded as a command to move forward in the file.

To see how the **a** command works, move the cursor until all four
of the preceding steps are on the screen, then move the cursor
to the beginning of the next line. Type **a**, then **hello**, and
then press Esc.

You should have seen the word **hello** appear on the screen as
you typed. You did not see the **a** for append — that was a
command to **vi**, not text to display on the screen. You might
also have noticed that the cursor changed from a line to a
block; **vi** doesn't do this on all systems, but it does on some
machines. For people who have such machines, the block
indicates when you are in Insert Mode.

Creating several lines of text is just as easy as creating one
line. Type an **a**, type your text lines, and press Esc. For
example, try entering the first few lines of Mary Had A Little
Lamb immediately after this line.

Correcting Mistakes:

Did you have any trouble? Perhaps you made a typing mistake.
If you make mistakes while typing text, they're easy to
correct. Press the Backspace key until you have backed up over
the error. After you have done this, you can type over the old
characters to correct them. Try it. Move the cursor to the
next blank line, then type an **a** to enter Insert Mode. Type
hello, backspace back to the **h** and type **hi!**. Then press
Esc.

Notice that before you pressed Esc, the line looked like **hi!lo**
— the old letters from the end of **hello** were still visible.
After you pressed Esc, the **lo** disappeared. Backing over
characters with the Backspace key removes the text, even if it
doesn't erase the characters from the screen. The characters
are only erased when you type over them or when you press Esc.

If you're like many writers, you may change your mind partway
through a line and want to get rid of the whole thing. If you
are in Insert Mode and you want to get rid of everything on the
line you have just typed, enter an at sign (@). You will see
the cursor jump back to the first character you inserted on the
current line. You can then type over the old line. (Note that
this does not work outside of Insert Mode.)

Adding Text in the Middle of a Line:

So far, I've just been talking about adding new lines. You can
add text to an existing line too. For example, move the cursor
to the end of the next line, type an **a**, enter the word
hello, and press Esc. When you moved the cursor to the end of
the line, it sat on the last character. When you pressed **a**,
it moved to the next position on the line. You could then type
your new text.

You can add text in the middle of a line too. For example, this
line contains the word **math**. Can you add text to change it to
mathematics? Try it. If you try to do it and find that the
text is being added in the wrong place, you started with the
cursor in the wrong place. Backspace over what you have typed,
press Esc, and move the cursor, so you can try again.

The Insert Command:

There are several other commands you can use for entering text.
The **i** (insert) command lets you insert text in front of the
current cursor position. For example, move the cursor to the
beginning of this line. Type an **i**, then **hello**, then press
Esc. You will see the text inserted in front of the cursor.

The Open Command:

The **o** (open) command creates a blank line after the line that contains the cursor and lets you append text there. For example, move the cursor anywhere on the next line, then type an **o**, then **hello**, then Esc. You will see that a blank line opens up when you type the **o**, and anything you type next is added to that line. Note that all the rest of the text in the file shifts down to make room for the new line.

The Write Command:

When you use commands like **a**, **i**, and **o**, you add text to the material shown on the screen. Before you quit **vi**, however, you should save these changes in a file. To do this, you can use the write command.

Using Enter or Ctrl-D, make sure that the entire next paragraph is on the screen. Now, type a colon (:). You will see the cursor move to the bottom line of the screen and display the colon there. Next, type a **w** (for write), then a space, then a file name like junk. If you make any typing mistakes while you do this, you can correct them in the usual way, using the Backspace key. When you have the command correct, it should look something like

:w junk

at the bottom of the screen. When it looks like this, press Enter.

You will see that **vi** pauses for a few moments, and then prints information on the bottom of the screen: the name of the file and how much text was written. The **w** command writes the text you have entered into the file called **junk**. This saves the text, so you can use it later. After you have written your text into a file, it is safe to quit **vi** by typing **:q** and pressing Enter. **(Don't do this now!)**

Limited Writing Capabilities

The vi that comes with the MKS Tools will only write out a maximum of 100 lines. The vi that comes with the full MKS Toolkit can write much larger files.

Quitting Without Writing:

If you try to quit with **:q** before writing out your text with
:w, **vi** will check to see if you've made changes since the
last time you wrote out the file. If you have, **vi** won't let
you quit. This is a safety measure — if you do not use **:w** to
write out your text before you quit **vi**, all the changes you
have made since the last write will be lost. Thus **vi** stops
you from quitting if you haven't saved your recent changes.

If you really want to quit without saving your changes, type
:q! and press Enter. You've probably used this while working
through this guide. **:q!** is just an emphatic **:q**. When you
are actually working with **vi**, you should probably use **:q**
instead of **:q!**. Leaving off the **!** gets you that safety
feature I just talked about.

If you want to quit now, use **:q!**. Otherwise, go on to the
next section.


```
*****************************************************************
*******            Part II: Simple Editing        *******
*****************************************************************
```

I've shown you how to add new text to a file. Now I'm going to
show you how to change the text that the file already contains.

Deleting Lines:

Look at deleting text first. The command to delete a line of
text is **dd**. Try it. Move the cursor to the next line and
type **dd**.

TWINKLE, TWINKLE, LITTLE STAR

You should see the line disappear on the screen. The other
lines on the screen close in to fill the gap.

To delete more than one line, type a number followed by **dd**.
This deletes the given number of lines, beginning at the line
that contains the cursor. Try **4dd** to delete the next four
lines.

TWINKLE, TWINKLE, LITTLE STAR
HOW I WONDER WHAT YOU ARE
UP ABOVE THE WORLD SO HIGH
LIKE A TEA TRAY IN THE SKY

164

Again, the lines disappear on the screen and the remaining lines close in.

The undo Command:

Now, type a **u**. You should see the lines reappear. **u** stands for undo, and it reverses the effect of commands like **dd**. This is a very useful command to remember. If you delete something by mistake, you can get it back again if you immediately type **u** for undo. However, you can only undo the most recent command that changed text. If you type **u** and **u** again, the second **u** will "undo the undo," so you'll go back to the way things were before the first undo. Try it.

Deleting Blocks of Text:

Another way to delete text is to type **d** followed by a command that moves the cursor. This deletes everything from the beginning cursor position to where the cursor ends up. For example, move the cursor to the * in the next line, then type **d$**.

*   AND AWAY WE GO!

You see that all the text from the * to the end of the line disappears. **$** moves the cursor to the end of the line, so **d$** deletes to the end of the line.

Move the cursor to the beginning of the word BACON in this line and type **dw**. You will see the word disappear. Remember that **w** moves the cursor forward one word, so **dw** deletes everything from the cursor to the beginning of the next word. What will **db** do? Try it on a word in this line.

You can even use searches after **d**. Type a / or a **?** to begin the search, then the pattern you want to search for, then a closing / or **?** (whichever you started with). When you're done, press Enter. **vi** will search forward or backward for a string that matches the desired pattern and delete everything from the cursor to the matching string. Move the cursor to the beginning of the next line and type

d/hello/

As you see, this deletes everything up to the **hello**.

Deleting a Single Character:

If you want to delete a single character, move the cursor on top of the character and type a lowercase **x**. Use this to get rid of the double quotation marks around "**x**" in this sentence.

Changing Lines:

The **cc** command changes a line. To see how it works, begin by getting this whole paragraph on the screen. Move the cursor to any part of the next line and type **cc**.

THE WALRUS AND THE CARPENTER WERE WALKING HAND IN HAND.

You will see the whole line disappear. The cursor can also change into a block. You are now in Insert Mode, and anything you type will be displayed on the screen. Type **hello**, press Enter, and type **hello** again. You will see the two new lines replace the one old one. To get out of Insert Mode, press Esc.

If you type a number followed by **cc**, **vi** will get rid of that number of lines and let you type new text to replace them. For example, move the cursor to the first of the new lines you entered in the last paragraph and type **2cc**. **vi** replaces the two lines with a single blank line. Just press Esc and that blank line will stay there in place of the two old lines.

Changing Blocks of Text:

A **c** followed by a command to move the cursor lets you change everything from the starting position of the cursor to its final position. To see how this works, begin by getting this whole paragraph on the screen. Move the cursor to the first letter of the word BACON on this line and type **cw**.

You will see that **vi** puts a **$** sign on the last letter of the word. This marks the end of the material that the command will change. The cursor will still be at the beginning of the word. Now type **VEGETABLE** and press Esc. You see that the characters which you type overstrike the characters that were there until you get to the **$** sign. Then the rest of the line moves over to make room for the extra characters that you add to the line.

Whenever you change text with a **c** command, you can enter as much or as little new text as you want. For example, you could have replaced **BACON** with many lines of text if you liked. The rest of the text would have moved to make room for the new text you entered.

Replacing a Single Character:

If you want to change a single character in your text, move the cursor to that character, type **r** (for replace) and then type the new character. You do not have to type Esc. The new character will replace the old one.

More About undo:

The **u** command undoes **c** and **r** commands as well as **d**. For example, move the cursor to the **X** on this line and type **rY** to change the **X** to a **Y**. If you now type **u**, you will see the **Y** change to an **X**. Keep pressing **u**, and the character will flip-flop back and forth between **X** and **Y**.

```
******************************************************************
*******          Part III: Moving Text Around          ******
******************************************************************
```

One common editing job is moving text from one part of a file to another. For example, you may want to move a sentence or paragraph from one section of a report to another. You may want to move whole sections around. You may also want to copy chunks of text and then modify them. For example, I made the heading for this part of the exercise file by making a copy of the heading for Part II and editing the title that was inside the stars. And, of course, I made the heading for Part II by copying the heading for Part I and editing that. There are repetitious aspects of most word processing jobs, and you can save yourself some typing by using the copy-and-edit process.

The yank Command:

There are two commands involved in the copy-and-edit process. The first is the **y** command, also called yank. The yank command makes a copy of a block of text. It works like **c** and **d** — you move the cursor to the beginning of the block you want to copy, then type **y** plus a cursor movement command that determines the end of the block you want to copy. For example, here's a line of text:

LITTLE BOY BLUE, COME BLOW YOUR HORN

Move the cursor to the beginning of the line and type **y$**. This makes a copy of the text from the cursor position to the end of the line. Not much happens when you make the copy — you may hear the disk do some writing and the screen may blink once, but that's about it. The text you just copied stays where it is.

The paste Command:

Now move the cursor to the empty line following this line

and type **p**. **p** stands for put or paste, and it puts copied
text back into the file you're editing. The text is written
down immediately after the cursor. Any text that was already
there moves to make room for the new text. Now move the cursor
to the beginning of the next blank line and type **p** again. As
you can see, typing **p** pastes down the same line of text again.
You can paste the same text any number of times. However, if
you use **y** to copy/yank some new text, **p** will paste the new
text instead of the old.

More on yank and paste:

If you want to yank an entire line, put the cursor anywhere on
the line and type **yy**. (You have already seen that **cc** changes
a line and **dd** deletes one.) If you want to yank several lines,
type the number and then **yy**. For example, move the cursor to
the beginning of this paragraph and type **7yy**. This yanks the
seven lines of this paragraph. Move the cursor to the next
blank line and type **p**. This pastes the whole paragraph.

Up to this point, you have been yanking text by going to the
beginning of what you want to copy and typing **y** followed by a
cursor movement command that determined the end of what you want
to copy. **vi** lets you do the opposite too. For example, move
the cursor to the end of this paragraph and type **yH**. You have
just yanked everything to the top of the screen. Go to the
blank line after this paragraph and type **p** to paste in what
you just yanked.

Cutting:

The yank process is similar to the copy operation in a number of
word processors. You might be wondering if there is an
operation similar to the cut operation in word processors (which
deletes text but saves the text so that you can paste it in
later).

The answer is that the **d** command automatically saves whatever
you delete so that you can paste it in later. For example, use
dd to delete the next line of poetry:

RUB A DUB DUB, THREE MEN IN A TUB

Now move the cursor to the end of this line and type **p**. You'll see that the line you just deleted comes back again when you paste it in. In short, **d** deletes something but saves it for later pasting; **y** copies text without deleting it.

Sentences:

Now suppose you want to copy a particular sentence. To do this, put the cursor at the beginning or end of the sentence, then type **y** followed by a cursor movement command that goes to the end or beginning of the sentence. What kind of cursor movement command would this be? Well, you could enter a search command that looked for the first or last word of the sentence, but that's a bit clumsy...and what happens if that word is somewhere in the middle of the sentence too?

To deal with problems like this, **vi** has a command that moves the cursor to the beginning of a sentence. This is the **(** command. For example, move the cursor to the **X** in this line and type the **(**. You will see the cursor move back to the beginning of the sentence. Move the cursor to the beginning of this line and type **(**. You will see the cursor jump back one line to the beginning of the sentence. So yanking a sentence is easy. Move the cursor to the space following the period at the end of this very sentence and type **y(**. Now move the cursor to the next blank line and type **p** to see what you've yanked.

You will see that the first part of the sentence is on one line and the rest of the sentence is on the next line. This is because the yanking process copies the line break after **the**. If you want to make things prettier, move the cursor to the word **the** and type **J**. **J** stands for join, and it joins two lines in the way you just saw. The cursor can go anywhere on the first line; when you type **J**, **vi** joins the next line onto the end of the current line.

By the way, I should point out what happens if you type the **(** command when the cursor is already at the beginning of a sentence. Move the cursor to the **X** in this line and type **(**. The cursor jumps to the beginning of the sentence. Type **(** again, and the cursor jumps to the beginning of the previous sentence. This shows that you can use **(** to go backward sentence by sentence.

```
******************************************************************
*******        Part IV: Contextual Cursor Movement        *******
******************************************************************
```

The (command is one example of contextual cursor movement.
It moves the cursor to a position that is important in the
context of your text. There are several others.

) goes to the beginning of the next sentence. Move the cursor
to the beginning of the previous line and type) to see what
happens. Now type it again.

{ (the opening brace) goes back to the beginning of a
paragraph. Move the cursor to the end of the preceding
paragraph and type { to see what happens. Now what do you
think will happen if you type }? Try it and find out.

The (,), {, and } commands all use technical
definitions for what a *sentence* and/or *paragraph* looks like.
These definitions are given in the man page for **vi**. Once in a
while, you and **vi** may disagree on what constitutes a sentence,
but most of the time, **vi** knows what it's doing.


```
******************************************************************
*******            Part V: Editing Options            *******
******************************************************************
```

vi has many options that change the way the editor behaves
during an editing session. The **vi** man page contains a
complete list of these options. In this exercise file, I'll
only discuss a few that can be immediately useful.

You must be in Command Mode to set options (that is, not appending
text). To set an option, begin by typing a colon (:). You will
see the cursor move to the bottom of the screen. Then type

:set *option*

I'll talk about option names in a moment. You can correct
typing mistakes by backspacing. When you have typed everything
correctly, press Enter.

Ignoring Case in Searches:

One commonly used option is **ignorecase**. If you type

:set ignorecase

170

vi will not pay attention to the case of letters when searching. For example, type the preceding **set** command, then move to the beginning of this paragraph and type /**for** (followed by Enter). You will see that the cursor moves to the *For* at the beginning of the previous sentence, even though the *F* is uppercase. Now type / followed by Enter. This time, you see that the search finds the word *for* with the *f* in lowercase. Many people prefer caseless searches over case-sensitive ones. If you want to go back to case-sensitive searches, type

:set noignorecase

Setting Tab Positions:

By default, **vi** sets tab stops every eight spaces. For example, if you begin a paragraph by typing a tab, the tab moves the cursor over eight spaces. If you are entering a program using tabs for indentation, each level of indentation will be eight spaces. Move the cursor to the next blank line, type an **a** to append text, then a tab and **Hello!** to see how much space is created for the tab. Press the Esc key to leave Insert Mode.

Many people feel eight spaces is too big for a tab stop. For example, when I took typing classes, I was told the "proper" indentation was five spaces. You can set tab stops of five spaces with

:set tabstop=5

When you press Enter, keep your eye on the **Hello!** line you entered a few lines back. You should see the word jump backward from column 8 to column 5. All tab stops in the file are changed with the one command. (Note: You are changing how **vi** displays tabs, but you are not changing the contents of the file. The file just contains a tab character.) Similar commands can set tab stops to any number of spaces.

```
**************************************************************
*******       Part VI: Editing Several Files       *******
**************************************************************
```

In a typical **vi** session, you may want to edit several files. When you have finished editing one file, you must first write out the text. If you do not save the text you have been editing, any editing you have done will be lost when you quit **vi**. If you started your **vi** session with the command

vi filename

you can save your text in that file just by typing

:w

and pressing Enter. You can try this now.

If you want to save your text in a new file, you can type

:w newfile

where *newfile* is the new filename. Try this now. Type

:w myjunk

and press Enter. When **vi** has finished writing the file, you will see that it prints the name of the file and some information about the file's size.

If you want to save your text in a file that already exists but was not the file you were originally editing, you have to type

:w! file

The exclamation point indicates that you know the write operation will overwrite the old contents of the file and that you want this to happen. (Don't try this unless you have some files you don't mind writing over.)

After you have written out your changes, you can start editing a different file by typing

:edit newfile

and pressing Enter. This will clear out the text you have been editing and set things up so that you can edit the new file. If the file already exists, its current contents will be read.

Now here's a trick I can't demonstrate in this guide, but it's something to remember when you want to edit several files. If you start **vi** with a command line of the form

vi *file1 file2 file3 ...*

you can edit several files one after the other. After you have finished editing a file and have written it (with **:w**), you can start editing the next file by typing

:next

```
or just

:n
```

It may be particularly useful to use wildcard characters on the
vi command line, as in

```
vi *.v
```

This will be expanded to a list of all the files under the
current directory that have the **.v** extension (the **vi**
exercise files).

Time to Experiment

I now recommend that you experiment with vi, creating small files of your
own and editing them. After you are familiar with the parts of the editor that
this guide has discussed, begin reading bits of the complete description of vi
in the man pages. vi has a great number of features. Some of them may be
useful in the work you do, while others are not. Just remember that vi has
something for everyone.

---

doc.v—Documentation Tips

The third vi exercise file is named doc.v. In order to work through the exercises in
the file, enter the command

```
cp doc.v mydoc.v
vi mydoc.v
```

The cp command creates a copy of the doc.v file, and the vi command lets you look
at that file. It's better to work with a copy instead of the real thing, in case you make
a mistake or someone else wants to try.

The exercise file contains several tips for people who might use vi in creating documents. As in the last section, I recommend that you enter the preceding command
now and work through the exercise file. The rest of this section essentially repeats
what you will see in the file.

The **browse.v** file explained how to read through a file using
vi. Unless the text suggests a different way to move through
the file, just read through this file by pressing Enter or
Ctrl-D.

```
*******************************************************************
******        Part I: General Tips              *******
*******************************************************************
```

The wrapmargin Option:

When you are typing lines of text in paragraph form, your job
is easier if you don't have to remember to press Enter when you
reach the end of a line. Try entering the following command.

:set wrapmargin=8

Now go to the next blank line, type **a** to begin appending text,
and start typing the contents of this paragraph, beginning
with *When you*. Don't press Enter when you start copying the
second line. Keep on going. Press Esc to leave Insert Mode
after a few lines.

You should see that the word *easier* automatically jumps down
to a new line. The option **wrapmargin=8** says that if you end a
word within eight spaces of the right margin of the screen, the
next word should wrap around to begin on the next line. You do
not have to press Enter. With this kind of wrap-around margin,
you can just keep on typing words. The only time you need to
press Enter will probably be at the end of paragraphs.

Abbreviations:

vi lets you define abbreviations for commonly used words and
phrases. This uses the **:ab** (abbreviate) command. As an
example, try typing

:ab xyz XYZ Widgets Inc. International

and then press Enter. This says that **xyz** will be an
abbreviation for **XYZ Widgets Inc. International**. To see how
it works, move the cursor to the next blank line, press **a** to
begin appending text, and type

xyz welcomes you!

You will see that as soon as you type the space after **xyz**, the
abbreviation is expanded into the associated phrase. Now move
the cursor to the next blank line, press **a** to begin appending
text, and type

This is the XYZ factory.

This time, you'll see that **XYZ** is not expanded into the abbreviation. The abbreviation feature pays attention to the case of letters. Now move the cursor to the next blank line, press **a** to begin appending text, and type

xyzwill not expand.

When you type this, you will see that the **xyz** is not expanded because it is part of another word. **vi** only expands abbreviations when they are not part of other words.

If you want to get rid of an abbreviation that has been set, use the **:una** (unabbreviate) command. For example, type

:una xyz

This tells **vi** to forget about the **xyz** abbreviation.

Command Files for vi:

An abbreviation only lasts for the duration of a **vi** session. If you set up an abbreviation now, it will be remembered as long as you stay in **vi**, but will be forgotten when you leave **vi**. This means that you have to set up common abbreviations every time you start **vi**. This would be a lot of work if you did it by hand, but you can simplify things quite a bit by setting up a command file.

A command file contains several commands that can be executed as if they were typed in a **vi** session. For example, you might use **vi** to create a file with the contents

```
set wrapmargin=8
set tabstop=5
ab mks Mortice Kern Systems Inc.
ab aa another abbreviation
ab bb another abbreviation
    ...and so on...
```

setting all the options you want to use and all the abbreviations you commonly need. The file can only contain instructions that normally start with a colon (:) in **vi**, and you omit the colons in the command file. You can execute all the instructions in the command file inside **vi** with the instruction

:so *filename*

where *filename* is the name of your command file. **so** stands
for *source*, and it tells **vi** that the given file should be
taken as the source of several commands.

As a matter of fact, you can execute the commands in a command
file when you first start **vi**. You do this by starting **vi**
with the command line

vi -c "so *cmdfile*" *editfile*

where *cmdfile* is the name of your command file and *editfile* is
the name of the file you want to edit. After I've discussed
aliases in Chapter 7, you might want to set up a KornShell alias
for

vi -c "so *cmdfile*"


```
****************************************************************
*******          Part II: Combining Files          *******
****************************************************************
```

Occasionally, you may want to combine several files into a
single document. For example, you may have a table of data
stored in one file and want to add the table to another file.
To demonstrate how this can be done, move the cursor to the next
blank line and type

:r sonnet

You should see the contents of the file read in after the line
that holds the cursor. **r** stands for read, and it reads in the
text of a file. This text is added to the current file after
the line indicated by the cursor.

The same sort of command can be used to combine the chapters of
a document into a single file. For example, consider the
following commands (but don't enter them):

```
:r chapter1
G
:r chapter2
G
:r chapter3
```

These will read in chapters that are stored in separate files.
Notice that you had to add **G** commands to go to the end of the
file after each **r** operation so that the next input file would
be added to the end of the text.

It's a good idea to store large documents in several smaller files and only combine them when you are ready to create the finished product. The smaller the file, the faster **vi** can read and write the text. Small files are also more convenient for you to edit, because it takes less time to find the text you want to change.

```
******************************************************************
*******              Part III: Sorting Data              *******
******************************************************************
```

In many types of reports, it is convenient to be able to sort a few lines of text (for a table of information). As an example, consider the following lines.

```
a  — append after cursor
o  — open an input line
dd — delete a line
cc — change a line
w  — move forward a word
b  — move backward a word
x  — delete a letter
u  — undo
```

I entered these descriptions of **vi** commands in the order I thought of them, but it would be nice to sort them into alphabetical order. To do this, you can send the preceding lines through the **sort** command.

First, you have to find out the line numbers of the lines you want to sort. To do this, move the cursor to the first line of the preceding table and press Ctrl-G. **vi** displays the name of the file and a notation of the form **line N of M**, where **N** is the line number of the current line and **M** is the total number of lines in the file. Note the line number (it should be 173, or a number close to that). Move the cursor to the last line of the table and press Ctrl-G again. You should find out the line number is 180. Now type

:173,180!sort

and press Enter. This asks **vi** to send lines 173 to 180 through the **sort** command. The lines will be replaced with the output of the sort command, namely the sorted lines. Go back and check the list, and you will see that it is now sorted.

The same technique can be used to send lines through other commands if you like. However, **sort** is probably used in this context more often than any other command.

If you do not specify a range of lines for a command, the command will just be executed. Its output will be displayed on the screen, but it will not replace any of the text of the file. For example, write out this file and then try the command

:!wc doc.v

Because **wc** prints the number of lines, words, and characters in a text file, this command gives you a quick word count for your document.

```
******************************************************************
*******            Part IV: Formatting by Hand          *******
******************************************************************
```

Most UNIX systems do not have word processors; the most common way to create documents on UNIX is to use a text formatting program named **troff**, discussed in Chapter 10. Using **troff** is definitely recommended for long documents, but for short documents like letters, you can often format text "by hand," using **vi** to create a text file that can be printed directly on a printer.

Page Breaks:

The Ctrl-L character is called the formfeed. You can use it to separate pages. However, there's a catch. On a UNIX system, you can't just append a Ctrl-L character to your text, since Ctrl-L is a special instruction that works even when you're in Insert Mode. This instruction tells **vi** to redraw the screen; it's needed because there are a variety of ways in which the text that is displayed on your screen can get messed up by output written by other processes. (It's too complicated to explain how this might happen, but take my word for it, once in a while you have to tell **vi** that some other program messed up your screen and you want **vi** to clean things up again.)

However, you can still add a Ctrl-L character to your text; you just have to be a little more clever about it. To see what you have to do, move the cursor to the next blank line and press **a** to begin appending text. First press Ctrl-V, then press Ctrl-L. The Ctrl-V tells **vi** to append the next character you enter, even if that character usually has a special meaning. After you do this, you should see that the screen displays ^**L**, standing for Ctrl-L. By inserting these formfeed characters, you can break a document into pages.

On a normal line printer, an 8 1/2- by 11-inch sheet of paper holds a maximum of 66 lines. For the purpose of formatting, 54 lines fit nicely on a page, with an inch of space at the top and the bottom for margins. Thus you should consider inserting formfeeds every 54 lines (give or take one or two).

If you indent a paragraph with a tab character, the amount of indentation is determined by the tab stops set for the printer on which the document is printed. If you indent a paragraph with spaces, the amount of indentation does not depend on the printer setting.

Indentation:

The > command can indent several lines in a uniform way. For example, try typing

`:1,275>`

and press Enter. This indents the first 275 lines of this file. You can get rid of the indentation by typing

`:1,275<`

and pressing Enter. As an instruction to try later, you can indent the entire file with

`:1,$>`

When you are giving a range of lines to a command, **$** is a special symbol that stands for the last line of the file. The reason I suggest you try this later is that the cursor will move to the last indented line (the end of the file), which would cause you to lose your place in this file.

After you have formatted a document, write it out to a file (with `:w`). On a true UNIX system, you could then print the file using the **lp** or **lpr** commands. On DOS, you can quit the MKS Tools and use **PRINT**.

program.v—Topics of Interest to Programmers

The final vi exercise file is named program.v. In order to work through the exercises in the file, enter the command

```
cp program.v myprog.v
vi myprog.v
```

As before, working with a copy of the file makes sure that accidents don't damage the original file.

This exercise file is intended for those who will use vi to enter program source code. Because vi originated on UNIX, the editor contains several features primarily aimed at programming in the C language. However, these same features are applicable to many other languages, particularly structured ones like Pascal, Modula-2, and Ada.

Even if you do not intend to program on UNIX, you'll find useful information by reading through this file. The examples may look a little odd if you aren't used to looking at programs, but the vi features are still applicable to other work.

As in the last section, I recommend that you enter the preceding command now and work through the exercise file. The rest of this section essentially repeats what you will see in the file.

```
The browse.v file explained how to read through a file using
vi.  Unless the text suggests a different way to move through
the file, just read through this file by pressing Enter or
Ctrl-D.


*****************************************************************
*******        Part I: Indentation Control        *******
*****************************************************************


The source code for a program differs from ordinary text in
several ways.  One of the most important of these is the way
source code uses indentation.  Indentation shows the logical
structure of the program: the way statements are grouped into
blocks.


The autoindent Option:

Issue the command

:set autoindent

(Don't forget to press Enter after you have typed this.)  The
command turns on a vi option that controls indentation when
you enter source code.  To see how it works, copy (append) the
next two lines into the blank line that follows them.

    if (a > b) max = a;
        else max = b;
```

(Make sure you add the blank space at the beginning of the first line, either with several spaces or by pressing the Tab key.) You will notice that when you press Enter after typing the first line, the cursor goes to the next line and automatically indents the same distance as the previous line.

The **autoindent** option automatically indents each line the same distance as the previous one. This can save quite a bit of work getting the indentation right, especially when you have several levels of indentation.

When you are entering code with **autoindent** in effect, pressing Ctrl-T gives you another level of indentation, and pressing Ctrl-D takes one away. For example, copy (append) the next four lines into the blank line that follows them.

To indent the next line, press Ctrl-T at the start of the line.
    The next line will be indented this same distance.
    On the next line, press Ctrl-D at the start of the line.
Notice how Ctrl-D moves the cursor back one level of indent.

I should point out that you press Ctrl-T and Ctrl-D while you are in Insert Mode.

The amount of indentation provided by Ctrl-T is one **shiftwidth**. Like tab stops, shiftwidths are set every eight spaces by default. A command like

:set shiftwidth=5

can change the shiftwidth for a **vi** session.

Try using the **autoindent** option when you are entering source code. It makes correct indentation easier. It can even help you avoid bugs — correct indentation often makes it easier to notice certain types of syntax errors.

Shift Commands:

The << and >> commands can also help you indent source code. By default, >> shifts a line right one shiftwidth; << shifts a line left one shiftwidth. For example, move the cursor to the beginning of this line and press > twice. You will see the line move right. If you now press < twice, the line will move back again.

You can shift several lines by typing the number followed by >> or <<. For example, move the cursor to the first line of this paragraph and type **5>>**. You will shift all five lines in the paragraph. What command will move the paragraph back? Try it to make sure.

Two Different Shift Commands

In doc.v, I discussed shift commands that started with a colon, as in

:1,200>

There's no significant difference between this kind of shift and >>. If you use the :> form, you can specify a range of lines. If you use the >> form, you can specify the number of lines. Use whichever form is more convenient to whatever job you're trying to do.

```
****************************************************************
*******        Part II: Special Search Commands       *******
****************************************************************

The characters (, [, {, and < can all be called opening
brackets.  When the cursor is resting on one of these
characters, pressing % moves the cursor from the opening
bracket forward to the corresponding closing bracket — ),
], }, or >, keeping in mind the usual rules for nesting
brackets.  For example, move the cursor to the first ( in

if ( cos(a[i]) > sin(b[i]+c[i]) )
{
    printf("cos and sin equal!");
}

and press %.  You will see that the cursor jumps to the
parenthesis at the end of the line.  This is the closing
parenthesis that matches the opening one.

Similarly, if the cursor is on one of the closing bracket
characters, pressing % moves the cursor backward to the
corresponding opening bracket character.  For example, move the
cursor to the closing brace after the preceding printf line
and press %.

Not only does % help you move forward and backward through a
program in long jumps, it lets you check the nesting of
parentheses in source code.  For example, if you put the cursor
on the first { at the beginning of a C function, pressing %
should move you to the } that (you think) ends the function.
If it doesn't, you've made a typing mistake somewhere.
```

```
*****************************************************************
******      Part III: Large-Scale Changes        ******
*****************************************************************
```

If the name of a data object or function has to be changed in a program for some reason, it becomes necessary to change every occurrence of that name. This would be a tedious process using the **vi** features I have discussed up to this point, because you would have to search through each source file for the name and then type the new name wherever the old one was found. To avoid much of this work, **vi** offers the substitute command.

The substitute Command:

The usual form of the substitute command is

:s/pattern/replacement/

where pattern is a regular expression and replacement is any string. For example, move the rest of this paragraph onto the screen, then move the cursor to THIS line and type

:s/THIS/this/

As soon as you type the colon, you see the cursor move to the bottom of the screen. Type the rest of the command and press Enter. You will see **THIS** turn into **this**. The command puts the given replacement string in the place of the first string that matches the given pattern.

What happens if a line has more than one string that matches the pattern? This line contains the word **the** several times. If you move the cursor to the line and type

:s/the/XXX/

what happens? **vi** only replaces the first matching string. The position of the cursor in the line does not matter.

If you want to change every occurrence of a string on a line, type a **g** (standing for global) after the last slash. For example, move the cursor to this line and type

:s/h/H/g

You will see both **h** characters change. Notice that **global** only refers to a single line in this context, not to the whole file.

Now how does the **s** command help you make large-scale changes?
In addition to applying **s** to a single line, you can apply it
to a range of lines. For example, type the following command
and press Enter:

:1,176s/^/!/

What happens? The **1,176** in front of the **s** indicates that
the command should be applied to the lines from 1 through 176
(everything up to the 176th line in the file). The **s** command
itself says that the beginning of the line ^ should be
replaced by an exclamation mark. So (as you have probably seen
by now), **vi** puts an exclamation mark at the beginning of every
line up to number 176. To get rid of the exclamation marks,
type

:1,176s/^!//

(which says, *Change every ! at the beginning of a*
line into nothing).

Line Numbers:

In the preceding instructions, I made use of line numbers to
refer to lines. How do you know what number a line has? If you
just want to know the number of one line, move the cursor to
that line and press Ctrl-G. For example, find out what the line
number of this line is. For another approach, type

:set number

and press Enter. As you can now see, this displays the number
of every line in the file. If you want the numbers to go away,
type

:set nonumber

It's up to you whether or not you want to keep the numbers.

Line Ranges:

There are several special symbols that can be used when
specifying a range of lines. The . stands for the line that
currently holds the cursor. For example, move the cursor to
this line and type

:1,.s/$/???/

This adds **???** to the end of every line from the start of the file to the line containing the cursor. Move the cursor down to this line and type

:1,.s/???$//

This removes the question marks. Notice that the command worked, even though the last few lines before the cursor did not end in **???**. When you issue a **substitute** command with a range, it is all right if some of the lines in the range do not contain the pattern you are replacing.

When specifying a range of lines, **$** stands for the last line in the file. Try this command

:1,$s/the/THE/g

What does it do? It changes every *the* in the file to uppercase (including within words like *there*, where *the* is part of the word). Now, just to put things back the way they were, type **u** to undo the change you just made. This demonstrates that the **u** command can undo changes made by **:s** as well as those made by **c** and **d**.

It should be obvious now how to make a global change in a file. For example, here's a small piece of program source code to change.

```
int bubble()
{
    extern int array[30];
    int i, j, temp;
    for (i = 0; i < 30; i++)
        for (j = 29; j > i; j—)
            if (array[j] < array[j-1])
            {
                temp = array[j];
                array[j] = array[j-1];
                array[j-1] = temp;
            }
    return array[0];
}
```

Now, use an **s** command to change every occurrence of *array* into *list*. Make sure you get the line range correctly; use Ctrl-G to find out the line numbers of the first and last lines if you no longer have the line numbers shown on your screen. You can also use

```
:set number
```

to make the line numbers reappear on your screen.

Now check the sample source code to make sure that you changed every occurrence of *array* into *list*. The command you should have used to do this was

```
:250,263s/array/list/g
```

If you forgot the **g** on the end, the lines that contain *array* twice will still have references to *array*. Without the **g**, the **s** command only changes the first occurrence of the given pattern.

Confirmation of Substitution:

What would you do if you wanted to change the variable **i** into a **k**? You can't just use an instruction like

```
:250,263s/i/k/g
```

because that changes the letter **i** into **k**, even when the letter appears in words like *int* and *list*. The solution is to add a **c** (for check) on the end of the **s** command. When you do this, **vi** checks with you before making every substitution. Before each possible change, **vi** prints the line at the bottom of your screen and puts a ^ under the string that is eligible to be changed. If you want the change to happen, press **y** followed by Enter. If you do not want the change to happen, press **n** followed by Enter. To see how this works, try

```
:250,263s/i/k/gc
```

and only change those occurrences of **i** that are related to the variable **i**.

Using **:s** is much faster (and less error-prone) than trying to change every occurrence of a symbol by hand. Remember the **c** option if you think there's a chance that the name you are trying to change might be part of a larger symbol.

```
*****************************************************************
*******        Part IV: Executing Commands          *******
*****************************************************************
```

Suppose you have just finished creating a source code file using
vi and you are ready to compile it. You can write out the
file, quit **vi**, and then compile it if you want...but everybody
knows that there are likely to be errors the first time you
compile a new file. To fix these compilation errors, you'll
have to use **vi** again to edit the source code.

To avoid the time and effort of quitting **vi** to compile, then
going back into **vi** to fix errors, you can invoke the compile
command directly from **vi**. A step-by-step description of how
you can do this follows; however, you can't do it right now
because you're looking at this exercise file, and not at a
program's source code.

(a) First, write out your source code to a file by saying

:w *filename*

You don't have to specify the *filename* if you've already
written to the file once before, or if you originally read the
text in from the file.

(b) Type a colon (:), followed by an exclamation mark (!),
followed by the command you would normally use to compile that
file. On a true UNIX system, this might be

:!cc filename

because **cc** is the usual command for compiling C code under
UNIX. This won't work on MKS Tools, because the software doesn't
include a C compiler. Press Enter when you have typed the line.
cc compiles the program, and displays any diagnostic messages
in the usual way.

(c) After the compilation is finished, you automatically return
to **vi**, where you can correct any errors that might have been
detected.

The ability to execute commands from inside **vi** has other
benefits. For example, enter

:!more sonnet

This shows that you can use **more** if you want to look up
information in some other file. If you were really programming,
you might want to check another source code file for the name of
a function or variable.

A Glimpse of *vi*'s Cousins

UNIX systems offer several other editors in addition to vi. I don't have the space here to provide a complete introduction to these programs, but I'll provide brief overviews in case you ever find the programs necessary.

The *sed* Editor

The sed editor is a noninteractive editor, sometimes called a *stream editor.* At the same time that you call sed to edit a file, you specify the editing commands that sed should perform on that file. In other words, you don't interact with the program; you specify all your commands up front. As an analogy, using an interactive program is like shopping in a store where you can decide what you want to buy as you go along; using a noninteractive program is like shopping through a mail-order catalog, where you write a complete list of everything you want, then send off your list and wait to have the order filled.

The advantage of sed is the same as the advantage of shopping through a mail-order catalog: lower overhead. The sed editor doesn't need any facilities for interacting with a user, so it can be smaller and faster than comparable interactive editors. Interactive editors like vi, on the other hand, require extra memory and execution time because they have to interact with the user, just as normal retail stores require extra staff because they need clerks to provide personal help for customers.

Obviously, you can only use sed when you know exactly what you want to do. Here are some cases when sed comes in handy:

- When you want to make the same simple changes in a large number of files. With an interactive editor, you would have to read in a file, make the changes, read in the next file, make the changes, and so on. With sed, you just give sed the list of files you want to change and a set of changes you want performed on each file. By using sed, you don't have to do a lot of work by hand, and you don't have to worry about the mistakes that inevitably happen when you do a lot of typing.

- When there's a particular editing job that you expect to perform frequently. For example, suppose a particular program produces output every day, and every day you have to modify that output slightly in order to include it in a report. You can save time by creating a file of sed commands that automatically do the editing for you. Then, instead of making the changes by hand every day, you can have sed do all the work for you. Again, you save time and you avoid mistakes; if you always use the same sed commands, you ensure consistency from day to day.

The commands of sed are not very different from the commands you use in vi. For example, the basic command for making a substitution is

```
s/pattern/replacement/
```

where pattern is a regular expression and replacement is what you want to substitute in place of the first string that matches the regular expression. For more information on sed, see the man page in this book.

Making sed Scripts

I've said that you write up instructions for sed before you actually call the editor. One way to do this is to create a text file containing the instructions you want sed to perform. Such a text file is called a sed *script*. How do you create a sed script? With vi, of course. vi is the natural way to create any text file.

The *ed* Line Editor

The ed editor is an interactive line editor with many of the same features as vi. It is an older editor, and many people believe vi makes ed obsolete because vi contains almost all of ed's commands.

ed is primarily of interest because of its connection with diff. diff's output resembles ed's input.

Chapter Review

vi is a screen editor, primarily intended to create text files. Table 6.1 lists the vi commands discussed in this chapter. For a full discussion of vi and its commands, see the vi man page.

Table 6.1. vi commands discussed in this chapter.

Command	Meaning
Movement Commands	
Ctrl-B	Go backward a full screen
Ctrl-D	Go down half a screen
Ctrl-F	Go forward a full screen
Ctrl-U	Go up half a screen
Enter	Go down a line
$	Go to the end of the line
%	Jump to the balancing bracket
(	Go to the beginning of the previous sentence
)	Go to the beginning of the next sentence
_	Go up a line
/string	Search forward for string
/	Search forward for the previous string
?string	Search backward for string
?	Search backward for the previous string
{	Go to the start of the previous paragraph
}	Go to the beginning of the next paragraph
0	Go to the beginning of the line
b	Move backward one word
G	Go to a specific line
h	Go left one character
H	(*High*) go to the top of the screen
j	Go down one line
k	Go up one line

Command	Meaning

Movement Commands

l	Go right one character
L	(*Low*) go to the bottom of the screen
M	(*Middle*) go to the middle of the screen
w	Move forward one word

Editing Commands

a	Append text (enters Insert Mode)
c	Change text (enters Insert Mode)
cc	Change line (enters Insert Mode)
d	Delete text
dd	Delete line
i	Insert text (enters Insert Mode)
J	Join two lines into one
o	Open a new line (enters Insert Mode)
p	Paste
r	Replace a single character
u	Undo
x	Delete a single character
y	Yank
yy	Yank line
<<	Shift left
>>	Shift right
:!command	Execute command

continues

Table 6.1. continued

Command	Meaning
Editing Commands	
`:<`	Shift left
`:>`	Shift right
`:ab`	Create abbreviation
`:edit file`	Edit new file
`:n`	Edit next file
`:next`	Edit next file
`:q`	Quit if you've already saved text
`:q!`	Quit immediately, without saving
`:r file`	Read file
`:s/X/Y/`	Substitute Y for the first X on the line
`:s/X/Y/c`	Confirm before substituting
`:s/X/Y/g`	Substitute Y for every X on the line
`:so file`	Get `vi` commands from `file`
`:una`	Get rid of abbreviation
`:w`	Write file
`:w!`	Overwrite file
Ctrl-G	Find out line number

`vi` has several options that let you control its behavior. Table 6.2 lists the options discussed in this chapter. Again, the `vi` man page provides the complete list.

Table 6.2. vi **options.**

Option	Meaning
:set autoindent	New lines automatically match the indentation of the previous line
:set ignorecase	Ignore the case of letters when matching
:set noignorecase	Pay attention to the case of letters when matching
:set nonumber	Do not show line numbers
:set number	Show line numbers
:set shiftwidth=n	Shift actions should shift by n columns
:set tabstop=n	Set tabs every n columns
:set wrapmargin=n	Wrap around if within n columns of the end of the line

Several other editors are available under UNIX. sed is a noninteractive editor with speed as its great virtue. ed is an older editor that is mainly of interest because of its connection with diff.

Exercises

1. Use vi to edit the file profile.ksh. Change the line that begins with PATH so that it reads

   PATH=".;c:/lu/bin"

   (This exercise is very important. It sets up a definition that will become important in later chapters.) If you installed the MKS Tools under a non-standard directory, change the line to refer to that directory instead of c:/lu. For example, if you installed the package under c:/lux, the line should read

   PATH=".;c:/lux/bin"

2. Starting with the command line

   vi *onnet

   use vi to edit all the onnet files so that the last two lines are not indented (they should line up with the rest of the poem).

3. Using vi, change all the colon (:) characters in comics.1st into semicolons. Sort the result according to month and year. (Note: if the sort command line refers to the semicolon character, you must put the character in quotation marks, as demonstrated in the exercises at the end of Chapter 4.)

4. Create a file containing the names of all files under your home directory, sorted in alphabetical order. Read this file into vi. Delete all the directory names. For all remaining lines of the form

filename

edit the line to read

cat *filename* >>junk

(Editing a list of files with vi is a simple way to produce *shell scripts,* as you'll see in Chapter 8.)

Using the
KornShell

THE KORNSHELL

The KornShell was developed by David Korn of AT&T laboratories. It is a descendant of the Bourne Shell, one of the first UNIX shells to gain wide popularity. The KornShell incorporates many of the features of the C Shell, another popular UNIX shell.

Every time you log into the MKS Tools that accompany this book, you use the KornShell. The KornShell reads the commands you type and executes them.

From time to time I've discussed what the shell does for you. For example, the shell expands glob constructs into the names of appropriate files and directories. However, I have concentrated primarily on commands rather than the shell itself.

This chapter introduces several of the most basic features and capabilities of the KornShell.

- Command substitution: the ability to use the output of one command as part of the command line for another command.

- Aliases: the ability to define short forms for frequently used commands, to save you time and help you avoid typing mistakes.

- Shell options: the ability to let you change the default behavior of the shell.

- Command history: the ability to keep a record of the commands you have entered most recently. Such a record preserves an exact history of what you do during your session with the KornShell. You can tell the shell to re-execute any command from the command history, thereby saving you the trouble of typing the command again.

- Command editing: the ability to edit and re-execute commands stored in your command history. For example, if you make a typing mistake while entering a command, you don't have to type the command all over again; you can just correct the mistake in the command and resubmit it.

- Variables: the ability to save information and pass that information on to commands, as well as using the information to construct command lines.

Information about the KornShell is provided by the sh man page and by the man pages of commands listed in the *See Also* section of the sh man page.

> **Note**
> On a system that has both the Bourne Shell and the KornShell, the Bourne Shell is called sh and the KornShell is called ksh.

Command Substitution

A pipe lets you use the output of one command as the input to another command. *Command substitution* is similar, but it lets you use the output of one command as part of the command line that invokes another command.

An example will make this situation easier to understand. To set this up, it's useful to create some junk files, so enter the following commands:

```
cp sonnet junk1
cp sonnet junk2
cp sonnet testdir/junk1
cp sonnet testdir/junk2
```

This creates two junk files under your home directory, and two more under testdir.

Now suppose that time passes, and a month from now you notice that you have some filenames that start with junk. You don't remember what these files contain, but they're taking up disk space and you want to know if you can get rid of them. To do this, you have to look at their contents.

You could examine their contents with the instruction

```
more junk1 junk2 testdir/junk1 testdir/junk2
```

but there are two problems to doing this. First, it's a lot of typing. Second, I'm assuming that you've forgotten why you created the files, so you've probably forgotten how many files you created and what names you gave them.

You already know how to get a list of all files with names beginning with junk. The basic command to do this is

```
find . -name "junk*" -print
```

Enter this command and you'll see that it displays the names of all the junk files you created. You may also find that you have other junk files left over from previous exercises.

Now that you know the names of the files, you could enter a more command to look at them all. However, there's an easier way. Whenever the shell finds a command line containing a construct of the form

```
$(command)
```

the shell executes the command, then replaces the $(command) with the output of the command. For example, enter

```
more $(find . -name "junk*" -print)
```

The shell executes this command in two stages. First, it executes the find command inside the parentheses in order to get a list of filenames; then the shell executes the more command, using those filenames as arguments. You'll find that you can use more to look at each junk file in turn.

Note that you can execute the preceding command without knowing how many junk files you have. The find command will find all the appropriate files, and then more will display those files one by one. You don't have to remember how many files there were, or what their names were.

It's important to distinguish between the command we've just discussed

```
more $(find . -name "junk*" -print)
```

and a command like

```
find . -name "junk*" -print ¦ more
```

The second form pipes the output of `find` into `more`, and `more` displays the list of filenames that `find` generates. The first form, however, displays the contents of the same files, not just the filenames. Therefore, the first command (the one with command substitution) lets you examine the files to see if you want to keep them; the second command (with the pipe) simply tells you the filenames.

You can use the same trick with the series of files with names ending with `onnet` (created several chapters ago). How can you find out what these files are and what they contain? Enter the command

```
more $(find . -name "*onnet" -print)
```

The form of the command is almost the same. You just change the options of the `find` command so that it finds a different set of files.

You can use similar constructs in many different contexts. For example, ask yourself how to get rid of the junk files you created at the beginning of this section. You should be able to figure out an easy way to do so. Enter the command

```
rm $(find . -name "junk*" -print)
```

The `find` command creates a list of names. The shell substitutes this list of names into the `rm` command, then executes the `rm` command to remove the files.

As you can see, the `find` command is well suited for use in command substitution. `cat` also lends itself to this purpose. As an artificial example, enter the following commands

```
find . -newer sonnet -print >out
ls -l $(cat out)
```

The first command obtains a list of all files newer than `sonnet` and stores this list in `out`. The second command uses `cat` in a command substitution. The result is that the `ls` command lists information on all the files newer than `out`. You could get the same results with

```
ls -l $(find . -newer sonnet -print)
```

but you may find there are times when it's useful to put the name list into a file rather than calling `find` in a direct command substitution.

One such time might be when you want to edit the list of files before you do the second command. For example, here's a situation for you to consider (but don't enter any of the commands). Suppose that your hard disk contains several old files. You intend to back up most of these files, then clear them off your disk.

To start this process, you want a list of all files that have been around a long time.

```
find / ! -ctime -365 -print >out
```

finds all files that haven't changed in the past year and writes the list into `out`.

Now, you may want to get rid of most of the files listed in `out`, but not all of them. You can therefore read `out` into `vi` and read through the list for files you don't want to delete. Using `vi` you can remove such files from the list so that the list only contains the names of files that you want to delete.

After you've written out the edited list, the file `out` contains the names of all the files you want to back up and then remove. To back them up, you might use a command along the lines of

```
tar -cvf a:archive $(cat out)
```

The `cat` command just outputs the file list contained in `out`. The shell replaces the `$(cat out)` with the actual file list, then calls `tar`. As a result, `tar` backs up all the files in the list. To get rid of the files after they've been backed up, you can use

```
rm $(cat out)
```

As these examples show, command substitution can save you a good deal of typing. Not only does this save time, but it also eliminates some possible errors. It's easy to make typing mistakes or to overlook files when you are trying to remember all the files you want to work with. By having commands like `find` generate file lists for you, you know that the lists are going to be right.

An Alternate Format for Command Substitution

The command substitution examples have used the format `$(command)`, as in

```
rm $(cat out)
```

for command substitution. You can get the same effect by enclosing `command` in grave accents, as in

```
rm `cat out`
```

This format has been in use for several years, but the POSIX.2 standard *deprecates* the form. This means that the form is considered obsolete and should not be used. I only mention it here because you may see it used in old UNIX applications.

Aliases

An *alias* is a personalized name that stands for all or part of a command. Typically, you set up your own personal aliases for commands that you intend to use frequently. Here are some reasons for setting up aliases:

- To reduce the amount of typing you have to do. For example, you can set up a short, easy-to-type alias that stands for a much longer command.

- To create easy-to-remember names that stand for hard-to-remember commands.

You'll see examples of these in the sections to come.

Creating an Alias

Begin by setting up a simple alias. Enter the command

```
alias p="more"
```

This is an example of the `alias` command. It says that when you issue a command named p, you want the shell to replace the p with the string `more`. This process is called *alias substitution*. For example, enter

```
p sonnet
```

The shell substitutes `more` in place of the p, then executes the command. As a result, the preceding command is equivalent to

```
more sonnet
```

This example only saves you a few characters, but for some people that's useful. Here's another example that shows the power of aliases more clearly. Enter the two commands

```
alias findnew="find / -ctime -7 -print"
findnew
```

The `alias` command tells the shell that the name `findnew` stands for the `find` command given inside the double quotation marks. You can then enter `findnew` as if it were a command; the shell replaces the alias with the associated `find` command and executes the command. This alias saves you typing, and also saves you the trouble of remembering the format of a complex command.

You can use an alias name any time you could use the string associated with the alias. For example, enter

```
findnew >out
```

The shell changes this to

```
find / -ctime -7 -print >out
```

and then executes the command. You can also use aliases in a pipeline, as in

```
findnew ¦ more
```

DOS-Like Aliases

If you're a DOS user, you may prefer to set up aliases that let you use DOS command names. For example, enter the commands

```
alias del="rm"
alias dir="ls -l"
```

After you have set up these aliases, you can use `del` to get rid of files, and `dir` to display the contents of directories. Notice that you set up `dir` to be equivalent to `ls -l`. For example, you can enter

```
dir /lu/etc
```
and the effect is the same as

```
ls -l /lu/etc
```

I chose to put the `-l` option into the alias because the output of the DOS DIR command is more like `ls -l` than the plain `ls` command. If you prefer, you can enter

```
alias dir="ls"
```

or

```
alias dir="ls -x"
```

so that the name `dir` is associated with one of the other forms of the `ls` command.

The Position of Aliases

Aliases normally only work when they're at the beginning of a command. For example, suppose you've set up the alias `dir` as in the previous paragraph. The shell only performs alias substitution when the alias appears in a place that a command can begin. For example, you can say

```
mkdir dir
```

to create a directory named `dir`. The shell won't replace `dir` because it's not at the beginning of a command.

Note that I say *the beginning of a command,* not *the beginning of a line.* You can use an alias in a pipeline or command substitution if it is appropriate. For example, enter

```
ls -l ¦ p
```

This uses the `p` alias that you created earlier. The preceding line is equivalent to

```
ls -l ¦ more
```

The General Form of the *alias* Command

The general form of the `alias` command is

```
alias name="string"
```

where `name` is a name you choose and `string` is all or part of a command. Remember that `string` must be the first part of a command, because the alias can only be used in a place where it's valid for a command to begin.

Built-In Aliases

If you just enter

```
alias
```

without any arguments, the shell displays all the aliases that are currently defined. This includes the aliases you've created in the past few sections. It also includes some aliases you won't recognize. These are *built-in aliases.*

Built-in aliases are automatically defined for you by the shell when you first log in. I'll be discussing the purpose of some of these built-in aliases in later sections. If you're eager to find out about them now, you can check the man pages for information.

> ### How Long Do Aliases Last?
>
> Aliases are created through the KornShell and, therefore, they always disappear when you log out. There is no such thing as a *permanent* alias. However, there is a way to tell the KornShell to set up aliases automatically for you every time you log in. This is discussed in Chapter 9, "Customizing."

Getting Rid of Aliases

Normally, an alias lasts from the time you define it until the time you log out. If you want to get rid of an alias before you log out, use the `unalias` command. For example, enter

```
unalias p
p sonnet
```

You'll see that you get the message

```
p: not found
```

The `unalias` command tells the shell to forget about a particular alias. After that, the shell doesn't recognize the alias any longer.

The general form of the `unalias` command is

```
unalias name name ...
```

where the *names* given on the command line are existing alias names that you want the shell to forget.

Shell Options

The KornShell lets you set various options to control its behavior. To do this, you use the `set` command. In this section you'll see a few simple options that you can set. As I discuss more KornShell features in later sections, I'll discuss other options that pertain to those features.

Glob Constructs

If you call the set command with the -f option, the shell will stop expanding glob constructs. For example, enter

```
set -f
echo *
```

If the shell were expanding glob constructs, it would expand the * in the echo command into a list of all the files and subdirectories under the current directory. However, set -f tells the shell not to expand glob constructs. As a result, the echo command simply displays the * character.

Now enter the commands

```
set +f
echo *
```

As you might guess, the +f option is the opposite of the -f option. It tells the shell to go back to expanding glob constructs. This time, the echo command displays the names of all the files and subdirectories under the current directory.

Plus and Minus Signs

In general, if set -option sets an option, set +option reverses the option setting. This works for any valid option.

Showing Expansions

The -x option (also called the xtrace option) tells the shell to display each command line after expansions have been performed and before the command is actually executed. For example, enter

```
alias dir="ls -l"
set -x
dir sonnet
```

You'll see that the shell displays the line

```
+ ls -l sonnet
```

before it calls `ls` to display the `listing` of the `sonnet` file. This shows you the command that the shell is actually executing; the shell has replaced the alias `dir` with its associated string `ls -l`. The + at the beginning of the line is added to make the command stand out from other information that's displayed on the screen.

Now enter

```
dir *onnet
```

and you'll see that the shell displays

```
+ ls -l bonnet connet sonnet
```

The shell replaced the alias `dir` with the command `ls -l` and expanded the glob construct `*onnet` into the three filenames. Once again, the shell shows you the actual command it is executing.

You may find that you like turning on the `xtrace` every time you log in. If you're confused about how the shell deals with complicated commands, `xtrace` helps clarify what's going on. For example, enter the command

```
ls -l $(find . -ctime -3 -print)
```

You'll see that the shell prints out two lines. The first is

```
+ find . -ctime -3 -print
```

This shows that the shell begins by executing the `find` command inside the parentheses. (This command finds the names of all files under the current directory that have changed in the last three days.) The second line that the shell prints begins with

```
+ ls -l
```

followed by the list of filenames obtained by the `find` command. These two lines show the two-stage process that the shell uses in order to execute the original command line: first the `find` command, and then the `ls` using the filenames obtained by `find`.

I suggest that you work with the `-x` option through the next few sections. If you decide you don't want to use the option, you can get rid of it with

```
set +x
```

> ### The Duration of Options
>
> Options only stay in effect until you log out. For example, if you use
>
> ```
> set -x
> ```
>
> in your current session, it will last until you log out (or until you change the option with `set +x`). The next time you log in, the option will not be in effect. In Chapter 9, "Customizing," I'll show how you can set things up so that your favorite options are turned on automatically every time you log in. For the time being, you'll just have to remember to set up the options by hand if you want to use them.

Command History

Enter the command

```
history
```

You'll see that it displays a list of the most recent commands that you've entered during this session. (If you have `set -x` in effect, you'll see that the `history` command is an alias and expands into a cryptic-looking command that begins with `fc`. Ignore this for the time being.)

As you enter commands, the KornShell keeps records of those commands. These records are called your *command history.* On UNIX, your command history is stored in a file named `.sh_history`. DOS won't accept filenames that begin with a dot, so the MKS Tools version of the KornShell stores your command history in a file named `sh_histo`. The file that contains your command history is called your *history file.*

The command history is useful in itself for providing a record of what you've done during your session with the computer. On the simplest level, suppose you enter a command and, due to a typing mistake, it doesn't do what you expect it to do. By the time you find out something went wrong, the command you entered may have disappeared from the top of the screen, especially if the incorrect command wrote a lot of text to the screen. However, you can still use `history` to display your command history and see what you actually typed. This can often help you correct the error.

You might also check your command history if you recently executed a complicated command and waNt p/ execute the saee command or a similar one. For example, many people find it hard to remember the tar command for backing up a directory. They usually have to look up the command to make sure they've got the right arguments in the right order. If you're backing up several directories, you may have to look up the tar command in the manual the first time; however, the next time you want to do the same backup operation (or a similar one), you can just check your command history to see what you did the last time (within the same session). This means you don't have to keep going back to the manual to see what you did.

> **Note**
>
> If you really do have this problem with tar, the simplest solution is to create an alias. For example, if you're using the MKS Tools you might define
>
> ```
> alias backup="tar -cvf a:archive"
> ```
>
> as your standard command for backing up a directory. When you have this alias, you can just say
>
> ```
> backup name
> ```
>
> to back up a directory or file named name. That way you don't have to look up the command at all; you can just use the alias. There are also more sophisticated solutions to this problem using shell functions or shell scripts. (You'll see these in later chapters.)

The output of history only shows the last 16 commands entered. The shell history file (.sh_history on UNIX, sh_histo on DOS) holds a much larger number of commands, but there's no point in showing all the commands if most of them just disappear off the top of your screen.

Re-Executing Commands with the *r* Command

Enter the command

```
history
```

again. You'll notice that the output of history shows a number beside each command. These numbers reflect how many commands you've entered since you logged in. The first command is number 1, the next is number 2, and so on. As I noted before, the history command only shows the 16 most recent commands, so if you've been working for a while, the numbers beside the commands can be quite large.

In the last section I mentioned that you could consult the history file if you wanted to retype a complicated command and needed to check the format of that command. But why should you have to go to the trouble of typing the command again when the system already has a copy of the command stored in the history file?

In fact, you don't have to retype such commands. You can simply tell the shell to read a command from the history file and re-execute that command. To see how this works, enter the two commands

```
ls -l
r
```

The r command re-executes a command from the shell history file. When you issue an r command without arguments, it runs the most recent command you executed. In the preceding example, it runs ls -l again.

Here's an example that's a bit more realistic. Enter

```
find / -ctime -3 -print
```

Suppose you issue the find command to display several files but discover that the number of files is larger than you expected and that the output runs off the top of the screen. You'd like to rerun the command, only this time you'd like to pipe the output through more so that you can read it screen by screen. You can rerun the command and pipe the output through more by entering

```
r ¦ more
```

The r command is equivalent to re-executing the original find command, and the addition of ¦ more pipes the result of the find command into more.

The r Command is an Alias for fc

If you are running with set -x, you'll notice that the r command is an alias for another command that begins with the name fc. The fc command is a multipurpose command for working with the history file. The trouble is that fc can be a complicated command, and many people have trouble remembering how to use it.

> The designer of the KornShell solved this problem by creating several built-in aliases that were easier to use than fc itself. The r command is one of these; history is another. Enter the command
>
> ```
> alias
> ```
>
> and you'll see that several of the built-in aliases are forms of the fc command. If you're interested in fc itself, see the man pages.

Re-Executing Other Commands by Number

You can use the r command to re-execute any command in the command history. For example, enter the commands

```
ls -l /lu/etc
history
```

The history command displays the numbers of all the recent commands. You can re-execute any command in the history file by entering

```
r number
```

where number is the number of the command, as shown in the output of history. Try this. Re-execute the ls -l command by entering r followed by the number of the command, as shown by history.

Re-Executing Other Commands by Name

There's an even easier way to re-execute commands with the r command. Enter the following command.

```
r ls
```

This version of the r command tells the shell to re-execute the most recent command that began with ls. In this case, it will be the command

```
ls -l /lu/etc
```

that you executed in the last section.

You don't even have to type the full name of the command. For example, enter

```
r l
```

and you get the same effect. The shell looks for the most recent command with a name beginning with `l` and executes the command. Once again, it will be the `ls` command.

Substitutions in Re-Executed Commands

Enter the commands

```
set -x
ls /lu/etc
```

The `ls` command displays the contents of `/lu/etc`. Now enter

```
r etc=bin
```

You'll see that the shell displays the contents of `/lu/bin` instead of `/lu/etc`. The output `-x` shows that the shell has run the command

```
ls /lu/bin
```

You should have no trouble guessing why the command has changed. The argument

```
etc=bin
```

tells the shell to change the first occurrence of the string `etc` into `bin`. By default, `r` runs the most recent command, so it runs `ls /lu/etc` but changes the `etc` to `bin`. As another example, enter the commands

```
ls /lu/etc
cd /lu
r etc=bin ls
```

Again, you'll see that the `r` command runs `ls /lu/bin`. The `ls` on the end of the `r` command says to reexecute the most recent `ls` command, and `etc=bin` says to change `etc` to `bin` before running the command.

This example shows that you can make simple substitutions in commands before reexecuting them with `r`. The general form is

```
r old=new indicator
```

The `indicator` indicates which command you want to run. This can either be a number (indicating that you want to execute the command that has that number) or it can be a string (indicating that you want to execute the most recent command that begins with that string). The `old=new` says that you want to replace the first occurrence of the string `old` with the string `new`. In the example, `old` was `etc` and `new` was `bin`.

You can do the same thing again, in reverse. Enter

```
r bin=etc ls
```

and the shell reexecutes the `ls` command you just executed, except that it changes `bin` back to `etc`. You'll see that the effect is the same as

```
ls /lu/etc
```

Typically, you use this kind of substitution when you want to execute a command that is nearly the same as a previous one. For example, enter

```
cd
```

to go back to your home directory. Then enter

```
cp sonnet testdir
r so=bo
```

The first command copies `sonnet` to `testdir`; the second copies `bonnet`. You save a small amount of typing by using `r` for the second command rather than another `cp`. Obviously, the longer the original command, the more typing you save by using a short substitution.

Substitutions Only Work for the First Occurrence

An `old=new` substitution only substitutes the first occurrence of `old`. You have to be careful about this. For example, suppose you want to rename `file1` to `f1` and `file2` to `f2`. You might try this with

```
mv file1 f1
    r 1=2
```

However, the result of the `r` command is

```
mv file2 f1
```

because the shell only changes the first 1 to a 2. In this instance, it would certainly be more useful for `r` to replace every occurrence of `old` with `new`...but the UNIX convention is to replace only the first occurrence (such as in `vi` s commands).

Command Editing

Command editing is a natural outgrowth of the action that was discussed in the previous section: obtaining a command from the history file, changing the command slightly, then reexecuting the command. With command editing, however, you have much more freedom to modify commands. In fact, you have most of the same editing features that vi has.

Activating Command Editing

To start up command editing, enter the command

```
set -o vi
```

This tells the shell that you want to be able to edit commands as if you were using vi.

Using Command Editing

As I've discussed, your history file records the commands you have entered most recently. Command editing is much like using vi to edit the history file, except that you only get to see one line at a time.

When the shell prompts you to enter a command, you are in Insert Mode. Press the Esc key. As with vi, this switches from Insert Mode to Command Mode. Pressing k moves back through the history file. The first time you press the key, you should see

```
set -o vi
```

This is the command that you just entered. Press k again and you'll see other commands that you entered recently.

Go back to the command

```
ls /lu/etc
```

that you entered a few sections ago. You're now going to edit this into

```
ls /lu/bin
```

You'll notice that the cursor is on the first character of the line. By entering w (for *move forward a word*) several times, you can move across until you get to the first character of etc. Now, you want to change the word etc into bin. Do this using standard vi commands. First you enter cw to say you want to change a word; then you enter bin as the new word. Press Enter when you're done, and the shell executes the command.

With command editing, you can't use the vi commands that begin with a colon (:). For example, you can't use :s. However, you can use most of the other vi commands with this form of command editing. For example, 0 goes to the beginning of the line and $ goes to the end. You can use c for changing text, d for deleting it, and a for adding to it. The j and k keys let you move from one command line to another.

After you've edited a command into the form you want, you can press Enter to execute the command. It doesn't matter whether you're in Insert Mode or Command Mode, and the cursor doesn't have to be at the end of the command line.

You should practice using command editing for a while until you're comfortable with it. Command editing is so useful that the designers of DOS copied it from UNIX. The standard DOS shell, COMMAND.COM, has command editing facilities, and many alternative DOS shells also have these facilities.

Why is the ability to reuse previous commands useful? Because most people use the same commands over and over again. For example, I'm writing this book with a word processor. From time to time I have to check the commands I'm talking about, so I quit the word processor to try out the commands. When I'm finished, I want to go back to the word processor to continue writing. Rather than writing out the command to invoke the word processor again, I just use command editing to go back through my history file to find the last time I invoked the word processor. I can find the command much more quickly than I can retype it, and I don't have to stop and remember the name of the file I was editing.

I use command editing all the time and I strongly recommend that you try it out for yourself. If you haven't used the facility on DOS, it may take a while for you to learn how to exploit its potential. Invest the time now; you'll save a good deal of time and trouble later.

Variables

Experienced DOS users are familiar with the concept of *environment variables*. In DOS, an environment variable is a piece of information with a name and a value. Any DOS program can consult the environment variables that are currently defined.

For example, the login procedure for the DOS MKS Toolkit defines an environment variable named HOME. The value of this variable is the name of your home directory. Any program that wants to determine the name of your home directory can ask DOS to look up the value of HOME.

UNIX also has variables that can be used in this way. However, DOS and UNIX variables differ in at least one important respect.

> In DOS, environment variables are stored in a single *table*. Every program has access to every variable in the table. If a program creates a new variable, it gets added to the table, and all other programs can use the new variable. If a program changes the value of a variable, all subsequent programs that consult the table will see the changed value.

> In UNIX, each program has its own separate table of variables. If a program creates a new variable or changes the value of an existing variable, it only affects the program's own table. It doesn't affect the variable table of any other program.

The variable table of a UNIX program is created by whatever invokes the program. For example, when you tell the shell to run a program, the shell loads the program into memory and creates a variable table for that program. The shell decides what to put into the table. To do this, the shell looks at its own variable table and decides which of those variables should be passed on to the program. When the shell passes some of its variables to a new program, we say that the shell *exports* those variables to the new program.

After the new program starts executing, it can change the value of its variables or add new variables to its table. These changes only affect the program's own table; normally, such changes do not affect the shell's table or the table of any other program. However, a program can explicitly ask the operating system to export selected variables back to the shell, in which case the shell's variable table is affected.

Variables Exported by the Shell

The KornShell works with many variables. You can create variables of your own, as you'll see in a later section; in addition, the shell automatically creates several variables by default when you first log in. The sh man page gives a complete list of these variables. In the sections to come, you'll only see some of the most basic variables.

> ### Displaying Your Shell Variables
>
> You can display the shell's list of variables at any time by entering the command
>
> ```
> set
> ```
>
> without any arguments. If you do, you'll probably see a lot of variables you don't recognize right now. These are set up automatically for you when the shell starts up. For more information on any of these variables, see the `sh` man page.

History Variables

The value of the `HISTFILE` variable is the name of your command history file. If HISTFILE isn't defined, the shell uses `.sh_history` on UNIX; `sh_histo` on DOS.

The value of the `HISTSIZE` variable is the maximum number of commands that the shell should record in the history file. If HISTSIZE is not defined, the shell uses a default value of 127. If you exceed this number of commands, the shell begins to discard old commands. For example, when the shell records command 128, it throws away its information about command 1.

Your Home Directory

The value of the `HOME` variable is the name of your home directory. This is set at the time that you log in.

Working Directories

The value of the `PWD` variable is the name of your current working directory. The shell automatically changes this every time you issue a `cd` command.

The value of the `OLDPWD` variable is the name of your previous working directory. Whenever you issue a `cd` command to change directories, the shell uses `OLDPWD` to record the name of the directory you're leaving. When you issue the command

```
cd -
```

to switch back to your previous working directory, the shell uses `OLDPWD` to determine the name of that directory.

Using Variables in Commands

If you want to use the value of a variable in a command, write a dollar sign ($) followed by the name of the variable. For example, enter the command

```
echo $HOME
```

This displays the value of the HOME variable, which is the name of your home directory. This is the same name that you'll see if you enter the pwd command right after logging in. The process of replacing a $name construct with the value of the variable name is called *variable expansion.*

Enter the command

```
cd /
```

This makes the root directory your current directory. If you enter the commands

```
echo $PWD
```

you'll see the output is

```
c:/
```

because PWD holds the name of your current directory, and your current directory is the root directory. Now enter

```
more $HOME/sonnet
```

This displays the sonnet file from your home directory. When the shell processes this command, it expands $HOME into the name of your home directory so that the argument of more is the absolute pathname of the sonnet file.

You can use $HOME to refer to your home directory, no matter what your current directory is. Constructs like this simplify the job of writing shell programs, as you'll see in Chapter 8, "An Introduction to KornShell Programming."

Creating Your Own Variables

You can create your own variables with a command of the form

```
name='string'
```

This is called an *assignment;* it assigns a value to a variable. For example, enter the command

```
TD='testdir'
```

This creates a variable named `TD` with a value equal to the string `testdir`. You can use this variable in commands. For example, enter the following:

```
echo $TD
ls -l $HOME/$TD
cd
ls -l $TD
```

The `echo` command simply echoes the string `testdir`. The first `ls` command displays the contents of the `testdir` directory under your home directory. The `cd` command returns to your home directory, and the last `ls` command displays the contents of `testdir` again. Of course, you could save more typing by defining

```
TD='$HOME/testdir'
```

This way, `TD` contains the full pathname of `testdir`, and you don't have to add things to the name when you change directories.

Variable Names

The first character of a variable name must be an upper- or lowercase letter, or the underscore character (_). The rest of the name (if any) can consist of upper- or lowercase letters, underscores, and/or the digits 0 through 9.

The case of letters is significant. For example, `VAR`, `Var` and `var` are all distinct variables.

Changing the Value of a Variable

You can change the value of a variable with another assignment. For example, enter

```
TD='sonnet'
```

This changes the value of `TD` to `sonnet`. Enter the command

```
ls -l $TD
```

and you'll see that it displays information about the file `sonnet` rather than the directory `testdir`.

You can change the value of built-in shell variables such as `HOME` and `HISTSIZE`. For example,

```
HISTSIZE=200
```

tells the shell that you want it to keep up to 200 history commands in your history file rather than the default value of 127.

Getting Rid of Variables

You can get rid of any variable using the `unset` command.

```
unset name
```

gets rid of the variable that has the given name. For example, enter

```
unset TD
```

This gets rid of the `TD` variable. Enter

```
set
```

and you'll see that `TD` is no longer in the list of defined variables. Also, enter

```
echo $TD
```

You'll see that the command just outputs a blank line. Because `TD` is no longer defined, `$TD` has no meaning and there's nothing for `echo` to display. Technically speaking, `$TD` is expanded into the *null string,* a string that has no characters. If a variable does not currently exist, its value is always taken to be the null string.

Arithmetic with Variables

Enter the following commands:

```
i=1
j=$i+1
echo $j
```

You'll see that `echo` displays the string `1+1`. Even though the assignments look like they're doing arithmetic, they're really just assigning strings of characters to variables. In

```
j=$i+1
```

the shell changes `$i` to the value of `i`, namely `1`. Thus the variable `j` is assigned the string `1+1`, and that's what the `echo` command displays.

If you want to perform true arithmetic with variables, you can do so using the `let` command. The command has the form

```
let variable=expression
```

where `variable` is the name of a new or existing variable, and `expression` is an arithmetic expression. For example, enter the commands

```
i=1
let j=$i+1
echo $j
```

This time the `echo` command displays 2. The `let` command evaluated the expression 1+1 and assigned the result to `j`.

You can also use `let` to change the value of `i` itself. For example, enter

```
i=1
let i=$i+1
echo $i
```

Again, the `echo` command displays 2. The `let` command works like this. First, the shell expands `$i` and replaces it with the value of `i`. Thus the command turns into

```
let i=1+1
```

As a result, `i` is assigned a new value of 2. The `echo` command shows you that the new value of `i` is 2.

Table 7.1 shows operations that can be used in expressions in a `let` command. In keeping with standard mathematical practice, all negation operations are evaluated first, then all `*`, `/`, and/or `%` operations (from left to right in the order they appear), then all + and _ operations (from left to right in the order they appear). I've grouped Table 7.1 to show this.

Table 7.1. Operations in a `let` Command.

Operation	Meaning
-A	Negative A
A*B	A times B
A/B	A divided by B
A%B	Remainder from A divided by B
A+B	A plus B
A-B	A minus B

As an example of the order of operations, enter

```
let i="5+2*3"
echo $i
```

Note that if the expression contains an asterisk (*), it should be put inside double or single quotation marks. This way, the shell doesn't interpret the asterisk as a glob construct and won't try to expand it into a file list.

The `echo` command displays the value 11, because the multiplication in the `let` command takes place before the addition. If you want to change the order in which the expression is evaluated, put parentheses around the operations you want `let` to evaluate first. For example, enter

```
let i="(5+2)*3"
echo $i
```

This time the `echo` command displays the value 21 because the addition takes place first.

Integers Only

The `let` command does not let you perform arithmetic with numbers that have fractional parts. You can only use whole numbers (integers).

Exporting Variables

I mentioned earlier that the shell can export variables to the programs that it invokes. However, the shell doesn't do so automatically. You have to tell it which variables it can export.

The `export` command tells the shell which variables it should export. It has the form

```
export name name name ...
```

where each `name` is the name of a variable. For example, enter

```
export HOME PWD
```

This says that the shell should export `HOME` and `PWD` to every command it invokes from now on.

When you issue an `export` command for a set of variables, we say that those variables are *marked for export.* They will be exported to every subsequent command that the shell executes. Remember, a program can't use a variable unless the shell exports that variable. Therefore, you must mark for export any variable that programs might want to use. We'll see examples of how this works in later chapters.

The command

```
set -a
```

tells the shell that it should export every variable that you define from now on. This means that when you create a new variable, the shell automatically marks it for export. Note that this only works for variables after you issue the `set` command. If you want to export a variable that existed before you issued the `set` command, you have to use the `export` command.

Quotation Marks and the KornShell

In previous chapters, you've seen how you can enclose arguments in quotation marks (single or double). Quotation marks enclose an argument when the argument contains whitespace. Quotation marks also tell the shell not to expand glob constructs that occur inside the quotation marks. In this section, you'll see the effects of quotation marks on other shell constructs.

The shell does not perform command substitutions, alias substitutions, or variable expansions inside single quotation marks. For example, enter

```
i=1
echo '$i'
```

and you'll see that the output is $i. The variable is not expanded because the $i construct appears inside single quotation marks. Enter

```
echo '$(ls)'
```

and you'll see that command substitution doesn't take place either. Finally, enter

```
alias p=more
p sonnet
'p' sonnet
```

You'll see that the p alias works when it isn't inside single quotation marks. However, when p is quoted, the shell doesn't perform alias substitution; instead, it just tries to execute a command named p. There is no such command, so you get the message

```
p: not found
```

Now, let's try the same sequence of commands with double quotation marks instead of single quotation marks. Enter

```
echo "$i"
echo "$(ls)"
"p" sonnet
```

Despite the double quotation marks, the shell expands the variable `$i` and the command substitution `$(ls)`. However, it doesn't recognize the alias `p`, so double quotation marks still turn off alias substitution.

In a sense then, double quotation marks are *weaker* than single quotation marks. With single quotation marks, the shell ignores all special constructs inside the quotation marks. With double quotation marks, the shell ignores glob constructs and aliases, but still performs command substitution and variable expansion.

There's one other special case to note. Enter the two commands

```
echo $(ls)
echo "$(ls)"
```

With the first command, the names under the current directory are displayed on one long line (which the shell *folds* several times so that the long line fits on the screen). With the second command, the names are displayed with one name per line.

Why does this happen? The output of the `ls` command normally shows one name per line when `ls` is used in command substitution. However, when the command substitution takes place in the unquoted form, the shell processes the output from `ls`, changing each line break into a single space. This long line is then given to `echo` as input. However, when `$(ls)` appears in double quotation marks, the shell doesn't process the line breaks. It leaves them as they are, so `echo` displays the line breaks as well as the names.

Line Breaks

In a UNIX text file, lines are separated by special characters called *newline* characters. Most UNIX systems use the ASCII linefeed character as their newline character, although this isn't necessary. The POSIX.1 standard lets you customize your system to use a different character as the newline if you want.

The KornShell

7

In a DOS text file, lines are usually separated by a pair of characters: the ASCII carriage return and the ASCII linefeed. Thus DOS text files usually have two characters between each pair of lines, while UNIX text files only have one.

Chapter Review

When a construct of the form

```
$(command)
```

appears in a command line, the shell performs command substitution. It executes the given `command` and puts the standard output of the `command` into the command line in place of the original `$(command)` construct.

An alias is a personalized name that stands for all or part of a command. To create an alias, use

```
alias name="string"
```

where `name` is the name of the alias you want to create. When the shell sees an alias at the beginning of a command, it replaces the alias `name` with its associated `string`. This process is called alias substitution. The command

```
alias
```

displays all aliases currently defined, and the command

```
unalias name name ...
```

gets rid of the aliases that have the given names.

Shell options are set with the `set` command. Table 7.2 shows the shell options discussed in this chapter. Options turned on with a minus sign (-) are turned off with a plus sign (+) in the same position.

Table 7.2. Shell options discussed in this chapter.

Option	Meaning
set -a	Export all variables defined in the future
set -f	Do not expand glob constructs
set +f	Expand glob constructs
set -o vi	Permit editing of commands with vi commands
set -x	Show all expansions and substitutions performed on commands (xtrace)
set +x	Turn off set -x

The history command displays a list of the most recent commands that you have executed with the shell. This list is called your command history and is stored in a history file.

The r command reexecutes a command from the history file. Table 7.3 shows various forms of the r command.

Table 7.3. Forms of the r command.

Form	Meaning
r	Executes the most recent command
r number	Executes the command with the given number
r string	Executes the last command to begin with string
r old=new X	Replaces the first occurrence of old with new in command X, then reexecutes the command

Command editing lets you edit and execute command lines from the history file in the same way that you edit text with vi. Most of the common vi operations can be used. When you press Enter, the (edited) command is executed. In order to activate command editing, enter the command

```
set -o vi
```

When you use command editing, pressing Esc switches from Insert Mode to Command Mode. Pressing k after that will move back through the history file, one line at a time.

UNIX lets you define variables for use by the shell. To create or change the value of a variable, use

```
name=value
```

where `name` is an appropriate variable name and `value` is a string. Each UNIX program keeps its own table of variables, so changes in the table of one program do not usually change the table of any other program.

Table 7.4 lists some of the variables that are used by the KornShell. A complete list is given in the `sh` man page.

Table 7.4. Shell variables discussed in this chapter.

Variable	Meaning
HISTFILE	The name of your history file
HISTSIZE	The maximum number of entries in your history file
HOME	The name of your home directory
OLDPWD	The name of your previous working directory
PWD	The name of your current directory

When the shell finds the construct

```
$name
```

in a command line, it expands the construct by replacing it with the value of the variable name. If there is no such variable, the shell replaces the construct with nothing (in other words, the null string, a string that contains no characters).

You can do arithmetic with variables using the `let` command. The general form of the command is

```
let name=expression
```

where `name` is a name for a new or existing variable and `expression` is an arithmetic expression.

The command

```
export name name ...
```

tells the shell to mark the specified variables for export. The names and values of these variables will be passed on to every subsequent command that the shell invokes.

The command

```
unset name name ...
```

gets rid of the specified variables.

When an argument is enclosed in single quotation marks, the shell does not attempt glob expansion, alias substitution, command substitution, or variable expansion on any part of the argument. When an argument is enclosed in double quotation marks, the shell does not attempt glob expansion or alias substitution, but does attempt command substitution and variable expansion on appropriate constructs within the double quotation marks.

Exercises

1. Create an alias named h5 that prints the first five lines of any text file. (Hint: use the head command, discussed in the exercises at the end of Chapter 4, "Five Ways to List a Current Directory.")

2. Create an alias named wcl that prints the number of lines in a text file.

3. Create an alias named rmi that works the same as rm except that it uses the -i option to query you about every file you ask to delete.

4. Consider the following commands:

```
ls >out1
r 1=2 1
```

What is the effect of the r command?

5. When set -o vi is not in effect, pressing Esc gets rid of the current input line so that you can retype the line from scratch. However, when set -o vi is in effect, Esc has a different meaning. (What is it?) When set -o vi is in effect, what can you type to get rid of the current input line? Read Appendix F, "KornShell Editing Features," to see other alternatives.

6. The env command displays all the environment variables currently defined;

see the env man page. What is the difference between this and the set command with no arguments? (See the Glossary for a definition of environment variables.) Try it and see.

7. What is the difference between

```
let x= 4
```

and

```
let x=" 4"
```

Try it and see.

8. Make sure that set -o vi is in effect. Type the following without pressing Enter:

```
more so
```

Now press Esc and *. What happens? Read Appendix F for an explanation of this feature and others related to it. Will this feature help reduce typing errors for you?

AN INTRODUCTION TO KORNSHELL PROGRAMMING

This chapter demonstrates how you can write programs for the KornShell to execute. Shell programs have many features in common with programs written in more conventional programming languages like BASIC, Pascal, and C; however, the "statements" of shell programs are commands like cp, find, and so on.

If you're an experienced DOS user, you may already be familiar with this type of programming; writing a DOS batch file (for example, with a .bat suffix) is a form of shell programming. However, you'll find that the KornShell's programming capabilities are much more extensive than DOS batch programming.

The chapter begins with an examination of *shell scripts*. A shell script is a file containing a sequence of commands that you want the shell to execute. The first sections discuss very simple scripts; later sections show more sophisticated features that can be used inside scripts, including the following:

The ability to pass *arguments* to shell scripts and shell functions

Control structures that can be used in shell scripts and shell functions; these include such constructs as if-else and for loops

The ability to define *shell functions*, comparable to subprograms in a programming language

Shell Scripts

A *shell script* is a file that contains input for the shell. You've already seen what kind of input the shell takes.

Utilities that you want to execute (such as cp, more, find)

Commands that set options for the shell (such as set)

Commands that create or manipulate variables (such as assignments or let)

Combined utilities (such as ones using pipes or command substitution)

Other special instructions (such as using alias to create aliases or r to re-execute a previous command)

A shell script can contain the same kind of instructions that you have been typing from the keyboard. In addition, it can contain more specialized instructions that control the behavior of the script. You'll learn about such instructions later in the chapter.

Creating a Shell Script

The easiest way to create a shell script is to use vi. It's best to start with something simple, so enter the command

```
vi simple
```

This command says that you want to edit a file named simple. Because there currently is no file with that name, vi knows you want to create a new file. Use the a command to enter the following text:

```
echo Hello there!
echo "How are you?"
```

Write out the file (using :w) and quit vi.

Needless to say, this shell script consists of only two echo commands. When you execute the script, the shell will read its input from the script file and execute these commands.

Making a Shell Script Executable

Before you can execute the script, you have to make the file executable. In Chapter 3, "The UNIX File System: Go Climb a Tree," I discussed how to do this: enter the command

```
chmod +x simple
```

This assigns execute permission to the simple file. If you use the preceding chmod command, anyone can execute the file. You could also use commands like

```
chmod -x simple
chmod u+x simple
```

if you wanted to be the only one who could execute the file. The first chmod command turns off execute permission for you, for those in your group, and for all other users on the system. The second chmod command turns execute permission back on, but only for you.

Executability on DOS

Several future sections ask you to create a shell script with vi and then to execute the shell script. On a true UNIX system, you would have to use chmod to make the scripts executable. On DOS, all files are considered to be executable, so you can skip using chmod.

Executing Shell Scripts

There are several ways to execute a shell script. The sections that follow examine some of these and discuss how the various approaches differ from one another.

233

Executing the Command Directly

The easiest way to execute a shell script is simply to enter the name of the script. Enter

```
simple.
```

(Notice that you need to put a dot on the end of the filename; this is explained in the **simple. Versus simple** sidebar.) After you enter the command, you'll see

```
Hello there!
How are you?
```

displayed on the monitor screen. The shell has executed the echo commands inside simple, and you see the result on the screen.

If you find that the simple. command doesn't work, you may have missed doing Exercise 1 in Chapter 6, "Text Files—Veni, Vidi, *vi*." Use vi to read in the file profile.ksh from your home directory and edit the PATH line so that it reads

```
PATH=".;c:/lu/bin"
```

When you have edited the file, write it back out, then log out and log in again. Now when you execute

```
simple.
```

it should work. In Chapter 9, "Customizing," you'll see why the PATH line in profile.ksh is important, and I'll discuss a number of points related to the format of PATH.

---

simple. Versus simple

You'll notice that you had to enter the name of the file as simple. with a dot on the end. This is a property of the DOS simulation of the KornShell. Remember that DOS usually expects filenames to have a suffix; however, the simple file doesn't have a suffix. More precisely, it has a *null suffix,* a suffix that doesn't contain any characters. To show that there is no suffix, you have to add the dot on DOS and type simple..

On a true UNIX system, you would only have to type simple (with no dot). UNIX doesn't require a suffix, so there's no need to worry about null suffixes. On UNIX you type the shell script's name exactly as it is; on DOS you have to add a dot if the shell script's name doesn't have a suffix.

> If you find the dot on the end of the name to be ugly or hard to remember, you can always create an alias. For example, if you enter
>
> ```
> Alias simple="simple."
> ```
>
> you can then execute the script under the name `simple` instead of `simple..`

As another example of executing a command file directly, enter the following commands:

```
cp simple testdir
testdir/simple.
```

The `cp` command creates a copy of `simple` under the `testdir` directory. The second line executes the copy of the shell script. (Notice that you need a dot on the end of the filename.)

Executing the Command with a Subshell

You can also execute a shell script with the `sh` command. As mentioned in earlier chapters, `sh` is the name of the KornShell. Enter

```
sh simple.
```

and you'll see

```
Hello there!
How are you?
```

displayed on the screen again. Enter

```
sh testdir/simple.
```

and you execute the shell script from the `testdir` directory.

Now what really happens when you execute a shell script with this form of the command? The shell you are using sees the `sh` command and recognizes that you want to execute a command named `sh`. The shell therefore goes looking for a file that contains a program named `sh`. The name `simple.` is just an argument for the `sh` command.

But it so happens that `sh` is the name of the KornShell program. This means that the `sh` command line starts a new copy of the KornShell. This new copy of the KornShell looks for arguments on its command line. It finds `simple.` and executes the contents

of the file. When it reaches the end of the `simple` file, the new KornShell has no more input to process, so it quits. After the new KornShell quits, the old KornShell comes back to start taking input again.

You might picture the process like this: Imagine that the KornShell is a butler who is always by your side to carry out your wishes. You ask the butler to do a job. Your butler rings a bell to summon another butler and tells that butler to do the job. The second butler does the job and reports back to the first butler. The first butler dismisses the second butler, then reports back to you and waits for new instructions.

Technically, your KornShell starts a *subshell* to execute the shell script. The subshell is entirely separate from the original shell, just as the second butler is entirely separate from the first.

You may be bothered by this indirect method of executing a shell script. Why start up a new copy of the shell when you're already running an old copy? Here are some simple reasons:

> When you invoke the `sh` command, you can specify *options*. The options for the subshell don't have to be the same as your original shell. It's like hiring a subcontractor with more specialized skills than the primary contractor. For a list of `sh` command line options, see the `sh` man page.

> You may want to execute the shell script in a *clean* environment. After all, you may have changed your shell session by defining variables or aliases, or by using `set`. When you create a subshell, the subshell can start again from scratch. The subshell inherits all variables marked for export in the original shell, but it doesn't inherit anything else. This can be an advantage.

> You may want to protect your original shell session from things that the shell script does. For example, suppose a shell script uses `let` and other commands to change the values of variables. If you already have variables of the same name defined in your current shell session, you may not want the script to change your variables. By using a subshell, you create a separate environment, making it difficult for the shell script to interfere with your original shell session.

The Dot Command

Enter the command

```
. simple.
```

This is an example of the *dot* command. The name of the command is just a dot character, and the argument is the name of the shell script you want to execute.

In a sense, the dot command is the opposite of the sh command. Instead of executing the shell script in a subshell, the script is executed by your current shell so that all the commands in the script affect the current shell. For example, if the script contains set commands or commands that change the value of variables, the commands affect the current shell.

In general, the only time you use the dot command is when you want the script to change options and/or variables in the current shell. In most other cases, you'll find it's better to execute the script directly or with a subshell.

What's the Difference?

You've now seen three ways to execute shell scripts: directly, in a subshell, and with the dot command. What's the difference?

The difference is related to the concept of *execution environments.* An execution environment is the collection of variables, aliases, options, and so on that are in effect when a command or shell script is executed. Here's what happens to the execution environment in each of the three ways of executing a script:

> If the script is executing under a subshell, the script gets an absolutely clean environment, running under an entirely separate shell. It is possible to specify options that will affect the behavior of this shell; for example, you can tell the shell to reinitialize itself as if you just logged in again.

> If the script is executed with the dot command, the script operates in the same environment as the shell itself, and can affect the shell's variables, aliases, options, and so on.

> If the script is executed directly, the shell creates a separate environment for the script. This is similar to running the script under a subshell, because the script's environment is separate from the shell's and cannot affect the original shell environment. However, it is not exactly like using a subshell because you can't specify options for the shell on the command line and the environment inherits some information from the original shell.

Explaining the exact differences between the subshell environment and the separate environment set up for a script executed directly would require more technical background than the average reader would like to handle. Just remember that using a subshell means a separate copy of the shell, while executing directly just means a separate environment (but the same copy of the shell).

Shell Scripts and Other Constructs

You can execute a shell script anywhere you can execute a normal command. For example, enter

```
simple. ¦ wc
```

This pipes the standard output of `simple` through the `wc` command. The output of `wc` is the number of lines, words, and bytes in the standard output of the shell script. You could also say

```
simple. ¦ more
```

to pipe the output of `simple` through `more`, although there isn't much point to this because `simple` doesn't produce much output.

The preceding examples show that you can use shell scripts in pipes. You can also use scripts in command substitutions. Enter

```
echo $(simple.)
```

and you'll see that the system displays

```
Hello there! How are you?
```

The `$(simple.)` construct tells the shell to execute the command and collect its standard output. The standard output is substituted into the `echo` command to produce

```
echo Hello there! How are you?
```

This explains why the output you see on your screen is all on one line.

You can create aliases for shell scripts. For example, enter

```
alias sim="simple."
sim
```

and you'll see that the `sim` line runs the `simple` shell script.

Comments

If a line in a KornShell script contains a number sign (#) symbol, the shell simply ignores everything after the #. This lets you place *comments* inside your shell scripts, which are explanations of what the script does or what a particular statement does. For example, use `vi` to edit the `simple` file, to change the changes into

```
# This script just prints two lines of messages
echo Hello there!   # The rest of this line is ignored
echo "How are you?"
```

Now execute `simple` in any of the ways discussed in previous sections. You'll see that `simple` behaves the same way it did before you edited the file. The comments have no effect on the script's behavior; they just provide information that helps you understand what the script does.

Comments make shell scripts more readable. I strongly recommend that you put a comment at the beginning of each script to explain what that script does. This will help other people who read the script and will also help you. A week or a month after writing a script, you may not remember what the script does. A comment helps clarify what the script is for.

You may also want to add comments to explain particularly complicated commands or command sequences. An explanation in plain English can be more comprehensible than a cryptic UNIX command.

Positional Parameters

As you've just seen, you can use shell scripts in the same way you might use an ordinary UNIX command like `cp` or `echo`. You can also pass arguments to shell scripts in the same way that you pass arguments to an ordinary command.

To see how this works, use `vi` to create a file named `easy` that contains the following:

```
# This script displays three lines of output
echo $1 $3 $2
echo "$1" "$3" "$2"
echo '$1' '$3' '$2'
```

When you have done so, quit `vi`, then enter

```
alias easy="easy."
```

With this alias, you can execute the script with `easy` instead of `easy.`, so you don't have to keep remembering that extra dot. Now enter

```
easy Hello there friends!
```

You'll see that the output is

```
Hello friends! there
Hello friends! there
$1 $3 $2
```

To understand this output, examine the first line of the shell script.

```
echo $1 $3 $2
```

The constructs $1, $3, and $2 are called *positional parameters*. A *parameter* is a name or symbol that stands for a command line argument. Inside a shell script, $1 stands for the first argument given on the command line that invokes the script, $2 stands for the second argument, and $3 stands for the third argument. Because the command line for the script was `easy Hello there friends!`, $1 stands for `Hello`, $2 stands for `there`, and $3 stands for `friends!` The order of the parameters given to the echo command explains the order in which echo displays the words `Hello`, `there`, and `friends!`.

The second echo command in the shell script is similar. In

```
echo "$1" "$3" "$2"
```

the parameters are again *expanded*, which means that they're replaced with the arguments in the corresponding positions on the command line. As discussed in Chapter 7, "The KornShell," double quotation marks are "weak" and don't prevent variable expansion in a command line. This example shows that double quotation marks don't prevent the expansion of parameters either.

The final echo command in the shell script is

```
echo '$1' '$3' '$2'
```

The output of this command is simply

```
$1 $3 $2
```

The single quotation mark characters are "strong" quotation marks. When the shell executes a shell script, it does not expand parameter constructs that are enclosed in single quotation marks.

Now enter the command

```
easy "Hi there" "How are you?" "Fine"
```

You'll see that the output is

```
Hi there Fine How are you?
Hi there Fine How are you?
$1 $3 $2
```

This shows that the first argument on the command line is `Hi there`. The argument has two words, but the double quotation marks serve to group the words into a single argument.

As another example, enter

```
easy Hello there!
```

The output is

```
Hello there!
Hello   there!
$1 $3 $2
```

In this case, there are only two arguments. When the shell sees the parameter $3 inside the shell script, the shell realizes there is no corresponding argument. Therefore, the shell expands $3 into a *null string* (a string that contains no characters). The shell script therefore becomes

```
echo Hello  there!
echo "Hello" "" "there!"
echo '$1' '$3 '$2'
```

In the first echo command, replacing $3 with a null string means that echo has only two arguments. Because echo puts a single blank between each of its arguments, the output is only Hello there! In the second echo command, there are three arguments; "" is a null string. This means that the second echo command outputs Hello followed by a space, the null string (no characters) followed by a space, and finally there! As you can see in the output, the result is an extra space between Hello and there!

Now enter

```
easy A B C D
```

This time the output is

```
A C B
A C B
$1 $3 $2
```

The original command line contained four arguments. However, the shell script only contains references to the first three arguments, $1, $2, and $3. You can specify as many arguments as you want on the command line; if the script doesn't happen to use some of those arguments, those arguments are simply ignored. You also could write a shell script that only uses arguments $2, $3, and $4, for example. You can ignore any or all arguments if you want.

Here's one last example to test your understanding of the way the shell works. Enter the following commands

```
easy *
easy "*"
```

Are you surprised by what you see? Here's how the two commands work and the output you'll see.

In the first easy command, the shell sees the * glob construct and expands it immediately. The shell then executes the easy script. The first three arguments to the script will be the first three files in the expansion of *. Other filenames in the expansion of * aren't used. Therefore you'll see the usual sort of three-argument output from easy, but the arguments will be the first three filenames under your current directory.

In the second easy command preceding, the shell doesn't expand the * immediately because it's enclosed in quotation marks. Instead, the shell believes that the first (and only) argument of the script is the * character. When the shell expands the contents of the shell script, the result is

```
echo *
echo "*" "" ""
echo '$1' '$3' '$2'
```

The first echo command displays all file and directory names under the current directory. The second echo just displays the * character; the shell doesn't expand * because it's enclosed in quotation marks. The final echo command is the same as usual.

Positional Parameter $0

The positional parameter $0 (zero) stands for the name of the shell script command itself. For example, in

```
easy A B C
```

$0 stands for easy., because that's the real name, not the alias of the script. If you specify a longer pathname to invoke the script, as in

```
./easy. A B C
```

$0 stands for the pathname you give.

The preceding examples show the dramatic difference that quotation marks can make inside shell scripts and on the command lines that invoke shell scripts. In the first example, you see a few filenames; in the second example, you see all the filenames under the current directory, plus the * character. Obviously, you have to be careful whenever you use quotation marks, inside or outside a script.

Special Parameters

The KornShell lets you use several special parameters inside shell scripts. To see how some of these work, use `vi` to create a file named `special` with the following contents:

```
# This script demonstrates special parameters.
easy. "$@"
easy. "$*"
```

Notice that this script makes use of the `easy` script you created earlier. This shows that you can call one script inside another script. Next use `vi` to change the existing `easy` script to

```
echo $1 $3 $2
echo This script has $# arguments
```

Entering an @

In `vi`, the @ character normally tells `vi` to delete everything you typed on the current line. To put @ in a file, enter Ctrl-V @.

The following list examines each of the special parameters used in these shell scripts:

$#Expands to the number of arguments passed to the script.

$@Expands to a list of all arguments, each as a separate argument in the list. This means that $@ is equivalent to $1 $2 $3 ...

$*Expands to a single argument that is a list of all the arguments passed to the shell script. This means that "$*" is equivalent to the single argument $1 $2 $3 ....

You'll understand the difference between $@ and $* after you see an example. When you have created the `special` file, exit `vi` and enter the command

```
special. A B C
```

Listing 8.1 shows the output from this command.

 **Listing 8.1. Output from the special script.**

```
A C B
This script has 3 arguments.
A B C
This script has 1 arguments.
```

The first two lines of output come from the first easy command.

```
easy. "$@"
```

The "$@" construct expands into a list of the arguments to the special script; each item in the list is a separate argument. Therefore, the preceding line becomes

```
easy. "A" "B" "C"
```

The results of the command are

```
A C B
This script has 3 arguments
```

The $# construct inside easy changes into the number of arguments.

Now, consider the second easy command in the special script.

```
easy. "$*"
```

The "$*" construct expands into a single argument made up of all the arguments passed to special. Therefore the preceding line becomes

```
easy. "A B C"
```

Because there is only one argument this time, $1 inside the easy script is "A B C" and $2 and $3 are null strings. The results of the command are

```
A B C
This script has 1 arguments.
```

Check the definition of the easy script to make sure you understand how this output was produced.

The *shift* Command

The shift command lets you adjust the list of arguments that a shell script receives. The easiest way to understand how the command works is to look at an example. Use vi to create a file named shifty that contains the following:

```
# This script demonstrates the shift command.
# You must specify at least six arguments.
echo "$*"
shift 3
echo "$*"
shift 2
echo "$*"
shift 1
echo "$*"
```

After you have created the file, exit `vi` and enter the following command:

```
shifty. A B C D E F
```

The output from this command is

```
A B C D E F
D E F
F
```

(with a blank line after the F).

Looking at the output, you should be able to figure out what the `shift` command does. Each `echo` command in the `shifty` script prints all the arguments to the script. The first `echo` command prints A B C D E F, as you probably would expect. After the `shift` command, however, the output is only D E F.

The `shift` command gets rid of the specified number of arguments from the beginning of the argument list. Therefore,

```
shift 3
```

gets rid of the first three arguments. Because you started with A B C D E F, the `shift` command reduces the argument list to D E F. The command

```
shift 2
```

gets rid of two more arguments, leaving only F. Finally,

```
shift 1
```

gets rid of the last argument. The final `echo` command therefore outputs a blank line.

The `shift` command gets its name because it shifts the parameter numbers of all the arguments. For example, if the original argument list is

```
A B C D E F
```

then A is $1, B is $2, and so on. In particular, D is $4. After

```
shift 3
```

the argument D is `$1`. As you can see, the argument has shifted from `$4` to `$1`. The other remaining arguments also shift their positions accordingly.

Now enter the command

```
shifty. a
```

This time, you'll see that the first `shift` command gets an error. The error occurs because you tried to `shift` three arguments but there was only one argument in the argument list. You'll get the same sort of error if you enter the command

```
shifty. a b c d e
```

The `shift 3` and `shift 2` commands get rid of all the arguments. Therefore the final `shift 1` command has nothing left to shift.

Redirection with Shell Scripts

Here's a simple example that shows how you can use redirection with shell scripts. Create a file named `sm` that contains the following line:

```
sort $@ ¦ more
```

This shell script simply takes all the command line arguments and uses them to create a `sort` command. The sorted output is then piped through `more` to make it easier to read. For example, enter

```
sm. -t: -k 4n,4 -k 3M,3 comics.1st
```

You'll see that it sorts the `comics.1st` file according to year and month, as discussed in Chapter 5. "Popular Tools." This is because the command inside the shell script expands to

```
sort -t: -k 4n,4 -k 3M,3 comics.1st ¦ more
```

once the `$@` construct is expanded to all the arguments on the `sm` command line. Now enter

```
sm. -t: -k3M,3 < comics.1st
```

This is almost the same as the last time, except that `comics.1st` is provided as input by redirection rather than by specifying it as an argument.

What happens this time? The `sort` command has a number of options like `-t:` and the `-k` options, but it doesn't have any input file. Therefore it reads the standard input. Because of the `comics.1st` on the command line, the standard input is read from `comics.1st`; therefore, you once again see the `comics.1st` file sorted according to year and month.

Control Structures

Control structures let you make more ambitious shell scripts. For example, there is a control structure that lets you test a condition and take different actions depending on the result. This lets you write "smarter" shell scripts that can take different possibilities into account and act accordingly.

Command Status Values

Before discussing control structures themselves, it's important to understand the idea of *command status values*.

When a command finishes execution, it reports back to the shell; this lets the shell know that the command is done and that it's time to execute a new command. When a command reports back to the shell, the command has the opportunity to give the shell a status report. Most UNIX commands limit their status reports to "I succeeded" or "I failed." Commands can fail for many reasons; for example, a command might fail because you made a typing mistake on the command line, or because you didn't have appropriate permissions to perform a particular action, or because it didn't have the right number of arguments to work with.

The status report that a command presents to the shell is really just a single integer number. This number is called the command's *status value* or *return value*. As a loose rule of thumb, commands use a status value of 0 (zero) to report success and a status value of 1 to report failure. However, there are several commands that don't follow this rule; to find out the status values used by a particular command, see the *Diagnostics* section of the man page for that command.

Some commands use a wider range of status values. For example, `diff` returns the following values:

0 If the files that `diff` compares are identical

1 If the files that `diff` compares are different

2 If `diff` fails for some reason (such as a typing mistake on the command line)

By looking at the status value, the shell can determine the results of a command after the command has finished executing. For example, you can tell the shell to take one action if a command succeeded and a different action if the command failed. The next section describes the shell instructions that make this possible.

DOS Versus UNIX Status Values

Experienced DOS users may be aware that DOS commands are also capable of returning status values. On DOS systems, status values are called *exit codes*.

The *if* Construct

The `if` construct has the form

```
if condition

then commands
fi
```

where `condition` is a command and `commands` is a list of commands.

When the shell sees this construct, it begins by executing the `condition` command. If the status value of this command is zero, the shell executes the list of `commands`; otherwise, the shell skips past the `commands` and executes whatever comes after the `fi` line. (Note that `fi` is `if` backwards.)

For example, enter the following

```
if diff sonnet bonnet
then echo No difference
fi
```

(You should type these commands directly to the shell; don't put them in a shell script file.) When the shell executes the `if` construct, it begins by executing the `diff` command. Because the files `sonnet` and `bonnet` are identical, `diff` returns a status of zero. Because of this status, the shell executes the `echo` command that comes after `then`, and you'll see the output

```
No difference
```

As contrast, enter the following

```
if diff sonnet nursery >junk
then echo No difference
fi
```

Again, the shell begins by executing the `diff` command. This time the files are not identical and the status value is 1. Because the status is not zero, the shell skips the command that follows `then`. As a result, you won't see any output. (Note that the `>junk` construct on the `diff` command redirected the normal `diff` output so that it didn't clutter up the screen. On a true UNIX system, you could redirect into the null file `/dev/null`, but that doesn't work with MKS Tools.)

Entering `if` Constructs

When you typed the lines

```
if diff sonnet bonnet
then echo No difference
fi
```

you probably noticed that the shell prompted for the `then` line with > instead of the shell's usual input prompt. This shows that the shell isn't expecting you to enter a new command; instead, it's expecting you to enter a continuation of the previous line. You'll keep on getting the > prompt until you enter `fi`.

The shell doesn't take any action until you enter the `fi` to finish the `if` construct. For example, the shell doesn't try to execute the `diff` command. An `if` construct is considered to be a single instruction, even though it can contain several commands. The shell won't do anything until you've typed the entire construct.

As noted earlier in this section, you can put several commands in the `then` part of an `if` construct. For example, enter the following:

```
if diff bonnet sonnet
then
    echo No difference
    cat sonnet
fi
```

This `if` construct has two statements in its `then` part: an `echo` command and a `cat` command.

DOS IF

DOS has an IF command that can be used in batch files for much the same purpose as the UNIX `if` construct. However, the DOS IF can only execute a single command if a condition is met, unlike the UNIX `if`, which can execute any number of commands. In addition, the DOS IF is limited in the kinds of conditions it can test.

Indentation Style

The last example put the `echo` and `cat` commands on separate lines, and indented them from the left margin. Indenting these statements serves several purposes.

It makes the keywords then and fi stand out more clearly, because they are flush with the left margin and because they are the only words on their lines.

It emphasizes that the `echo` and the `cat` commands are grouped together: the shell either executes both commands or neither of them.

Some people prefer to put the `condition` of an `if` construct on its own line too, as in

```
if
    diff bonnet sonnet
then
    echo No difference
    cat sonnet
fi
```

With this style, only the keywords are flush with the left margin. In this way, the keywords stand out more clearly.

These techniques of indentation are all part of *programming style*. A good programming style arranges commands to make them more readable and to emphasize the underlying logic of the statements. The indentation in the preceding code section shows that the `if` construct is broken into two chunks: the first chunk (from `if` to `then`) is the `condition` part, and the second chunk (from `then` to `fi`) tells what to do if the condition is met.

Good programming style can actually help you avoid errors. For example, indenting commands makes it harder to forget the `fi` required to mark the end of the `if` construct. When you see

```
if
    condition
then
    command
    command
```

it's easier to remember that you need some kind of marker to indicate the end of the construct; you need something special to *cancel the indentation*.

You should work to develop a good programming style. A clear and consistent style makes your shell scripts easier to understand when you're writing them and when you're reading them later on.

The *else* Clause

if constructs can have the form

```
if condition
then commands
else commands
fi
```

If the condition command returns a status value of zero, the shell executes the commands that follow the keyword then. However, if the condition command returns any other status value, the shell executes the commands that follow the keyword else. For example, use vi to create a file named dif that has the contents shown in Listing 8.2.

 Listing 8.2. The dif shell script (first draft).

```
# This script finds the difference between two files.
# Differences are displayed with the more command.
# Uses "junk" as a temporary working file.
if
    diff $1 $2 >junk
then
    echo No difference
else
    more junk
fi
rm junk
```

This shell script uses diff to compare two files whose names are given as arguments to the script. The set of differences are written into a file named junk; again you could use /dev/null on a true UNIX system. If the two files are identical, the shell executes

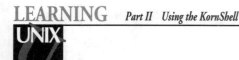
the echo command that follows then; otherwise, the shell executes the more command that follows else. After the fi that marks the end of the if construct, the script removes the junk file.

After you have created the dif file, leave vi and enter the command

```
alias dif= "dif."
```

so you don't have to worry about the trailing dot. Then enter

```
dif bonnet sonnet
dif sonnet nursery
```

You'll see that dif works very much like the usual diff command. However, when two files are identical, dif displays the message No difference (unlike the usual diff command, which does not display any output if the files are identical). In addition, dif displays diff's output with more so that you can look at the differences a screenful at a time rather than everything sliding by too fast to read.

Improving *dif*

In some ways, dif is superior to the normal diff command, because it displays a message if the files are identical and because it uses more to show its output. dif certainly has its weaknesses too. For example, you can specify several options with the command diff, but not with dif. However, this weakness in dif is easily overcome. Use vi to edit dif and change the diff command, as shown in Listing 8.3.

 Listing 8.3. The **dif** shell script (second draft).

```
# This script finds the difference between two files.
# Differences are displayed with the more command.
# Uses "junk" as a temporary working file.
# You may specify any options you like for the diff command.
if
    diff $@ >junk
then
    echo No difference
else
    more junk
fi
rm junk
```

This version of the command does not single out $1 and $2 as the only arguments to pass to diff. The special parameter $@ expands into all the arguments specified on the shell script's command line. For example, enter

```
dif -b -C 4 sonnet bonnet
```

As you might guess, `-b` and `-C 4` are possible options for `diff`. You can read about them in the `diff` man page if you want, but their meaning isn't really relevant to this example. The important thing to notice is that the `diff` command inside the shell script receives all the arguments that you specified on the `dif` command line, in the same order that the arguments were specified. With the preceding command line for `dif`, the `diff` command inside the script becomes

```
diff -b -C 4 sonnet bonnet >junk
```

The revised `dif` script is a reasonable substitute for the `diff` command in many instances. There are still times that you might want to use the real `diff` command, such as if you want to pipe the output to another command rather than just reading it on the display screen. However, you may find that most of the time you prefer using `dif` to `diff`.

This is one of the virtues of using shell scripts. With scripts, you can write your own versions of basic UNIX commands that are just as easy to use as the original commands but are better suited to your personal preferences.

The *elif* Clause

It's time now to return to other forms of the `if` construct. `if` constructs can also have the form

```
if condition1
then commands1
elif condition2
then commands2
elif condition3
then commands3
    ...
else commands
fi
```

`elif` is short for *else if.* If the `condition1` command returns a status value of zero, then the shell executes `commands1`. Otherwise, the shell goes on to execute the `condition2` command. If that returns a status value of zero, the shell executes `commands2`. Otherwise, the shell goes on to execute the `condition3` command, and so on. If none of the `condition` commands returns a status value of zero, the shell executes the `commands` after the `else` keyword.

As an example of this, use `vi` to create a file named `dif3` containing the shell script given in Listing 8.4. You pass this script three filenames as arguments. The script compares the files and tells you if any pair of files is identical.

 **Listing 8.4. The `dif3` shell script.**

```
# This script takes three filenames as arguments
# and determines if any pair of the files is identical.
if
    diff $1 $2 >junk
then
    echo $1 and $2 are identical
elif
    diff $2 $3 >junk
then
    echo $2 and $3 are identical
elif
    diff $1 $3 >junk
then
    echo $1 and $3 are identical
else
    echo No files match
fi
rm junk
```

When you have created the `dif3` file, leave `vi` and enter the following commands

```
dif3. bonnet sonnet nursery
dif3. bonnet nursery sonnet
dif3. bonnet nursery comics.lst
```

In each case, the script should tell you if any pair of files is identical.

Notice that the script contains three `diff` commands, to compare each possible pair of files. If a `diff` command finds a match, the following `echo` command displays an appropriate message and the shell proceeds to the end of the `if` construct. If a `diff` command finds that two files are not identical, the shell goes down to the next `elif` clause to compare another pair of files. If no files are identical, the shell goes to the `else` clause and executes the `echo` command to display `No files match`.

The script redirects all `diff` output into a file named `junk` and removes `junk` when all comparisons have been made. This is because the script is only interested in finding out if files are identical; if files are different, the script doesn't really care what those differences are.

The *test* Command

The `test` command returns a status value that indicates whether or not a particular condition is true. For example, the command

```
test -f name
```

returns a status of zero if name is the name of an existing file and returns a status of 1 otherwise. Table 8.1 shows many other uses of the test command.

Table 8.1. Uses of the `test` command.

Command	Meaning
Testing Pathnames	
`test -d name`	Is name a directory?
`test -f name`	Is name an ordinary file?
`test -r name`	Can you read name?
`test -w name`	Can you write to name?
Testing the Age of Files	
`test file1 -ot file2`	Is `file1` older than `file2`?
`test file1 -nt file2`	Is `file1` newer than `file2`?
Comparing Two Integers A and B	
`test A -eq B`	Is A equal to B?
`test A -ne B`	Is A not equal to B?
`test A -gt B`	Is A greater than B?
`test A -lt B`	Is A less than B?
`test A -ge B`	Is A greater than or equal to B?
`test A -le B`	Is A less than or equal to B?
Comparing Two Strings `str1` ***and*** `str2`	
`test str1 = str2`	Is str1 equal to str2?
`test str1 != str2`	Is str1 not equal to str2?
Testing a String to Be Null	
`test string`	Does string contain any characters?

test commands are obviously useful in if constructs. As an example, use vi to create a file named list that contains the text shown in Listing 8.5.

 Listing 8.5. The list shell script.

```
# This script displays information about files,
# directories, or other arguments.
if
    test -f $1
then
    more $1
elif
    test -d $1
then
    ls $1
else
    echo $1
fi
```

This script is designed to be called with a single argument. If the argument is a filename, the script uses more to display the contents of the file. If the argument is a directory name, the script uses ls to display the contents of that directory. Otherwise, the script merely echoes the argument. Notice that this example shows you can use positional parameters in test commands (you can use positional parameters anywhere in any script).

When you have created the list file, quit vi and enter the following commands:

```
list. sonnet
list. testdir
list. $HOME
```

You'll see that in all cases list provides information about the contents of the argument. You might use list as a general purpose utility for displaying information about things: list gives useful information about files, directories, and other arguments.

Reversing Tests

By putting an exclamation mark (!) as the first argument of a test command, you can reverse the sense of a test. For example,

```
test -d name
```

---

returns a status of 0 if name is a directory and returns a status of 1 otherwise.

```
test ! -d name
```

returns a status of 0 if name is not a directory and returns a status of 1 otherwise.

The *[]* Structure

The KornShell offers an alternate format for executing test commands. Instead of putting the word test at the beginning, omit the word and put the rest of the command in square brackets. With this technique, you can rewrite the list script, as shown in Listing 8.6.

 Listing 8.6. The `list` script with `[ ]`.

```
# This script displays information about files,
# directories, or other arguments.
if [ -f $1 ]
then
    more $1
elif [ -d $2 ]
then
    ls $1
else
    echo $1
fi
```

This format is slightly more compact than the test format, but doesn't really offer any other advantage. Some people prefer it, but the examples in this book will continue to use test.

The *for* Loop

The for loop is another control structure often used in shell scripts. Like loop structures in normal programming languages, the shell's for loop repeats a set of commands several times until a given condition is met. The format of the for loop is

```
for name in list
do commands
done
```

where `name` is a name that can be used as a variable name, `list` is a list of arguments, and `commands` is a list of commands. The shell begins executing the loop by assigning the first argument in `list` to the variable `name`. The shell then executes all the commands. When the last command has finished, the shell goes back to the top of the loop, assigns the next argument in `list` to `name`, and executes the commands again. The shell keeps repeating this process until it has executed the commands once for each argument in `list`.

You'll understand this more easily with an example. Enter the following as a command (not as a shell script):

```
for file in ?onnet
do
    echo $file
done
```

In this case, `name` is `file` and the `list` is created by the glob construct `?onnet`. This will be a list of all the files in the current directory with names ending in `onnet`. The `list` will therefore be

```
bonnet connet sonnet
```

To execute the `for` loop, the shell begins by assigning the name `bonnet` to the variable `file`. It then executes the `echo` command; the construct `$file` expands to `bonnet`, so the `echo` command displays this name. The result of the `for` loop is that it displays the names of all the files with names ending in `onnet`, one name per line.

The preceding `for` loop isn't very useful; you could do almost the same thing in several different ways.

```
echo ?onnet
find . -name "?onnet"
ls | grep "^.onnet$"
```

(Ask yourself how these three approaches differ. Enter the commands to see if you were right.) Listing 8.7 gives an example of a `for` loop that does a job that isn't as easy to do with other commands.

Listing 8.7. Counting the number of lines in files.

```
total=0
for file in ?onnet
do
    let j="$(wc -l <$file)"
    let total=$total+$j
done
echo $total
```

The commands in Listing 8.7 count the total number of lines in the onnet files. To understand how this works, you have to look at

```
let j="$(wc -l <$file)"
```

The $file construct expands to the name of one of the onnet files each time through the for loop. The command substitution uses wc -l to count the number of lines in the file given by $file. This results in a number that is assigned to the variable j. The next line is

```
let total=$total+$j
```

which adds the value of j to the current value of total. Just before the for loop, you set total to zero, so the total variable represents a running total of the number of lines in all the files examined so far. After the end of the loop, the command

```
echo $total
```

displays the final total of lines.

Niceties in the `let` Command

You may wonder why the command

```
let j="$(wc -l <$file)"
```

has this form. You can't just say

```
let j="$(wc -l $file)"
```

because wc will output the name of the file as well as the number of lines, and you can't assign a name to a numeric variable. However, wc doesn't display a filename if it is counting the number of lines in the standard input. Thus you might write

---

```
let j=$(wc -l <$file)
```

to get rid of the filename. But there's one more problem: the output of wc begins with blank spaces and you can't have blanks immediately after the = in a let statement. You can get around this problem by enclosing the command substitution in double quotation marks.

```
let j="$(wc -l <$file)"
```

This expands into a line of the form

```
let j="    integer"
```

where integer is the number of lines in the file. There are no blanks after the = and the let command works properly.

To expand on the previous example, use vi to create a file named linecnt that contains the text given in Listing 8.8.

 Listing 8.8. The `linecnt` shell script.

```
# This script counts the total number of lines in
# a set of files.
#
total=0
for file in $@
do
    let j="$(wc -l <$file)"
    let total=$total+$j
done
echo $total
```

This script is almost exactly the same as the previous example, except that it uses the $@ in the for statement. This stands for all the argument names given on the linecnt command line. Quit vi and enter the command

```
linecnt. sonnet nursery
```

You'll see that the script prints the total number of lines in the two files sonnet and nursery. In general, you can give the linecnt script any number of filenames and it will display the total number of lines in the entire set of files.

There are many ways you can produce a list of files for `linecnt`. For example,

```
linecnt. $(find . -type f -print)
```

uses command substitution to produce the list of files whose lines you want to count. The `find` command obtains the names of all files under the current directory, and the `linecnt` command counts all their lines. As another example,

```
linecnt. s*
```

produces a line count for all the files whose names begin with `s`.

Local Variables

The `linecnt` script creates variables named `total` and `j`. If the script is executing in a subshell, these variables will exist in the subshell but not in the original shell that invoked the script. Remember that the subshell's environment is separate from the original shell's environment, and the subshell variables are not shared by the original shell.

Variables like `total` and `j` are said to be *local* to the subshell and are called *local variables*. You can only use them inside the shell script itself. They cannot be used outside the script and they cannot affect anything outside the script.

On the other hand, if you execute a script with the period command, the script executes inside the original shell environment. When the script creates a variable, the variable is created in the original shell. In this case, the variables aren't local because they are considered part of the original shell's environment.

Combining Control Structures

You can combine several control structures at once. For example, enter the following:

```
for file in $(find . -name "?onnet" -print)
do
    if
        test $file -nt nursery
    then
```

```
        more $file
    fi
done
```

This uses find to produce a list of all names ending in onnet under the current directory. The for loop repeats the if construct for each one of those names. The if construct tests to see if each file is newer than nursery; if so, it displays the file contents with more.

Notice that I used several levels of indentation to make it easier to understand the different sections of the command. As shell input becomes more complicated, indentation becomes more important if you want to be able to make sense out of what you are writing.

Other Control Structures

The shell offers several other control structures that you may find useful for writing shell scripts. The following list gives an overview of these structures; the sh man page gives full descriptions.

- The while loop repeats a set of commands while a given condition is true.

- The until loop repeats a set of commands until a given condition becomes true.

- The case construct lets you break a given situation up into cases and take a different set of actions in each case.

- The select construct can be used inside shell scripts to prompt a user for a reply and to take different actions depending on the reply. This is useful if you want to set up scripts that offer users a *menu* of possible actions.

- The time construct lets you time how long it takes the shell to execute a given command or pipeline.

Shell Functions

A *shell function* is similar to a subprogram in a programming language like Pascal or C. A shell function is a collection of shell commands that can be executed together as a single command, in much the same way that shell scripts let you execute a collection of commands with a single command line. Shell functions can be executed inside shell scripts or in normal interactive sessions.

Shell functions are well suited to jobs you perform frequently. As with shell scripts, aliases, and other features, you can use functions to reduce the amount of typing you have to do, and to make it unnecessary to remember complicated commands or command sequences.

Before you can use a shell function, you must *define* the function. The definition of a shell function looks like this:

```
function name
{
    commands
}
```

where `name` is the name you choose to give the function and `commands` are the commands that make up the function. Notice that the `commands` are enclosed in *braces*. The part inside the braces is called the *body* of the function.

Function Names

Function names have the same form as variable names. They can contain uppercase characters, lowercase characters, digits, and the underscore (_) character. The first character cannot be a digit.

As a simple example of a function, enter the following:

```
function cdl
{
    cd $1
    ls
}
```

This defines a function named `cdl`. After you type the function definition, nothing special happens; the shell just prompts you for a new command. When you type a function definition, the shell just stores the definition until you actually use the function. I'll show you how to use the `cdl` function in a moment. Right now, notice that the statements in the body of the function look much like statements in a shell script. In particular, you see the `$1` construct. This stands for the first argument of the function, just as it stands for the first argument of a shell script when it appears in a shell script.

To use the function, you just enter the function name followed by any arguments to the function. For example, enter

```
cdl /
```

When the shell tries to execute this line, it goes back to the definition of the `cdl` function and executes the commands in the body of the function. As you might guess, it substitutes the appropriate function argument in place of each positional parameter. Thus the shell executes

```
cd /
ls
```

when it executes the function. In this way, `cdl` uses `cd` to go to a new directory, then uses `ls` to list the contents of the directory. I find that I use this function a lot when I'm working with UNIX. When I `cd` to a new directory, I almost always want to list the contents of that directory before I do anything else; by using `cdl`, I can `cd` and list the contents with a single command. Now enter

```
cdl -
```

and you'll go back to your previous directory. Again, `cdl` lists the contents of that directory as well.

Shell functions can use control structures such as `if` constructs and `for` loops. A shell function can call other functions and shell scripts.

Shell Functions Versus Shell Scripts

Anything you can do with a shell script you can do with a shell function, and vice versa. However, there are a few differences between the two.

Shell functions are always executed within the shell's own execution environment. This means that instructions within a function can affect the shell's variables, options, and so on; shell scripts can't affect the shell's environment unless you execute them with the dot command.

Also, the shell saves shell functions directly in memory. This means that functions can be executed faster than shell scripts. The shell can execute a function immediately, but to execute a script, the shell has to search for the appropriate file containing the script, the read in the file.

As a general rule of thumb, then, shell functions are good for things that you do a lot, where small savings in time can add up to something significant. Shell scripts are good for jobs that you do less often; they are also good for very lengthy sets of instructions, since shell functions occupy memory inside the computer, and the more memory you use to store a function, the less memory you have for other purposes.

The *exit* and *return* Commands

Earlier sections explained that normal UNIX commands return status values. Shell scripts and shell functions also can return status values, using the exit and return commands. These commands have the form

```
exit expression
return expression
```

where expression is the same sort of expression that you use with let commands. The exit command is used to return a status value from a shell script; the return command is used to return a status value, either from a shell function or from a shell script executed with the dot command. When the shell encounters either of these commands inside a shell function or shell script, it evaluates the expression and immediately returns the result as the status value of the function or script. Notice that these commands tell the shell to return immediately, even if there are more commands left in the function or script.

As an example of exit, use vi to edit the dif shell script created in an earlier section so that the contents are as shown in Listing 8.9.

 Listing 8.9. The dif shell script (third draft).

```
# This script finds the difference between two files.
# Differences are displayed with the more command.
# Uses "junk" as a temporary working file.
# You may specify any options you like for the diff command.
if
    diff $@ >junk
then
    echo No difference
    rm junk
    exit 0
else
    more junk
    rm junk
    exit 1
fi
```

In this version, I have introduced two exit statements. The script returns a status value of 0 if there are no differences and returns a status value of 1 if differences are found. In this way, dif sets its status values in much the same way that diff does.

Notice that the `then` and `else` clauses both contain `rm` commands before the `exit` command. The script has to get rid of the `junk` file before executing an `exit` command; after you execute an `exit` command, the script is finished, so you have to make sure that all the necessary work is done before you `exit`.

Just for the sake of interest, Listing 8.10 shows another way you could rewrite `dif`. Inside the `if` construct, the script assigns an appropriate status value to the variable `stat` but doesn't actually return. After the end of the `if` construct, the script executes an `rm` command to remove the `junk` file, and then executes `exit` to return the value of `stat`. In this way, you don't have to put an `rm` command in each part of the `if` construct; you put it after the end of the construct and then return.

 Listing 8.10. The `dif` shell script (fourth draft).

```
# This script finds the difference between two files.
# Differences are displayed with the more command.
# Uses "junk" as a temporary working file.
# You may specify any options you like for the diff command.
if
    diff $@ >junk
then
    echo No difference
    stat=0
else
    more junk
    stat=1
fi
rm junk
exit $stat
```

Chapter Review

A shell script is a text file that contains shell instructions. In order to execute a shell script on a UNIX system, you must have execute permission on the file.

There are three ways to execute a shell script. You can execute a command whose command name is the name of the script file, as in

```
scriptname
```

You can execute the script in a subshell by using a `sh` command and specifying the name of the script file as an argument, as in

```
sh scriptname
```

Finally, you can execute the script with the dot command, as in

```
. scriptname
```

When you use the dot command, the script is executed in your current shell's environment; this means that commands in the script can affect your current shell, by setting options, creating variables or aliases, and so on. If you execute the script directly or in a subshell, the script is executed in a separate environment and it cannot affect your current shell's environment.

If a line of input to the shell contains a number sign (#), the rest of the line is ignored. This lets you put comments into shell input (such as in shell scripts or shell functions).

You can pass arguments to shell scripts and shell functions. Inside the script or function, the symbol $1 stands for the first argument value, the symbol $2 stands for the second argument value, and so on. The symbols $1, $2, and so on are called *positional parameters.* The shell also recognizes several special parameters, shown in Table 8.2. Parameters are not expanded if they are enclosed in single quotation marks, but they are expanded if they appear in double quotation marks.

Table 8.2. Special parameters discussed in this chapter.

Parameter	Meaning
$#	The number of arguments passed to the script or function.
$@	A list of all arguments, each a separate argument.
$*	A list of all arguments, as a single argument.

The shift command gets rid of arguments in the list of arguments passed to a shell script or function. For example,

```
shift 2
```

gets rid of the first two arguments in the list so that the third argument becomes $1.

When a command finishes execution, it returns a status value (or return value) to the shell. A status value of zero usually indicates that the command succeeded and a higher status value indicates that the command failed. However, some commands use their status values in different ways.

The most general form of an `if` construct is

```
if condition1
then commands1
elif condition2
then commands2
elif condition3
then commands3
    ...
else commands
fi
```

In this construct, all conditions are commands. If `condition1` returns a status value of zero, the shell executes `commands1`. Otherwise, the shell executes `condition2`. If this returns a status of zero, the shell executes `commands2`, and so on. If none of the `condition` commands returns a value of zero, the shell executes the commands following the `else`. You can omit the `elif` or `else` clauses if you don't need them.

The `test` command lets you test a variety of conditions about pathnames, the age of files, numbers, and strings. It is often used in `if` constructs. The following command forms are equivalent:

```
test expression
[ expression ]
```

Table 8.1 lists many uses of the `test` command.

The `for` loop has the form

```
for name in list
do commands
done
```

The shell executes the `commands` once for each item in the `list`. Each time it executes the `commands`, it assigns one of the items in the `list` to the variable `name`.

A shell function is like a subprogram in a programming language. The definition of a shell function has the form

```
function name
{
    commands
}
```

When a command line begins with the name of the shell function, the shell executes the `commands` specified in the definition of the function. You can pass arguments to the function and refer to the values of those arguments using positional parameters.

Inside shell scripts, you can use the statement

```
exit expression
```

to return a status value to the shell. Similarly, you can use the statement

```
return expression
```

from inside shell functions or shell scripts executed with the dot command. As soon as the shell encounters an `exit` or `return` statement, it evaluates the `expression` and immediately quits the shell script or shell function that contains the statement.

Exercises

1. Create a file containing the names of all the files under your home directory and its subdirectories. Use `vi` to edit this file into a shell script that performs `ls -l` on each of these filenames. Run the shell script.

2. Create a shell script named `finds` that takes exactly the same kind of arguments as `find`. The difference between `finds` and `find` should be that the output of `finds` is sorted in alphabetical order.

3. Create a shell script named `last` that just displays its last argument, no matter how many arguments it is passed. For example,

   ```
   last A B C D
   ```
   displays D.
   ```
   last A
   ```

   displays A. (Hint: $# tells how many arguments there are.)

4. Create a shell script named `run` that takes a command line as its argument. The script runs the command line as it is specified, except that the standard error for the command is redirected to a file named `err`.

5. Rewrite the `last` shell script (which was written in an earlier exercise) as a shell function.

6. Suppose that the shell variable `re` contains a regular expression. Write a shell function named `gp` with arguments that are text filenames and that searches for the value of `re` in all those files. For example, if you assign

   ```
   re = "^T.*e$"
   ```

   the `gp` function should search for lines that begin with T and end in e.

7. Suppose your favorite word processor is named wpr and you invoke this word processor with a command line of the form

```
wpr filename
```

You can only specify one filename on the wpr command line, so you can only edit one file at a time. However, you want to be able to edit a list of files, such as a list produced by the glob construct *.doc. Write a shell function that accepts a list of filenames as its arguments and that invokes the wpr word processor on each filename in the list. (As soon as you quit using wpr to edit one file, the function will start wpr again to edit the next file.)

CUSTOMIZING

As mentioned in earlier sections, UNIX can be customized to a greater extent than almost any other operating system. This chapter examines some approaches to customizing, primarily with the KornShell but also with vi.

The key to customizing the KornShell is to create a *profile file*. Typically, a profile file is a shell script containing instructions that set shell options, create aliases, define shell functions, and do any other work that you'd like to automatically do each time you log in.

The chapter also examines the role that certain shell variables play in customizing. In particular, you'll see how to change the string that the shell uses to prompt you for input. You'll also see how to use the UNIX PATH variable (analogous to the DOS PATH command) to tell the shell where to find the programs you want to run. The which and WHENCE commands can help you find out where the shell finds particular programs if you become confused.

Next, the chapter examines the *passwd file.* This file contains information about all the authorized users of a UNIX system, and provides such information as the name of your home directory and the shell that you've chosen to use.

Finally, the chapter looks at *initialization files:* files that contain commands to set up sessions with software packages like vi. With an initialization file, you can automatically set up options for your vi sessions, without having to type a lot of commands every time you start the editor.

Profile Files

Over the past few chapters you've seen several useful options that control the behavior of the shell. Among these are

```
set -a
```

which marks all subsequently created variables for export,

```
set -o vi
```

which lets you edit commands with vi editing facilities and

```
set -x
```

which shows you the expansions of all commands that the shell executes. You've also seen how aliases and shell functions can save you time and trouble as you work with the shell.

One drawback to the way you've used the shell so far is that your entire environment disappears whenever you log out. This means that every time you log in, you have to remember to set up the options that you want, any aliases you'd like to use, and so on. This is more than just an annoyance; if you want to set up a lot of things when you log in, you have to do a lot of typing, and the more typing you do, the more likely it is that you'll make a mistake.

If you think a little, you should be able to come up with a solution to this problem. The easiest approach is to write a shell script that sets all your options, creates any aliases and shell functions that you want, and does any other work you'd like to do before you start using the shell. Each time you log in, you could execute the shell script to do all your set-up work. Note that you'd have to execute the script with the period command so that the instructions affect your original shell environment; otherwise the script executes in a separate environment and does not affect the shell environment.

In fact, the KornShell makes this process even easier. Whenever you log in to the shell, the shell automatically tries to execute a *profile file* before it does anything else. For most people, a profile file is a shell script that sets options, creates aliases, and so on. After you've created that profile file, the shell automatically executes the instructions in the file each time you log in. In this way, your session is automatically customized according to your tastes whenever you start up.

Types of Profile Files

There are two types of profile files.

- A *global* profile file sets up the environment for everyone using your UNIX system.

- A *personal* profile file sets up the environment for a single user.

On a true UNIX system, the global profile file is stored in the file

```
/etc/profile
```

With MKS Tools, there is no global profile file, but you can create one if you want, under the name

```
/lu/etc/profile.ksh
```

On a true UNIX system, your personal profile file should be named

```
.profile
```

under your home directory. With the MKS Tools, your personal profile file should be named

```
profile.ksh
```

under your home directory. Table 9.1 summarizes these names.

Table 9.1. Profile filenames.

Name	Description
`/etc/profile`	Global profile on true UNIX
`/lu/etc/profile.ksh`	Global profile for MKS Tools
`$HOME/.profile`	Personal profile on true UNIX
`$HOME/profile.ksh`	Personal profile for MKS Tools

When you log in, the KornShell executes the instructions in the global profile file first (if there is one). Then the shell looks to see if you have a personal profile file. If so, the shell executes that file too. On most UNIX systems, the global profile file sets up some *default* options, aliases, and so on. You can then use your personal profile file to change those defaults or to add to the environment.

Your Personal Profile File

If you look at the file `profile.ksh` under your home directory, you'll see that it contains the following:

```
PATH=".;c:/lu/bin"
export PATH
```

This is an extremely simple profile; it just sets a single variable named PATH and marks that variable for export. Later in this chapter you'll see what the PATH variable is used for.

It's time now to create a more sophisticated profile file. For the purposes of this book, please use `vi` to edit `profile.ksh` under your home directory so that it contains the shell commands given in Listing 9.1. This suggested profile file contains a more sophisticated setting for PATH than your old profile file. It also sets the three options mentioned earlier, creates the alias p for the more command, and defines the shell function `cdl` discussed in the last chapter. Make sure that you put in all the quotation marks shown.

 Listing 9.1. Suggested personal profile file (first draft).

```
# Sample profile file
PATH="c:/lu/bin;."
export PATH
set -a
set -o vi
set -x
alias p="more"
function cdl
{
    cd $1
    ls -x
}
```

After you've created the `profile.ksh` file, log out and log in again. During the log-in process, the shell automatically finds your personal profile file and executes its contents. To see that this has actually happened, enter the command

```
p profile.ksh
```

This should display the contents of `profile.ksh`, because your profile has set up `p` as an alias for `more`. The shell should also display

```
+ more profile.ksh
```

Because the profile file `set` the `-x` option, the shell displays the expansion of each command before executing it.

Future sections will suggest additions and changes to this personal profile. The file is the key to automatic customizing of all your interactions with the shell. You should also think about what you would like to see in your profile file.

> What aliases will make your life easier? Consider an alias for every lengthy command that you type frequently.

> What shell functions would you find convenient to have available? Consider a shell function for any series of commands that you tend to type frequently.

> What variables would you like to define or change? Consider a variable for any piece of information you want to remember.

> What actions do you commonly perform when you first log in? For example, I usually list the contents of my home directory whenever I start a session, so I've put that command directly into my profile file.

Shell Variables and Customizing

Shell variables play a major role in customizing UNIX sessions. The sections that follow discuss some of the most useful of these.

Changing Your Prompt

The `PS1` variable controls what the shell uses to prompt for input. For example, enter the command

```
echo "$PS1" test
```

and you'll see that the command displays

```
$  test
```

There are two blank spaces between the $ and the word test. This is because the value of PS1 is actually "$ " (with a blank after the dollar sign). This is what the shell has used to prompt for commands since you started these exercises. The value of PS1 is called your *command prompt string.* The echo command displays the value of PS1 (ending in a blank), then another blank and the word test, because echo always puts a single blank between output arguments.

To change your command prompt string, you just have to change the value of the PS1 variable. For example, enter

```
PS1="What now? "
```

After you press Enter, you'll see that the shell prompts you for your next command by saying

```
What now?
```

Notice that there's a blank after the question mark; a little bit of whitespace makes it easier to distinguish the prompt from the commands you enter. If the command prompt string contains an exclamation mark (!) character, the shell replaces the character with the number of the command in the shell history file. For example, enter

```
PS1="now-!% "
```

and you'll get prompts of the form

```
now-1%
now-2%
   . . .
```

You'll probably see different numbers than the ones shown previously; the numbers are based on your shell history, and everyone has a different shell history.

Many people find that this kind of prompt makes it easier to use the r command to re-execute previous commands. The prompt shows you the number of each command, so you don't have to look up the appropriate number by typing history.

Putting the Current Directory in Your Prompt

You'll recall that the value of the PWD variable is the name of your current working directory. Many people find that it's useful to have this directory name as part of their prompt; this reminds you what your current directory is, no matter where you cd to. You can put the current directory name into your prompt by making PWD part of your command prompt string. Enter

```
PS1='$PWD-!% '
```

It's important to enclose the string in single quotation marks as shown previously. If you only use double quotation marks, the shell immediately expands the $PWD into the name of your current working directory, and then assigns the result to PS1. This means that you'll always see the name of your working directory at the time that you assigned the string to PS1. However, if you enclose the prompt string in single quotation marks, the shell doesn't try to expand anything inside the quotation marks immediately. PS1 is assigned the value

```
$PWD-!%
```

Whenever the shell displays a prompt, it expands the $PWD into the name of the current directory. To see this in action, enter the commands

```
cd testdir
cd ..
```

You'll see that the prompt changes as your current directory changes.

Choosing a Prompt

You may want to experiment now with various prompt formats until you get one that you like. When you do, you can add an appropriate

```
PS1=prompt
```

line to your personal profile file so that the shell will use this prompt every time you log in.

The Secondary Prompt

You'll recall that when you enter a multiline construct like a for loop or a function definition, the shell uses a > to prompt for input. This is called the *secondary prompt string,* and it can be changed as easily as you changed your command prompt string.

The variable that controls the secondary prompt is named PS2. For example, enter

```
PS2="More> "
if
    diff sonnet bonnet
then
    echo No difference
fi
```

You'll see that the shell uses the string `"More> "` to prompt for the internal lines of the `if` construct. When you reach the `fi` that ends the construct, the shell executes the construct, then goes back to prompting with your command prompt string.

If you want to go back to the default secondary prompt, you can enter the command

```
PS2="> "
```

Notice that there's a space after the > character; this puts a little gap between the > prompt and whatever you type, making it easier for you to read what's on the screen.

Search Paths

One of the major purposes of the shell is to read the commands you want to execute and then to execute those commands. Some commands (such as `set`) are built into the shell, but most are not. When a command is not built into the shell, the shell must find a file containing the command and execute that command. This file may be a normal program (in a binary file), or it may be a shell script (in a text file). Both these types of files are called executable files, or *executables*.

When you issue a command, the shell has to find the appropriate executable for that command. To do so, the shell looks through a sequence of directories and sees if any of the directories contains a file with a name that matches the command name. If you're an experienced DOS user, you know how DOS lets you use the PATH command to tell the shell which directories to examine. The UNIX approach is similar. However, less-experienced DOS users may not be familiar with PATH and related concepts, so this section will deal with the subject from scratch.

A *search path* is a list of directories. On true UNIX systems, the names in this list are separated by colon (:) characters. With the MKS Tools, the names in the list should be separated by semicolon (;) characters. The MKS Tools can't use colons because these might be confused with DOS device names (such as C:).

When you log in, the shell sets up a default search path and assigns this to the shell variable PATH. To see what your current search path is, enter

```
echo $PATH
```

The value of PATH is sometimes called your list of *search rules*.

When you enter a command, the shell first checks to see if the command name is an alias, the name of a shell function, or one of the built-in commands of the shell. If not, the shell checks under the first directory in your search path to see if that directory contains a file matching the command name. If the directory contains such a file, and if the file is executable, the shell executes the contents of the file. Otherwise, the shell checks the next directory in the search path for a matching file that is executable. The shell goes through the directories in the order specified until it finds a match or it gets to the end of the list.

On true UNIX and UNIX look-alike systems, a file only matches the command name if the names are identical. For example, if you have asked to execute the diff command, the shell looks for a file named diff under one of the directories in the search path. The case of letters is important; for example, a file named DIFF or Diff doesn't match the command name diff.

With the MKS Tools, the differences of the DOS system force some changes. The following list gives the rules for matching filenames and command names:

- The case of letters isn't important. diff is the same command as DIFF, Diff, and so on.

- If a command name has a suffix, the shell looks for a file with the same basename and suffix. For example, if the command name is xyz.abc, the shell looks for a file named xyz.abc.

- If a command name has a null suffix, the shell looks for a file with the same name and with no suffix. This is why the previous chapter executed the simple file by specifying the simple. command. You had to specify a null suffix (just the .) to tell the KornShell to look for a file without a suffix.

- If the command name doesn't have a suffix, the shell looks for a file with the same basename and with any one of the suffixes

  ```
  .com    .exe    .bat    .ksh
  ```

  For example, if the command name is xyz, the shell looks for xyz.com, xyz.exe, xyz.bat, or xyz.ksh (in that order).

To see this in action, use vi to create three shell scripts. The first should be written into the file /lu/bin/showpath.ksh and should contain the command

```
echo Hello! /lu/bin/showpath.ksh
```

The second should be written into the file showpath.ksh under your home directory, and should contain the command

```
echo Hello! showpath.ksh
```

The third should be written into the file testdir/showpath.ksh under your home directory, and should contain the command

```
echo Hello! testdir/showpath.ksh
```

Obviously, each of these three scripts is designed simply to tell the name of the file that contains the script.

When you've created the file, enter the command

```
PATH="/lu/bin;$HOME;$HOME/testdir"
```

(It's very important to use double quotation marks as shown previously.) This setting for PATH says that you want the shell to look for commands in the /lu/bin first, then in your home directory, and then in the directory testdir under your home directory. Now enter the command

```
showpath
```

You'll see that the output is

```
Hello! /lu/bin/showpath.ksh
```

The shell looked for showpath under the /lu/bin directory first and found a matching file. (Remember that when a command name doesn't have a suffix, the shell accepts a filename made out of the command name with the suffix .ksh.) The shell therefore executed the shell script from /lu/bin/showpath.ksh.

It's important to stress that there are three shell scripts that could be executed as the showpath command: the one in /lu/bin, the one under your home directory, and the one in testdir. The shell executes the first one it finds as it goes through your search rules, and it ignores the presence of the other two candidates.

Now enter the commands

```
rm /lu/bin/showpath.ksh
showpath
```

The rm gets rid of the showpath.ksh under the /lu/bin directory. Now when you execute the showpath command, the output is

```
Hello! showpath.ksh
```

In accordance with your search rules, the shell looked under the `/lu/bin` directory, but couldn't find any matching files. It therefore looked under the next directory in the search path, namely your home directory. It found a matching file and executed it. The output shows that the shell executed the `showpath.ksh` file under your home directory.

Now, enter the commands

```
PATH="/lu/bin;$HOME/testdir;$HOME"
showpath
```

(Make sure you put in the quotation marks when you assign the value to `PATH`.) The assignment to `PATH` changes the order of directories in the search path. Now, the output of the `showpath` command is

```
Hello! testdir/showpath.ksh
```

because the shell executes the `testdir` version of the script. The shell finds the `testdir` version of `showpath` before it finds the version in your home directory, so that's the one that the shell executes.

PATH in Your Profile File

The best way to specify your search path is to add an appropriate line to your profile file, setting your `PATH` variable to your desired search rules. In this way, you don't have to set `PATH` manually and risk the possibility of making a typing mistake.

The *whence* Command

As the previous section shows, it's possible to have several different versions of the same command. Your `PATH` variable determines which version the shell will execute.

The `showpath` scripts were written to make it easy for you to tell which version was executing. With other commands, the situation can be more confusing. Therefore the KornShell offers the `whence` command that can clarify the situation. Enter

```
whence showpath
```

and the KornShell tells you the name of the file it would execute if you issued a `showpath` command. Using `whence`, you can see how your search rules affect which command version gets executed.

The whence command can give information on other types of commands. For example, enter

```
whence -v p set cdl
```

whence tells you that p is an alias (set up in your profile file), set is a built-in command, and cdl is a shell function. The -v option tells whence to indicate the type of each command.

The /lu/bin Directory

If you experiment with setting your own search rules, make sure that the directory /lu/bin is always somewhere in the search path. This is the directory where the MKS Tools package stores all the common commands like cp, rm, more, and so on. If you leave out /lu/bin, the shell won't find any of the everyday UNIX commands and you won't be able to do much work.

Search Paths and the Current Directory

Experienced DOS users know that the DOS COMMAND.COM command interpreter always searches for executables under your current directory before it searches through any of the directories in your search path. It does this regardless of whether you explicitly specify your current directory in the search path.

With UNIX shells, the situation is different. A UNIX shell only searches the directories given in your search path. If you want the shell to search your current directory, you have to put the directory into your path.

You'll recall that the dot . character stands for the current directory. For example, enter

```
PATH= "/lu/bin;."
```

(Make sure you put in the quotation marks.) This setting for PATH says that you want the shell to search /lu/bin first, then your current directory. Note that the . stands for whatever is your current directory at the time that you enter the command. Enter the commands

```
cd $HOME
showpath
cd testdir
showpath
cd
```

When you are in your home directory, the shell executes showpath from your home directory; when you are in testdir, the shell executes showpath from testdir.

As a short form, the KornShell lets you omit the dot from the search path. For example, you can write either

```
PATH= "/lu/bin;."
PATH= "/lu/bin;"
```

and get the same effect. Similarly you can write either

```
PATH="/lu/bin;.;$HOME/testdir"
PATH="/lu/bin;;$HOME/testdir"
```

to say that the shell should search /lu/bin, then the current directory (whatever that is at the time), then testdir under your home directory. I think omitting the dot is confusing, but it is a very common practice in some circles, so you should be prepared for it.

What Your Search Path Should Be

Until you get more experience with UNIX, you probably shouldn't try to set your own search path, by hand or in your profile file. During the log-in process, the system sets a default PATH that will let the shell find all the standard UNIX commands.

When you start writing your own commands (programs and shell scripts), you'll have to change your PATH so that the shell can find those commands. The most common technique is to create a directory named bin under your home directory and to store all your personal executables under that directory. You would then change your profile to create a PATH that had your bin directory as the first directory in the list. In this way, the shell always starts by seeing if you have a personal version of a command in your bin directory; if you don't, the shell then goes on to check other directories.

The first directories in your search path should be the ones where standard commands like cp and rm are found. For MKS Tools, this is

/lu/bin. Most UNIX users prefer to put the current directory . (dot) as the last in the list, or else omit . altogether.

Always remember to mark PATH for export. Other software may need to search for commands too.

The *passwd* File

On every UNIX and UNIX look-alike system, there is a file named /etc/passwd that holds information about all the authorized users of the system. With the MKS Tools, the file is named /lu/etc/passwd, but it serves the same purpose.

Enter the command

more /lu/etc/passwd

and you'll see what the file looks like. There is one line for each authorized user.

You're the One...

In most cases, your user ID will be the only one in the passwd file, because the MKS Tools are geared toward one student at a time. However, there are ways to obtain passwd files for several users at once, as explained in Appendix G, "Installing the MKS Tools Package."

Each line in the passwd file is divided into fields. The fields are separated by colon : characters on a true UNIX system, and by semicolons on DOS. Each line contains the following fields:

- A *user name* (log-in id). the rest of the line provides information about that user.

- An *encrypted password.* this is a version of the password you enter when you log in. However, the password has been *encrypted.* This means that it has been put into a special code so that people reading the password file cannot figure out what your true password is. The encryption technique is sometimes called a *one-way scheme.* Such a scheme makes it easy for the computer to encrypt the password, but very difficult for someone to decrypt the result. On true UNIX systems, the encrypted password is always 13 characters long, but UNIX look-alikes may differ.

■ Your *user number*. On a true UNIX system, each user is assigned a number as well as a log-in name. With the MKS Tools, this number is always 0.

■ Your *group number*. On a true UNIX system, this number would indicate your primary group. With the MKS Tools, this number is always 0.

■ A *comments field*. This can contain anything, but most sites use the field to give a user's full name. With the MKS Tools, the comment field contains `Learning UNIX`. This field is also called the GECOS or GCOS field.

■ The *name of your home directory*. This is how the log-in procedure finds out the name of your home directory. It assigns this directory name to the `HOME` variable.

■ A *command line* for invoking your shell-previous chapters have mentioned that different users can have different shells. When you log in, the log-in procedure checks your entry in the `passwd` file to find out which shell you want to use. The log-in procedure then uses the command line from `passwd` to invoke your chosen shell.

Various commands let you change parts of your `passwd` entry for the purpose of customizing. For example, you've already seen how the `passwd` command lets you change your password.

vi Initialization Files

The shell's profile file is an example of an *initialization file*. Whenever you invoke a new copy of the shell (either when you log in or when you start a subshell with `sh -L`), the shell executes the commands in your profile file as if you were typing those commands as input. In this way, the profile file *initializes* your shell session, by creating aliases, setting options, defining functions, and so on.

Several other UNIX programs accept initialization files too. For example, you can create an initialization file for `vi`. Such a file would have the same form as the command files discussed in Chapter 6, Text Files—Veni, Vidi, *vi*:" a sequence of `vi` commands that would normally begin with the colon : character. Chapter 6 showed that you could use command lines of the form

```
vi -c "so cmdfile" editfile
```

With this command line form, vi executes the commands from cmdfile first, then reads in editfile so that you can begin editing it.

In order to see how initialization files work, use vi to create two command files in your home directory. First, create a file named viab that contains

```
ab xyz XYZ Widgets Inc. International
```

This instruction says that xyz is an abbreviation for XYZ Widgets Inc. International. Next create a file named ex.rc that contains

```
set tabstop=4
```

This instruction sets tab stops every four columns. When you have created the two files, quit vi.

Now, enter the command

```
vi
```

to start editing a new file. When the MKS Tools version of vi begins executing, it automatically looks for a file named ex.rc under your home directory. If it finds such a file, it executes the commands in the file before it does anything else. To see how this works, enter a to begin appending text, and then enter a tab and the string xyz!.

You'll see that vi displays four blank spaces in place of the tab. Your ex.rc file contained the instruction to set tabs every four columns. vi automatically executed this instruction when it started, so your tabs are set every four columns automatically.

The Name of the vi Initialization File

On a true UNIX or UNIX look-alike system, the name of the vi initialization file is .exrc, not ex.rc. However, DOS doesn't allow filenames that begin with a dot, so the MKS Tools have to use ex.rc.

Now press Esc and quit vi by typing

```
:q!
```

This just quits without saving the text. Now enter the command

```
vi -c "so viab"
```

This starts vi again, but this time it specifies that vi should read viab as a command file. Press a to begin entering text again, and then enter a tab and the string xyz!.

Once again, you'll see that `vi` displays four blank spaces in place of the tab. This is because `vi` has read your `ex.rc` file again. However, you'll also see that the string `xyz` changes into `XYZ Widgets Inc. International`. The `-c "so viab"` option told `vi` to read initialization commands from `viab` as well as from the `ex.rc` file. In this way, you've specified two initialization files, not just one.

Quit `vi` by pressing Esc and typing

```
:q!
```

```
alias vix = 'vi -c "so viab"'
```

This sets up an alias that automatically specifies the `viab` initialization file. Notice that you must put double quotation marks around `so viab`, and single quotation marks around everything after the = sign. After you have set this alias, a command like

```
vix connet
```

lets you edit the `connet` file. Whenever you want, you can use the abbreviation `xyz` as you edit `connet`.

This kind of setup can be very useful. You can create any number of abbreviations in the `viab` file. When you start an editing job where those abbreviations might come in handy, you can use the `vix` alias to set up those abbreviations automatically. In other editing jobs, however, where the presence of the abbreviations would just be confusing, you can use the `vi` command directly; this doesn't use `viab` as a command file, so you don't have to worry about the abbreviations.

Note that both `vix` and `vi` itself read the `ex.rc` file. Thus you can use `ex.rc` to set up options and initializations that you would like every time you use `vi`. For example, your `ex.rc` can set tab stops, set your `wrapmargin`, and so on.

Other Initialization Files

Several other UNIX commands accept initialization files. For example, electronic mail packages often accept initialization files named `.mailrc` and the RCS revision control system (discussed in the next chapter) uses `.rcsrc`. The `rc` at the end of such names could be taken as a short form for *reconfigure,* because the initialization files let you reconfigure the way the software behaves.

Discussing software packages like `mail` is outside the scope of this book. The important point to remember is that initialization files are used by many software packages, to let you customize the way that the software behaves.

Chapter Review

A profile file is typically a shell script containing shell instructions. Whenever the shell starts up, it looks for your profile file and executes the instructions in that file. This means that you can use your profile file to set options, create aliases, define shell functions, and do any other work you would like to do every time you log in.

Profile files often set variables that control the behavior of the shell. Table 9.2 summarizes the shell variables discussed in this chapter.

Table 9.2. Shell variables discussed in this chapter.

Variable	Meaning
PS1	Command prompt string
PS2	Secondary prompt
PATH	Search path

If the PS1 string contains the ! character, the shell replaces that character with the command number each time the shell prompts you to enter a command.

A search path is a list of directories. When you enter a command that is not a built-in command, shell function, or alias, the shell searches through the directories in your search path, looking for an executable file whose name matches the command name. If and when the shell finds a matching file, it executes that file in order to carry out the command.

The whence command provides information about command names. It can identify aliases, shell functions, and built-in commands. It can also tell you the file that will be executed to carry out a normal command.

Unlike DOS, a UNIX shell will not search the current directory unless its name appears in the search path. This means that you must put . as one of the directory names in the search path if you want the shell to look for commands in the current directory.

The file /etc/passwd (/lu/etc/passwd with the MKS Tools) contains a line for each authorized user of a UNIX system. This line provides such information as the name of the user's home directory and the user's chosen shell. Thus, the file controls some of the most basic facets of your use of the system.

The profile file is an example of an initialization file. An initialization file supplies instructions that a particular command carries out whenever that command begins execution. `vi` accepts an initialization file in your home directory named `.exrc` (`ex.rc` with the MKS Tools). This file should be a `vi` command file, containing `vi` instructions that you would normally enter beginning with a colon `:`. One good use of `vi` command files is to create a series of abbreviations that you can use when creating files.

Exercises

1. Change your profile file so that it uses `banner` to say `Hello!` every time you log in. When you've made this change, log out and log in again to make sure you've done it correctly. Then edit your profile file to get rid of this silly instruction.

2. Change the definition of `PATH` in your profile file so that the shell only searches the `/lu/bin` directory, then your home directory, then the current directory.

3. Make a copy of `/lu/etc/passwd` named `/lu/etc/oldpass`. Use `:` to edit `/lu/etc/passwd` to change your home directory to `/lu`. Log out and log in again to see if the change worked. Then copy `/lu/etc /oldpass` back to `/lu/etc/passwd` so that things go back to the way they were.

# Chapter 10

Specialized Topics

This chapter surveys several topics that, although they are important for understanding the current state of UNIX, didn't fit into previous chapters. There are no exercises in this chapter, and no instructions for you to try on your machine. The MKS Tools do not support the software discussed in this chapter, either because of the limitations of the DOS system or the limited amount of space on the disks that accompany *Learning UNIX*. Unlike the rest of the book, this chapter is not a how-to guide; instead, it's an armchair travelogue, intended to provide further glimpses of the UNIX world.

The travelogue starts with a quick tour of some of the useful software packages commonly associated with UNIX.

- *Revision control* software enables you to keep a complete history of the changes that take place in a file. For example, I used a revision control package to keep track of the various drafts of this book, as the text went through copyediting, technical editing, proofreading, and all the other stages of preparation. This let me see what changes were made along the way, and also gave me a chance to recover older drafts of the book when that became necessary.

- The awk programming language is a cross between a programming language like C and a noninteractive text editor like sed. It is particularly good for *rapid prototyping:* the quick production of programs to solve an immediate need or to test aspects of software design.

- The make program automatically keeps a collection of related files in synch with each other. It was originally created to help programmers make and remake programs, but it can be used in almost any situation where a set of files must be kept up-to-date with each other.

- The troff program lets you create formatted documents for hard copy or display on the terminal screen.

After looking at these software packages, the chapter turns to a few facts about running UNIX systems. The job of being a UNIX system administrator is worthy of a complete book, all on its own, and it's impossible to do more here than sketch some of the simplest principles. However, in the future some readers may find themselves in charge of a microcomputer that runs UNIX, and such people may be grateful for any sort of help.

Finally, the chapter turns its attention to a feature that can't be simulated on DOS, but one that gives UNIX much of its appeal: its ability to run several programs simultaneously. In particular, you'll learn about *foreground* and *background* jobs and how you can use them productively.

A Taste of Popular UNIX Software

As mentioned in Chapter 1, "Operating Systems," some of the most inventive and popular software of the past two decades was created on UNIX systems. The sections that follow offer a taste of what's available on UNIX systems today. The list is highly selective and doesn't begin to cover many important software packages; nevertheless, it should give you a head start on a few programs you may want to learn more about.

Revision Control

Computer files are seldom fixed; they change with time. Documents are edited and revised. Spreadsheets receive new data and expand to fit more sophisticated needs. Software packages are updated as new releases are issued. More than 40 percent of the files on my personal computer have changed in the past year, and I suspect that percentage is low compared to those of many other users.

A *revision control* software package lets you keep track of the changes in your files. In effect, it keeps a *history* of all the revisions you make. This has several useful aspects.

It provides a record of what changes were made and the reasons for them. This is particularly important if several people are working on the same project. Suppose, for example, that Clark and Lois are working together on a report. If Clark makes several changes to Chapter 1 of the report, Lois can use the revision control software to identify the changes that Clark made and keep up-to-date on what's happening. Clark can also remind himself what he did, in case he forgets later on.

You can recover earlier versions of a file. For example, suppose that Clark and Lois create a report and take the document to their boss, Perry. Perry tells them to make some revisions, but when they present him with a new draft, he decides he liked the first one better. (We've all had bosses like that!) With revision control software, Clark and Lois can immediately go back to the previous version. The package can restore any earlier version of the file in almost no time.

You can avoid interfering with each other. For example, suppose both Clark and Lois decide they want to change Chapter 1 of the report at the same time. (Remember, several people can use the same UNIX system simultaneously.) If Clark is the first one to start editing the report, the revision control software will prevent Lois from starting too; it will tell her that Clark is already at work on the file. This warning system prevents people from getting in each other's way and working at cross purposes.

There are several popular revision control software packages on UNIX, but the two most prominent are Revision Control System (RCS) and Source Code Control System (SCCS). The two work in different ways.

With RCS, every file on the system has an associated *history file*. The history file has a complete copy of the most recent version of the file. It also has a record of the changes between the most recent version and the second most recent, the changes between the second most recent and the third, and so on back to the original version. Because changes tend to be minor from one version to the next, the history file doesn't take up nearly as much disk space as storing complete copies of all versions would. However, the history of changes is enough to let you reconstruct any version of the file. You can start with the current version of the file and work backwards through the changes to reproduce any earlier version. Usually, history files are only a little larger than the current version of the file, but they provide information on all versions.

SCCS also uses history files, but the information is stored in an entirely different way. The history file is modeled after the original version of the associated file. At points where the original file has changed, there are records showing what changes were made. As more and more changes are made, more and more change records are embedded into the history file at the locations where the changes are made.

In summary then, an RCS history file starts with one complete copy of the associated file, then has a list of all the changes made from the previous file, a list of all changes made from the one before that, and so on. An SCCS history file is one big file, with entries scattered throughout the file showing how versions of the file differ at those locations.

The *awk* Programming Language

awk was developed by Aho, Weinberger, and Kernighan of AT&T Bell Laboratories. As a programming language, it is closely related to the C programming language. Many statements in awk look the same as statements in C, so awk is a good stepping stone toward C. awk is found on most UNIX systems, and is a good program to turn to when you want to perform single actions on text files quickly.

awk is also a good first language for people who would like to learn how to program. It's simple, and you can write useful programs soon after you start learning the language. (With many other languages, you have to learn a great deal of background before you can understand the simplest programs.) This short section can't do justice to awk's versatility, but it can give an overview of how awk works.

All awk programs perform operations on text input. The general form of an awk program is

```
criterion { actions }
criterion { actions }
criterion { actions }
criterion { actions }
    ...
```

awk reads a specified data file line by line. After awk reads a line of input, it checks to see if that line meets one or more of the specified criteria. If so, awk executes the actions associated with the matching criteria. After awk has finished checking the line against all the given criteria, it reads the next line and does the same thing all over again.

Here's a simple example of an awk program:

```
/^abc/  { print }
/^def/  { print "Hello!" }
```

This program has two statements. The criteria of the statements are both regular expressions, of the sort accepted by vi, grep, and other commands. The first statement says that if a line begins with the string abc, awk should print the line. The second statement says that if a line begins with the string def, awk should print Hello!. When you use this awk program, you specify a data file; awk then reads through the data file line by line, checking each line against the specified criteria, and taking appropriate action for lines that meet the criteria.

There is a great deal more to the awk programming language, but this gives you the general idea. Because of its extreme simplicity, I often turn to awk when I want to whip off a program quickly. awk automatically takes care of tedious details that other programming languages make you deal with from scratch.

The *make* Program

People who program on UNIX like to break their programs into a lot of small files. As a rule, they use a separate file for each subprogram, and they try to keep each subprogram short (usually no more than 50 lines of text, unless there's a very good reason for going longer). This means that a single program can be produced from a huge number of smaller files; more than 100 files is not an unusual amount for large software packages.

Typically, the programmer creates many *source files,* containing instructions in a programming language like C or Pascal. Next these source files are sent through a compiler program to produce *object files.* An object file is a translation of the original source file into a format that is close to the internal language of the machine. The object files are often gathered together into an *object library,* which is a single file containing all the separate object files. Object libraries usually take up less disk space and can be easier to work with than a lot of little object files. Finally, separate object files and object libraries must be *linked* together to form a single, unified program.

This means that a programmer has many files to keep track of: source files, object files, object libraries, and final programs. If the programmer changes one of the source files, it's necessary to remake the corresponding object file, the object library, and the final program. This is a lot of work, and if you're changing a lot of source files, it's easy to forget to update some of the corresponding object files. The problem is multiplied if several people are working on the program; a change made by one worker can affect a file belonging to another worker, and keeping track of which files have to be updated can get very confusing.

make avoids this confusion. To use make, you create a *makefile,* which shows the interdependencies between the files that make up a program. For example, object files depend on source files, object libraries depend on object files, and the final program depends on its object libraries. When you run make, it checks the *change times* of all these files to determine which files need to be updated. For example, if the change time on a source file is more recent than its corresponding object file, the object file must be updated to stay in synch with the source. But make also realizes that a change in the object file necessitates updating the object library, which necessitates updating the final program.

The makefile doesn't just show interdependencies; it also tells how to update any file that needs to be updated. Thus make uses the information in the makefile and automatically updates every part of the program that needs updating. Programmers don't have to keep track of what work needs to be done; make figures out what needs to be done and does it for you.

The *troff* Text Formatter

The troff text formatting program is frequently used for producing documents on UNIX and UNIX look-alike systems. It is quite different from word processors like WordPerfect or Microsoft Word. troff has more in common with programming languages than it does with conventional word processors.

The input to troff is a text file containing the text of the document, interspersed with instructions for formatting that text. Formatting instructions are also given in text format. For example

```
.sp 1v
```

is a formatting instruction that tells troff to space down one vertical line. There are similar instructions for all the usual text formatting operations: changing font, indenting lines, adding headers and footers to the page, and so on.

When you want to create a document with troff, you process this kind of input with the troff program itself. You don't actually interact with troff; you prepare the input file ahead of time (with a text editor such as vi), then simply submit the file to be processed by troff. Thus, you can start the formatting process, then go off and do other work while the job is running.

troff formatting instructions are very basic. For example, there is no single instruction to start a paragraph; you might have to issue several instructions to do the job. For example, you might have to put an instruction that spaces down from the previous paragraph, and another instruction to indent the next output line by an appropriate amount. Obviously, this situation has drawbacks; you have to do a lot of typing to get a simple effect (such as starting a paragraph), and there's always the possibility you'll forget one of the instructions and mess up the document.

For this reason, troff lets you create *macros,* which are combinations of several simple instructions. For example, you can create a "start paragraph" macro, a "put this in italics" macro, and so on. Most UNIX systems have several standard macro packages already provided for you, so you don't have to create macros of your own. The most popular macro packages are named mm, me, and ms, names derived from the command line option that lets you specify what macro package you want to use.

In recent years, another text-formatting program called TeX (pronounced *Teck*) has been increasingly popular on UNIX systems. TeX works in the same way as troff, although the format of the input is different. One popular macro package for TeX is called LaTeX (pronounced *Lay Teck*).

Basic System Administration

Historically, UNIX systems have offered few software tools for system administration. In the absence of such tools, each manufacturer of UNIX or a UNIX look-alike system has created its own software packages to do these jobs.

This situation complicates any discussion of UNIX system administration. For example, consider the process of making backup copies of UNIX files. Many UNIX and UNIX look-alike systems offer their own backup software, and each of these software packages is different. This book can't examine all the different packages, so it can only discuss techniques that work on all UNIX and UNIX look-alike systems. Such techniques are probably inferior to the specialized software offered by individual manufacturers; therefore, if you find yourself in charge of a UNIX machine, you are strongly advised to read the system administration documentation and to seek out any special commands especially designed for your specific system.

The Superuser

On every UNIX and UNIX look-alike system, one user ID is designated as the *superuser*. The superuser has user number zero, and often has the user name root. However, this can vary from system to system.

The superuser can do anything on the system. The kernel never checks the superuser's permissions, so the superuser can access any file. The superuser can also control any of the programs running on the system, and can terminate those programs if necessary.

Various system administration jobs can only be performed by the superuser. For example, the superuser is the only user who can create new device files, in order to make new devices available to other users. In addition, the superuser is often the only user who can create new userids or new groups.

In order to use the superuser's powers, you must log in as the superuser. To do so, you must know the superuser's password, which is set up at the time that UNIX is installed on the machine. The superuser can change the password with the usual passwd command.

At large UNIX sites, several people may be told the superuser password. Because the superuser can do anything on the system, you don't want too many people knowing the password, because that can cause security problems. On the other hand, it's risky for only one person to know the password; if something happens to that person, many system administration jobs (like backups) can come to a halt.

Backups

If a system doesn't offer its own backup software, the tar command is often used as an alternative. Usually, system backups must be run by the superuser, because the superuser is the only person who has permission to access every file on the system.

Chapter 5, "Popular Tools," showed how you can use the tar command to write directories to a diskette. To make backups, you use the same principle. However, there's a catch. You must make sure that the backup medium (whether it's a diskette or tape) has enough space to hold all the data you want to back up. Ideally, of course, you want your backup software to be smart: if it fills up one diskette, it should ask you to put in another diskette, then continue writing to the new diskette. However, most versions of tar don't work that way. If they run out of space on a diskette, they just give up. Fortunately, the MKS Tools tar command is smart enough to know when it needs another diskette and will prompt you accordingly.

If you have a lot of data to back up and you want to use tar, you're forced to do the backups in chunks. Make a list of all the files you want to back up, then break this list into subsets, where each subset is small enough to fit on a diskette. Run tar for each of these subsets, using an empty diskette each time.

Alternatives to `tar`

The cpio and pax commands are alternatives to tar. They work on the same basic principle. They can save many directories and files in a single file archive. If you find a UNIX or UNIX look-alike that doesn't have tar, look for cpio or pax instead.

The tar command is often used to transfer sets of files from one machine to another. For example, software packages are often distributed as tar archives. If you want to transfer several files to another system, you might put copies of all those files together in one directory, then use tar to save that directory on diskette. Take the diskette to the destination system, and use tar to extract the files from the diskette.

Background and Foreground Modes

Chapter 1, "Operating Systems," mentioned that UNIX can run several programs simultaneously. This is one of the system's greatest strengths: it lets you do several things at once. Pipelines are one example of this capability. The programs in the pipeline start simultaneously. As soon as the first program begins producing output, the output is piped to the second program so that it can start working too, and so on all through the pipeline. By running several programs simultaneously, you can get results faster and more easily than if you ran them one at a time.

There are many kinds of jobs that take a long time to complete and don't produce output directly on the screen. For example, most of the stages of writing programs—compiling, linking, and so on—fit into this category. With many operating systems, you type a command line, then sit around waiting for the job to finish. This can take minutes or even hours if the job is big enough.

On UNIX, you don't have to sit and wait. Instead, you can tell the system to run such jobs in the *background* while you do other work at the keyboard. It works like this:

1. When you issue a command, you can put an ampersand (&) at the end of the command line. This tells the shell that you want the command to run in the background.

2. The shell starts the command running, then immediately prompts you for another command. The first command keeps running, but you can do other work in the meantime. For example, a programmer can start compiling one file, then immediately go on to edit additional files. The job that is running on its own is called a *background job;* the jobs that you are doing at the terminal are called *foreground jobs.*

3. If the background job produces output, the output appears on your screen as it is produced. Because this can get in the way of other work, you usually redirect the output of the background job.

4. When the background job finishes, it may notify the shell that it's done. The shell then displays a message telling you that the job has been completed.

You can have any number of jobs running in the background. For example, you might use

```
cc file1 >out1 2>err1 &
cc file2 >out2 2>err2 &
cc file3 >out3 2>err3 &
cc file4 >out4 2>err4 &
```

to start compiling four files in the background. (cc is the usual UNIX command for compiling C programs.) Notice that the command lines redirect both the standard output (into the out files) and the standard error (into the err files) so that this output doesn't get lost and doesn't get in the way of what you're doing in the foreground.

The ps command tells you what programs you currently have running, both in the foreground and the background. Each program is identified by a number, called the program's *process ID.* This number is used to identify programs for various purposes. In particular, the kill command lets you terminate a background job if there's some good reason to do so (such as you suddenly realize you made a mistake); to kill the correct job, you have to specify that job's process ID, as reported by ps.

None of these commands can really be simulated on DOS, because DOS can only run one job at a time. This overview has been provided to let you know about the possibility of running jobs in the background on UNIX. When you start using a real UNIX or UNIX look-alike system, read the man pages for ps and kill to see how they work.

Chapter Review

Revision control software keeps track of all the changes that have been made to a file. It helps you identify what changes have been made from one version to the next, lets you recover previous versions of a file, and can prevent people from interfering with each other as they work on the same project.

The awk programming language is a simple language well suited to being a novice's first programming language. An awk program takes the form

```
criterion { actions }
criterion { actions }
criterion { actions }
criterion { actions }
    . . .
```

When you apply such a program to a data file, awk reads through the data file line by line. If a line meets one or more of the specified criteria, awk executes the actions associated with those criteria. awk then reads the next line, checks the criteria, and so on.

The make program helps keep a collection of files in synch with each other. It does so by consulting a makefile, which states all the interdependencies of the files in question. The makefile also tells make how to update any file that needs updating.

The troff program takes text files as input and produces formatted documents. troff input consists of the words of the document interspersed with formatting instructions. Macro packages make it easier to produce documents, by combining basic formatting instructions into more sophisticated actions.

Most UNIX systems offer their own system administration software, and there is little uniformity in the way that different systems approach system administration tasks. One common facet of system administration is the use of a user ID called the *superuser*. The kernel lets the superuser access any file on the system and control all executing processes.

While individual systems can offer their own backup software, many sites use tar, cpio, or pax for backing up files. These commands can also be used to create archives, convenient for transferring several files or directories to other systems.

Programs can run in two modes on a UNIX system. In foreground mode, the process can interact with the terminal in the normal way. In background mode, the process is cut off from the terminal to some extent, executing on its own without interacting with the user. Background mode is ideal for commands that take a long time to do the work and that do not need to interact with you, such as compiling programs.

Part
III

COMMAND
MANUAL
PAGES

INTRODUCTION TO
MANUAL PAGES

The documentation describing UNIX commands is made up of *man pages,* which is short for *reference manual pages.* This section of the book contains man pages for the MKS Tools package. Before I get to the actual man pages, however, I'll discuss the format of the pages and how to understand them.

How to Read a Manual Page

UNIX documentation is traditionally divided into several numbered sections.

Section 1 describes the standard utility commands (cp, vi, and so on).

Section 2 describes the basic services provided by the kernel. These man pages are organized according to *system calls* that programmers can use in their programs. A system call looks like a subprogram written in the C programming language. For example, the kernel provides facilities that let a program open a file. The open system call is presented as a C subprogram that programs can use when they want to open files.

Section 3 describes additional subprograms that programmers can use when they are writing programs. For example, this section would contain an explanation of the C programming language's fopen subprogram. fopen stands for *file open;* the fopen subprogram calls open to open a file, then does some additional work to prepare the file for use by the C program. Writing programs with Section 3 subprograms is like building a house with prefabricated parts; you still use the same basic materials (the system calls), but someone else has already put them together to make your job faster and easier.

Section 4 describes the formats of files used by various utilities. For example, Section 4 would show what a tar archive looks like inside.

Section 5 provides supplementary information on various topics. For example, several of the appendixes to this book are based on Section 5 documentation from the MKS Toolkit package.

Within each section, topics are in alphabetical order. Additional sections may be added for such topics as system administration procedures, communication features, games, and so on. Section 3 is often divided into subsections, one for each programming language. For example, subprograms for the C programming language would be in Section 3C, while subprograms for the FORTRAN programming language would be in Section 3F.

It's common to refer to man pages by name and section. For example, the description of the tar utility in Section 1 would be tar(1). The description of the tar archive file format in Section 4 would be tar(4).

The rest of this chapter describes the parts of a Section 1 man page as used in this book. The format of this book's man pages is similar to the format of man pages for any UNIX or UNIX look-alike system; when you can find your way through a *Learning UNIX* man page, standard UNIX documentation should look familiar to you.

Section 1 Only

Learning UNIX only offers Section 1 man pages. This book doesn't deal with programming, so there's no point in providing Sections 2 or 3. Section 4 information tends to vary from one UNIX system to another, because different manufacturers use different file formats with their software. Finally, the appendixes provide as much Section 5 information as you'll need to use the MKS Tools productively.

Parts of a Manual Page

Man pages are divided into parts, with each part providing a different kind of information. The following sections describe the various parts of a man page for a utility command.

The Synopsis Section

Every Section 1 man page begins with a Synopsis section that gives a quick summary of the command's format. For example, here is the synopsis of the `ls` command.

```
ls [-AabCcdFfgiLlmnopqRrstux1] [pathname ...]
```

The synopsis takes the general form of a command line; it shows what you can type, and the order in which the arguments should appear. The parts that are enclosed in square brackets are optional; you can omit them if you choose. Parts that are not enclosed in square brackets must be present for the command to be correct. (Note that the square brackets are just markers to make the synopsis easier to read. You shouldn't enter these square brackets when you type an actual command.)

The synopsis begins with the name of the command itself. After the command name comes a list of options, if the command accepts any. UNIX options generally consist of a minus sign (-) followed by a single character, usually an upper- or lowercase letter. For example, `-l` and `-x` are two of the valid options for `ls`.

Unless otherwise stated, the order of options is not important. If you are going to specify several of this type of option for the same command, you can put all the option characters after the same dash; for example,

```
ls -l -x
ls -x -l
ls -xl
ls -lx
```

are all equivalent.

Because you can put a group of options together in one string, the synopsis usually puts them together. In the `ls` synopsis, for example, the options are given as

```
-AabCcdFfgiLlmnopqRrstux1
```

This means that the valid options are `-A`, `-a`, `-b`, and so on.

Some commands have options of the form

```
-name value
```

where `name` is the name of the option and `value` is some value for the option. For example, the `banner` command synopsis is

```
banner [-c char] [-f fontfile] [-w n] [text ...]
```

This synopsis shows several options of this form. For example, consider

```
-w n
```

This option controls how many characters wide the output of `banner` will be. In this case, the `name` of the option is `w` and the value is `n`. Notice that `n` is written in italics. In a command synopsis, arguments written in italics are *placeholders* for information that you should supply when you enter the command. In this case, `n` stands for an integer that specifies the actual output width. When you type a `banner` command and choose to specify a `-w` option, you would put a number in place of `n`, as in

```
banner -w 72 "Hello"
```

Note

Whenever a synopsis contains a *placeholder* in italics, the rest of the man page will tell you what kind of value you should use to fill the placeholder.

Some commands contain options of the form

`-xvalue`

where there is no space between the letter of the option and its value. For example, the synopsis of the `sort` command contains an entry of the form

`-tx`

This is similar to the previous option type, except that there is no space between the argument `name` and its `value`. In this example, the name is `-t` and the value is represented by a placeholder `x`. As the rest of the `sort` man page explains, this placeholder stands for a single character. If you want to use the `-t` option for `sort`, you would type `-t` immediately followed by another character, as in

`sort -t:`

The `banner` synopsis ends with

`[text ...]`

As the italics suggest, this is another placeholder. The `...` indicates that you may enter a list of `text` strings, as in

`banner Each of these is a text argument`

The list supplied in the preceding command consists of the arguments

```
Each
of
these
is
a
text
argument
```

There are a few arguments that are used frequently:

`[file ...]`

stands for a list of filenames.

`[pathname ...]`

stands for a list of pathnames (which can be either filenames or directory names). It is common to use glob constructs to create lists of filenames or pathnames; for more information on glob constructs, see Chapter 4, "Five Ways to List a Directory."

The synopsis shows the order in which command line arguments should be specified. Typically, options must come immediately after the command name, and other

arguments come after the options. If a command has a special format that does not follow this order, the synopsis will show the order you must use.

The Description Section

The *Description* section describes what the command does and how you can use the command productively. It usually starts by explaining the command line synopsis, and telling what happens if you omit any of the optional arguments.

For complex utilities like the KornShell and vi, the *Description* section may be divided into subsections, each dealing with a particular aspect of using the utility.

The Options Section

The *Options* section lists the options accepted by the utility and what each of these options means. The options are often described in a table format to make it faster for you to pick out the options you want to use.

If a utility only takes a few options, there may not be a separate *Options* section. Instead, the options are discussed in the *Description* section.

The Examples Section

Some man pages have an *Examples* section, giving examples of how the utility can be used. The man page tries to give a mix of simple examples that show how the utility works on a basic level, plus more complex examples that show how the utility can perform sophisticated tasks.

The Diagnostics Section

The *Diagnostics* section shows the status values that the utility returns; status values are discussed in Chapter 8, "An Introduction to KornShell Programming." The *Diagnostics* section may also show some of the error and warning messages that the utility can display. Usually, the man pages only show messages that might be difficult to understand; the man pages often omit messages that are self-explanatory.

The Files Section

The *Files* section lists any *supplementary* files to which the utility may refer. Supplementary files are files that are not specified on the command line. Such files usually provide information that the command needs. For example, the *Files* section of the passwd man page mentions the /etc/passwd file because that is where a UNIX system stores password information.

The *Files* section may also mention temporary files that the command creates as it does its work. For example, the *Files* section of the sort command shows that sort may create temporary files with names of the form /tmp/stm* to hold partially sorted data.

The Limits Section

The *Limits* section lists any limits on the operation of the utility. For example, the *Limits* section of the diff command mentions that diff cannot handle files with lines longer than 1024 characters. Limits of this sort are inevitable when writing software, but MKS does its best to set the limits high enough so that they don't get in your way.

Some limits may depend on how much other work you are doing with the computer. For example, the amount of memory available to any DOS program depends on how many other programs you are already executing (Terminate-and-Stay-Resident programs, the shell, and so on). Such limits are seldom described in the *Limits* section because they are dictated by factors outside the utility's control.

The Portability Section

The *Portability* section lists other systems where the utility command is available. This information is important because of the many "flavors" of UNIX currently in use. As discussed in Chapter 1, "Operating System," there are many differences between UNIX and UNIX look-alikes, and utilities that are standard on one version may not be found on another version.

Most of the commands provided with MKS Tools are based on the POSIX.2 standard. MKS has taken great care to agree with the standard to the maximum amount possible on a non-UNIX system. Because the MKS Tools are based on the MKS Toolkit, the *Portability* section always mentions the MKS Toolkit. There are versions of the MKS Toolkit available for DOS, OS/2, and Windows NT.

The Portability section may also mention the X/OPEN standard. The X/OPEN corporation is a consortium of companies that leads in UNIX systems sales. Current members include Amdahl, Bull, DEC, Fujitsu, Hewlett-Packard, Hitachi, IBM, ICL, NCR, NEC, Olivetti, Siemens Nixdorf, Sun Microsystems, and Unisys. X/OPEN has produced a Common Applications Environment standard to ensure portability and connectivity of applications, and to allow users to move between systems without retraining. The X/OPEN specification is committed to conformance with POSIX, and defines a commercially viable operating environment.

Finally, the *Portability* section often discusses ways the MKS Tools version of a utility differs from other commonly available versions of the same utility.

The See Also Section

The *See Also* section refers to other man pages that may contain information relevant to the man page you have just read. For example, the man page for `alias` refers to the man page for `sh`, because aliases are handled by the shell. The man page for `alias` also refers to `unalias`, the command that can get rid of the aliases you create with `alias`.

The Warning Section

If a man page has a *Warning* section, the section contains important advice for using the command. In MKS Tools documentation, the *Warning* section is often aimed at those who are already familiar with UNIX; it tells how the MKS Tools may differ from the utilities on a true UNIX system.

The Notes Section

The *Notes* section offers additional notes about using the software. The *Notes* section serves approximately the same purpose as the *Warning* section: it provides important information that you shouldn't overlook. However, the *Notes* section usually addresses issues that are less serious than those covered by *Warnings*.

COMMAND MANUAL PAGES

alias—Display or Create Command Alias

Synopsis

```
alias [-tx] [name[=value] ...]
```

Description

alias displays or creates command *aliases*. alias is built into the KornShell.

How Aliases Work

When you type a command line, the shell checks to see if the first word of the line is a shell keyword (like cd, set, and so on). If it isn't, the shell checks to see if the word appears in the list of currently defined aliases. If it does, the shell replaces the alias with its associated string value. The result is a new command line that might begin with a shell function name, a built-in command, an external command, or another alias.

Generally, the shell only checks to see if the first word on the line is an alias. However, if the substituted value ends with a blank, the next word of the command line is also checked for aliases. This means that you can have aliases for things in the middle of a command line (such as filenames or options) as well as for the part of the command line that comes at the beginning.

When all aliases have been expanded on the original command lines, the shell checks the new command line for aliases and follows these same rules to expand the aliases. This process continues until no aliases are left on the command line or recursion occurs in the expansion of aliases.

Typically, you use aliases to simplify the job of entering a command. For example, you might set up a short alias to stand for a command that you type a lot (to save typing) or for a command that is complicated and hard to type (so that you only have to remember the alias, not the full command).

The Form of the *alias* Command

If alias is called without arguments, it displays all the currently defined aliases and their associated values.

If alias is called with arguments of the form

```
name=value
```

it creates an alias for each *name* with the given string *value*. From this point on, when the shell sees a command line that begins with *name*, it will replace *name* with *value*.

If alias is called with parameters of the form name without any value assignment, name and its associated value are displayed.

Options

The -x option marks each alias *name* on the command line for *export*. If -x is specified without any names on the command line, alias displays all exported aliases. Only exported aliases are understood in a *subshell* (a child process of the shell).

If you use the -t option, each *name* specified on the command line becomes a *tracked* alias. A tracked alias is assigned its full pathname the first time that the alias is used. Whenever you use the alias after this, the shell can find the appropriate command immediately using the full pathname, without doing the usual search through the directories in PATH. If you change PATH, the shell will reexamine the tracked alias the next time you use it, and assign a new value to the alias based on the new PATH. The same type of reexamination happens if you execute the shell command cd. Invoking alias with the -t option but without any specified names displays all currently defined tracked aliases.

If you issue the command

```
set -h
```

each command that you use in the shell automatically becomes a tracked alias.

There are several aliases built into the shell. These are described in Table M.1.

Table M.1. Aliases built into the KornShell.

Alias	Value
functions	typeset -f
hash	alias -t
history	fc -l
integer	typeset -i
nohup	"nohup "
r	fc -s

Any of these aliases can be removed or changed. See the relevant manual pages for details.

Examples

The command

```
alias
```

simply displays all currently defined aliases.

```
alias rm="rm -i"
```

defines rm as an alias. From this point on, when you issue an rm command, it automatically turns into rm -i and asks you to confirm each file being removed.

```
alias ls="ls -x"  p= "more"
```

defines two aliases: ls stands for ls -x, and p stands for more.

Diagnostics

Possible exit status values are

      0   Successful completion

      1   Failure because an alias could not be set

      2   Failure because of an invalid command-line option

If you ask alias to determine the values of a set of names, the exit status is the number of those names that are not currently defined as aliases.

Portability

KornShell. POSIX.2. MKS Toolkit. On UNIX, alias is a built-in command of the KornShell, but not of the Bourne Shell.

See Also

cd, fc, history, r, set, sh, typeset, unalias

banner—Display Text in Large Type

Synopsis

```
banner [-c char] [-f fontfile] [-w n] [text ...]
```

Description

If text arguments are specified, banner writes the arguments on the standard output in large letters according to a default font. If no such arguments are present, text is read from the standard input. Listing M.1 shows a typical example of banner output.

 Listing M.1. A typical use of banner.

```
banner hello
XXX                     XXX     XXX
 XX                      XX      XX
 XX          XXXXX       XX      XX         XXXX
 XX XXX   XX      X      XX      XX       XX   XX
 XXX XX   XXXXXXX        XX      XX       XX   XX
 XX  XX XX               XX      XX       XX   XX
XXX   XXX  XXXXX        XXXX    XXXX       XXXX
```

Options

By default, banner does not check the output line length or truncate the output to fit the line. If you specify the -w n option, the output width is limited to n characters at the most.

Output characters are normally formed from the X character. You can use the -c option to use any other single character in the output. The character used to make the large letters is called the *fill character*.

If you specify the -f option, banner obtains the output font from the specified fontfile instead of using the default font. To create your own fontfile, follow the fontfile examples mentioned in the following *Files* section.

Diagnostics

Possible exit status values are

0	Successful completion
1	Failure because of an unknown command line option, inability to open or missing font file, invalid font file format, missing fill character, or missing width

Files

/etc/small.fnt	Optional small font file
/etc/italic.fnt	Optional italic font file

Portability

X/Open Portability Guide. All UNIX systems. MKS Toolkit.

bc—Arbitrary-Precision Arithmetic Calculation Language

Synopsis

```
bc [-l] [-i] [file ...]
```

Description

bc is a programming language that can perform arithmetic calculations to arbitrary precision. It can be used interactively, by entering instructions from the terminal. It can also run programs taken from files.

If file arguments are specified on the command line, they should be text files containing bc instructions. bc will execute the instructions from those files, in the order that they appear on the command line. Then bc will execute instructions from the standard input. bc terminates when it executes a quit instruction or reaches the end-of-file character on standard input.

The *bc* Language

bc is a simple but complete programming language with a syntax reminiscent of the C programming language. This version of bc is a superset of the standard language available on most systems. It has several additional features intended to make the language more flexible and useful. Features that are unique to this implementation are noted in the text.

Input consists of a series of instructions that assign values to variables or make calculations. You can also define subprograms called *functions;* functions perform a sequence of instructions to calculate a single value.

bc displays the result of any line that calculates a value but does not assign the value to a variable. For example, the instruction

2+2

displays

4

bc saves the last value displayed in a special variable denoted by the dot character (.).

Numbers

Numbers consist of an optional minus sign (-) followed by a sequence of zero or more digits, followed by an optional decimal point (.), followed by a sequence of zero or more digits. Digits can be the usual 0 through 9, plus the hexadecimal digits A through F. These uppercase letters represent the values from 10 through 15. They must be uppercase.

A number must have at least one digit, either before or after the decimal point. If not, bc interprets the decimal point as the special variable (.) mentioned in the previous section.

A number can be arbitrarily long and can contain spaces. Here are some valid numbers with an input base of 10:

0   0.   .0   -3.14159   +09.   -12   1 000 000

Here are some valid numbers with an input base of 16:

0   FF   FF.3   -10.444   A1

See the following *Bases* section for more information on input bases.

You can break up numbers using spaces but not commas. For example, you can write `1000000` or `1 000 000`, but not `1,000,000`.

Identifiers

Identifiers consist of any number of letters, digits, or the underscore (_) character; the first character must be a lowercase letter. Spaces are not allowed inside identifiers. (Note: some versions of bc only let you use identifiers that are a single character long.)

Identifiers are used as names for *variables, functions,* or *arrays.*

■ A *variable* holds a single numeric value. Variables that are *local* to a function are declared using the `auto` statement, described in the *Functions* section. All other variables are *global* and can be used inside any function or outside all functions. You do not have to declare global variables. Variables are created as required, with an initial value of zero. Remember that there is also the special dot variable (.), which contains the last value displayed. Single numeric values and variables are sometimes called *scalars.*

■ A *function* is a name for a sequence of instructions that calculate a single value. Function names are always followed by a list of zero or more values enclosed in parentheses, as in `my_func(3.14159)`. Functions are discussed in more detail in the *Functions* section.

■ An *array* is a list of values. Values in the list are called the *elements* of the array. These elements are numbered; the first element in the array is always numbered `0` (zero). The number of an element is called the *subscript* or *index* of the element. Subscripts always appear in square brackets after the array name. For example, `a[0]` refers to element zero in the array `a` (the first element in the array). If a subscript value is given as a floating point number, bc discards the fractional part to make the subscript into an integer. For example, all of the following expressions refer to the same element.

```
a[3]   a[3.2]   a[3.999]
```

The valid array subscripts range from 0 to 32767 inclusive. In bc (unlike many other programming languages), you don't need to declare the size of an array. Elements are created dynamically as required, with an initial value of zero.

Because function names are always followed by parentheses and array names are always followed by square brackets, bc can distinguish among all three types of names.

Therefore, you can have variables, functions, and arrays with the same name. For example, `sample` can be a variable, while `sample()` is a function and `sample[]` is an array.

Built-In Variables

bc has several built-in variables that are used to control various aspects of the interpreter. These are described in the sections that follow.

Scale

The *scale* value is the number of digits to be retained after the decimal point in arithmetic operations. For example, if the scale is 3, at least three digits after the decimal point will be retained in each calculation. This would mean that

```
5 / 3
```

would have the value

```
1.666
```

If you specify the `-l` option on the bc command line, the scale starts with the value 20; otherwise it starts with the value 0.

The variable `scale` holds the current scale value. To change scales, assign a new value to `scale`, as in

```
scale = 5
```

Because `scale` is just a regular bc variable, it can be used in any bc expression.

The number of decimal places in the result of a calculation is affected by the scale but also by the number of decimal places in the operands of the calculation. Details are given in the *Operations* section that follows.

There is also a function called `scale()`, which can determine the scale of any expression. For example,

```
scale(1.1234)
```

returns a result of 4, which is the scale of the number 1.1234. The result of the `scale()` function is always an integer.

Bases

bc lets you specify numbers in different bases besides decimal, including octal (base 8) and hexadecimal (base 16). bc lets you input numbers in one base and output them in a different base, simplifying the job of converting from one base to another. It does this using the built-in variables ibase and obase.

ibase is the base for input numbers. It has an initial value of 10 (normal decimal numbers). To use a different base for inputting numbers, assign an integer to ibase, as in

```
ibase = 8
```

This says that all future numbers will be input in base 8 (octal). The largest input base accepted is 16.

When the base is greater than 10, use the uppercase letters as digits. For example, base 16 will use the digits 0 through 9, and A through F. The digits larger than 9 are allowed in any number, regardless of the setting of ibase, but they are usually inappropriate if the base is smaller than the digit. There is one useful exception: the constant A always has the value 10 no matter what ibase is set to, so

```
ibase = A
```

always sets the input base to 10, no matter what the current input base is.

obase is a variable that controls the base in which numbers are output. It has an initial value of 10 (normal decimal numbers). To change output bases, assign an appropriate integer to obase.

If the output base is 16 or less, bc displays numbers with normal digits and hexadecimal digits (if needed). The output base can also be greater than 16, in which case each "digit" is printed as a decimal value, and digits are separated by a space. For example, if obase is 1000, the decimal number 123456789 is printed as

```
123 456 789
```

Here, the "digits" are decimal values from 0 through 999. As a result, all output values are broken up into one or more "chunks," with three decimal digits per chunk. Using output bases that are large powers of 10, you can break your output into columns; for example, many people find that 100000 makes a good output base because numbers are grouped into chunks of five digits each.

Long numbers are output with a maximum of 70 characters per line. If a number is longer than this, bc puts a backslash (\) at the end of the line, indicating that the number is continued on the next line.

Internally, bc performs all calculations in decimal, regardless of the input and output bases. The number of places after the decimal point is therefore dictated by the scale when numbers are expressed in decimal form. For example, if the scale is 5, bc does calculations with five base-10 digits after the decimal point. If the result of a calculation is displayed in some other base, you might get less than five digits of accuracy in the new base because of the conversion from base 10 to the new base.

Arithmetic Operations

bc can perform a large number of arithmetic operations. In accordance with the usual arithmetic conventions, some operations are calculated before others; for example, multiplications take place before additions, unless you use parentheses to change the order of calculation. Operations that take place first are said to have a higher *precedence* than operations that take place later.

Operations also have an *associativity*. The associativity dictates the order of evaluation when you have a sequence of operations with equal precedence. Some operations are evaluated left to right while others are evaluated right to left. Table M.2 shows the operators of bc from highest precedence to lowest.

Table M.2. bc operators from highest precedence to lowest.

Operator	Associativity
( )	Left to right
unary ++, —	Not Applicable
unary -, !	Not Applicable
^	Right to left
*, /, %	Left to right
+, -	Left to right
=, +=, -=, *=, /=, ^=	Right to left
==, <=, >=, !=, <, >	Left to right
&&	Left to right
||	Left to right

If you're familiar with the C programming language, you should notice that bc's order of precedence is not the same as C's. In C, the assignment operators have the lowest precedence.

Next I describe what each operation does. In the descriptions, A and B can be numbers, variables, array elements, or other expressions. V must be either a variable or an array element.

(A)	An expression in parentheses is evaluated before any other operations are performed.
-A	Is the negation of the expression A.
!A	Is the logical complement of the expression. This means that if A is zero, !A is 1. If A is not zero, !A is 0. This operator may not be found in other versions of bc.
++V	Adds 1 to the value of V. The result of the expression is the new value of V.
— V	Subtracts 1 from the value of V. The result of the expression is the new value of V.
V++	Adds 1 to the value of V, but the result of the expression is the old value of V.
V —	Subtracts 1 from the value of V, but the result of the expression is the old value of V.
A^B	Calculates A to the power B. B must be an integer. If you let a be the scale of A and b be the absolute value of B, the scale of A^B is min(a * b, max(scale,a)), where min calculates the minimum of a set of numbers and max calculates the maximum.
A*B	Calculates A multiplied by B. If you let a and b be the scales of the two expressions, the scale of the result is the expression min(a+b,max(scale,a,b)).
A/B	Calculates A divided by B. The scale of the result is the value of scale.
A%B	Calculates the remainder from the division of A by B. This is calculated in two steps. First, bc calculates A/B to the current scale. It then obtains the remainder through the formula A-(A/B)*B calculated to the scale max(scale + scale(B), scale(A)).

A+B   Adds A to B. The scale of the result is the maximum of the two scales of the operands.

A-B   Calculates A minus B. The scale of the result is the maximum of the two scales of the operands.

The operators in the next group are all *assignment* operators. They assign values to objects. An assignment operation has a value: the value that is being assigned. Therefore, you can write operations such as

$a=1+(b=2)$

In this operation, the value of the expression inside parentheses is 2 because that is the value assigned to b. Therefore, a is assigned the value 3.

The recognized assignment operators are

V=B   Assigns the value of B to V

V^=B   Is equivalent to V=V^B

V*=B   Is equivalent to V=V*B

V/=B   Is equivalent to V=V/B

V%=B   Is equivalent to V=V%B

V+=B   Is equivalent to V=V+B

V-=B   Is equivalent to V=V-B

The following expressions are called *relations,* and their values can be either true or false. In some versions of bc, you can only use relations in the conditional parts of if, while, or for statements; however, this version of bc lets you use relations in any expression.

Relations work in exactly the same way as their counterparts in the C language. This means that the result of a relation is a number: 1 if the relation is true and 0 if the relation is false. For example, consider

V = (A > B)

If A is greater than B, the relation is true and therefore V is assigned a value of 1. If A is not greater than B, the relation is false and V is assigned a value of 0. The following list shows all the relations recognized by bc.

A==B   Is true if and only if A equals B.

A<=B   Is true if and only if A is less than or equal to B.

A>=B   Is true if and only if A is greater than or equal to B.

A!=B   Is true if and only if A is not equal to B.

A<B   Is true if and only if A is less than B.

A>B   Is true if and only if A is greater than B.

A&&B   Is true if and only if A is true (non-zero) and B is true. If A is not true, the expression B is never evaluated because bc can already tell the relation is false. This operator is an extension to the POSIX.2 standard.

A¦¦B   Is true if either A or B is true (or both). If A is true, the expression B is never evaluated, because bc can already tell the relation is true. This operator is an extension to the POSIX.2 standard.

Comments and Whitespace

A *comment* has the form

```
/* Any string */
```

Comments can extend over more than one line of text. When bc sees /* at the start of a comment, it discards everything up to the next */ and replaces the whole comment with a single blank.

As an extension to the POSIX.2 standard, this version of bc provides an additional comment convention using the # symbol. All text from a # to the end of the line is treated as a single blank, as in

```
2+2 # this is a comment
```

bc is *free format*. This means that you can insert blanks or horizontal tab characters anywhere you like to improve the readability of the code. Instructions are assumed to end at the end of the line. If you have an instruction that is so long you need to continue it on a new line, use a backslash (\) as the last character of the first line and continue on the second, as in

```
a = 2\
 + 3
```

The \ indicates that the instruction continues on the next line, so the preceding is equivalent to

```
a = 2 + 3
```

Instructions

A bc instruction can be an expression, an assignment, a function definition, or a statement. If an instruction is not an assignment, bc displays the result of the instruction after the calculation has been carried out. For example, if you enter

```
3.14 * 23
```

bc displays the result of the calculation. However, with

```
a = 3.14 * 23
```

bc does not display anything because the expression is an assignment. If you want to display the value of an assignment expression, put parentheses around the expression. For example,

```
(a=2)
```

displays the result 2.

Here are the instruction forms recognized by bc:

`expression`	Calculates the value of the `expression`.
`"string"`	Is a string constant. When bc sees a statement of this form, it displays the contents of the string. For example, the instruction `"Hello world!"` tells bc to display Hello world!. bc doesn't output a newline character after the string. This lets you issue such commands as `foo = 15 "The value of foo is "; foo`. With these commands, bc displays The value of foo is 15.
`statement ; statement ...`	Is a sequence of statements on the same line. In bc, a semicolon (;) and a newline character have the same effect: they both

| | indicate the end of a statement. bc executes the given statements in order from left to right. |
| {statement} | Is a brace-bracketed statement. Brace brackets are used to group sequences of statements together, as in |

```
{
statement
statement
 ...
}
```

As shown, brace brackets can group a series of statements that are split over several lines. Braces are usually used with control statements such as `if` and `while`.

| print expression, expression, ... | Displays the results of the argument expressions. Normally bc displays the value of each expression or string it encounters. This can make it difficult to format your output in programs. For this reason, the MKS bc has a `print` statement to give you more control over how things are displayed. `print` displays all of its arguments on a single line. It places a single space between adjacent numbers, but not between numbers and strings. A `print` statement with no arguments displays a newline. If the last argument is null, subsequent output will con- |

tinue on the same line. Here are some examples of how to use print:

```
/* basic print statement */
print "The square of ", 2,
"is ",2*2 The square of 2 is
4
/* insert a space between
adjacent numbers */
print 1,2,3
1 2 3
/* note - no spaces because
of null strings */
print 1,"",2,"",3
123
/* just print a blank line
*/ print
/* two statements with
output on same line */
print 1,2,3,"" ; print 4, 5,
6
1 2 3 4 5 6
```

void expression

void throws away or *voids* the result of the evaluation of the expression instead of displaying it. This is useful when using ++ and — operators or when you want to use a function but don't want to display the return value. For example void sample++ increments sample but does not print the result. The void statement is not found in other versions of bc.

if (relation) statement

Tests whether the given relation is true. If so, bc executes the statement.

Otherwise, bc skips over the statement and goes to the next instruction. For example,

```
if ( (a%2)==0 ) "a is even"
```

displays a is even if a has an even value.

```
if (relation) statement1
else statement2
```

Is similar to the simple if statement. It executes *statement1* if *relation* is true. Otherwise it executes *statement2*. It can be used as follows:

```
if ( (a%2)==0 ) "a is even"
else
"a is odd"
```

Note that there is no statement separator between a is even and the else keyword. Here is another example:

```
if (a<10) {
   "a "
   "is "; "less than 10 "
   a
} else {
   "a is"
   " greater than or equal
to 10 "
   a
}
```

The braces must be on the same line as the if and the else keywords. This is because a newline or a semicolon immediately after the conditional part of the statement tells bc that the body of the conditional is the null statement. One common source of errors in bc programs is typing the statement body portion of an `if` statement on a separate line. If you specify `-i` on the bc command line, bc displays a warning when an `if` statement has a null body.

The `else` form of `if` is an extension to the POSIX.2 standard.

`while (relation) statement`

Repeatedly executes the given statement -while `relation` is true. For example,

```
i = 1
a = 0
while (i <= 10) {
    a += i
    ++i
}
```

adds the integers from 1 through 10 and stores the result in a.

If `relation` is not true when bc encounters a `while` loop, bc will not execute `statement` at all.

```
for (initexp ; relation ;
endexp)
```
is equivalent to

```
initexp
while (relation) {
    statement
    endexp
}
```

where `initexp` and `endexp` are expressions and `relation` is a relation. For example,

```
a = 0
for (i = 1; i <= 10; ++i) a
+= i
```

is equivalent to the `while` example given earlier. C programmers should note that all three items inside the parentheses must be specified; unlike C, `bc` doesn't let you omit any of these expressions.

break

Can only be used inside a `while` or `for` loop. `break` terminates the loop.

sh command

Lets you send a line to the shell for execution, as in `sh more myfile`.

This command passes to the command interpreter for execution everything from the first nonblank character until the end of the line. The preceding command would use `more` to display the contents of `myfile.sh`. It is an extension to the POSIX.2 standard.

quit

Terminates `bc`. In other implementations of `bc`, the interpreter exits as soon as it reads this word. This version of bc treats quit as a real statement, so you can use it in loops, functions, and so on.

Several other types of statements are only relevant in function definitions. These are described in the *Functions* section.

Functions

A function is a *subprogram* that calculates a result based on *argument* values. For example, the following function converts a temperature given in Fahrenheit into the equivalent temperature in Celsius.

```
define f_to_c(f) {
    return ( (f-32) * 5 / 9 )
}
```

This defines a function named f_to_c that takes a single argument called f. The *body* of the function is enclosed in braces. Note that the opening brace must be on the same line as the define keyword. The function body consists of a sequence of statements that calculate the *result* of the function. An expression of the form

```
return (expression)
```

returns the value of expression as the result of the function. The parentheses around the expression are compulsory according to the POSIX.2 standard, but optional in this version of bc.

To make use of a subprogram, you create a *function call*. A function call has the form

```
name(expression,expression,...)
```

where name is the name of the function, and the expressions are argument values for the function. A function call can be used anywhere you can use any other expression. The value of the function call is the result value of the function, as calculated using the given expressions as argument values. For example, with the function f_to_c() defined previously, f_to_c(41) has the value 5 (because 41° Fahrenheit is equivalent to 5° Celsius).

The general form of a function definition is

```
define name(parameter,parameter,...) {
    auto local, local, ...
    statement
    statement
        ...
}
```

The `parameters` on the first line can be variable names or array names. Array names are indicated by putting square brackets after them. For example, if `addvec` is a function that adds two vectors, the function definition might start with

```
define addvec(a[],b[]) {
```

Parameter names do not conflict with arrays or variables of the same name. For example, you can have a parameter named a inside a function and a variable named a outside; the two are separate entities. Assigning a value to the variable will not change the parameter, and assigning a value to the parameter will not change the variable.

All parameters are passed *by value.* This means that a copy is made of the argument value and the copy is assigned to the formal parameter. This also applies to arrays. If you pass an array to a function, a copy is made of the whole array, so any changes made to the array parameter don't affect the original array. If you want to change the original array, don't pass it as an argument; simply refer to the array by name inside the function.

You might create a function that does not need any arguments. In this case, the `define` line will not have any parameters inside the parentheses, as in

```
define f() {
```

Local Variables

The `auto` statement declares one or more *local* variables. When a variable or array name appears in an `auto` statement, the current values of those items are saved away and the items are initialized to zero. For the duration of the function, the items have their new values. When the function terminates, the old values of the items are restored.

For example, `addarr` in Listing M.2 is a function that adds the elements in an array. The argument l stands for the number of elements in the array. The function uses two local names: a variable named i and a variable named s. These variables are local to the function `addarr` and are unrelated to any objects of the same name outside the function (or in other functions).

 Listing M.2. A function that sums the elements of an array.

```
define addarr(a[],l) {
    auto i, s
    for (i=0; i < l; ++i) s += a[i]
    return (s)
}
```

Objects that are named in an auto statement are called *autos*. Autos are initialized to zero each time the function is called. In addarr, the sum s is set to zero each time the preceding function is called.

Listing M.3 shows that you can also have local arrays that are specified by placing square brackets after the array name in the auto statement. This defines a local array called local_array. Local arrays start out with no elements in them.

 Listing M.3. A function with local_array.

```
define func_with_local_array() {
    auto local_array[];
    for(i=0; i<100; i++) local_array[i] = i*2
}
```

If a function refers to an object that is not a parameter and is not declared auto, the object is assumed to be *global*. Global objects can be referred to by other functions or by statements that are outside functions. In Listing M.4, the sum_c function references a global array named c that is the element-by-element sum of two other arrays. If c did not exist before you called sum_c, bc creates the array when it is referenced. After the program has called sum_c, statements in the program or in functions can refer to c.

 Listing M.4. Reference to a global array.

```
define sum_c(a[],b[],l) {
    auto i
    for (i=0; i < l; ++i) c[i] = a[i] + b[i]
}
```

Functions usually require a return statement. This has the form

```
return (expression)
```

The expression is evaluated and used as the result of the function. The expression must have a single numeric value; it cannot be an array.

A return statement terminates a function, even if there are more statements left in the function. Listing M.5 shows a function that returns the absolute value of its argument. If i is less than zero, the function takes the first return; otherwise, it takes the second.

Listing M.5. Absolute value function.

```
define abs(i) {
    if (i < 0) return (-i)
    return (i)
}
```

A function can also terminate by executing the last statement in the function. If so, the result of the function is zero. The function sum_c in Listing M.4 is an example of a function that doesn't have a return statement. The function doesn't need a return statement, because its work is to calculate the global array c, not to calculate a single value. If you want to return from a function but not return a value, you can use

```
return ()
```

or simply

```
return
```

If there are no parameters to the return statement, a default value of zero will be returned.

Built-In Functions

bc has several built-in functions that perform various operations. These functions are similar to user-defined functions but you don't have to define them yourself; they are already set up for you. The recognized functions are

length(expression)	Calculates the total number of decimal digits in the value of expression. This includes digits both before and after the decimal point. The result of length is an integer. For example, length(123.456) returns 6.
scale(expression)	Returns the scale of the value of expression. For example, scale(123.456) returns 3, because there are three digits after the decimal point. The result of scale is always an integer. Subtracting the scale of a number from the length of a number lets you determine the number of digits before the decimal point.

`sqrt(expression)`	Calculates the square root of the value of `expression`. The result is truncated in the least significant decimal place (not rounded). The scale of the result is the scale of the value of `expression` or the value of `scale`, whichever is larger.

The following functions can be used if you specify `-l` on the bc command line. (The `-l` option is discussed in the *Options* section.) If you do not specify `-l`, the function names will not be recognized. Note that there are two names for each function: a full name, and a single-character name for compatibility with the POSIX.2 standard. The full names are the same as the equivalent functions in the standard C math library.

`atan(expression)` or `a(expression)`	Calculates the arctangent of `expression`, returning an angle in radians
`cos(expression)` or `c(expression,`	Calculates the cosine of `(expression)` where this is taken to be an angle in radians
`exp(expression)` or `e(expression)`	Calculates the exponential of `expression` (that is, the value e raised to the power of `expression`)
`jn(integer,expression)` or `j(integer, expression)`	Calculates the Bessel function of `expression`, with order integer
`log(expression)` or `lexpression`	Calculates the natural logarithm of `expression`
`sin(expression)` or `expression, sexpression)`	Calculates the sine of where this is taken to be an angle in radians

Options

The `-l` option loads a library of standard mathematical functions before processing any other input. This library also sets the *scale* to 20.

The `-i` option puts bc into *interactive mode*. In this mode, bc displays a prompt when it is waiting for input. In addition, errors are handled somewhat differently. Normally, when bc encounters an error while processing a file, it prints an error message and exits. In interactive mode, bc prints the message, then returns to the interactive mode to allow debugging. `-i` is unique to this version of bc.

Examples

Listing M.6 shows a simple function that calculates the sales tax on a purchase. The amount of the purchase is given by purchase, and the amount of the sales tax (in percent) is given by tax. For example,

```
sales_tax(23.99,6)
```

calculates six percent tax on a purchase of $23.99. The function temporarily sets the scale value to 2 so that the monetary figures will have two figures after the decimal point. Remember that bc truncates calculations instead of rounding, so some accuracy might be lost. It is better to use one more digit than needed and perform the rounding at the end.

 Listing M.6. Function to calculate sales tax.

```
define sales_tax(purchase,tax) {
    auto old_scale;
    old_scale = scale
    scale = 2
    tax = purchase*(tax/100)
    scale = old_scale
    return (tax)
}
```

Division resets the scale of a number to the value of scale. Listing M.7 shows how you can use this to extract the integer portion of a number.

 Listing M.7. Extracting the integer part of a number.

```
define integer_part(x) {
    # a local to save the value of scale
    auto old_scale;

    # save the old scale, and set scale to 0
    old_scale = scale; scale=0

    # divide by 1 to truncate the number. Truncate means scale is 0
    x /= 1

    # restore the old scale
    scale=old_scale
    return (x)
}
```

Using the `integer_part` function, Listing M.8 shows how to define a function to return the fractional part of a number.

 Listing M.8. Obtaining the fractional part of a number.

```
define fractional_part(x) {
    return (x - integer_part(x))
}
```

Listing M.9 shows a function that lets you set the scale of a number to a specified number of decimal places.

 Listing M.9. Setting the scale of a number.

```
define set_scale(x, s) {
    auto os;
    os = scale
    scale = s
    x /= 1
    scale = os
    return (x)
}
```

Listing M.10 shows how the `set_scale()` function can be used in a function that will round a number to two decimal places. This is a useful function if you want to work with monetary values.

 Listing M.10. Rounding a number to two decimal places.

```
define round(num) {
    auto temp;
    if(scale(num) < 2) return (set_scale(num, 2))
    temp = (num - set_scale(num, 2)) * 1000
    if(temp > 5) num += 0.01
    return (set_scale(num,2))
}
```

A *recursive* function calls itself. Listing M.11 shows a recursive function that calculates the factorial of its argument. (The factorial of a positive integer is the product of the integer with all the positive integers that are smaller. For example, `fact(3)` returns 3*2*1, or 6.)

Listing M.11. Recursive factorial function.

```
define fact (x) {
    if(x < 1) return 1
    return (x*fact(x-1))
}
```

Listing M.12 shows a nonrecursive way to write the same function.

 Listing M.12. Nonrecursive factorial function.

```
define fact (x) {
    auto result
    result = 1;
    while(x>1) result *= x—
    return (result)
}
```

Listing M.13 shows another recursive function. This one calculates the nth element of the Fibonacci sequence.

Listing M.13. Recursive Fibonacci function.

```
define fib(n) {
    if(n < 3) {
        return (1)
    } else {
        return (fib(n-1)+fib(n-2))
    }
}
```

Listing M.14 defines functions that convert radians to degrees and vice versa.

 Listing M.14. Radian/degree conversion.

```
define rad_to_deg(n) {
    auto pi
    pi = 4 * atan(1)
    return (n * 180/pi)
}
define deg_to_rad(n) {
```

```
    auto pi
    pi = 4 * atan(1)
    return (n * pi/180)
}
```

Diagnostics

Possible exit status values are

0	Successful completion
1	Failure due to any of the following errors
	Break statement found outside of a loop
	Parser stack overflow
	Syntax error
	End-of-file in comment
	End-of-file in string
	Numerical constant is too long
	String is too long
	Unknown option
	Empty evaluation stack
	Can't pass scalar to array
	Can't pass array to scalar
	Invalid array index
	Built-in variable can't be used as a parameter or auto variable
	"Name" is not a function
	Invalid value for built-in variable
	Shell command failed to execute
	Division by 0
	Invalid value for exponentiation operator
	Attempt to take square root of negative number
	Out of memory
2	Failure due to an invalid command line option

341

Portability

POSIX.2. All UNIX systems. MKS Toolkit.

Notes

Unlike the C language (which uses lexical scoping rules), bc uses dynamic scoping. This is most easily explained by examining the example in Listing M.15.

 Listing M.15. Scoping example.

```
a=10
define f1() {
    auto a;
    a = 13;
    return (f2())
}
define f2() {
    return (a)
}

f1()
13
f2()
10
```

If you call f1(), bc displays the number 13 instead of the number 10. This is because f1() hides away the old (global) value of a (which is 10) and then sets a to 13. When f2() refers to a, it sees the variable that was dynamically created by f1() and so it prints 13. When f1() returns, it restores the old value of a. When f2() is called directly instead of through f1(), it sees the global value for a and prints 10. The corresponding C code would print 10 in both cases. Whenever possible, you should avoid situations where dynamic scoping makes a difference, since it can be confusing and it can foster bad habits that won't work if you ever try to program in C.

bc stores numbers as strings and converts them into numbers each time they are used. This is important because the value of a constant number can change depending on the setting of the ibase variable. For example, consider the instructions in Listing M.16. When the base is set to 10, ten() returns the decimal value 10. However, when the input base is changed to 16, the function returns the decimal value 16. This can be a source of confusing errors in bc programs.

Listing M.16. Example of number storage.

```
define ten() {
    return (10)
}

ten()
10
ibase=16
ten()
16
```

The library of functions loaded using the `-l` option is stored in the file `/lib/lib.b` under your root directory. This is a simple text file that you can examine and change to add new functions as desired.

break—Exit from the Shell Loop

Synopsis

```
break [number]
```

Description

break exits from a `for`, `select`, `until`, or `while` loop. It is built into the shell.

If number is given, break exits from the given number of enclosing loops. The default value of number is 1.

Diagnostics

break always returns an exit status of zero.

Portability

POSIX.2. X/Open Portability Guide. MKS Toolkit. break is a built-in command of the Bourne Shell and KornShell on UNIX systems.

See Also

continue, sh

cal—Display a Calendar for a Month or Year

Synopsis

cal [*month*] [*year*]

Description

cal displays a simple calendar on the standard output.

With no arguments, cal displays a calendar for the current month of the current year.

If there is one argument and it is numeric, it is interpreted as a year (such as 1995). If there is one argument and it is not numeric, it is interpreted as the name of a month, possibly abbreviated (such as apr).

When two arguments are given, the first is assumed to be the month (either a number from 1 to 12 or a month name) and the second is the year.

Diagnostics

Possible exit status values are

0	Successful completion
1	Failure due to an invalid command line argument, an invalid date, or a year outside the range of 1 A.D. to 9999 AD

Portability

X/Open Portability Guide. All UNIX systems. MKS Toolkit.

Note

Year numbers less than 100 refer to the early years A.D., not the current century. September 1752, the month when most of Europe switched from the Julian calendar to the Gregorian calendar, is handled correctly.

cat—Concatenate and Display Text Files

Synopsis

```
cat [-su] [-v[et]] [file ...]
```

Description

cat is most often used to display or concatenate files. It copies each `file` argument to the standard output. If you do not specify any files on the command line or give - as a filename, cat reads the standard input.

Options

Normally, cat buffers its output (which means that output is only written to the terminal when cat has accumulated several lines to display). The -u option tells cat to display output as soon as it is produced.

Cat normally produces an error message if one of the specified files does not exist or cannot be read. Specifying the -s option prevents such error messages.

If the -v option is specified, cat displays all characters including those that are unprintable. If a character is unprintable, one of three representations is used. If the top bit in a byte is on, cat outputs the character without that bit but precedes the character by the two characters M-; Control characters are displayed with ^ followed by the character representing the control character (for example, ^A for Ctrl-A); all other unprintable characters are represented by \xxx, where xxx is the octal representation of the character.

To use the -e and -t options, you must also specify -v. If -e is specified, cat indicates the end of each line with a $ character. If -t is specified, tab characters are represented as ^I.

Diagnostics

Possible exit status values are

0   Successful completion.

1   Failure due to an inability to open the input file, inability to write to the standard output, or the input file being the same as the output file. (This version of cat does not check to see whether the input and the output are the same file.)

2   Failure due to an invalid command line option.

Portability

POSIX.2. X/Open Portability Guide. All UNIX systems. MKS Toolkit. Berkeley UNIX systems have a cat command, but the command has different options.

See Also

cp, more, mv, pg

cd, chdir—Change Working Directory

Synopsis

```
cd [directory]
cd old new
```

Description

The command

```
cd directory
```

changes the working directory to directory. If directory is an absolute pathname (one that begins with /), cd goes to that directory. If directory is a relative pathname, cd takes it to be relative to the current working directory.

In the KornShell, if the variable CDPATH is defined, the built-in cd command searches for relative pathnames under each of the directories defined in CDPATH. If the directory is found outside the current working directory, cd displays the name of the new working directory.

The value of CDPATH should be a list of directory names separated by colons on UNIX, and by semicolons on DOS. To specify the current directory in CDPATH, use a null string. For example, if the value of CDPATH begins with a separator character, cd searches the current directory first; if the value of CDPATH ends with a separator character, cd searches the current directory last. To see how CDPATH works, consider

```
CDPATH="/dir1;/dir2;"
cd mydir
```

The cd command looks for mydir under /dir1, then under /dir2, then under the current directory.

In the KornShell, the special command

```
cd -
```

changes the working directory to the previous working directory by exchanging the values of the variables PWD and OLDPWD. Repeating this command switches back and forth between the two directories.

If you call cd without arguments, cd sets the working directory to the value of the HOME environment variable, if this variable exists. If there is no HOME variable, the current directory is not changed.

The form

```
cd old new
```

is specific to the KornShell. The KornShell keeps the name of the current directory in the variable PWD. The preceding cd command scans the current value of PWD and replaces the first occurrence of the string old with the string new. cd displays the resulting value of PWD and makes it the new working directory.

Diagnostics

Possible exit status values are

0	Successful completion
1	Failure due to no previous directory, a search for directory failed, or an old/new substitution failed
2	Failure because of an invalid command line option

Possible error messages include

`"directory" bad directory`	The target directory could not be located. The working directory is not changed.
`Restricted`	You are using the restricted version of the KornShell (for example, by specifying the `-r`, option for `sh`). The `cd` command is not allowed under the restricted shell.
`No HOME directory`	You have not assigned a value to the HOME environment variable. Thus when you just say `cd` to return to your home directory, the command can't figure out which directory is your home directory.
`No previous directory`	You tried the command `cd -` to return to your previous directory. However, there was no record of what your previous directory was.
`Pattern "old" not found in "dir"`	You tried a command of the form `cd old new`. However, the name of the current directory `dir` does not contain any string matching the regular expression `old`.

Portability

POSIX.2. X/Open Portability Guide. MKS Toolkit. The first form of the command is found on all UNIX systems. All forms are built into the KornShell.

See Also

`sh`

Note

Unlike the command of the same name under the DOS COMMAND.COM, `cd` can change the current disk as well as the current directory.

chmod—Change Access Permissions of a File or Directory

Synopsis

```
chmod [-fR] mode pathname ...
```

Description

chmod changes the access permissions or *modes* of the specified files or directories. Modes determine who can read, change or execute a file.

Options

The -R option can be used when a directory is specified on the command line. chmod will give all subdirectories and files under that directory the attributes specified for the directory itself.

The -f option forces chmod to return a successful status and no error messages, even if errors are encountered. This is useful if you're using -R to change a lot of files but you don't really care if chmod changes everything, provided that it changes a particular subset of the files.

Modes

The mode value on the command line can be specified in symbolic form or as an octal value.

A symbolic mode has the form

```
[who] op permission [op permission ...]
```

The who value can be any combination of the following:

u	Sets user (individual) permissions
g	Sets group permissions
o	Sets other permissions
a	Sets all permissions; this is the default

On DOS, there are no group or other permissions. Therefore, they always match the individual permissions.

The op part of a symbolic mode is an operator telling whether permissions should be turned on or off. The possible values are

+	Turns on a permission
-	Turns off a permission
=	Turns on the specified permissions and turns off all others

The permission part of a symbolic mode is any combination of the following:

r	Read permission. If this is turned off, you will not be able to read the file. On DOS, all files are always readable, so this permission is ignored.
w	Write permission. If this is turned off, you will not be able to write to the file.
x	Execute permission. If this is turned off, you will not be able to execute the file. On DOS, all files are considered to be executable, so this permission is ignored.
h	Hidden attribute. This is only recognized under DOS.
a	Archive bit. This is only recognized under DOS.
s	On UNIX, this stands for *setuid or setgid on execution* permission; discussion of this concept is outside the scope of this book. On DOS, this stands for a system file.
t	On UNIX, this stands for the "sticky" bit; discussion of this concept is outside the scope of this book. On DOS, it refers to the archive bit (so it is equivalent to a).

Multiple symbolic modes can be specified, separated by commas.

Absolute modes are supported for conformance to UNIX versions of chmod. Absolute modes are octal numbers specifying the complete list of attributes for the files; attributes are specified by ORing together these bits:

```
4000   Hidden file; setuid bit
2000   System file; setgid bit
1000   Archive bit; sticky bit
0400   Individual read
0200   Individual write
```

```
0100    Individual execute (or list directory)
0040    Group read
0020    Group write
0010    Group execute
0004    Other read
0002    Other write
0001    Other execute
```

The first three bits are shown with their meanings on DOS. These bits have different meanings on UNIX. This version of chmod tries to handle options in a way that parallels the UNIX approach. In the following list, each line shows a group of calls that are all equivalent.

```
chmod 0000    chmod o=s
chmod 2000    chmod g=s    chmod =s
chmod 4000    chmod u=s    chmod =h
chmod 6000    chmod a=s    chmod ug=s    chmod =hs
```

Note that +s is equivalent to 2000 on DOS; on UNIX, +s is equivalent to 6000. All of these equivalences are intended to support commands ported to DOS from UNIX. Such ported commands will not do the same thing that they do on UNIX (because DOS does not have the same file attributes as UNIX), but the commands will work in a consistent manner.

To make a DOS file read-only, all three write permission bits must be turned off. If any of the three is on, DOS considers the file to be writeable.

On DOS, the ls command indicates the mode settings of files. The DOS DIR command does not show these attributes.

Examples

```
chmod -w nowrite
```

makes a file named nowrite read-only.

```
chmod +hrs sysfile
```

sets the hidden, read-only, and system attributes for a file named sysfile.

```
chmod a=rwx file
```

turns on read, write, and execute permissions, and turns off the hidden, archive, and system attributes. This is equivalent to

```
chmod 0777 file
```

Diagnostics

Possible exit status values are

0	Successful completion
1	Failure because chmod couldn't access a specified file, couldn't change the modes on a specified file, couldn't read the directory containing the directory entry to change, or encountered a fatal error when using the -R option
2	Failure because the command line was missing the mode argument, had an invalid mode argument, or had too few arguments

Possible error messages include

`Fatal error during "-R" option`	The -R option was specified but some file or directory in the directory structure was inaccessible. This can happen because of permissions or because a removable unit has been removed.
`Read directory "name"`	You do not have read permissions on the specified directory.

Portability

POSIX.2. X/Open Portability Guide. MKS Toolkit. Different systems interpret some mode bits in different ways.

See Also

ls

: (colon)—Do Nothing, Successfully

Synopsis

```
: [argument ...]
```

Description

The : (colon) command simply yields an exit status of zero (success). This can be surprisingly useful, such as when you are evaluating shell expressions for their side effects. This command is built into the KornShell.

Diagnostics

Because this command always succeeds, the only possible exit status is

    0   Successful completion.

Examples

```
: ${VAR:="default value"}
```

sets VAR to a default value if and only if it is not already set. This is because the := construct inside the parameter expansion assigns the value to VAR if VAR doesn't have a value. The result of the parameter expansion is the value of VAR, and this is an argument to :. As usual, : just ignores this argument and returns a zero exit status. For more details, see the Parameter Substitution section of the sh man page.

Portability

POSIX.2. X/Open Portability Guide. All UNIX systems. MKS Toolkit.

See Also

alias, sh

continue—Skip to Next Iteration of Enclosing Loop

Synopsis

```
continue [number]
```

Description

continue skips to the next iteration of an enclosing for, select, until, or while loop. It is built into the shell.

If number appears on the command line, execution continues at the loop—control of the numberth enclosing loop (when loops are nested inside other loops). The default value of number is 1.

Diagnostics

continue always returns an exit status of zero.

Portability

POSIX.2. X/Open Portability Guide. MKS Toolkit. continue is a built-in command of the Bourne Shell and KornShell on UNIX systems.

See Also

break, sh

cp—Copy Files

Synopsis

```
cp [-cfimp] file1 file2
cp [-cfimp] file ... directory
cp -R [-cfimp] source ... directory
cp -r [-cfimp] source ... directory
```

Description

cp copies files (called the *sources*) to a target named by the last argument on its command line.

If the target is an existing file, it is overwritten. If it does not exist, it is created.

If there are more than two pathnames, the last pathname (the target) must be a directory. If the target is a directory, the sources are copied into that directory with names given by the final component of the source pathname. For example,

```
cp file1 file2 file3 dir
```

would create `dir/file1`, `dir/file2`, and `dir/file3`.

Options

If the target file already exists and does not have write permission, `cp` normally denies access and continues with the next copy. If you specify the `-f` (force) option, `cp` will overwrite such files immediately, without asking the question. The `-i` (interactive) flag always asks the question before overwriting an existing file, whether or not the file is read-only.

The `-m` flag sets the modify and access time of each destination file to that of the corresponding source file. Normally, the modification time of the destination file is set to the present.

The `-p` option also preserves the modify and access times. In addition, it preserves the file mode, owner, and group owner, if possible.

Problems can arise when copying files to diskettes. You might expect that

```
cp *.c a:
```

copies all `.c` files to drive A:. If, however, the diskette in drive A: fills up before all files are copied, it becomes difficult to construct a wildcard to copy only the remaining files to the next diskette. If you specify the `-c` (change) flag, `cp` will prompt you to change the diskette if there is insufficient room to complete a copy operation. Note that the parent directories must already exist on the new target diskette.

The `-R` option lets you clone an entire directory. It copies all the files and subdirectories of `dir1` into `dir2`. The `-r` option does almost the same thing. The difference is that `-R` is careful to duplicate all special files (for example, device files), where `-r` makes no special allowance for special files. Because DOS doesn't have special files, there is no difference between `-R` and `-r` in the MKS Tools.

Diagnostics

Possible exit status values are

0   Successful completion.

1   Failure because an argument had a trailing / but was not the name of a directory; a file could not be found; an input file could not be opened for reading; an output file could not be created or opened for output; a read error occurred on an input file or a write error occurred on an output file; the input and output files were the same file; a fatal error was encountered when using `-r` or `-R`. Possible fatal `-r` or `-R` errors include

                The inability to access a file

                The inability to chmod a target file

                The inability to read a directory

                The inability to create a directory

                A target that is not a directory

                The source and destination directories being the same

2   Failure because of

                An invalid command line option

                Too few arguments on the command line

                A target that should be a directory but isn't

                No space left on the target device

                Out of memory to hold the data to be copied

                The inability to create a directory to hold a target file.

Possible error messages include

`cannot allocate target string`	cp has no space to hold the name of the target file. Try to free up some memory to give cp more space.
`copying directory "name" as` `plain file`	You did not specify `-r` or `-R`, but one of the names you asked to copy was the name of a directory. cp will create a file corresponding to the original directory, but this file will probably be useless.
`"target name"?`	You are attempting to copy a file, but there is already a file with the target name, and the file is read-

only. If you really want to write over the existing file, enter y and press Enter. If you do not want to write over the existing file, enter n and press Enter.

source "name" and target "name" are identical	The source and the target are actually the same file (because of links) on UNIX systems. In this case, cp does nothing.
unreadable directory "name"	cp cannot read the specified directory (because you do not have appropriate permissions).

Portability

POSIX.2. X/Open Portability Guide. All UNIX systems. MKS Toolkit. The -c and -m flags are specific to MKS Tools and are not found on UNIX systems.

On DOS, if the target of cp is a device, the device is put into binary mode for the duration of the copy.

See Also

cat, mv, rm

date—Set and Display Date and Time

Synopsis

```
date [-ctu] [timespec]
date [-cu] [+format]
```

Description

date can display the operating system's idea of the current date and time or set the date to a new value. The default format of the date is given by the following example:

```
Wed Feb 26 14:01:43 EST 1992
```

Options

The -u option displays or sets the date and time according to Greenwich Mean Time (also called Coordinated Universal Time). When displaying the date, -u uses GMT as the time zone. The -c option is exactly the same as -u except that it uses CUT as the time zone. The -t option specifies that the BSD format is used when setting the date and time.

If the argument to date does not begin with +, date assumes it is a timespec to set the date and time. The timespec can have the form [[mm]dd]hhmm[.ss] or mmddhhmmyy[.ss] where mm is the optional number of the month (01–12), dd is the optional day of the month, hh is the hour in 24-hour format (required), mm is the minutes (required), yy is the optional last two digits of the year, and ss is the optional seconds.

date uses these values to set the date and time. Note that you must specify the hours and minutes; other arguments are optional. The year can be specified only if you have specified the month and day.

The -t option allows you to use the BSD date format, which is [[[[cc]yy]mm]dd]hhmm[.ss] where cc is the optional first two digits of the year

If the argument to date begins with a + character, it is treated as a format to use when displaying the date. All characters of the format, excluding the + character, are written directly to the standard output, with the exception of *placeholders* consisting of a % character immediately followed by another character. Placeholders are described in the *Placeholders* section. The format should be enclosed in single or double quotation marks if it contains blanks or other special characters.

date outputs a newline character after the format string is exhausted.

Placeholders

The % character introduces a placeholder, similar to those in the printf function of the C programming language. The following special formats are recognized.

%%	Displays the % character literally
%a	Displays the three-letter abbreviation for the day of the week (for example, Sun)
%A	Displays the full name of the day (for example, Sunday)
%b	Displays the three-letter abbreviation for the month (for example, Feb)

%B	Displays the full month name (for example, February)
%c	Displays the local representation of the date and time (see %D and %T)
%C	Displays the first two digits of the year
%d	Displays the two-digit day of the month as a number
%D	Displays the date in the form mm/dd/yy
%e	Displays the day of the month in a two-character, right-justified, blank-filled field
%h	Displays the three-letter abbreviation for the month (for example, Feb)
%H	Displays the two-digit hour (00 to 23)
%I	Displays the hour in the 12-hour clock representation (01 to 12)
%j	Displays the numeric day of the year (001 to 366)
%m	Displays the month number (01 to 12)
%M	Displays the minutes (00 to 59)
%n	Displays a newline character
%p	Displays the local equivalent of AM or PM
%r	Displays the time in AM/PM notation (for example, 11:53:29 AM)
%R	Displays the 24-hour time (for example, 14:53)
%S	Displays the seconds (00 to 59)
%t	Displays a tab character
%T	Displays the time in 24-hour notation (for example, 14:53:29)
%u	Displays the number for the day of the week, with Monday being 1 and Sunday being 7
%U	Displays the week number in the year, with Sunday being the first day of the week (00 to 52)
%V	Displays the week number in the year, with Monday being the first day of the week (01 to 53). If the week containing January 1 has four or more days in the new year, it is week 1 of the new year; otherwise it is week 53 of the previous year

%w	Displays the number for the day of the week, with Sunday being 0 and Saturday being 6
%W	Displays the week number in the year, with Monday being the first day of the week (00 to 52)
%x	Displays the local date representation (see %D)
%X	Displays the local time representation (see %T)
%y	Displays the two-digit year (for example, 95)
%Y	Displays the full year (for example, 1995)
%z	Displays the time zone name (for example, EDT)
%Z	Displays the time zone name (for example, EDT)

Examples

Assume that it is Thursday, January 10, 1991, 6:55 p.m., Eastern Standard Time. Listing M.17 displays a variety of date commands and the resulting output. Output is indented to distinguish it from the date commands.

 Listing M.17. Samples of date output.

```
date
    Thu Jan 10 18:55:00 EST 1991
date '+%A, %B %d'
    Thursday, January 10
date '+%a, %b %d'
    Thu, Jan 10
date '+The time is %T'
    The time is 18:55:00
```

Diagnostics

Possible exit status values are

| 0 | Successful completion |
| 1 | Failure due to a bad date conversion, a formatted date that was too long, or no permission to set the date |

| 2 | Failure due to an invalid command line argument, inability to open one of the input files or too many arguments on the command line |

Possible error messages include

`No permission to set date`	The system denies you the right to set the date.
`Bad format character x`	A format string contained something of the form %x, but it wasn't a recognized placeholder.
`Bad date conversion in "string"`	The date and/or time specified on the command line has an invalid format (for example, the hour might be greater than 24).

Portability

AT&T System V. X/Open Portability Guide. All UNIX systems. MKS Toolkit.

Note

On machines that have a time-of-day clock with battery backup, using date will not necessarily change this real-time clock. You may have to use a special command that is unique to your system.

df—Display Amount of Free Space Remaining on Disk

Synopsis

```
df [-kP] [[device] [pathname]] ...
```

Description

df shows the amount of free space left on a disk device, and the total amount of space that the device has (both used and unused). Space is measured in units of 512-byte disk sectors. A device is specified either by name or by naming any file or directory on that device. If no argument is given, space is reported for all devices known to the system.

Options

If you specify the -k option, df uses 1024-byte (1K) units instead of the default 512-byte units when reporting space information.

The -P option lists complete information on space used, in the following order: file system name, total space, space used, space free, percentage of space used, and file system root.

Diagnostics

Possible exit status values are

0	Successful completion
1	Failure because of an inability to access pathname, inability to access device, or device is not a device
2	Failure because of an invalid command line option

Portability

AT&T System SVID. X/Open Portability Guide. All UNIX systems. MKS Toolkit.

See Also

du, ls

diff—Compare Two Text Files and Show Differences

Synopsis

```
diff [-befhHimnrsw] [-c[n]] [-C n] [-Difname] path1 path2
```

Description

`diff` attempts to determine the minimal set of changes needed to convert one file into another.

If either (but only one) pathname is `-`, `diff` uses the standard input for that file. If one of `path1` or `path2` is a directory, the filename of the other file is used in the specified directory. For example,

`diff dir1/filex dir2`

compares `dir1/filex` and `dir2/filex`.

If both names are directories, files with the same filenames under the two directories will be compared. However, files in subdirectories are not compared unless the `-r` option is specified.

Output consists of descriptions of the changes in a style reminiscent of the `ed` text editor. Each set of differences begins with a line indicating the type of difference. These lines have the form

`a1,b1 code a2,b2`

This indicates that lines `a1` through `b1` in `path1` are different from lines `a2` through `b2` in `path2`. The code tells the nature of the difference. Possible codes are a (for append), d (for delete), and c (for change). For example, if lines 3–5 in `path1` have been replaced with lines 3–10 in `path2`, the set of differences would begin with the line

`3,5c3,10`

After the line giving the type of change, deleted or added lines are displayed. Lines from `path1` have the < prefix. Lines from `path2` have the > prefix.

Options

Options that control the output or style of file comparison are

`-b`	For the purpose of comparing lines from `path1` and `path2`, trailing blanks and tabs are ignored. Adjacent groups of blanks and tabs elsewhere in input lines are considered equivalent.

-c[n]	With each difference, n lines of context before and after each change are shown. The default value for n is 3. Lines removed from path1 are marked with -; lines added to path2 are marked with +. Lines changed in both files are marked with !.
-C n	Equivalent to -cn, except that n must be specified.
-Difname	Under this option, the output of diff is the appropriate input to the C preprocessor to generate path2 when ifname is defined and path1 when ifname is not defined.
-e	Writes a script of commands for the ed text editor, which will convert path1 to path2. Output is printed to the standard output.
-f	Produces a script similar to the one produced under -e, but the line numbers are not adjusted to reflect earlier editing changes. Instead, they correspond to the line numbers in path1.
-h	Uses a fast algorithm instead of the normal diff algorithm. This algorithm is able to handle arbitrarily large files. However, it is not particularly good at finding a minimal set of differences in files with many differences.
-H	Uses the -h algorithm only if the normal algorithm runs out of memory.
-i	Ignores the case of letters when doing the comparison.
-m	Produces the new file with extra formatter request lines interspersed to show which lines were added (those with vertical bars in the right margin) and deleted (indicated by a * in the right margin). These are nroff/troff requests.
-n	The differences are displayed in a form that is usable by the MKS Revision Control System (RCS).
-r	Can be used when two directory names are specified on the command line. diff compares corresponding files under the directories and recursively compares corresponding files under corresponding subdirectories under the directories.

-t	Expands tabs into spaces before doing the comparison. Tab stops are set every eight columns (columns 1, 9, 17, and so on).
-w	Ignores whitespace when making the comparison.

Diagnostics

Possible exit status values are

0	No differences between the files compared.
1	The files were successfully compared and found to be different.
2	Failure due to an invalid command-line argument, inability to open one of the input files, out of memory, or a read error on one of the input files.
4	At least one of the files is not a text file (that is. the file is a binary file). For the purposes of `diff`, text files are files that have no NUL characters and no lines longer than 1024 characters.

Possible error messages include

`Binary files filename and filename differ`	The two specified files are binary files. `diff` has compared the two files and found that they are not identical. With binary files, diff does not try to report the differences.
`File "filename": no such file or directory`	The specified filename does not exist. filename was either typed explicitly, or generated by diff from the directory of one file argument and the basename of the other.
`Common subdirectories: name and name`	This message appears when `diff` is comparing the contents of directories but -r is not specified. When `diff` discovers two subdirectories with the same name, it reports that the directories exist, but it does not try to compare the contents of the two directories.

`Insufficient memory (try` `diff -h)`	`diff` ran out of memory for generating the data structures used in the file differencing algorithm (see the *Limits* section). The `-h` option of `diff` will handle any size file without running out of memory.
`Internal error—cannot create` `temporary file`	`diff` could not create a working file. You should ensure that you either have a writeable directory `/tmp` or that the environment contains a variable `TMPDIR`, which names a directory where temporary files can be stored. Also be sure there is sufficient file space in this directory.
`Missing #ifdef symbol` `after -D`	No conditional label was given on the command line after the `-D` option.
`Only one file may be "-"`	Of the two input files normally may be found on the command line of `diff`; only one is allowed to be the standard input.
`Too many lines in "filename"`	`diff` was asked to work with a file that contains more than the maximum number of lines (see the *Limits* section). This limitation does not apply to the `-h` option, and on DOS you are unlikely to get this message because of other memory limitations.

Limits

The longest input line is 1024 bytes. Files are limited to 32000 lines, except when `-h` is specified.

Memory to compute differences is limited to 64K. This memory limit will normally further restrict the number of lines (except with `-h`).

Portability

POSIX.2. X/Open Portability Guide. All UNIX systems. MKS Toolkit. The `-H`, `-m`, and `-n` options are specific to this implementation. The `-c` and `-D` options are only available on Berkeley systems.

See Also

Hunt, J.W. and M.D. McIlroy. "An Algorithm for Differential File Comparison." *Computing Science Technical Report 41*. Bell Telephone Laboratories.

. (dot)—Execute Shell File in Current Environment

Synopsis

```
. file [argument ...]
```

Description

. (dot) executes a KornShell script in the current environment and then returns. The command is built into the shell.

Normally the shell executes a command file in a subshell so that changes to the environment by commands like cd, set, trap, and so on are local to the command file. The . (dot) command circumvents this feature.

The variable `PATH` is used to find the file you want to execute. If you try to use dot to execute a file under the current directory but your search rules don't look at the current directory, the shell won't find the file. If you have this problem, you can use

```
. ./file
```

This explicitly indicates that the shell file you want to run is in the current directory.

If the command line contains an argument list `argument ...`, the positional parameters are set to this list before execution.

Diagnostics

Possible exit status values are

1   Returned if the path search fails or `file` is unreadable.

Otherwise, the exit status is the exit status of the last command executed from the script.

Portability

POSIX.2. X/Open Portability Guide. MKS Toolkit. On DOS, `.ksh` is added as a suffix to *file* if *file* doesn't already have a suffix. To execute a DOS file that has no suffix, add a dot, as in

```
. file.
```

. (dot) is a built-in command of the Bourne Shell and the KornShell on UNIX systems.

See Also

`cd`, `set`, `sh`, `trap`

du—Summarize Disk Space Usage by Directory

Synopsis

```
du [-a¦-s] [-ktx] [pathname ...]
```

Description

`du` reports the amount of disk space used by the given pathname arguments. If *pathname* is a directory, `du` reports the total amount of file space used by all files in that directory and each subdirectory in its hierarchy. If you don't specify a pathname, `du` assumes the current directory. Disk space is measured in disk sectors, which are 512 bytes long.

Options

Normally, du reports disk usage in all the subdirectories of the directories under examination. The -s (summary) option suppresses the subdirectory display; the -a option shows the sizes of all files and subdirectories under all the directories.

The -t option displays the total amount of space used by all the pathnames examined.

The -k option displays sizes in 1024-byte (1K) units, instead of the default 512-byte units.

The -x option only reports on the disk usage of files contained on the same device as the specified directory. This has no effect on DOS, because DOS files are always on the same device as the directory that contains the files. On UNIX, files and directories may be on different devices because of links.

Diagnostics

Possible exit status values are

0	Successful completion
1	Failure because of an invalid command line option, inability to access a directory, inability to read a directory, or inability to access file information

Portability

POSIX.2. AT&T SVID. X/Open Portability Guide. All UNIX systems. MKS Toolkit.

See Also

df, ls

Note

The disk space usage is computed in units of disk sectors (512 bytes). The actual disk space used by files and directories may be more, because some systems allocate space in units of some multiple of a sector. On versions of DOS before 3.1, this allocation unit is usually eight sectors for disks of size 20M or greater; on DOS 3.1, it is four sectors. On UNIX System V, it is usually two sectors, and on Version 7 UNIX, it is one sector.

echo—*echo* Command Arguments

Synopsis

```
echo [argument ...]
```

Description

echo writes its arguments to the standard output. You can represent special characters in the arguments by using the substitutes shown in Table M.3. These substitutes are called escape sequences and are based on the escape sequences of the C programming language. For example,

```
echo "This is broken\nover two lines"
```

displays

```
This is broken
over two lines
```

because the \n escape sequence is replaced by a newline character.

Table M.3. Escape sequences.

Escape Sequence	Meaning
\a	Bell
\b	Backspace
\c	Removes any following characters including \n and \r
\f	Formfeed
\n	Newline (linefeed on UNIX, carriage return and linefeed on DOS)

Escape Sequence	Meaning
\r	Carriage return
\t	Horizontal tab
\v	Vertical tab
\\	Backslash
\ooo	Three octal digits used to represent the octal value of a character

The final argument on the command line is followed by a newline unless \c is found somewhere in the arguments.

Arguments are subject to standard argument expansions. For example, in

```
echo *
```

the * undergoes the usual wildcard expansion and is replaced by the name of all files under the directory. As a result, the command displays all the filenames under the directory.

As always, arguments may be enclosed in double or single quotation marks. See the sh man page for more about quoting.

Examples

```
echo *.[ch]
```

displays the names of all files with names ending in .c or .h, typically C source and header files. The names will be displayed on a single line.

echo is also convenient for passing small amounts of input to other filters.

```
echo 'this is\nreal handy' | banner
```

passes two lines to the banner program.

Diagnostics

echo always returns the status value.

    0   Successful completion.

Portability

POSIX.2. X/Open Portability Guide. AT&T SVID. MKS Toolkit. On older UNIX systems, the escape sequences are not available. The -n option is equivalent to \c embedded in an argument.

On UNIX systems using the C Shell, echo is built-in and follows the older UNIX echo syntax.

DOS COMMAND.COM includes a command of the same name but with a somewhat different function.

See Also

sh

env—Print Environment, Set Environment for Process

Synopsis

```
env [-i] [variable=value ...] [command argument ...]
env [-] [variable=value ...] [command argument ...]
```

Description

If env is called with no arguments, it displays the value of the environment variables that it received from its parent (presumably the shell).

Arguments of the form

```
variable=value
```

enable you to add new variables or change the value of existing variables of the environment.

If the command line includes a *command*, env calls *command* with the arguments that appear on the command line. The accumulated environment is passed to this command. The command is executed directly as a program found in the search PATH and is not interpreted by the shell.

Options

If the first argument is -i or -, the environment inherited by env is not used.

Examples

Compare the output of the following two examples that illustrate the use of env:

```
env foo=bar PATH=xxxx env
env - foo=bar PATH=xxxx env
```

Diagnostics

Possible exit status values are

0	Successful completion
1	Failure due to insufficient memory, or a name that is too long
2	Failure due to an invalid command line argument
126	Failure due to an inability to invoke command
127	Failure due to an inability to find command

Possible error messages include

Too many environment variables	The maximum number of environment variables that can be specified in a single env command is 512.

Portability

POSIX.2. X/Open Portability Guide. AT&T SVID. MKS Toolkit. printenv on Berkeley UNIX systems has similar functionality.

See Also

sh

eval—Execute Arguments as if Typed to Shell

Synopsis

```
eval [argument ...]
```

Description

The shell evaluates each argument as it would for any command. eval then concatenates the resulting strings, separated by spaces, re-evaluates this string, and executes it in the current environment. eval is built into the shell.

Example

The command

```
for a in 1 2 3
do
      eval x$a=fred
done
```

sets variables x1, x2, and x3 to fred (because $a expands to the value of the variable a each time through the loop). After the for loop is finished, entering the command

```
echo $x1 $x2 $x3
```

produces

```
fred fred fred
```

since $x1, $x2, and $x3 will expand to the value of the variables x1, x2, and x3.

Diagnostics

Possible exit status values are

0   No arguments were specified or the specified arguments were empty strings.

Otherwise, the exit status of eval is the exit status of the command that eval executes.

Portability

POSIX.2. X/Open Portability Guide. MKS Toolkit. `eval` is a built-in command of the Bourne Shell and the KornShell on UNIX.

See Also

`exec, sh`

exec—Execute a Command in Place of the Current Shell

Synopsis

`exec [command_line]`

Description

The argument to `exec` is a *command line* for another command. `exec` executes this command without creating a new process. Some people picture this action as *overlaying* the command on top of the currently executing shell. Thus when the command exits, control returns to the parent of the shell. For example,

`exec echo Bye-bye!`

replaces your shell with the `echo` command. When `echo` is finished, you will be logged off unless you were in a subshell, The original shell is gone, so your session is over.

Input and output redirections are valid in the `command`. Input and output descriptors of the shell can be modified by giving only input and output redirections in the command. For example

`exec 2>errors`

redirects the standard error stream to `errors` in all subsequent commands executed by the shell. You can picture this as replacing your original shell with a shell that has its standard error stream redirected.

If no `command` is specified, `exec` simply returns a successful exit status. `exec` is built into the shell.

Diagnostics

If you specify *command line,* exec does not return to the shell. Instead, the shell exits with the exit status of command line or one of the following exit status values:

1-125   Failure due to a redirection error

126   Failure due to an inability to execute the command in command_line

127   Failure due to an inability to find the command in command_line

Portability

POSIX.2. X/Open Portability Guide. MKS Toolkit. exec is a built-in command of the Bourne Shell and the KornShell on UNIX.

See Also

sh

exit—Exit from the Shell

Synopsis

```
exit [expression]
```

Description

exit terminates the shell. The command is built into the shell. If exit is issued from a subshell, it terminates the subshell; otherwise it terminates the original shell, logging you off.

Diagnostics

The shell returns the value of the arithmetic expression to the parent process as the exit status of the shell. If expression is omitted, the shell returns the exit status of the last command executed.

Portability

POSIX.2. X/Open Portability Guide. MKS Toolkit. `exit` is a built-in command of the Bourne Shell and the KornShell on UNIX systems. However, the Bourne Shell only accepts a number, while the KornShell accepts any valid expression.

See Also

`return, sh`

fc—Display, Edit, and Re-Enter Previous Commands

Synopsis

```
fc [-r] [-e editor] [first [last]]
fc -l [-nr] [first [last]]
fc -s [old=new] [specifier]
```

Description

`fc` displays, edits, and reenters commands that have been input to an interactive shell. `fc` stands for *fix commands*.

The environment variable `HISTSIZE` controls how many commands the shell keeps in its history. If `HISTSIZE` is defined and has a numeric value N, the shell keeps the N most recent commands in its history file. If the variable `HISTSIZE` is not defined, 128 commands are accessible.

Commands are stored in a *history file*. If the `HISTFILE` environment variable is defined as the name of a writeable file, the shell uses this as the history file. Otherwise, the history file is `$HOME/sh_history`, if `HOME` is defined and the file is writeable. If the `HOME` variable is not defined or the file is not writeable, the shell attempts to create a temporary history file.

Note that any invocation of the shell shares its history with all shells that have the same history file. This means that the contents of the history file will contain all the commands executed under different invocations of the shell.

Normally, the shell will not keep a history of commands executed from a profile file or the `ENV` file. By default, however, the shell begins recording commands in the history file if it encounters a function definition in either of these setup files. This means that the HISTSIZE and HISTFILE variables must be set up appropriately before the first function definition. If you do not want the history file to begin at this time, use

```
set -o nolog
```

For further information, see sh and set.

The first form of fc shown in the synopsis puts you into an editor and lets you edit a range of commands. When you leave the editor, the edited commands are input to the shell. If you specify the -e *editor* option, the specified editor is used to edit the commands.

If you do not specify the -e option, fc looks for an environment variable named FCEDIT. If this variable is defined, its value is taken to be the pathname of the editor you want to use; fc therefore invokes that editor. If you do not have FCEDIT defined, fc uses $ROOTDIR/bin/ed (the ed editor, not discussed in this book).

The *first* and *last* arguments let you specify one or more commands that you want to edit and re-execute by specifying a range of commands. There are several ways to specify a command for *first* and/or *last*.

1. If one of these arguments is an unsigned number, fc edits the command with that number.

2. If one of these arguments is a negative number -*n*, fc edits the command that came *n* commands before the current command.

3. If one of these arguments is a string, fc edits the most recent command beginning with that string.

The default value of *last* is *first*. If neither *first* nor *last* is given, the default command range is the previous command entered to the shell.

Options

-e   Specifies an editor, as explained earlier.

-l   Displays the specified range of commands, rather than editing them or reentering them. With this option, the default command range is the 16 most recently entered commands.

-n   Suppresses command numbers when commands are displayed or edited.

-r   Reverses the order of the commands in the command range.

-s   Reenters exactly one command without going through an editor.
          If a command *specifier* is given, the command to reenter is
          selected as described previously. Otherwise, fc uses the last
          command entered.

          fc can perform a simple substitution on the command before
          reentry by using a parameter of the form *old=new*. The first
          occurrence of string *old* is replaced with the string *new*.

Diagnostics

Possible exit status values are

0   If -l was specified, the 0 indicates successful completion

1   Failure because of a missing history file or inability to find the
         desired line in the history file

1   Failure because of an invalid command-line option or argument

If fc executes one or more commands, the exit status of fc is the exit status of the last
executed command.

Possible error messages include

Cannot create temporary file   fc must create a temporary file to do
                                     some operations. This message is
                                     printed if fc cannot create the tempo-
                                     rary file (for example, because the disk
                                     is full or because /tmp doesn't exist).

No command matches *string*   You asked to edit a command begin-
                                     ning with a particular *string*, but there
                                     was no such command in the history
                                     file.

Out of space on temporary file   fc cannot increase the size of its
                                     working file. This suggests that the disk
                                     is full.

Files

/tmp   Used to store temporary files. The ROOTDIR environment variable
is used to find /tmp. The TMPDIR environment variable can be
used to dictate a different directory to store temporary files.

Portability

MKS Toolkit. This is a command built into the KornShell on UNIX, but it is not
built into the Bourne Shell. On UNIX, the KornShell does not truncate the history
file at log in.

See Also

alias, print, read, sh, vi

Note

This command is built into the shell. r is a built-in alias for fc -s. history is a built-in alias for fc -l.

find—Find Files Within File Tree

Synopsis

find directory ... expression

Description

find walks through a directory structure, finding files that match a set of criteria.
Each directory, file, and special file is *passed through* the expression given. If the
-exec or -ok option is used, the expression has the side effect of invoking some command on the file found. In this version of find, an expression with no side effects
automatically displays the name of any file that meets the requirements of the expression; on a stock UNIX system, you must specify the -print option if you want
to display the filenames.

Options

The expression is built from a set of options; the juxtaposition of two options implies a logical AND. The -a and -o options are also used between options for logical AND and logical OR operations. You can precede an expression with a !, which negates the expression. You can group options with parentheses. All options, numbers, arguments, parentheses, and the terminal semicolon on the -exec option, must be delimited by whitespace.

Each *number* argument noted next is a decimal number, optionally preceded by a plus or minus sign. If a number is given without a sign, find tests for equality; a plus sign implies *greater than* and a minus sign implies *less than*.

-print	Displays the current filename. It is always true.
-name *pattern*	The current filename must match the pattern given or the expression fails. The pattern may compare glob constructs, and is compared to the final component of the name of the file. It matches as many trailing pathname components as specified in *pattern*.
-perm *mask*	The permissions on the file must exactly match the ones given in *mask*. The mask is given in octal. On DOS file systems, the only useful permissions are 0777 (read/write for all) and 0555 (read-only for all). In this form, only the bottom nine bits of the file mode are used; an exact match is required.
	If the mask is preceded by a dash (-), 12 bits of the file mode are permitted. In this form, an exact match is not required; find only ensures that all the bits given in the mask are turned on. That is, *(mask&mode)==mask*.
	-perm may also be followed by a symbolic mode. For more information on symbolic modes, see the man page for chmod.
-type c	The type of the file must match the type given by the character c. Table M.4 gives possible values of the character. On DOS, only directories and regular files exist.

Table M.4. File types for **find**.

Code	Type
b	Block-special
c	Char-special
d	Directory
f	Regular file
n	Network file
p	FIFO (named pipe)
-links *number*	There are *number* links to the file. DOS does not have links.
-user *name*	The owner of the file is *name*. *Name* can also be a userid number. The *name* on DOS must be the name of user 0 (zero), which owns all files.
-nouser	The file is not owned by any user with a name in /etc/passwd.
-group *name*	The group owner is *name*. The same conditions apply as for -user.
-nogroup	The file is not owned by any group with a name in /etc/group.
-size *number*	The size of the file is *number* blocks long, where a block is 512 bytes.
-atime *number*	The file was last accessed *number* days ago.
-mtime *number*	The file was last modified *number* days ago.
-ctime *number*	The file was last changed *number* days ago.
-exec *command*;	All arguments after -exec are taken until find reaches an argument consisting only of the semicolon. Any argument that is exactly {} (that is, the two brace characters) is replaced by the current filename. The resulting command string is then executed. A return status of zero from this command is treated as success; a nonzero return status is treated as failure.

Code	Type
-ok *command*;	This is similar to -exec, but before find executes the command, it displays the command to make sure that you really want to go ahead. The command string is executed only if you type y (for *yes*). If you type n (for *no*), find treats the situation as if the command was executed but failed.
-newer *file*	Compares the modification date on this file to that on the file given. The expression is true if this file is more recently modified than *file*.
-depth	Processes directories after their contents. If present, this option is always true.
-prune	Stops traversing lower into the tree at this point. If present, this option is always true.
-xdev	Does not cross device boundaries from the root of the tree traversal. If present, this option is always true.
-none	Indicates that some action has been taken; thus, the default -print action will not be invoked. If present, this option is always true.

Examples

Here is an extreme example:

```
find . "(" -name "tmp.*" -o -name "*.tmp" ")" -perm 0555 -exec rm "{}" ";"
```

On DOS, this finds all read-only files that have tmp in either part of their names, and deletes all such files. Various parts of this expression are quoted because of the command-line filename expansion facility.

Diagnostics

Possible exit status values are

0   Successful completion

1   Failure due to insufficient memory, an invalid character specified after `-type`, inability to obtain information on a file for `-newer`, permissions for `-perm` that do not match, an unknown user or group name, inability to access the PATH variable, inability to execute a command specified for `-exec` or `-ok`, a syntax error, or a stack overflow caused by an expression that is too complex

2   Failure due to an invalid command-line argument, not enough arguments on the command line, a missing option, or an argument list that isn't terminated properly

Possible error messages include

`bad number specification in "string"`	You specified an option that takes a numeric value (for example `-atime`, `-ctime`), but did not specify a valid number after the option.
`cannot stat file "name" for -newer`	You used a `-newer` option to compare one file to another. However, `find` could not obtain a modification time for the specified file. Typically, this happens because the file does not exist or you do not have appropriate permissions to obtain this information.

Portability

POSIX.2. X/Open Portability Guide. All UNIX systems. MKS Toolkit. Obviously, many of the options are of dubious portability to DOS, but MKS has tried to supply approximations. The `-depth` option is unique to this implementation. On DOS, `-mtime`, `-ctime`, and `-atime` are always the same.

Stock UNIX systems do not have a default action of `-print`; hence, they do not need the `-none` option. The `-a` operator is undocumented on stock UNIX systems.

grep, egrep, fgrep—Match Patterns in a File

Synopsis

```
grep [-EFbcilnqsvx] [-e pattern] ... [-f patternfile] ... [pattern] [file ...]
egrep [-bcilnqsvx] [-e pattern] ... [-f patternfile] ... [pattern] [file ...]
fgrep [-bcilnqsvx] [-e pattern] ... [-f patternfile] ... [pattern] [file ...]
```

Description

fgrep searches files for one or more *pattern* arguments. It does not use regular expressions; instead, it does direct string comparison to find matching lines of text in the input.

egrep works in a similar way but uses extended regular expression matching, as described in Appendix C, "Summary of Filename Generation with Glob Constructs." This means that regular expression metacharacters in *pattern* will normally have their special meanings. If you want to "turn off" the special meaning of a metacharacter, put a backslash (\) in front of the character. In general, it is simpler to use fgrep when you don't need special pattern matching.

grep is a combination of fgrep and egrep. If you specify the -F option, grep behaves like fgrep. If you specify the -E option, it behaves like egrep. If you don't specify -E or -F, grep behaves like egrep but matches basic regular expressions instead of extended ones. For more information on basic and extended regular expressions, see Appendix C.

If one of the grep commands finds a line that matches a *pattern*, it displays the entire line. If the command line gives more than one input file, the command labels each output line with the name of the file in which the line appeared.

Options

All three commands accept similar options. Multiple patterns can be specified either through the -e option or by reading from a file using the -f option. The -e option also provides a means of defining a pattern that begins with - (dash). If neither of these options is specified, the first nonoption argument is taken as a single search pattern.

The following options can alter the usual behavior of the grep family.

-b	Precedes each matched line with its file block number
-c	Displays only a count of the number of lines that were matched and not the lines themselves
-e *pattern*	Searches for lines matching the regular expression *pattern*. To search for several different patterns, use several -e options
-f *patternfile*	Reads the file *patternfile* and searches for regular expressions given in the file. The *patternfile* should contain one regular expression per line; the command will print lines that match any or all of the regular expressions
-i	Ignores the case of the letters being matched
-l	Lists only the filenames that contain the matching lines
-n	Precedes each matched line with its file line number
-q	Suppresses output and simply returns appropriate return code
-s	Suppresses the display of any error messages
-v	Complements the sense of the match; that is, displays all lines not matching a pattern
-x	Requires a string to match an entire line

Examples

To display every line mentioning a classical element,

```
grep -E "earth¦air¦fire¦water" astro.log
```

Diagnostics

Possible exit status values are

0	The command found at least one match for *pattern*.
1	The command found no matches for *pattern*.

<table>
<tr><td>2</td><td>Failure because a -e option was missing a *pattern*, a -f option was missing a *patternfile*, an input file could not be opened, the program ran out of memory for input or to hold a pattern, the program could not open a *patternfile*, a regular expression was invalid, a command-line option was invalid, or the command line had too few arguments. If the program fails to open one input file, it tries to go on to look at any remaining input files, but it will return 2 even if it succeeds in finding matches in other input files.</td></tr>
</table>

Possible error messages include

`out of space for pattern "string"`	grep did not have enough memory available to store the code needed to work with the given pattern (regular expression). The usual cause is that the pattern is very complex. Make the pattern simpler, or try to free up more memory so that grep has more space to work with.

Limits

The longest input record (line) is restricted to 1024 bytes. Longer lines are treated as two or more records.

Portability

POSIX.2. X/Open Portability Guide. All UNIX systems. MKS Toolkit.

See Also

`find`, Appendix C

head—Display Beginning of File

Synopsis

```
head [- bcklmn number] [file ...]
head [-number] [file ...]
```

Description

By default, head displays the first 10 lines of each *file*. If no *file* is specified, head reads the standard input.

Options

-b *number*	Displays the first *number* 512-byte blocks of each file
-c *number*	Displays the first *number* characters of each file
-k *number*	Displays the first *number* kilobytes (1024 bytes) of each file
-l *number*	Displays the first *number* lines of each file
-m *number*	Displays the first *number* megabytes of each file
-n *number*	Displays the first *number* lines of each file
-*number*	Displays the first *number* lines of each file

Diagnostics

Possible exit status values are

0	Successful completion
1	Failure because of an inability to open an input file, a read error on the standard input, or a write error on the standard output
2	Failure because of an unknown command-line option or a missing or invalid number in an option

Possible error messages include

Badly formed line/character	In an option of the form -n *number* count "*string*" or -*number*, the *number* was not a valid number.

Portability

POSIX.2. X/Open Portability Guide. MKS Toolkit. This program is a Berkeley idea and a frequent add-on to UNIX systems.

See Also

cat, pg, sed, tail

history—Display Command History

Synopsis

```
history [-nr] [first [last]]
```

Description

history displays commands that you executed previously. These commands make up your *command history*. history is built into the shell.

By specifying values for *first* and *last*, you can display a specified range of commands rather than the 16 most recent. For example,

```
history 1 10
```

displays commands 1 through 10.

Your command history is stored in the file given by the variable HISTFILE; by default, this is sh_histo on DOS, .sh_history on UNIX. The number of commands kept in the file is given by the variable HISTSIZE. If HISTSIZE is not defined, the default is 128.

history is an alias defined with

```
alias history='fc -l'
```

For further information, see the manual page for fc.

Options

By default, history displays the 16 most recent commands, from the earliest to the most recent. -r displays commands in reverse order, from the most recent to the earliest.

By default, commands are numbered beginning at 1 (for the first command you execute during this KornShell session). -n displays the commands but not the command numbers.

Diagnostics

Possible exit status values are

0	Successful completion
1	Failure because of a missing history file or inability to find the desired command in the history file
2	Failure because of invalid command-line option or argument

Portability

POSIX.2. X/Open Portability Guide. All UNIX systems. MKS Toolkit.

See Also

alias, fc, sh

let—Evaluate Arithmetic Expressions

Synopsis

```
let expression ...
((expression))
```

Description

`let` evaluates each arithmetic *expression* from left to right, using long integer arithmetic with no checks for overflow. The command is built into the shell.

`let` does not generate output; it simply sets an exit status. The exit status is 0 if the last *expression* has a nonzero value, and 1 otherwise.

The following two lines are equivalent: the second form avoids quoting and enhances readability.

```
let "expression"
((expression))
```

The portable way to write these commands is to use the POSIX command.

```
: $((expression))
```

Expressions consist of named variables, numeric constants, and operators. Variables are shell variables. see Chapter 7, "The KornShell," for details. Numeric constants have the form

```
[base#]number
```

where *base* is a decimal integer between 2 and 36 inclusive, and *number* is any non-negative number expressed in the given base. For example, 8#12 stands for 12 base 8 (which is 10 base 10). For digits greater than 10, use the lowercase letters a through z. For example, 20#a stands for a base 20 (which is 10 base 10). The default base is 10. Undefined variables evaluate to zero.

Table M.5 lists operators in decreasing order of precedence. Operators sharing a line in the table have the same precedence, and are called a *precedence group*. Evaluation within a precedence group is from left to right, except for the assignment operator, which evaluates from right to left. For example, + and - operators are in the same precedence group, so additions and subtractions are performed in the order they appear in an expression.

Table M.5. Summary of operators for `let`.

Operators	Meaning
Unary Operators	
-	Unary minus
!	Logical negation

continues

Table M.5. continued

Operators	Meaning
Arithmetic Binary Operators	
* / %	Multiplication, division, and remainder
+ -	Addition, subtraction
Relational Operators	
< >	Less than, greater than
<= >=	Less than or equal to, greater than or equal to
== !=	Equal to, not equal to
Assignment Operator	
=	Assignment

Example

The commands

```
let a=7 'b=4*2' c=b+1
echo $a $b $c
```

produce the output

```
7 8 9
```

because $a expands to the value of variable a, $b expands to the value of b, and $c expands to the value of c. See Chapter 7 for more about variables.

Diagnostics

Possible exit status values are

0	The last argument evaluated to a nonzero value
1	The last argument evaluated to a zero value or the expression contained a syntax error or tried to divide by zero

Portability

MKS Toolkit. `let` is a command built in to the KornShell on UNIX, and is not a Bourne Shell command.

See Also

`sh`

ls—List File and Directory Names and Attributes

Synopsis

`ls [-AabCcdFfgiLlmnopqRrstux1] [pathname ...]`

Description

`ls` is the command most often used on UNIX to list files and directories. If the *pathname* is a file, `ls` displays information on the file according to the requested options. If *pathname* is a directory, `ls` displays information on the files and subdirectories therein.

Options

If no options are specified, `ls` displays only the filename(s). If output is being sent to a pipe or a file, `ls` writes one name per line; if output is being sent to the terminal, `ls` uses `-C` (multicolumn) format.

The information displayed is at least the name; more information can be requested with various options. The many options are briefly described next. Those marked [UNIX] are only meaningful on UNIX systems, not DOS.

`-A`	List all entries, including those starting with dot (.), but excluding any . or .. entries.
`-a`	List all entries, including those starting with dot (.).
`-b`	Display nonprintable characters in octal, as in \ooo.

-C	Put output into sorted columns, with output going down the columns.
-c	Sort according to the last time the file's attributes were modified [UNIX].
-d	Give information on a directory itself instead of its contents.
-F	Put a / at the end of each directory name and a * at the end of every executable file.
-f	Force argument to be a directory [UNIX].
-g	Do not display userid of owner [UNIX].
-i	Display inode number(s) along with filename(s) [UNIX]. (Explaining what inodes are is outside the scope of this book.)
-L	Follow symbolic links [UNIX].
-l	Display permissions, links, owner, group, size, time, name; see *Long Output Format.*
-m	Display the list of names in one long line, with commas separating names.
-n	Display userid and group id numbers [UNIX].
-o	Do not display group id numbers [UNIX].
-p	Put a / at the end of the directory name.
-q	Display nonprintable characters as ?.
-R	List subdirectories recursively.
-r	Sort in reverse of usual order; can be combined with other options that sort the list.
-s	Display size in blocks (after the inode number but before other information).
-t	Sort by time. This is normally the time of the last modification; however, with -c, it will be the time of the last change, and with -u, it will be the time of the last access.
-u	Sort by last access time [UNIX].

-x   Put output into sorted columns, with output going across the rows.

-1   Use single-column output on terminal.

Long Output Format

The output from `ls -l` summarizes all the most important information about the file on one line. Here is a sample and what it means:

```
-rw-rw-rw- 1 root  dir 104 Dec 25 19:32 file
```

The first character is - for files, and d for directories.

The next nine characters are in three groups of three; they describe the permissions on the file. The first group of three describes owner permissions; the second describes group permissions; the third describes other (or *world*) permissions. On DOS, there is no support for group permissions and other permissions, so these are the same as the owner. Table M.6 gives characters that may appear.

Table M.6. Possible permission characters.

Character	Meaning
r	Permission to read file
w	Permission to write on file
x	Permission to execute file
a	Archive bit is on (file has not been backed up)
s	System file
h	Hidden file

On DOS, most of the permissions shown will be artificial, with no real meaning. Some permissions can be set with the `chmod` command.

After the permissions comes a number telling the number of links to a file. Because DOS does not support links, this will always be 1 when you use the MKS Tools.

Next comes the name of the owner of the file or directory. Because DOS does not support the concept of ownership, this will always be the name of the first user in the `passwd` file when you use the MKS Tools.

Next comes the name of the group that owns the file or directory. Because DOS does not support the concept of groups, this will always be group 0 (zero) when you use the MKS Tools.

Next comes the size of the file, expressed in bytes.

After this comes a date and time. For a directory, this is the time that the directory was created. For a file, it is normally the time that the file was last modified; however, with -c, it is the time of the last change, and with -u, it is the time of last access.

The last item on the line is the name of the file or directory.

Diagnostics

Possible exit status values are

0	Successful completion
1	Failure because of an invalid command-line option, out of memory, inability to find a file's information, too many directories specified on the command line, or file/directory not found
2	Failure because of an invalid command-line option

Possible error messages include

File or directory "name" is not found	The requested file or directory does not exist.
Cannot allocate memory for sorting	In order to sort its output, ls needs to use a certain amount of memory; this message says that there was not enough memory for the sorting operation.
Too many directory entries in "dir"	The maximum number of entries allowed in a directory is 2,048.

Portability

POSIX.2. X/Open Portability Guide. All UNIX systems. MKS Toolkit. Because DOS doesn't keep track of much file structure information, the options -cfginou have no effect. On DOS, files and directories marked with the *hidden* attribute are treated like UNIX filenames beginning with . (dot).

Note

On DOS, all files are considered executable. Thus the -F option shows a lot of * characters.

mkdir—Create a New Directory

Synopsis

```
mkdir [-p]  [-m mode] directory ...
```

Description

mkdir creates a new directory for each named *directory* argument.

Options

-m   Use to specify permissions for the directories. The *mode* argument can have the same value as the *mode* for chmod. See the manual page for chmod for more details.

-p   Creates intermediate directory components that don't already exist. For example, if one of the *directory* arguments is dir/subdir/subsub and subdir doesn't exist already, it will be created. Directories are created with the *mode* u+wx, which gives full permissions to the owner.

Diagnostics

Possible exit status values are

0   Successful completion

1   Failure because of a missing *mode* after -m, an invalid *mode*, an invalid command-line option, a missing *directory* name, or the inability to create the directory

Possible error messages include

`Path not found`	The parent directory of the named *directory* does not exist.
`Access denied`	The requested directory already exists or is otherwise inaccessible.
`Cannot create directory`	Some other error occurred during the creation of the directory.

Portability

POSIX.2. X/Open Portability Guide. All UNIX systems. MKS Toolkit.

A command of the same name is built into COMMAND.COM, which is supplied with DOS. This MKS command is provided as an alternative because it accepts multiple names and UNIX-style filenames.

See Also

rm, rmdir

more—Interactively View Files on the Screen

Synopsis

```
more [-ceiSs] [-A¦-u] [-n number] [-P prompt] [-p command] [-t tag] [file ...]
more [-ceiSs] [-A¦-u] [-n number] [-P prompt] [-t tag] [+command] [file ...]
```

Description

more displays files one page at a time. It obtains the number of lines per page from the environment or from the -n option. If the standard output is not a terminal device, the number of lines per page is infinite.

If more than one file is specified, they are displayed one at a time. When more fin-ishes displaying one file, it begins displaying the next one in the list. If you give - as one of the filenames, more reads the standard input at that point in the sequence.

more allows paging forwards and backwards and searching for strings.

Options

more accepts the following options:

-A	Causes the display of all characters, including unprintable ones. Normally unprintable characters are displayed in a printable format. Further, ANSI escape sequences for display modes are processed. This option cannot be used with -u. Note: The character in the upper-left corner of the screen always appears in normal mode.
-c	Clears the screen before displaying a new file. If at any time, the new screen to be displayed does not have any lines in common with the current screen, more does not scroll, but instead, redraws the screen one line at a time, starting from the top. more may ignore this option if the terminal doesn't support such operations.
-e	Exits immediately after displaying the last line of the last file. Normally, if standard output is a terminal device, more stops after displaying the last line of the last file and prompts for a new command. If the command that displays text causes more to reach the end of the file again, more exits.
-i	Ignores case during searches.
-n *number*	Specifies the number of lines per page. This overrides any values obtained from the environment.
-P *string*	Sets the prompt that appears at end of each page of text to *string*. The default prompt is [filename]. more normally displays the prompt in reverse video.

-p *command* +*command*	Initially executes the more command on each file. If it executes successfully and *command* is a positioning command, such as a line number or a regular expression search, more displays the resulting page; otherwise more displays the first page of the file. If both the -t and -p options are specified, the -t option is processed first.
-S	Displays the prompt in normal mode rather than reverse video mode.
-s	Replaces consecutive empty lines with a single empty line.
-t *tag*	Searches for the named tag and displays the page of text containing it. A discussion of the ctags command is beyond the scope of this book.
-u	Displays all backspaces as ^H. Normally, *characterbackspace_* (underscore) displays character as underlined, and *characterbackspacecharacter* displays character as boldfaced. -u also displays all carriage returns as ^M. This option cannot be used with -A.

Interactive Commands

more also accepts the following interactive commands.

[*n*]b [*n*]CTRL-B [*n*]PgUp	Moves backward n lines, with a default of one page. If n is more than the page size, more displays only the final page.
[*n*]d [*n*]CTRL-D	Scrolls forward *n* lines, with a default of one half of the page size. If you specify *n*, it becomes the new default for subsequent *d* and *u* commands.

[*n*]f

[*n*]CTRL-F

[*n*]PgDn   Moves forward *n* lines, with a default of one page. At end-of-file, *more* continues with the next file in the list or exits if the current file is the last one in the list.

[*n*]G   Goes to the *n*th line in the file. If you do not specify *n*, *more* advances to the end of the file.

[*n*]g   Goes to the *n*th line in the file, with the default being the first line of the file.

h   Displays a summary of interactive commands.

[*n*]j

[*n*]SPACE

[*n*]ENTER

[*n*]downarrow Scrolls forward *n* lines, with a default of one line for *j*, ENTER and downarrow and a default of one page for SPACE. This command displays the entire *n* lines even if *n* is more than the page size. At end-of-file, these commands cause more to begin displaying the next file in the list or to exit if the current file is the last one in the list.

[*n*]k

[*n*]uparrow   Scrolls backward *n* lines, with a default of one line. This command displays the entire *n* lines even if *n* is more than the page size.

m*letter*   Marks the current position with the lowercase letter. When you view a new file, all previous marks are lost.

[*n*]N   Repeats the previous search, but in the opposite direction. If you specify *n*, *more* repeats the search *n* times.

[*n*]n	Repeats the previous search. If you specify *n*, more repeats the search *n* times. For example, if there are eight occurrences of pattern in the file and /pattern found the second occurrence, a follow-up command of 5n finds and sets the current position to the seventh occurrence of pattern.
q	
:q	
ZZ	Exits more.
R	Refreshes the screen and discards any buffered input.
r	
CTRL-L	
	Refreshes the screen.
[*n*]s	Skips forward *n* lines (with a default of one line) and displays one page beginning at that point. If *n* would cause less than a full page to be displayed, more displays the last page in the file.
[*n*]u	
[*n*]CTRL-U	Scrolls backward *n* lines, with a default of one-half the page size. If you specify *n*, it becomes the new default for subsequent d and u commands.
v	Invokes an editor to edit the current file. more uses the editor named by the environment variable EDITOR. The default editor is vi.
'*letter*	Returns to the position marked with *letter*.
' '	Returns to the position from which you last issued a movement command of greater than one page or the beginning of the file if you have issued no such commands.

:e [*filename*]ENTER
> Stops viewing the current file and views *filename* instead. If you do not specify *filename*, more returns to the beginning of the current file. If *filename* is #, more returns to the last file viewed before the current one.

[*n*]:n
> Views the next file from the list given on the command line. If you specify *n*, more views the *n*th next file from the list.

[*n*]:p
> Views the previous file from the list given in the command line. If you specify *n*, more views the *n*th previous file from the list.

:t *tagname*
> Goes to *tagname*

:w *filename*
> Writes the contents of the current file to the file *filename*.

!*shell-command*
> Escapes to shell and executes *shell-command*.

=

CTRL-G
> Displays, where possible, the name of the file currently being viewed, its number (relative to the total number of files specified in the command line), the current line number, the current byte number, the total bytes to display and what percentage of the file has been displayed.

[*n*]/[!]pattern
> Searches forward in the file for the *n*th line containing pattern. *n* defaults to one if not specified. If pattern is the null regular expression (/), more uses the previous pattern. If the character ! precedes pattern, more searches for lines that do not contain pattern.

[*n*]?[!]pattern
> Searches backward in the file for the *n*th line containing pattern. The search begins at the line immediately before the top line displayed. *n* defaults to one if not specified. If pattern is the null regular expression (?),

more uses the previous pattern. If the character ! precedes pattern, more searches for lines that do not contain pattern.

HOME   Goes to the first line in the file.

END   Goes to the last line in the file.

Diagnostics

Possible exit status values are

0   Successful completion

>0   Failure due to any of the following: filename not a text file, -n option too large, syntax error in regular expression, inability to create a file, inability to open input file, insufficient memory, invalid command, inability to access the terminal, or missing string after -p option

Portability

POSIX.2. X/OPEN Portability Guide. All UNIX systems. MKS Toolkit.

The -A, -P, and -S options, and the :w and ! commands are extensions to the POSIX standard. The HOME, END, PgDn, PgUp, downarrow, and uparrow commands are extensions to traditional implementations of more, available only on terminal types that support these keys.

See Also

cat, head, pg, tail, vi

mv—Rename and Move Files and Directories

Synopsis

```
mv [-fi] file1 file2
mv [-fi] file ... directory
mv -Rr [-fi] directory1 directory2
```

Description

mv can rename files or move them to a different directory. If you specify more than one file, the target must be a directory. mv moves the files into that directory and gives them names that match the final components of the source pathnames. For example,

```
mv file1 file2 dir
```

moves file1 to dir/file1 and moves file2 to dir/file2.

When a single source file is specified and the target is not a directory, the source is moved to the new name.

Options

If a destination file exists and does not have write permission, mv normally asks whether it is all right to overwrite the existing file. If you answer y or yes, the destination is deleted and the source is moved. The -f (*force*) flag suppresses the question; in other words, it automatically behaves as if you answered yes. The -i (interactive) flag always asks the question before overwriting an existing file, whether or not the file is read-only.

The -R (recursive) flag copies a directory and all its contents (files, subdirectories, files in subdirectories, and so on). For example,

```
mv -R dir1 dir2
```

moves the entire contents of dir1 to dir2/dir1. Any directories that need to be created will be created in the process. The -r option is equivalent to -R.

Diagnostics

Possible exit status values are

0   Successful completion.

1   Failure because an argument had a trailing / but was not the name of a directory, a file could not be found, an input file could not be opened for reading, or an output file could not be created or opened for output. Other possible reasons for failure include a read error occurred on an input file or a write error occurred on an output file, the input and output files were the same file, the input file was on a different file system than the output, the input file could not be unlinked, the input file could not be renamed, or a fatal error was encountered when using the -R option.

Possible fatal -R errors include

The inability to access a file

The inability to read a directory

The inability to remove a directory

The inability to create a directory

A target that is not a directory

The source and destination directories being the same

2   Failure because of an invalid command-line option, too few arguments on the command line, a target should be a directory but isn't, no space left on target device, out of memory to hold the data to be copied, or the inability to create a directory to hold a target file.

Possible error messages include

`Cannot allocate target string`	No space to hold the name of the target file. Try to free some memory to give mv more space.
`read only?`	You are attempting to move a file, but there is already a file with the target name and the file is read-only. If you really want to write over the existing

	file, enter y and press Enter. If you do not want to write over the existing file, enter n and press Enter.
`source "name" and target "name" are identical`	The source and the target are actually the same file (for example, because of links, on UNIX systems). In this case, mv will do nothing.
`unreadable directory "name"`	mv cannot read the specified directory, for example, because you do not have appropriate permissions.

Portability

POSIX.2. X/Open Portability Guide. All UNIX systems. MKS Toolkit.

Although you can move files around easily under DOS, it is not so easy to move a DOS directory. You can rename a directory, but you cannot move it to another directory. Renaming directories is allowed only under DOS 3.0 and later versions.

See Also

cp, rm

passwd—Change User Log-In Password

Synopsis

passwd [*username*]

Description

passwd changes your log-in password. The superuser (user number 0 in /etc/passwd) can also change other users' passwords. If *username* is given, passwd changes the password for that user.

If you (or the specified *username*) already have a password, passwd asks you to enter the old password. passwd then prompts you to enter a new password, and then prompts you to enter the same new password to verify that you typed it correctly.

If you are the superuser, passwd prevents you from choosing a password with less than six characters.

Some versions of UNIX have facilities that do not let you change a password too soon after the last time you changed it (to prevent you from changing your password, and then changing right back to the old one).

Diagnostics

Possible exit status values are

0	Successful completion
1	Failure because of an unknown command-line option, an invalid number of arguments, an error opening or writing to a temporary working file, an error opening or writing to the password file, or an error message, such as the ones that follow

Possible error messages include

Sorry.	When passwd asked you to enter the current (old) password, you did not do so correctly.
Passwords do not match. Try again.	The new password and the verification copy do not match. passwd asks you to enter both again.
Password is too easily broken. Try again.	As the superuser, you tried to use too simple a password. Try something longer.
$LOGNAME is not a user in /etc/passwd	The current setting of the LOGNAME environment variable is not one of the user names in the /etc/passwd file. In other words, you are not one of the recognized users, and passwd cannot determine what your password should be. (This problem happens only on DOS where you are free

to choose any value for LOGNAME. On UNIX, security measures ensure that the system can always identify you.)

`No permission to change user's password`

You tried to change the given user's password, but you were not the superuser (user number 0 in /etc/passwd).

`Too many tries. Try again later.`

If you make too many mistakes trying to change the password, passwd simply quits. This is intended to slow down unauthorized users who are trying to guess your password.

`Password may not be changed for` *number* `weeks`

You are required to change your password when it becomes too old. The theory is that it's been around long enough for someone to guess. In this situation, people sometimes try to change their old password to something new, and then immediately change back to the old one again. To prevent this, passwd will not let you change your password again until a certain amount of time has passed.

Files

`/etc/passwd` File where passwords are stored. This is found under $ROOTDIR if the ROOTDIR environment variable exists.

Portability

AT&T UNIX SVID. X/Open Portability Guide. All UNIX systems. MKS Toolkit. With the MKS Toolkit, the encrypted password is binary-compatible with the encryption scheme used on both UNIX System V.2 and 4.2 BSD systems.

Warning

For this command to work properly within a network, you should lock the /etc/
passwd file while you are updating it.

pg—Interactively View Files on the Screen

Synopsis

pg [-acefnst] [-p *prompt*] [-*n*] [+*n*] [+/*pattern*/] [*file* ...]

Description

pg makes it easy for you to read text files, or output piped from another command,
a screenful at a time. pg displays the contents of each *file* named on the command
line. If you haven't specified any filenames on the command line, pg displays the
standard input. To specify the standard input explicitly, use - in place of a filename.

Options

The following command-line options control the way you read files with pg:

-*n*	Sets the window size (in other words, the number of lines displayed in each interaction) to *n* lines. When this option is not present, the default window size is one line shorter than the number of lines on the screen. Also see the w command in the *Commands* section.
-p *prompt*	Displays a prompt at the end of each screenful of text. The -p option sets this prompt to the string *prompt*. The default prompt is :. If the *prompt* string contains the characters %d, as in "[Page %d]", the command will replace those characters with the current page number as it displays each file.
-a	Forces pg to work in *ANSI mode*. This means of display can be more portable to non-PC-compatibles.
-c	Clears the screen before printing each new screenful of text.

| -e | Eliminates the (EOF): prompt at the end of each file. |

-f   Normally, lines longer than the screen width are *folded* into multiple lines. -f tells pg not to fold lines in this way. This can be useful for files containing device-specific escape sequences.

-n   Normally, when you enter a command while reading a file, you must press Enter at the end of the command. However, if you specify -n on the command line, you won't have to press Enter for most commands; pg will execute the command immediately upon receipt of the command character.

-s   Displays all interactive command prompts in a form that stands out on the screen (most often in reverse video).

-t   Normally, pg lets you go backward and forward when you are reading a file. However, with some types of input files (for example, pipes), there's no direct way to go back to an earlier part of the text. To make going back possible, pg stores the input from such sources in a temporary file. Inside this temporary file, you can go backward and forward, even if you couldn't do so in the original source.

-t   Tells pg not to save such input in temporary files. This saves time and disk space. However, it means that you cannot go back and read text that has disappeared from the screen.

+n   Starts printing at line n of the first file. The default is to start printing at line 1.

+/pattern/   Starts printing at the line containing the first occurrence of the regular expression *pattern*. Regular expressions are summarized in Appendix C, "Summary of Filename Generation with Glob Constructs."

Commands

Depending on the options that are specified on the command line, pg pauses at several points as you read through a file. It pauses between windows (screensful) of text, at the end of each file, and before starting any file other than the first. At these pauses, pg lets you enter commands to dictate what pg does next.

Typically, you will just press Enter or Space when pg pauses. This tells pg to display the next screenful of text. If you want a different action, you can type one of the commands described in this section.

You can precede these commands with an optional sign (+ or -), followed by an optional numeric address. Addresses are measured in *screensful*. Normally, an address without a sign refers to an *absolute* position (counting from the beginning of the file). An address with a sign is a *relative* position, relative to the current position in the file. Thus, 1 is an absolute line number, referring to the first screenful of text in the file. -1 is a relative position referring to the screenful of text immediately before the current screen, and +1 is the screenful of text immediately after the current one.

As you type commands, you can make corrections with the standard *erase* and *kill* characters. The complete set of interactive commands is

h	Displays a summary of the interactive commands.
q	Quits pg immediately.
Q	Same as q.
!*command*	Executes the string *command* as if it were typed to the default shell. You must press Enter at the end of the line, whether or not you specified the -n option on the pg command line.
d	Displays a half-screenful of text. The address is measured in half-screenful and defaults to the next half-screenful.
Ctrl-D	Same as d.
l	With no address, l displays the next line of the file. With an address, l displays a screenful starting at the position addressed, with distances measured in lines rather than screensful.
$	Displays the last screenful of text in the file.
.	Redisplays the most recent screenful of text (redraws the screen).
Ctrl-L	Same as . (dot).
s *file*	Saves the entire contents of the file you are looking at in *file*. You must press Enter at the end of the line, whether or not you specified the -n option on the pg command line.

n	If no address is specified, this starts displaying the next file. If an address *n* is specified, it must be an unsigned number, and pg displays the *n*th next file, counting from the current file.
p	If no address is specified, this starts displaying the previous file. If an address *n* is specified, it must be an unsigned number, and pg displays the *n*th previous file, counting from the current file.
w	If an address is specified, w sets the window size to that (unsigned) value. In any case, it displays the next screenful of (the new) window size lines.
/*pattern*/[tmb]	Searches forward within the current file for the first occurrence of a line matching the regular expression *pattern*. An optional character on the end controls where the matching line is displayed on the screen. The letter t is the default and displays the line at the top of the screen. m displays it in the middle of the screen. b displays it at the bottom of the screen. When no letter is present, pg uses the last letter entered (or t if no letter has been entered). You must press Enter at the end of the line, whether or not you specified the -n option on the pg command line.
?*pattern*?[tmb]	Same as the previous example, but searches backward instead of forward.
^*pattern*^[tmb]	Same as ?*pattern*?[tmb].

Examples

The following interactive commands illustrate pg's flexibility. Suppose that you entered the command

```
pg -n *.c
```

and that there are a large number of files with the .c suffix in the current directory.

```
1
```

redisplays the first screenful of the current file.

`-4`

goes back four screens in the current file and displays a screenful of text.

`p`

displays the first screenful of the previous file.

`10w`

sets the window size to 10 lines.

`/Fred/m`

finds the first line containing Fred after the current position in the file, and displays a screenful of text with that line in the middle of the screen.

Diagnostics

Possible exit status values are

0	Successful completion
1	Failure because of an unknown command-line option, insufficient memory, inability to create a temporary file, inability to access the terminal, or a missing *prompt* after a `-p` option

Portability

X/Open Portability Guide. MKS Toolkit. pg is available on UNIX System V, while more is available on POSIX.2-compliant and Berkeley UNIX systems.

On DOS, the character erase is Backspace and the line kill is Esc.

On DOS, if the `ansi.sys` driver (or its equivalent) is loaded, pg automatically uses ANSI-compatible escape sequences. Otherwise, BIOS calls are used to write characters and attributes on the screen. The `-a` option forces ANSI mode.

Files

`/tmp/pg*` Temporary files to allow backward reading. The `/tmp` directory is found using the `ROOTDIR` environment variable. You can specify a different temporary directory using the `TMPDIR` environment variable. For more information, see Appendix E, "POSIX.2 Utility Summary."

See Also

alias, head, more, sh, tail, vi

pr—Print and Format Files

Synopsis

```
pr [-adFfmprtW] [-c n] [-e[c][n]] [-H header-fmt] [-h header] [-i[c][n]]
[-l n] [-n[c][n]] [-o n] [-s[c]] [-w n] [+n] [-n] [file ...]
```

Description

pr displays the given files on its standard output in a paginated form. pr uses the standard input if no files are given on the command line, or if - appears in place of a filename.

Each file is formatted into pages. Each page has a header containing the filename and its last modified date, and the current page and line number. Note that pr only formats the pages and displays them on standard output; if you want to get hard copy, you must use an lp or lpr command to send pr's output to the printer.

By default, output is placed in columns of equal width separated by at least one space. If there is more than one column, each line is truncated to fit the column. pr can order items either down the columns or across the page. It can also use multiple columns to represent different files.

Options

+n	Starts printing with the *n*th page of each file; in other words, it skips the first *n*-1 pages. The default for *n* is 1.
-n	Prints *n* columns of output.
-a	Orders input lines across the page when they are output. If -a is not specified, pr orders items down columns (vertically instead of horizontally).
-c n	Displays n columns of output. When you specify this option, pr behaves as though you had also specified the

-e and -i options. When you specify both this option
and -t, pr uses the minimum number of lines possible to
display the output. You should not specify this option
with -m.

-d   Double-spaces output.

-ec*n*   Expands tabs on input. If given, *c* is taken to be the
character indicating a tab; the default is the ASCII
horizontal tab character. Tabs are set every *n* positions;
the default for *n* is 8. This option is always on, and is
used to change the character and settings. Every occurrence of the input tab character is turned into a sequence
of spaces.

-F   Uses formfeeds to separate pages. pr normally separates
pages by sending a series of newline characters to fill the
length of a page.

-f   Uses formfeeds to separate pages. When output is to a
terminal, pr sounds the bell and waits for you to type a
carriage return before displaying the text. pr normally
separates pages by sending a series of newline characters
to fill the length of a page.

-H header_fmt   Use to customize your header line by specifying a format
with the string header_fmt. pr recognizes the following
special formatting commands:

       %c   Date and time
       %F   Current filename or header string given by -h
       %P   Page number
       %L   Line number
       %D   Date
       %T   Time
       %u   Current user name

The default header format is equivalent to the option
-H "%c %F Page %P".

-h header   Uses the *header* string on each succeeding page header.
This option can be specified between files; however, if
you also specify -m, only the final -h option has an effect.
If you do not specify -h, pr creates a header that contains
the name of the current input file.

-i*cn*	Replaces whitespace with tabs on output. If given, *c* is taken to be the character indicating a tab; the default is the ASCII horizontal tab character. Tabs are set every *n* positions; the default for *n* is 8. If this tab character differs from the input tab character and the input contains this tab character, the output is likely to be messy.
-l*n*	Sets the number of lines per page of output. The default is 66. The actual number of lines printed per page is this number less five lines for the headers and two for the trailers. If you specify both -t and -l, all lines of the page are used.
-m	Outputs each file in its own column down the page. -m overrides the -a option, and forces the -*n* option to the number of files given.
-n*cn*	Numbers the lines of each file. Each number is *n* characters wide; the default for *n* is 5. Each line number is separated from the rest of the line by the character *c*; the default is the ASCII horizontal tab character. If *c* is the same as the input tab character, pr follows the line number with the number of spaces needed to reach the next tab stop. These spaces can in turn be replaced by the output tab character if you specify -i. For multicolumn output, pr adds line numbers to each column. If you specify both -m and -n, pr only puts line numbers in the first column.
-o *n*	Offsets each line of output by *n* character positions.
-p	Pauses between pages if output is going to a terminal device. pr sounds the terminal's bell, then waits for you to press Enter.
-r	Does not print any error messages that might arise when opening files.
-s*c*	Normally each column is padded with spaces or truncated to the exact column width. With -s, each column is printed at its correct length and separated from the

next column with the character c. The default for c is the ASCII horizontal tab character. The given character c is never replaced by the output tab character.

-t   Does not print headers or trailers. The full length of the page is used for file output.

-w*n*   Sets the width of the page to *n*. The default is 72. The width is ignored for output using the -s option. It is also ignored for single-column output, unless you specify the -F option.

-W   Normally, lines are truncated at the column width if you don't use -s. -W folds lines instead; each separate part of the line is treated as a separate line.

Diagnostics

Possible exit status values are

0   Successful completion

1   Failure due to insufficient memory, insufficient line width, or a write error on the standard output

2   Failure due to invalid command-line syntax or option

Possible error messages include

Missing header   You specified -h but did not supply a *header* string after the -h.

Width is insufficient   The line is not wide enough to hold the given number of columns with the given column width; or a column is not wide enough to hold the minimum amount of data.

Files

/dev/tty   pr writes prompts to this on UNIX (which means that prompts appear on your terminal).

CON: pr writes prompts to this on DOS (which means that prompts should appear on your terminal).

Portability

POSIX.2. X/Open Portability Guide. MKS Toolkit. This version of pr is compatible with UNIX System V, which differs substantially from previous UNIX prs.

See Also

`cat`

print—Output Arguments from the Shell

Synopsis

```
print [-npRrs] [-u[descriptor]] [argument ...]
```

Description

If `print` is called without options or with only the - option, the command outputs each *argument* to the standard output using the same escape conventions as `echo`. In this form, `print` and `echo` have the same functionality; see the `echo` man page. `print` is built into the KornShell.

Options

The difference between `print` and `echo` is that `print` takes several options.

If you specify the -n option, `print` does not automatically add a newline to the end of the output.

With the -r and -R options, `print` ignores escape sequences. Also, with -R, `print` treats all subsequent command-line options (except -n) as arguments rather than as options.

The -p option sends output to a coprocess. This is not useful on DOS, because DOS does not have coprocesses.

If you specify the -s option, `print` appends its output to the command history file rather than sending the output to the standard output. Similarly, if you use -u[*descriptor*], `print` writes its output to the file corresponding to the file *descriptor*. The default file descriptor is 1. File descriptors are single digits between 0 and 9.

419

Diagnostics

Possible exit status values are

0   Successful completion

1   Failure because of an invalid command-line option, an invalid *descriptor* specified with -u, or a nonexistent coprocess

Possible error messages include

Cannot print on file descriptor ...   You tried to print on a file descriptor that was not opened for writing.

History not available   You specified the -s option to write into a history file, but at present you are not using a history file.

Portability

MKS Toolkit. print is a built-in command of the KornShell on UNIX, but not of the Bourne Shell.

See Also

echo, fc, read, sh

pwd—Display Working Directory

Synopsis

pwd

Description

pwd writes the pathname of the current working directory to the standard output.

Diagnostics

Possible exit status values are

0	Successful completion.
1	pwd cannot determine the current working directory.

Portability

POSIX.2. X/Open Portability Guide. All UNIX systems. MKS Toolkit.

On DOS, the CD command in COMMAND.COM has a similar function. On DOS, the output of PWD includes the current drive specification.

See Also

sh

Note

pwd exists both as a command built into the shell and as a separate command. In the shell, pwd is defined as

```
alias pwd='print - $PWD'
```

r—Edit and Re-Execute Previous Command

Synopsis

```
r [old=new] [specifier]
```

Description

The r command re-executes a command that you ran previously, possibly editing the command first. Commands are obtained from your *command history* file; see the man pages for fc and sh for more details.

The *specifier* argument tells which command you want to re-execute. It can have any of the following forms:

- An unsigned number: r runs the command that has that number.

- A negative number *-n*: r runs the command that came *n* commands before the current one.

- A character string: r runs the most recent command line beginning with that string.

If you do not give a *specifier*, r runs the most recent command.

The *old=new* feature lets you edit a command before running it. *old* and *new* must be character strings. r replaces the first occurrence of *old* with *new* and then re-executes the command.

Examples

```
r sh
```

Runs the most recent command beginning with the characters sh. The sh could be the whole command name, or it could be part of a longer command name (for example, shift).

```
cp file1 /dir
r 1=2
r 2=3
```

This is equivalent to

```
cp file1 /dir
cp file2 /dir
cp file3 /dir
```

Compare this with

```
cp file1 /dir/file1
r 1=2
```

which is equivalent to

```
cp file1 /dir/file1
cp file2 /dir/file1
```

Because r only replaces the first occurrence of the *old* string 1, the second 1 does not change. This shows that you have to be careful when you use the substitution feature.

r is an alias built into the shell. It is defined as

```
alias r='fc -s'
```

Diagnostics

Possible exit status values are

0	Successful completion
1	Failure due to a missing history file, or inability to find the desired command in the history file
2	Failure because of an invalid command-line option or argument

Portability

POSIX.2. X/Open Portability Guide. All UNIX systems. MKS Toolkit.

See Also

alias, fc, sh

read—Input a Line to the Shell

Synopsis

```
read [-prs] [-u[descriptor]] [variable?prompt] [variable ...]
```

Description

When read is called without options, it reads one line from the standard input, breaks the line into fields, and assigns the fields to each *variable* in the order they appear on the command line.

To determine where to break the line into fields, read uses the built-in variable IFS (Input Field Separator). When read encounters any of the characters in IFS, it

interprets that character as separating the end of one field from the beginning of the next. The default value of IFS is a blank, a tab, and a newline indicating that fields are separated by whitespace.

If read finds two IFS characters in a row, it usually assumes there is an empty field between the two characters. For example, if IFS is :, the input a::b has three fields: a, an empty field, and b. However, if IFS contains whitespace, a sequence of multiple spaces and/or tabs and/or newlines is considered to be a single field separator. For example, "a   b" is considered to have two fields, even though there are several spaces between the a and the b.

The *n*th *variable* in the command line is assigned the nth field read in. If there are more input fields than there are variables, the last variable is assigned all of the unassigned fields. If there are more variables than fields, the extra variables are assigned the null string ("").

When no variables appear on the command line, read assigns the input to an environment variable named REPLY.

Options

If you specify the -r option, input is read in *raw mode*. This means that escape sequences are ignored. For example, a backslash (\) is simply part of the input, not a line continuation character.

If you specify the -p option, input is read from a coprocess. This is meaningless on DOS because DOS doesn't have coprocesses.

If you specify the -s option, read adds its input to the command history file as well as assigning the input to the variables.

If you specify -u[*descriptor*], read takes its input from the file associated with the single digit file *descriptor*, rather than from the standard input. The default file descriptor is 0.

The first *variable* parameter may take the form

variable?prompt

If so, read outputs the string *prompt* to prompt for input, provided that the shell is interactive. The *prompt* is sent to the file *descriptor* if it is open for write and is a terminal device. If you do not specify -u*descriptor*, read writes the prompt to the standard error.

Example

Listing M.18 shows a short sequence of commands that provides a list of users from the /etc/passwd file.

 Listing M.18. Listing the system's users.

```
IFS=';'
while read name junk
do
     echo $name
done </etc/passwd
```

Diagnostics

Possible exit status values are

0	Successful completion
1	Failure due to an end-of-file on input, an invalid *variable*, an incorrect *descriptor* specified after -u, or a missing coprocess
2	Failure due to an invalid command-line argument

Possible error messages include

Cannot read on file descriptor ..."	You tried to read a file descriptor that was not opened for reading.

Portability

POSIX.2. X/Open Portability Guide. MKS Toolkit. read is a built-in command of the Bourne Shell and the KornShell on UNIX. The Bourne Shell does not implement parameters of the form *variable?prompt*, or any options.

See Also

continue, fc, print, sh

Note

This command is built into the shell.

return—Return from Shell Function or . (Dot) Script

Synopsis

```
return [expression]
```

Description

return returns from a shell function or . (dot) script. It is built into the shell. The exit status is the value of *expression*. The default value of *expression* is the exit status of the last command executed.

Diagnostics

The current function or script will return the value of *expression*. If no *expression* is given, the exit status will be the exit status of the last command executed.

Portability

POSIX.2. X/Open Portability Guide. MKS Toolkit. return is a built-in command of the Bourne Shell and KornShell on UNIX.

See Also

exit, sh

rm—Remove Files

Synopsis

```
rm [-fiRr] file ...
```

Description

rm removes (deletes) the files named on the command line.

Options

If you specify -r, names on the command line may be directories as well as files. If so, rm removes all files and subdirectories under the given directories. The option -R is exactly equivalent to -r.

Normally, if you ask rm to remove a read-only file, rm asks if you are sure you want to delete the file. Type y or yes if you really want the file deleted. The -f option tells rm to delete read-only files immediately, without asking for confirmation. -f also suppresses error messages for files that do not exist.

The -i (interactive) option displays the name of every file that might be deleted and prompts you for confirmation. Enter y or yes if you really want to delete the file. Enter n or no if you want to keep the file.

Diagnostics

Possible exit status values are

0	Successful completion
1	Failure because of an inability to remove a file, an attempt to remove a directory without specifying -r, or a fatal error during an operation when -r is specified (either the inability to find file information or the inability to read a directory)
2	Failure because of an invalid command-line option, or no filenames specified

Portability

POSIX.2. X/Open Portability Guide. All UNIX systems. MKS Toolkit.

See Also

cp, mv, rmdir

rmdir—Remove Directory

Synopsis

```
rmdir [-p] directory ...
```

Description

rmdir removes (deletes) each requested *directory*. rmdir only works on directories that are entirely empty (containing no files or subdirectories).

If -p is specified, rmdir removes all intermediate component directories. For example

```
rmdir -p abc/def/ghi
```

is equivalent to

```
rmdir abc/def/ghi
rmdir abc/def
rmdir abc
```

Diagnostics

Possible exit status values are

0	Successful completion
1	Failure because *directory* is not a directory, or because it still contains files or subdirectories
2	Failure because of an invalid command-line option, or no *directory* names specified

Possible error messages include

`Non-empty directory`	A directory contains files or subdirectories. Use rm -r to remove the directory.
`No such directory`	The requested *directory* does not exist or is otherwise inaccessible.
`Current directory illegal`	Indicates that you should use cd to change to another directory before removing the current directory.

Portability

POSIX.2. X/Open Portability Guide. All UNIX systems. MKS Toolkit. A command of the same name is built into the command.com shell supplied with DOS. However, the MKS version accepts multiple directory names and UNIX-style filenames.

See Also

```
mkdir, rm
```

sed—Stream Editor (Noninteractive)

Synopsis

```
sed [-En] [script] [file ...]
sed [-En] [-e script] ... [-f scriptfile] ... [file ...]
```

Description

sed edits text files. More precisely, sed reads a set of editing commands from *script* and applies those commands to each *file* named on the command line. If the command line does not specify any files, the editing commands in *script* are applied to the standard input. A script is simply a list of one or more sed commands. For example, in

```
sed "s/Athletics/Blue Jays/g" file
```

the script is the instruction

```
s/Athletics/Blue Jays/g
```

which is performed on the given file.

Commands in a sed script are similar to commands of the interactive text editor ed, but sed commands view the input text as a stream of characters rather than a directly addressable file.

Options

If -E is specified, sed uses extended regular expressions. Otherwise, it uses basic regular expressions. For more information, see Appendix C, "Summary of Filename Generation with Glob Constructs."

Each input line is read into a special area known as the *pattern buffer*. A second area, called the *hold buffer*, is used by certain sed commands [gGhHx]. By default, the final contents of the pattern buffer are written to the standard output after each pass through the script. The -n option prevents this automatic write; with -n, sed only produces output through explicit commands in the *script* [acilnpPr].

There are three ways to specify scripts on the command line.

- If the -e option appears on the command line, the string argument after the -e is used as the sed *script*. By specifying several -e options, you can create a script that contains several commands.

- If the -f option appears on the command line, the script is read from the file named scriptfile. By specifying several -f options, you can create a script that spans several files.

- If neither -e nor -f appears on the command line, the first argument (after -E and/or -n) is used as the (single) script.

Addresses

As in ed, sed commands may begin with zero, one, or two addresses. Zero-address commands reference every input line. One-address commands select only those lines matching that address. Two-address commands select those input line ranges commencing with a match on the first address up to an input line matching the second address, inclusive. Permissible addressing constructions are

n	Refers to the *n*th input line.
$	Refers to the last input line.
/regexp/	Selects an input line that matches the specified regular expression *regexp*. If you do not want to use slash (/) characters around the regular expression, you can use a different pair of characters but you must put a backslash (\) before the first one. For example, if you want to use % characters to enclose the regular expression, write \%*regexp*%.

Commands

Each line of a script contains up to two addresses, a single letter command, possible command modifiers, and a terminating newline character. The newline is optional in script strings that are typed directly on the command line.

The following list shows the commands and the maximum number of addresses they can take. You can give a command fewer than the number of addresses specified, but not more. Addresses appear before the command name; for example, the b command is shown as

```
a,bb label
```

This shows that b can take a range of addresses *a,b*, and is followed by another argument written as *label*.

`aa\`	The append command copies subsequent text lines from the script to the standard output. sed outputs the text after all other script operations are completed for the line and just before the next record is read. If you want to append several lines of input text, put a \ on the end of every line but the last. The first line without a \ character is taken as the end of the input text. The \ characters on the ends of lines are not considered to be part of the text.
`a,bb label`	The branch command branches to the given label. Labels are created with the : command.
`a,bc\`	The change command changes the addressed lines by deleting the contents of the pattern buffer (input line) and writing new text on the standard output. The new text lines are input in the same way as for a\. When two addresses are specified, sed delays text output until the final line in the range of addresses; otherwise, the behavior would probably surprise many users. sed skips the rest of the script for each addressed line.
`a,bd`	The delete command deletes the contents of the pattern buffer (input line). The script is restarted with the next input line.

`a,bD`	This is identical to the d command except that sed only deletes the pattern buffer up to and including the first newline. sed then starts the script again from the beginning and applies it to the text left in the pattern buffer.
`a,bg`	sed copies the text in the hold buffer into the pattern buffer, overwriting the pattern buffer's original contents.
`a,bG`	sed appends the text in the hold buffer to the end of the pattern buffer.
`a,bh`	This copies the text in the pattern buffer into the hold buffer, overwriting the hold buffer's original contents.
`a,bH`	This appends the text in the pattern buffer onto the end of the hold buffer.
`ai\`	The insert command is identical to the a\ command, except that sed outputs the text immediately.
`a,bl`	The list command prints the pattern buffer (input line) onto the standard output in a way that makes non-printable characters visible.
`a,bn`	After copying the pattern buffer to the standard output, sed reads the next line of input into the pattern buffer.
`a,bN`	sed appends the next line of input to the end of the pattern buffer.
`a,bp`	The print command places the text in the pattern buffer onto the standard output. This form of output is not disabled by the -n option. If you do not use -n, p prints the pattern buffer twice.
`a,bP`	This operates like the p command, except that it prints the text in the pattern buffer only up to and including the first newline character.
`aq`	The quit command quits sed. The rest of the script is skipped, and no more input lines are read. Outstanding operations (for example, a\) are still honored.

`a,b``r` *file*

The read command reads text from `file` and places this text onto the standard output after all other script commands have been processed. The timing of this operation is analogous to the a command.

`a,b``s/`*regexp*`/`*substitution*`/[gpn][`*wfile*`]`

The substitute command puts the string *substitution* in place of the first occurrence of text matching the regular expression *regexp*. If *regexp* contains the sequence \n, the sequence matches an embedded newline in the pattern buffer (for example, one resulting from an N command). The s command can be followed by a combination of the following:

p	This executes the print (p) command only if a successful substitution occurs.
g	Puts *substitution* in place of all occurrences matching *regexp,* instead of just the first.
n	Puts *substitution* in place of only the *n*th occurrence matching *regexp.*
wfile	If a substitution occurs, the contents of the pattern buffer (after substitution) are written to the end of the specified *file.*

`a,b``t` *label*

The test command branches to the indicated *label* if any successful substitution has occurred since reading the last input line or executing the last t command.

`a,b``w` *file*

The write command writes the text in the pattern buffer to the end of *file.*

`a,b``x`

The exchange command switches the text in the hold buffer with the text in the pattern buffer.

`a,b``y/`*set1*`/`*set2*`/`

This construction transliterates any input character occurring in *set1* to the corresponding element of *set2*. The sets must be the same length. For example,

```
y/abcdefghijklmnopqrstuvwxyz/
ABCDEFGHIJKLMNOPQRSTUVWXYZ/
```

changes lowercase letters to their uppercase counterparts.

433

`a,b{`	This command groups all commands until the next matching } command so that the entire group is executed only if the { command is selected by its address(es).
`: label`	This command has no action. It serves only as a placeholder for the *label* that may be the destination of a b or t command.
`a,b!cmd`	The negation command executes the specified *cmd* only if the addresses do not select the ! command.
`#`	Any empty script line is treated as a comment. A script line beginning with the # character is also treated as a comment, except for the first line in a script. If the first line in a script is #n, it is equivalent to specifying -n on the command line.
`a=`	This writes the decimal value of the current line number onto the standard output.

Examples

Here is a filter to switch political allegiance:

```
sed 's/democrat\(ic\)*/republican/g'
```

Diagnostics

Possible exit status values are

0	Successful completion
1	Failure because of any of the following:

> Missing script
> Too many script arguments
> Too few arguments
> Unknown option
> Cannot use both -f and -e options
> Can't open script file
> Must have at least one (noncomment) command

Label not found in script
Unknown command
Cannot nest ! command
\ must terminate command
End-of-file in command
Command needs a label
Badly formed filename
Cannot open file
Insufficient memory to compile command
Bad regular expression delimiter
No remembered regular expression
Regular expression error
Insufficient memory for buffers
y command must be followed by a printable character as
separator
Nonmatching { and } commands
Garbage after command
Too many addresses for command
Newline or end-of-file found in pattern

Possible error messages include

`badly formed filename for "command" command`	The given command required a filename, but its operand did not have the syntax of a filename.
`cannot nest "!" command`	A ! command cannot contain a ! command of its own.
`"command" command needs a label`	The specified command required a label, but you did not supply one.
`must have at least one (non-comment) command`	The input to sed must contain at least one active command (that is, a command that is not a comment).
`no remembered regular expression`	You issued a command that tried to use a remembered regular expression, such as //abc. However, there is no remembered regular expression yet. To correct this, change the command to use an explicit regular expression.

Portability

POSIX.2. X/Open Portability Guide. All UNIX systems. MKS Toolkit. The -E option is unique to this version of sed.

See Also

diff, grep, vi

set—Set Shell Flags and Positional Parameters

Synopsis

```
set [±abCefhiKkmnpsTtuvXx-] [±Aname] [±o[flag]] [parameter ...]
```

Description

If set is called without arguments, it displays the names and values of all the environment variables. Otherwise, set changes the values or the characteristics of shell variables or options.

Options

Arguments of the form -option set each shell flag specified as an option. Similarly, arguments of the form +option turn off each of the shell flags specified as an option.

Shell flags are also turned on with command-line arguments of the form -o flag and turned off with command-line arguments of the form +o flag. The command set -o lists the shell flags that are currently set.

If a *parameter* list is given, the positional parameters are set to the ones specified.

All the set options except ±A, -s, -, and -- are shell flags. Shell flags can also be set on the sh command line at invocation. The following list summarizes shell flags. The manual page for sh gives further information on many of these flags.

- -a   All subsequently defined variables are set for export.
- -b   Notifies you when background jobs finish running.

-C   Prevents the output redirection operator > from overwriting an existing file. Use the alternate operator >¦ to force an overwrite.

-e   If the shell is noninteractive, this tells the shell to execute the ERR trap and then exit. This flag is disabled when reading profiles.

-f   This disables filename generation.

-h   All commands used from now on become *tracked aliases*. See the alias manual page for an explanation of tracked aliases.

-k   Tells the shell that assignment parameters can be placed anywhere on the command line and will still be included in the environment of the command.

-K   Tells the shell to use Korn-compatible behavior in any case where the POSIX.2 behavior is different from that specified by Korn.

-L   Makes the shell a login shell. Setting this flag is effective only at shell invocation.

-m   Each background job is run in a separate process group and is reported on when completed.

-n   If the shell is noninteractive, commands are read but not executed.

-p   Resets PATH variable to a default value, disables processing of $HOME/.profile ($HOME/profile.ksh on DOS), and uses the file /etc/suid_profile (/etc/suid_pro.ksh on DOS) instead of the file in the ENV variable.

-t   Exits after reading and executing one command.

-T   Disables the shell's timer interrupt. This is useful when a program causes a TSR to enable a timer interrupt that would be disabled when the shell exits.

-u   Tells the shell to give an error message if an unset parameter is used in a substitution.

-v   Shell input lines are printed as they are read.

-x   Commands and their arguments are printed as they are executed.

The following options can be turned on with -o or turned off with +o.

allexport	Same as the -a option.
errexit	Same as the -e option.
bgnice	Background jobs run at a lower priority.
ignoreeof	Shell does not exit on end-of-file.
keyword	Same as the -k option.
markdirs	Trailing / added to filename-generated directories.
monitor	Same as the -m option.
noclobber	When set, the output redirection operator > will not overwrite an existing file. Use the alternate operator >¦ to force an overwrite.
noexec	Same as the -n option.
noglob	Same as the -f option.
nolog	When set, function definitions are not recorded in the history file.
nounset	Same as the -u option.
protected	Same as the -p option.
verbose	Same as the -v option.
trackall	Same as the -h option.
vi	Specifies vi style in-line editor for command entry.
xtrace	Same as the -x option.

In addition, set accepts the following options

+Aname	Assigns the parameter list to the elements of *name*, starting at *name[0]*.
-Aname	Unsets name, then assigns the parameter list to the elements of *name*, starting at *name[0]*.
-s	Sorts the positional parameters.

-	Turns off the -v and -x flags. Also, parameters that follow this option do not set shell flags, but are assigned to be positional parameters (see the manual page for sh).
- -	Parameters that follow this option do not set shell flags, but are assigned to positional parameters.

See Appendix F, "KornShell Editing Features," for a description of the effect of setting the vi option.

Diagnostics

Possible exit status values are

0	Successful completion
1	Failure due to an invalid command-line argument

Portability

POSIX.2. X/Open Portability Guide. MKS Toolkit. set is a built-in command of the Bourne Shell and KornShell on UNIX. Several shell flags are extensions only in the KornShell: noglob, ignoreeof, trackall, monitor, bgnice, and markdirs.

The -m and -o bgnice options are not useful on DOS. Under DOS, the value of the ROOTDIR environment variable determines where to find the /etc directory.

See Also

alias, export, sh, trap, typeset

Note

This command is built into the shell.

sh—Invoke the KornShell (Command Interpreter)

Synopsis

```
sh [±abCefhiKkLmnprTtuvXx] [-0 executable] [±o option] [-R address]
[cmd_file [argument...]]
sh -c cmdstring [±abCefhiKkLmnprTtuvXx] [-0 executable] [±o option] [-R address]
[cmd_name [argument...]]
sh -s [±abCefhiKkLmnprTtuvXx] [-0 executable] [±o option] [-R address]
[argument...]
```

Description

This manual page for sh contains the following subsections:

- Options and Invocation
- Command Syntax
- Command Execution
- Word Expansion
- Directory Substitution
- Parameter Substitution
- Arithmetic Substitution
- Command Substitution
- Quoting
- File Descriptors and Redirection
- Filename Generation
- Variables
- Shell Execution Environments
- Built-In Commands

Subsections dealing with substitution and interpretation of input appear in the order in which the shell performs those substitutions and interpretations.

Much of the functionality of the shell comes from built-in commands like `cd` and `alias`. The man pages for such commands describe additional features of the shell not included here.

Options and Invocation

MKS KornShell (`sh`) is a sophisticated command interpreter which is upwardly compatible with the Bourne Shell. It can serve as a replacement for the standard DOS command interpreter.

Normally you invoke the shell by logging in. You can also invoke the shell by typing an explicit `sh` command. On DOS, you can invoke the shell by putting an appropriate entry in config.sys or autoexec.bat. Some people find it useful to copy the sh.exe file into a file named rsh.exe. If you invoke the shell under the name `rsh`, the shell operates in *restricted* mode. This mode is described in connection with the `-r` option.

If you invoke the shell with a name that begins with the `-` character, it is a *login shell*. (You can also get a login shell if you invoke the shell with the `-L` option.) A login shell begins by executing the file

```
/etc/profile
($ROOTDIR/etc/profile.ksh on DOS)
```

It then executes

```
$HOME/.profile
($HOME/profile.ksh on DOS)
```

using the `.` command (see the `dot` man page). If `$HOME` is not set, the shell searches the current directory for

```
.profile
(profile.ksh on DOS)
```

and executes this file with the `.` command, if it exists. The shell does not complain if it cannot find any of these files.

You can use profile files to customize your session with `sh`. For example, your profile files can set options, create aliases, or define functions and variables.

If there is at least one argument on the `sh` command line, `sh` takes the first argument as the name of a shell script to execute. (The exception to this is when `-s` is used.) Any additional arguments are assigned to the positional parameters; usually, these serve as arguments to the shell script. See *Parameter Substitution* for information about positional parameters and the `set` man page for information about changing these parameters.

If sh finds the ENV environment variable set when it begins execution (after profile processing), it executes the file named by the expansion of the value of this variable (see *Variables*).

The shell accepts the following options on the command line:

-c *cmdstring*
: Executes *cmdstring* as if it were an input line to the shell and then exits. This is used by programs (for example, editors) that call the shell for a single command. sh assigns arguments in *cmdstring* to the positional parameters. If you specify *cmd_name,* special parameter 0 is set to this string for use when executing the commands in *cmdstring*.

-i
: Invokes an interactive shell, as opposed to running a script. With -i, the shell catches and ignores interrupts. Without -i, an interrupt terminates the shell. For shells which read from the terminal, -i is the default.

-K
: Specifies Korn-compatible behavior in any case where the POSIX.2 behavior is different from the behavior specified by Korn. Without -K, the shell defaults to POSIX.2 behavior.

-L
: Makes the shell a *login shell* as described earlier.

-0 *file*
: Specifies the name of the file that contains the shell program. This option is required for DOS 2.0. For DOS, it is only useful in conjunction with -R; -0 must come before -R on the command line. -R may require the reloading of the text area from disk. Normally, the shell can determine the name of the file used to load the shell; however in some cases, such as DOS release 2, that information is not available. With -0 *file*, you can give the name of the file that contains the shell program.

  This option may also be required on DOS version 6.0 if you set the shell in your config.sys file with the -R flag.

-r
: Invokes a restricted shell (as noted earlier, you can also invoke a restricted shell by using the name rsh). In a restricted shell, you cannot do any of the following: use the cd command; change the values of the variables ENV,

442

PATH, or SHELL; use > or >> to redirect output; specify command names containing /. These restrictions do not apply during execution of *profile* files.

-R *address*

Enables transient shell feature (under DOS only). This feature allows the shell's code space to be reloaded so that programs invoked by the shell have an additional 64K of space for execution. If *address* is zero, the code is placed at the highest part of normal DOS memory. As the shell completes each command, code within the shell's data area checksums the code in high memory. If that checksum fails, the code is reloaded from the original shell executable on disk. At start-up time, the shell opens the shell executable; then at reload time, it simply issues a seek and a read on the open file descriptor. This implies that the option should only be used when the shell is run from a hard disk.

If *address* is non-zero, it is assumed to be a hex segment address. Rather than being located in high DOS memory, the text is placed at this given address. sh assumes that this memory exists and is not part of any DOS memory chain. sh checksums the memory but does not reload on checksum failure. This is useful if you have a 64K memory area discontiguous from normal DOS memory, or a 386 protected mode program that causes the area to page to high memory.

-s

Reads commands from standard input and assigns all *arguments* to the positional parameters. Normally, if there is at least one *argument* to the shell, the first such *argument* is the name of a file to execute.

-T

Disables the shell's timer interrupt. This can be used when a program causes a TSR to enable a timer interrupt, which would be disabled when the shell exits. This is typically used for Sun's PC-NFS net start rdr command in a shell script. This option is only available on DOS.

If you specify `cmd_file` without either the `-c` or `-s` option, the shell takes it as the name of a file which contains commands to be run. Special parameter 0 is set to this name.

In addition, you can use the `-a`, `-b`, `-C`, `-e`, `-f`, `-h`, `-i`, `-k`, `-L`, `-m`, `-n`, `-o`, `-p`, `-r` `-T`, `-t`, `-u`, `-v`, `-X`, and `-x` options. You can specify these options with either a `-` to turn them off or a `+` to turn them on. The set man page describes these options.

Command Syntax

The shell implements a sophisticated programming language that gives you complete control over the execution and combination of individual commands. When the shell scans its input, it always treats the following characters specially.

```
; & ( ) < > ¦ ' \
space tab new-line
```

To use any of these characters inside an actual argument, you must quote the argument (so that the shell doesn't use the special meanings of the characters). See *Quoting* for more information.

A *simple command* is a list of *arguments* separated by blanks or tabs.

When a word begins with an unescaped hash mark (#), the remainder of the line is treated as a *comment,* and the shell discards input up to but not including the next newline.

When a command starts with a defined alias, `sh` replaces the alias with its definition (see the man page for `alias`).

A *reserved word command* starts with a *reserved word* (for example, `if`, `while`, `for`). Reserved word commands provide flow of control operations for the shell. These are described later in this section.

A *command* may be any of the following:

```
command: simple command
reserved word command
(command)
command ¦ command
command && command
command ¦¦ command
command & command
command &
command ¦&
command ; command
command ;
command <newline>
```

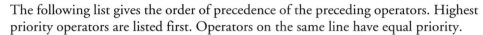

The following list gives the order of precedence of the preceding operators. Highest priority operators are listed first. Operators on the same line have equal priority.

```
( )
¦
&&
¦ ¦
&
;
```

You can also combine commands into a structure known as a *compound-command* which is simply a series of individuals commands joined together by these operators. The following list shows the meaning of these operations.

(*compound-command*)	Executes the commands in *compound-command* in a subshell. This means that the current shell invokes a second shell to execute the commands. In this way, *compound-command* executes in a completely separate execution environment; it can change working directories, change variables, open files, and so on, without affecting the first shell. The subshell's environment begins as a copy of the current environment, so the value of the ENV environment variable is not used when a subshell starts.
¦	Creates a pipe between the two *commands* that the ¦ operator connects. This means that the standard output of the first *command* becomes the standard input of the second *command*. A series of commands connected by pipes is called a *pipeline*. The exit status is that of the last command in the pipeline.
&&	Is the logical AND operator. The shell executes the second *command*—if and only if—the first *command* returns a true (zero) exit status.
¦ ¦	This is the logical OR operator. The shell executes the second *command*—if and only if—the first *command* returns a false (non-zero) exit status.

&   Asynchronously executes the *command* that
precedes it. This means that the shell just starts
the *command* running and then immediately goes
on to take new input, before the *command*
finishes execution. On systems such as DOS
where asynchronous execution is not possible,
this operation is effectively equivalent to ; .

¦&   Executes the *command* that precedes it as a *coprocess.* The *command* runs asynchronously, as
with the & operator, but *command*'s standard
input and standard output are connected to the
shell by pipes. The shell sends input to *command*'s
standard input with the print -p command and
reads from *command*'s standard output with the
read -p command. The *command* should not
buffer its output. Because of this and other
limitations, coprocesses should be designed to be
used as coprocesses. On systems such as DOS
where asynchronous execution is not possible,
coprocesses are not supported.

;   Is the sequential execution operator. The second
command is executed only after the first *command*
has completed.

\<newline\>   The unescaped newline is equivalent to the ;
operator.

The shell contains a rich set of *reserved word
commands* which control the flow of a shell
script and let you create compound commands.
In the following list, a *command* can also be a
sequence of *commands* separated by *new-lines*.
Italic square brackets (*[ ]*) indicate optional
portions of commands and are never part of the
command syntax.

! *command*   The exclamation point is the logical NOT
command. When its operand is false (non-zero),

this command returns true (zero). When its operand is true (zero), this command returns false (non-zero).

`{ compound-command;}`	Enclosing a command in braces is similar to the (*compound-command*) construct except that the shell executes the *compound-command* in the same environment rather than under a subshell. { and } are simply reserved words to the shell. To make it possible for the shell to recognize these symbols, you must put a blank or newline after the { and a semicolon or newline before the }.

```
case word in
[(][pattern[¦pattern] ...)compound-command ;;] ...
[(][pattern[¦pattern] ...)compound-command ;;] ...
esac
```

The case statement is similar to the switch statement of the C programming language or the case statement of Pascal. If the given *word* matches any one of the *patterns* separated by or-bar (¦) characters, sh executes the corresponding *compound-command*. The *patterns* should follow the rules given in *Filename Generation* except that the period (.) and slash (/) are not treated specially. Patterns are matched in the order they are given, so more inclusive patterns should be mentioned later. Once a pattern matching *word* has been found, no further patterns are expanded. You must use the double semicolon (- ;;) to delimit *compound-command* and introduce the next *pattern*.

```
for variable [in word ...]
do compound-command
done
```

The for statement sets variable to each word argument in turn, and executes the set of commands once for each setting of variable. If you omit the in word part, sh sets variable to each positional parameter. You may divert the flow of control within the loop with the break or continue statements. The exit status of a for command is the exit status of the last command in the loop to execute. If the loop contains no commands, the exit status is zero.

```
function funcname {
compound-command
}
funcname() {
compound-command
}
```

Either of these forms defines a `function` named *variable,* the body of which consists of the sequence of *command*s. You invoke a function just like any other command; when you actually call the function, `sh` saves the current positional parameters. The function's command-line arguments then replace these parameters until the function finishes. If the option flag `-K` is set, `sh` also saves the current ERR, EXIT traps and any flags manipulated with the `set` command; these are restored when the function finishes. The function terminates either by falling off the end of the code of the function body or by reaching a `return` statement. If the function uses `typeset` to declare any variables in the function body, the variables are local to the function. The exit status of a function definition is zero, if the function was declared successfully; otherwise, it is greater than zero. The exit status of an invoked function is the exit status of the last command executed by the function.

```
if compound-command
then compound-command
[elif compound-command
then compound-command] ...
[else compound-command]
fi
```

In the `if` statement, if the first (leftmost) *compound-command* succeeds (returns a zero exit status), `sh` executes the *compound-command* following `then`; otherwise, `sh` executes the *compound-command* (if any) following the `elif` (which is short for *else if*); if that succeeds, `sh` executes the *compound-command* following the next `then`. If none of these cases holds, `sh` executes the *compound-command* following the `else` (if any). The exit status of an `if` command is the exit status of the `then` *compound-command* or `else` *compound-command* that was executed, or zero if none was executed.

```
select variable [in word ...]
do compound-command
done
```

The `select` statement can handle menu-like interactions with the user. Its syntax is like the `for` statement. Each *word* is printed on the standard error file, one per line, with an accompanying number. If you omit the `"in word..."` part, `sh` uses the positional parameters. `sh` then displays the value of the variable `PS3` to prompt the user to enter a numerical reply. If the reply is an empty line, `sh` displays the menu again; otherwise, `sh` assigns the input line to the variable `REPLY`, sets *variable* to the *word* selected, and then executes the *compound-command*. `sh` does this over and over until the loop is terminated by interrupt, end-of-file, or an explicit `break` statement in the *compound-command*.

```
until compound-command1
do compound-command2
done
```

The until statement executes *compound-command1* and tests its exit status for success (zero) or failure (non-zero). If *command1* succeeds, the loop terminates; otherwise, sh executes *compound-command2*, and then goes back to execute and test *compound-command1* again. Including break or continue commands in *compound-command2* can affect the operation of the loop. The exit status of an until command is the exit status of the last *compound-command2* executed, or zero if none was executed.

```
while compound-command1
do compound-command2
done
```

The while statement works like the until statement; however, the loop terminates whenever *compound-command1* is unsuccessful (non-zero exit status). The exit status of a while command is the exit status of the last *compound-command2* executed, or zero if none was executed.

Shell reserved words are recognized only when they are the unquoted first token of a command. This lets you pass these reserved words as arguments to commands executed from the shell. The full list of reserved words is

```
! { }
case do done
elif else esac
fi for function
if select then
until while
```

Command Execution

A simple command consists of three optional parts: arguments, variable assignments, and redirection, which may appear in any order. For example,

```
variable=value argument0 argument1 <filename
```

is a simple command with one variable assignment, two arguments, and a redirection.

The command is processed as follows:

1. sh performs word expansion on command arguments (see *Word Expansion*). The first word of the expanded arguments is the command name. If there are no arguments, sh only performs variable assignments and temporary redirection.

2. sh performs word expansion on variable assignments. If there is no command or the command is a special built-in command (see *Built-In Commands*), variable assignments affect the current environment; otherwise, variable assignments affect the execution environment of the command.

3. sh does redirection, performing word expansion on any filenames (see *File Descriptors and Redirection*).

sh next searches for the command name and executes the command. If the command name is a special built-in command, sh invokes it. Most errors in special built-ins cause a noninteractive shell to exit.

If the command name is a function, sh executes the function. You can disable the search for functions with the built-in command named command

If the command name is a regular built-in command, sh invokes it.

If the command name is not a regular or special built-in command or a function, sh searches for an executable file containing a shell script or a program. The shell uses one of the following two methods to locate this file.

> If the command name typed to the shell has slash (/) characters in its name, the command is taken to be a full pathname (absolute or relative). The shell tries to execute the contents of that file.
>
> Otherwise, the shell performs a *path search.* To do this, the shell obtains the value of the PATH variable. The value should be a list of directory names. sh searches under each directory for a filename that matches the command name and executes the first matching file found.

Extra rules apply when searching paths on DOS. If the command name does not contain a dot, the shell looks for a file that has the given name plus any of the following suffixes:

.com	This is a DOS memory image file, used mostly for older software.
.exe	This is the standard DOS executable file format.
.ksh	This is a KornShell shell script. Such scripts are executed in a subshell of the current shell.
.bat	On DOS, any such file is passed to command.com and executed as a standard DOS batch file.

If the command name has a dot in it, the shell searches under PATH directories for files that have the name exactly as given. If the suffix after the dot is not one of these suffixes, the shell executes the file as if it contains a KornShell script.

If the path search fails, the command exit status is 127. If sh cannot execute the program and it is not a shell script, the exit status is 126.

Command names may be marked as tracked aliases. The first time you execute a command with a tracked alias, the shell does a normal PATH search. If the search is successful, the shell remembers the file it finds. The next time you execute a command with the same name, sh immediately executes the file found on the last PATH search; there is no new search. This speeds up the search for the appropriate file.

The set -h command tells the shell that all commands should be treated as tracked aliases. See the man pages for alias and set for more information.

Word Expansion

sh performs word expansion for simple commands, some reserved word commands, redirection filenames, some shell variables (ENV, MAILPATH, PS1, and PS4), and unquoted here documents. There are four steps to expansion: substitution, word splitting, path expansion, and quote removal.

Directory substitution, parameter substitution, command substitution, and arithmetic substitution are each described in the appropriate section of this man page.

After substitution, each word which underwent parameter substitution is checked for the characters in the IFS variable (by default, space, tab, and newline). If the word contains these characters, it is split into multiple words. When IFS contains an empty string, this word splitting is not performed.

If a word contains an unquoted *, ?, or], that word is subject to pathname expansion (see *Pathname Expansion*). Pathname expansion is disabled if the -f or -o noglob shell flag is set (see the man page for set).

Finally, sh removes any quote characters (\, ', and ") from the original word. In here documents (see the description of *number*<<[-]*name* in the section *File Descriptors and Redirection*) and shell variables that expand, single and double quotes have no special meaning and are not removed.

Directory Substitution

When a word begins with an unquoted tilde (~), sh tries to perform *directory substitution* on the word. sh obtains all characters from the tilde (~) to the first slash (/) (or \ on DOS) and uses this as a *user name*. sh looks for this *name* in the *name* field of $ROOTDIR/etc/passwd, the file that contains information on all the system's users. If sh finds a matching name, it replaces ~*name* with the name of the user's *home directory*, as given in the matching $ROOTDIR/etc/passwd, entry.

For example, if you specify a filename as

`~jsmith/file`

sh would look up jsmith's home directory and put that directory name in place of the ~jsmith construct.

If you just specify a ~ without an accompanying name, sh replaces the ~ with the current value of your HOME variable (see *Variables*). For example,

`echo ~`

displays the name of your home directory. Similarly, sh replaces the construct tilde plus (~+) with the value of the PWD variable (the name of the your current directory), and replaces tilde dash (~-) with the value of OLDPWD (the name of your previous current directory). In variable assignments, tilde expansion is also performed after colons (:).

Parameter Substitution

The shell uses three types of parameters: positional parameters, special parameters, and variables. A positional parameter is represented with either a single digit (except 0) or one or more digits in curly braces (for example, 7 and {15} are both valid representations of positional parameters). Positional parameters are assigned values from the command line when you invoke sh.

A special parameter is represented with one of the following characters:

`* @ # ? ! - $ 0`

The values to which special parameters expand are listed later in this section.

Variables are named parameters. For details on naming and declaring variables, see *Variables*.

The simplest way to use a parameter in a command line is to enter a dollar sign ($) followed by the name of the parameter. For example, if you enter the command

`echo $x`

sh replaces $x with the value of the parameter x and then displays the results (because echo displays its arguments). Other ways to expand parameters are shown later in this section.

Some parameters are built-in to the shell. These are as follows:

$1, $2, ... $9   Expands to the *d*th positional parameter (where *d* is the single digit following the $). If there is no such parameter, $*d* expands to a null string.

$0   Expands to the name of the shell, the shell script, or a value assigned when you invoked the shell.

$#   Expands to the number of positional parameters. The parameter assigned to $0 is not counted in this number, since it is a special parameter, not a positional parameter.

$@   Expands to the complete list of positional parameters. If $@ is quoted, the result is separate arguments, each quoted. This means that

"$@"

is equivalent to

"$1" "$2" ...

$*   Expands to the complete list of positional parameters. If $* is quoted, the result is concatenated into a single argument, with parameters separated by the first character of the value of IFS (see *Variables*). For example, if the first character of IFS is a space

"$*"

is equivalent to

"$1 $2 ..."

If IFS is unset, the parameters are separated by a space.

Note that setting IFS is not the same as unsetting it. In this case, the parameters are separated by the null string and, as a result, concatenated.

$-   Expands to all options that are in effect from previous calls to the set command and from options on the sh command line.

`$?`	Expands to the exit status of the last command executed.
`$$`	Expands to the process number of the original parent shell.
`$!`	Expands to the process number of the last asynchronous command.

These constructs are called *parameters* of the shell. They include the positional parameters, but are not restricted to the positional parameters.

We have already mentioned that you can expand a parameter by putting a $ in front of the parameter name. More sophisticated ways to expand parameters are

`${parameter}`	Expands any parameter.
`${number}`	Expands to the positional parameter with the given number. (When using $*d* to refer to the *d*th positional parameter, *d* must be a single digit; with brace brackets, *number* can be greater than nine.) Because braces mark the beginning and end of the name, you can immediately follow the expression with a letter or digit.
`${variable[arithmetic expression]}`	Expands to the value of an element in an array named *variable*. The `arithmetic expression` gives the subscript of the array. (See *Arithmetic Substitution*.)
`${variable[*]}`	Expands to all elements in the array *variable*, separated by the first character in IFS.
`${variable[@]}`	When unquoted, is the same as `${variable[*]}`. When quoted as `"${variable[@]}"`, it expands to all the elements in the array *variable*, each quoted individually.

`${#parameter}`	Expands to the number of characters in the value of the given `parameter`.
`${#*}`, `${#@}`	Expands to the number of positional parameters.
`${#variable[*]}`	Expands to the number of elements in the array named `variable`. Elements that do not have assigned values do not count. For example, if you only assign values to elements 0 and 4, the number of elements is 2. Elements 1 through 3 do not count.
`${parameter:-word}`	Expands to the value of `parameter` if it is defined and has a nonempty value; otherwise, it expands `word`. This means that you can use `word` as a default value if the parameter isn't defined.
`${parameter-word}`	Is similar to the preceding construct, except that the parameter is expanded, if defined, even if the value is empty.
`${variable:=word}`	Expands `word` with parameter expansion and assigns the result to `variable`, provided that `variable` is not defined or has an empty value. The result is the expansion of `variable`, whether or not `word` was expanded.
`${variable=word}`	Is similar to the preceding construct, except that the `variable` must be undefined (it can't just be null) for `word` to be expanded.

`${parameter:?word}` Expands to the value of *parameter* provided it is defined and nonempty. If *parameter* isn't defined or is null, sh expands and displays *word* as a message. If *word* is empty, sh displays a default message. Once a noninteractive shell has displayed a message, it terminates.

`${parameter?word}` Is similar to the preceding construct, except that sh displays *word* only if *parameter* is undefined.

`${parameter:+word}` Expands *word*, provided that *parameter* is defined and nonempty.

`${parameter+word}` Expands *word*, provided that *parameter* is defined.

`${parameter#pattern}` Attempts to match *pattern* against the value of the specified *parameter*. The *pattern* is the same as a case *pattern*. sh searches for the shortest prefix of the value of *parameter* that matches *pattern*. If sh finds no match, the previous construct expands to the value of *parameter*; otherwise, the portion of the value that matched *pattern* is deleted from the expansion.

`${parameter##pattern}` Is similar to the preceding construct, except that sh deletes the longest prefix that matches *pattern* if it finds such a match.

`${parameter%pattern}` Searches for the shortest suffix of the value of *parameter* matching *pattern* and deletes the matching string from the expansion.

${*parameter*%%*pattern*}

Is similar to the preceding construct, except that sh deletes the longest suffix that matches *pattern* if it finds such a match.

Arithmetic Substitution

Arithmetic substitution is available with the syntax

```
$((arithmetic expression))
```

or

```
$[arithmetic expression]
```

sh replaces this sequence with the value of *arithmetic expression*. Arithmetic expressions consist of expanded variables, numeric constants, and operators.

Numeric constants have the form

```
[base#]number
```

where the optional *base* is a decimal integer between 2 and 36 inclusive, and *number* is a non-negative number in the given base. The default base is 10. Undefined variables evaluate to zero.

In Table M.7, operators are listed in decreasing order of precedence. Operators sharing a heading have the same precedence, and are called a *precedence group*. Operators within the same precedence group are evaluated from left to right, except for assignment operators which are evaluated from right to left.

Table M.7. Arithmetic expression operators in precedence order.

Operator	Performs
Unary Operators	
-	Unary minus
!	Logical negation
+ ~	Identity, bitwise negation

continues

457

Table M.7. continued

Operator	Performs
Multiplicative Operators	
* / %	Multiplication, division, remainder
Additive Operators	
+ -	Addition, subtraction
Bitwise Shift Operators	
<< >>	Bitwise shift right, bitwise shift left
Relational Operators	
< >	Less than, greater than
<= >=	Less than or equal, greater than or equal
== !=	Equal to, not equal to
Bitwise AND Operator	
&	Bitwise AND
Bitwise Exclusive OR Operator	
^	Bitwise exclusive OR
Bitwise Inclusive OR Operator	
¦	Bitwise inclusive OR
Assignment Operator	
=	Assignment

Arithmetic expressions may be used without the enclosing $((and)) in assignment to an integer variable (see the man page for `typeset`); as an argument to the following built-in commands:

```
break continue exit let return shift
```

Command Substitution

In *command substitution,* sh uses the expansion of the standard output of one command in the command line for a second command. There are two syntaxes.

The first syntax (called *backquoting*) surrounds a command with grave accents `, as in

```
ls -l `cat list`
```

To process this command line, sh first executes the cat command and collects its standard output. The shell then breaks this output into arguments and puts the result into the command line of the ls command. The previous command therefore lists the attributes of all files, the names of which are contained in the file list.

This syntax is easy to type, but is not useful if you want to put one command substitution inside another (*nesting* command substitutions). A more useful syntax is

```
$(command)
```

as in

```
vi $(fgrep -l function $(find . -name '*.c'))
```

This command uses find to search the current directory and its subdirectories to find all files, the names of which end in .c. It then uses fgrep to search each such file for those that contain the string function. Finally, it calls vi to edit each such file.

There is an historical inconsistency in the backquoting syntax. A backslash (\) within a backquoted command is interpreted differently depending on its context. Backslashes are interpreted literally unless they precede a dollar sign ($), grave accent (`), or another backslash (- \); in these cases, the leading backslash becomes an escape character to force the literal interpretation of the $, `, or \. Consequently, the command

```
echo '\$x'
```

issued at system level produces the output

```
\$x
```

while the same command nested in a backquoted syntax

```
echo `echo '\$x'`
```

produces the output

```
$x
```

We recommend the $(*command*) syntax for command substitutions.

sh performs command substitutions as if a new copy of the shell is invoked to execute the command. This affects the behavior of $- (standing for the list of options passed to the shell). If a command substitution contains $-, the expansion of $- does not include the -i option, since the command is being executed by a noninteractive shell.

Quoting

To let you override the special meaning of certain words or special characters, the shell provides several quoting mechanisms. In general, you can turn off the special meaning of any character by putting a backslash (\) in front of the character. This is called *escaping* the character.

You can also use this method to tell the shell to disregard the special meaning of the newline character by putting a backslash at the end of a line. The shell ignores the escaped newline and joins the next line of input to the end of the current line. In this way, you can enter long lines in a convenient and readable fashion.

Escaping characters by putting a backslash in front of them is the most direct way of telling the shell to disregard special meanings; however, it can be awkward and confusing if you have several characters to escape.

As an alternative, you can put arguments in various types of quotes. Different quote characters have different *strengths*. The apostrophe (single quote) characters are the strongest. When you enclose a command line argument in apostrophes, the shell disregards the special meanings of everything they contain. For example,

```
echo '*'
```

displays the * character, rather than interpreting the * as a special character.

Double quote characters are weaker. Inside double quotes, the shell performs command substitutions of the form

```
$(command)
```

or

```
`command`
```

(See *Command Substitution*.) The shell does not perform such substitutions when they appear inside apostrophes. In addition, the shell performs parameter substitutions of the form

```
$parameter
```

when they are inside double quotes but not when they're inside apostrophes (see *Parameter Substitution*). As well, you can use the backslash to escape another character inside double quotes, but inside apostrophes, the shell ignores this special meaning.

The shell treats internal field separator characters (that is, characters in the value of the IFS variable) literally inside quoted arguments, whether they're quoted with double quotes or apostrophes. This means that a quoted argument is considered a single entity, even if it contains IFS characters.

Quoting can override the special meanings of reserved words and aliases. For example, in

```
"select" program
```

the quotes around select tell the shell not to interpret select as a shell reserved word. Instead, sh does a normal command search for a command named select.

You must always quote the following characters if you want sh to interpret them literally:

```
¦ & ; < > ( ) $ ' " ` \
<space> <tab> <new-line>
```

The following characters need to be quoted in certain contexts if they are to be interpreted literally.

```
* ? [ # % = ~
```

File Descriptors and Redirection

The shell sometimes refers to files using *file descriptors*. A file descriptor is a number in the range 0 through 9. It may have any number of digits. For example, the file descriptors 001 and 01 are identical to file descriptor 1. Various operations (for example, exec) can associate a file descriptor with a particular file.

Some file descriptors are set up at the time the shell starts up. These are the standard input/output streams:

Standard input (file descriptor 0)

Standard output (file descriptor 1)

Standard error (file descriptor 2)

Commands running under the shell can use these descriptors and streams too. When a command runs under the shell, the streams are normally associated with your

terminal; however, you can *redirect* these file descriptors to associate them with other files (so that I/O on the stream takes place on the associated file instead of your terminal). In fact, the shell lets you redirect the I/O streams associated with file descriptors 0 through 9, using the following command line constructs.

number<*file*   Uses `file` for input on the file descriptor *number*. If you omit *number*, as in <*file*, the default is 0; this redirects the standard input.

number>*file*   Uses `file` for output on the file descriptor *number*. If you omit *number*, as in >*file*, the default is 1; this redirects the standard output. The shell creates the file if it doesn't already exist. The redirection fails if the file already exists and `noclobber` is set (see the man page for `set`).

number>¦*file*   Is similar to *number*>*file* but if `file` already exists, it overwrites the current contents of the file.

number<>*file*   Uses `file` for input and output with the file descriptor *number*. This is most useful when the file is another terminal or modem line. If you omit *number*, as in <>*file*, the default *number* is zero; this redirects the standard input. Output written to the file overwrites the current contents of the file (if any). The shell creates the file if it doesn't already exist.

number>>*file*   Is similar to *number* > *file* except that output is appended to the current contents of *file* (if any).

number<<[-]*name*   Enables you to specify input to a command from your terminal (or from the body of a shell script). This notation is known as a *here document*. The shell reads from the standard input and feeds that as input to file descriptor *number* until it finds a line that exactly matches the given *name*. If you omit *number*, the default is the standard input. For example, to process the command

```
cat <<abc >out
```

The shell reads input from the terminal until you enter a line that consists of the word `abc`. This input is passed as the standard input to the `cat` command, which then copies the text to the file `out`.

If any character of *name* is quoted or escaped, sh does not perform substitutions on the input; otherwise, it performs variable and command substitutions, respecting the usual quoting and escape conventions. If you put - before *name*, sh deletes all leading tabs in the *here document.*

number<&word

Makes the input file descriptor *number* a duplicate of the file descriptor identified by the expansion of *word*. If you omit *number*, the default is the standard input (file descriptor 0). For example, <&4 makes the standard input a duplicate of file descriptor 4. In this case, entering input on 4 has the same effect as entering input on the standard input. If *word* expands to p, the input file descriptor *number* becomes a duplicate of the current coprocess' standard output.

number1>&word

Makes the output file descriptor *number* a duplicate of the file descriptor identified by the expansion of *word*. If you omit *number*, the default is the standard output (file descriptor 1). For example, >&2 makes the standard output a duplicate of file descriptor 2 (the standard error). In this case, writing output on the standard output has the same effect as writing output on the standard error. If *word* expands to p, the input file descriptor *number* becomes a duplicate of the current coprocess' standard input.

number<&-

Closes input descriptor *number*. If you omit *number*, it closes the standard input.

number>&-

Closes output descriptor *number*. If you omit *number*, it closes the standard output.

Normally, redirection only applies to the command where the redirection construct appears (see the exec man page).

The order of *redirection* specifications is significant, since an earlier redirection can affect a later one; however, these specifications may be freely intermixed with other command arguments. Since the shell takes care of the redirection, these constructs are not passed to the command itself.

Note: The shell performs the implicit redirections needed for pipelines before performing any explicit redirections.

Filename Generation

The characters *, ? and [are called *glob characters* or *wildcard characters*. If an unquoted argument contains one or more glob characters, the shell processes the argument for *filename generation*. The glob characters are part of *glob patterns* which represent file and directory names. These patterns are similar to regular expressions, but differ in syntax, since they are intended to match filenames and words (not arbitrary strings). The special constructions that may appear in glob patterns are

?	Matches exactly one character of a filename, except for the separator character / and a . at the beginning of a filename. (On DOS, it does not match the separator character \ either.) Unlike a similar notation used by some standard DOS programs, ? only matches an actual filename character and does not match nonexistent characters at the end of the filename. ? is analogous to the metacharacter . in regular expressions.
*	Matches zero or more characters in a filename, subject to the same restrictions as ?. * is analogous to the regular expression .*. Unlike the standard DOS wildcard syntax, *x.c is a valid pattern.
[*chars*]	Defines a *class* of characters; the glob pattern matches any single character in the class. A class may contain a range of characters by writing the first character in the range, a dash - and the last character. For example, [A-Za-z], in the POSIX locale, stands for all the uppercase and lowercase letters. If you want a literal - character in the class, put it as the first or last character inside the brackets. If the first character inside the brackets is an exclamation mark (!), the pattern matches any single character that is *not* in the class.

Some sample patterns are

```
[!a-f]*.c
```

matches all .c files beginning with something other than the letters a through f.

```
/???/?.?
```

matches all files under the root directory in a directory that has a three letter name, and which have a base name containing one character followed by a . and another single character.

```
*/*.[chyl]
```

matches all .c, .h, .y, and .l files in a subdirectory of the current directory.

```
~mks/*.ksh
```

matches all shell scripts in the home directory of user mks (see *Directory Substitution* for the use of ~).

If no files match the pattern, sh leaves the argument untouched. If the set option -f or -o noglob is in effect, the shell does not perform filename generation.

Variables

The shell maintains variables and can expand them when they are used in command lines; see `Parameter Substitution` for details.

A variable name must begin with an upper- or lowercase letter or the underscore (_). Subsequent characters in the name, if any, may be upper- or lowercase letters, underscores, and/or digits 0 through 9. You can assign a value to a variable with

```
variable=value
```

You may implicitly declare a variable as an array by using a subscript expression when assigning a value, as in

```
variable[arithmetic expression]=value
```

You can use a subscripted array variable anywhere that the shell allows an ordinary variable. See the section on *Arithmetic Substitution* for the syntax of an `arithmetic expression`. Also see the typeset man page for details about the attributes of shell variables and how shell variables may be exported to child processes.

For a list of variables that the shell either sets or understands, see *Environment Variables.*

Shell Execution Environments

A shell execution *environment* is the set of conditions affecting most commands executed within the shell. It consists of

> Open files
>
> The current working directory (see the man page for cd)
>
> The file creation mask

The traps currently set (see the man page for `trap`)

The shell parameters (see the man page for `set`)

The shell functions currently defined (see *Command Execution*)

Options (see the man page for `set`)

A *subshell environment* starts as a duplicate of the shell environment, except that traps caught by the shell are set to default values in the subshell. Since the subshell environment starts as a duplicate, the value of the ENV environment variable is not run. Changes made to a subshell environment do not affect the shell environment.

Command substitutions, commands within parentheses (for example, `(command)`), and commands to be run asynchronously (for example, `command&`) all run in subshell environments. Each command in a pipeline `command ¦ command` runs in a subshell environment.

Shell utilities also run in a separate environment which does not affect the shell environment, except for certain built-in utilities (for example, `cd` and `umask`) which explicitly alter the shell environment. The shell sets up a shell utility's environment to include the following

Open files, subject to redirection

Current working directory (see the man page for `cd`)

File creation mask

Traps; traps caught by the shell are set to default values and traps ignored by the shell are ignored by the utility

Variables defined inside the shell and having the export attribute

Built-In Commands

The following commands are built into the shell. Building such commands into the shell increases the performance of shell scripts and allows access to the shell's internal data structure and variables. For details on a command, see its man page. These internal commands have semantics indistinguishable from external commands.

```
: . [ alias break
cd continue echo eval exec
exit export false fc getopts
jobs kill let newgrp print
pwd read readonly return set
shift test time times trap
```

```
type typeset ulimit unmask unalias
unset wait whence
```

POSIX.2 recognizes a subset of these commands as *special* built-ins. Syntax errors in special built-in commands cause a noninteractive shell to exit with the exit status set by the command. The special built-in utilities are

```
: . break continue
eval exec exit export
readonly return set shift
trap typeset unset
```

The newgrp internal command does not work under DOS, because those operating systems do not have the functionality to support the command.

Under DOS, the wait and umask commands also do nothing. In the interest of compatibility with POSIX and UNIX systems, the DOS version of the shell still recognize such do-nothing commands, but they have no effect.

As well as built-in commands, the shell has a set of predefined aliases.

```
functions hash history integer
nohup r stop suspend
```

See the alias man page for details.

Examples

Software distributed over computer networks such as Usenet is often distributed in a form known as a *shell archive*. In essence, a shell archive is a shell script containing the data of one or more files, plus commands to reconstruct the data files and check that the data was transmitted correctly. The following shows a sample shell archive.

```
# This is a shell archive.
# It contains the one file "frag.ksh"
# To extract contents, type
# sh file
#
if [ -f frag.ksh ]
then echo frag.ksh exists: will not overwrite
else
        echo extracting frag.ksh
        sed 's/^X//' >frag.ksh <<_EOF_
X# This is frag.ksh
X# Not very interesting, really.
Xecho frag.ksh here!
_EOF_
```

```
        if [ "`sum frag.ksh¦awk '{print $1}'`" != 52575 ]
        then echo frag.ksh damaged in transit
        fi
fi
```

The following simple script produces as much of the Fibonacci sequence as can be calculated using integers.

```
# Print Fibonacci sequence; start sequence
# with first two positional parameters:
# default 1 1
typeset -i x=${1:-1} y=${2:-1} z
while [ x -gt 0 ] # until overflow
do
        echo $x
        let z=y+x x=y y=z
done
```

The following implements the basename utility as a shell function.

```
# basename utility as shell function
function basename {
        case $# in
        1) ;;
        2) eval set \${1%$2} ;;
        *) echo Usage: $0 pathname '[suffix]'
        return 1 ;;
        esac
        echo ${1##*/}
        return 0
}
```

Environment Variables

sh uses the following environment variables:

_(underscore)   Expands to the last argument of the previously executed command. For every command that is executed as a child of the shell, sh sets this variable to the full pathname of the executable file and passes this value through the environment to that child process. When processing the MAILPATH variable, this variable holds the value of the corresponding mail file.

CDPATH   Contains a list of directories for the cd command to search. Directory names are separated with colons on POSIX and UNIX systems, semicolons on DOS. CDPATH works in a similar way to the PATH variable.

COLUMNS	Contains the maximum width of the edit window in the KornShell Vi or EMACS editing modes. It is also used by several other commands to define the width of the terminal output device.
EDITOR	Enables the corresponding editing mode (see the set man page) when using vi, emacs, or gmacs.
ERRNO	Contains the system error number of the most recently failed system call. The shell only sets this variable for errors that occur in the current environment. Assigning a value of 0 to this variable clears it.
ENV	Contains a value on which sh performs parameter substitution and uses the result as the name of an initialization file. This file is executed with the . command (see the dot man page). You can use this facility to define functions (see *Command Syntax*), aliases (see the man page for alias), and other nonexported items during shell initialization.
FCEDIT	Contains the name of the default editor for the fc command. If this variable is not set, the default is the ed command.
HISTFILE	Contains the pathname of a file to be used as the history file. When the shell starts, the value of this variable overrides the default history file. See *Files.*
HISTSIZE	Contains the maximum number of commands that the shell keeps in the history file. If this variable contains a valid number when the shell starts, it overrides the default of 127.
HOME	Contains your home directory. This is the default directory for the cd command.
IFS	Contains a series of characters to be used as *internal field separator* characters. During word expansion (see *Word Expansion*), the presence of any of these characters within a word causes it to be split. In addition, the shell uses these characters to separate values put into variables with the read command. Lastly, the first character in the value of IFS separates the positional parameters in $* expansion. By default, IFS contains space, tab, and newline.

LINENO	Contains the number of the line currently being executed by a shell script.
LINES	Contains a numeric value that limits the number of output lines used by the select statement in printing its menu.
MAIL	Contains the pathname of a *mailbox*. If MAILPATH is not set, the MKS KornShell tells you when new mail arrives in this file. The shell assumes that new mail has arrived if the file modify time changes.
MAILCHECK	Contains the number of seconds of elapsed time that must pass before checking for mail; if not set, the default value is 600 seconds. When using the MAIL or MAILPATH variables, the MKS KornShell checks for mail before issuing a prompt.
MAILPATH	Contains a list of mailbox files. This overrides the MAIL variable. The mailbox list is separated by colons on POSIX and UNIX systems, and by semicolons on DOS. If any name is followed by ?*message* or %*message*, sh displays the message if the corresponding file has changed. sh performs parameter and command substitution on *message* and the variable _ (temporarily) expands to the name of the mailbox file. If no ?*message* or %*message* is present, the default message is you have mail in $_..
OLDPWD	Contains the name of the previous directory. The cd command sets this variable.
PATH	Contains a list of directories that constitute the search path for executable commands. Directories in this list are separated with colons on POSIX and UNIX systems and by semicolons on DOS. sh searches each directory in the order specified in the list until it finds a matching executable. If you want the shell to search the current directory, put a null string in the list of directories (for example, starting the list with a colon/semicolon tells the shell to search the current directory first).
PPID	Contains the decimal value of the process ID (PSP on DOS) of the parent of the shell.

PS1	Contains the primary prompt string used when the shell is interactive. The default value is a dollar sign followed by a space ($). The shell expands parameters before the prompt is printed. A single exclamation mark (!) in the prompt string is replaced by the command number from the history list (see the man page for fc); for a real exclamation mark in the prompt, use !!.
PS2	Contains the secondary prompt, used when completing the input of such things as *reserved word commands*, quoted strings, and here documents. The default value of this variable is a greater than sign followed by a space (>).
PS3	Contains the prompt string used in connection with the select reserved word. The default value is a number sign followed by a question mark and a space (#?).
PS4	Contains the prefix for traced commands with set -x. The default value is a plus sign followed by a space (+).
PWD	Contains the name of the current working directory. When the shell starts, the current directory name is assigned to PWD unless the variable already has a value.
RANDOM	Expands to a random integer. Assigning a value to RANDOM sets a new seed for the random number generator.
REPLY	Contains the user input from the select statement (see *Command Syntax*). The read command also sets this variable if no variable is specified.
SECONDS	Contains elapsed time. The value of this variable grows by 1 for each elapsed second of real time. Any value assigned to this variable sets the SECONDS counter to that value; initially the shell sets the value to 0.
SHELL	Contains the full pathname of the current shell. It is not set by the shell, but is used by various other commands to invoke the shell.
TMOUT	Contains the number of seconds before user input times out. If user input has not been received within this length of time, the shell terminates.

VISUAL   Overrides the EDITOR variable in setting vi, emacs, or gmacs
                editing modes.

Files

sh uses the following files:

.sh_history   Default history storage file (sh_history on DOS).

.profile   Profile for login shell ($HOME/profile.ksh on DOS).

/etc/profile   System-wide profile for login shells ($ROOTDIR/etc/
                     profile.ksh on DOS).

/tmp/sh*   Temporary files for here documents, command substitu-
                     tion, history re-execution, and so on. ($ROOTDIR/
                     tmp/sh* on DOS.) The default directory /tmp
                     ($ROOTDIR/tmp on DOS) can be overridden by
                     setting the shell variable TMPDIR to the name of some
                     other directory. The /etc and /tmp directories are found
                     using the ROOTDIR environment variable, if it exists.

Diagnostics

Possible exit status values are

0   Successful completion.

1   Failure due to any of the following: shell is invoked with an
           invalid option, shell is invoked to run a shell script and the
           command to run the script had a command syntax error, a
           redirection error, variable expansion error

Otherwise, the exit status of the shell defaults to the exit status of the last command
executed by the shell. This default may be overridden by explicit use of the exit or
return commands. The exit status of a pipeline is the exit status of the last command
in the pipeline.

Most diagnostics are self-explanatory. See separate man pages for diagnostics from
built-in commands.

Messages

Ambiguous redirection

A redirection construct expanded to more than one pathname.

Cannot exit from top level shell

On DOS, the top level shell is the command interpreter invoked at the time that your system is booted. You cannot exit from this shell, because there is nowhere left to go.

Coprocess not implemented-cannot reload shell

On DOS, you attempted to use an operation or option that depends on coprocesses. DOS does not support coprocesses. For the -R option, sh gives this error if the reloaded text segment still fails to checksum correctly. This probably means that the shell executable has changed.

File "*file*" already exists

You are attempting to redirect output into an existing file, but you have turned on the noclobber option (see the man page for set). If you really want to redirect output into an existing file, use the construct >¦*filename*, or turn off the option with set +o noclobber

File descriptor *number* already redirected

You attempted to redirect a file descriptor that was already being redirected in the same command. You can only redirect a file descriptor once.

Hangup

The shell received a *hangup* signal. This signal typically arises when a communication line is disconnected. (for example, when a phone connection is cut off).

In *base#number:* base must be in [2,36]

In a number with the form *base#number*, the value of the base was larger than 36 or less than 2. The only valid range for bases is from 2 through 36.

`Invalid subscript`	A shell array was indexed with a subscript outside the defined bounds.
`Insufficient memory ...`	Because the DOS-based versions of the shell runs in the small memory model, its data area is limited to 64K. The message appears if allocated data within the shell outgrows this limit. Possible causes include too many bytes of shell variables, too many functions, too complex an expression tree, and so on. If it is impossible to free any memory (for example, via unset), you should leave the shell or reboot the machine.
	Note: The amount of memory available for the shell's use may be limited by TSRs loaded after the shell is invoked. Such TSRs limit the amount of memory available for the shell's growth.
`Insufficient memory` `to reload shell text image`	For the -R option, this error indicates that the shell text image in memory was corrupted, but DOS didn't have enough available memory to reload it from disk.
`Illegal instruction`	The shell received an *illegal instruction* signal. This typically occurs when a process tries to execute something that is not a valid machine instruction recognized by the hardware.
`Misplaced subscript` `"array name"`	The subscript for an array was missing or invalid.
`Name is not an identifier`	You attempted to use a nonalphanumeric *Name*.
`Name: readonly variable`	The given *Name* is a read-only variable and cannot be removed or changed.

Name: no expansion of unset variable	The shell is operating with set -u, and you used an unset variable in a substitution. For more information, see the man page for set.
No file descriptor available for redirection	When a file descriptor is redirected, the shell remembers the old value by duplicating it to another file descriptor. Because the total number of file descriptors is limited by the system, the shell may run out of descriptors although it looks like your command is using far fewer than the maximum number allocated.
...: restricted	If the shell has been invoked as a restricted shell, certain things are disallowed (for example, the cd command, setting PATH, and output redirection).
Temporary file error using document	sh tried to create a here temporary file to hold the contents of a *<<word here document*, but the temporary file could not be created. This may indicate a lack of space on the disk where temporary files are created.

Portability

POSIX.2. X/OPEN Portability Guide. MKS Toolkit. Upward compatible with the Bourne Shell on UNIX systems.

Available as the boot-level shell from config.sys only in DOS 3.0 and up

DOS imposes a number of functional limitations. There is no multitasking and, therefore, no coprocesses, no background tasks, and no job control. Thus, the & operator is effectively equivalent to ;, except that commands invoked with the & operator return a process number to the shell that executes them. The ¦& operator is not supported on DOS. There is no bg command. The fg, jobs, and kill commands are not built-in. The commands set -o bgnice, set -o monitor, and wait have no effect.

On DOS, attempts to execute the `newgrp` built-in cause your current shell to exit.

The `select` and `function` reserved word commands are from the KornShell. The shell variables `ERRNO`, `LINENO`, `PS3`, `PWD`, `OLDPWD`, `TMOUT` are from the KornShell. Arrays and subscripted variables are from the KornShell. All the predefined aliases are from the KornShell. The restricted shell and invocation option `-r` are from SVID and the KornShell.

The construct `$[arithmetic expression]` is an extension to the POSIX standard.

Limits

The size of the command argument and exported variables passed between the shell and the utilities it runs depends upon the operating system. Because the shell has no way of knowing the type of command it is calling, it performs two expansions.

The first expansion is placed in the environment, to be read by utilities which receive their command line arguments from the environment (all MKS Tools utilities). This first expansion is restricted in size by the amount of memory available to the shell.

The second expansion is performed for commands which need their command arguments passed directly to them (for example, DOS commands). This second expansion is restricted by the limits of the native command interpreters (127 bytes under DOS).

The number of files that may be open simultaneously under DOS currently defaults to 8. Since you will require a substantial number of open files when using the shell (to accommodate pipes, for example), you'll want to increase the number of files you may have open. You do this by setting a value for the files variable in config.sys (a reasonable value is 20).

```
files=n
```

The maximum length of an executable filename, including subdirectories and extensions, depends upon the operating system. See your DOS documentation for specific restrictions on filenames.

See Also

`alias`, `break`, `cd`, `colon`, `continue`, `dot`, `echo`, `eval`, `exec`, `exit`, `fc`, `let`, `print`, `pwd`, `read`, `return`, `set`, `shift`, `test`, `trap`, `typeset`, `unalias`, `unset`, `whence`

shift—Shift Positional Parameters

Synopsis

```
shift [expression]
```

Description

`shift` renames the positional parameters. It is built into the shell.

If n is the value of the given arithmetic *expression*, the i+nth positional parameter becomes the ith positional parameter. You can think of this as getting rid of the first n parameters and shifting everything that's left to fill the resulting gap.

If you omit *expression*, the default value of n is 1. The value of *expression* must be between one and the number of positional parameters ($#), inclusive.

Example

The commands

```
set a b c d
shift 2
echo $*
```

produce

```
c d
```

Diagnostics

Possible exit status values are

0	Successful completion
1	Failure because the *expression* had a negative value or was greater than the number of positional parameters

Possible error messages include

`count cannot be negative`	You tried to pass a negative argument to `shift`; the argument must be positive (or zero).

too few positional parameters to shift by *number*	The number you specified was greater than the number of remaining positional parameters.

Portability

POSIX.2. X/Open Portability Guide. MKS Toolkit. shift is a built-in command of the Bourne Shell and the KornShell on UNIX. Note that the optional *expression* is an extension in the KornShell.

See Also

set, sh

sort—Sort/Merge Utility

Synopsis

```
sort [-cmu] [-o outfile] [-t x] [-y [n]] [-zn] [-bdfiMnr]
[-k startpos[,endpos]] ... [file ...]
```

Description

The sort command provides a full sort and merge facility. sort operates on input files containing records that are separated by the newline character.

Options

The following options select particular operations:

-c   Checks the input files to ensure that they are correctly ordered according to the key position and sort ordering options specified. With -c, sort does not modify the input files or produce output. sort displays a message if the files are not correctly sorted.

-m   Assumes that each input file is already ordered correctly according to the other options on the command line. sort merges these presorted files into a single sorted output stream.

With neither -c nor -m, sort sorts the concatenation of all input files and outputs the sorted result on the standard output.

Options that control the operation of sort are

-o *outfile*   Writes output into *outfile*. *outfile* can be one of the input files, in which case sort makes a copy of the input data to allow the (potential) overwriting of the input file. If this option is not specified, sort writes output onto the standard output.

-tc   Indicates that input fields are separated with the character *c*. When no -t option is specified, fields are separated by any number of whitespace (blank or tab) characters.

-u   Ensures that output records are unique. If two or more input records have equal sort keys, only one record is written to the output. When -u is used with -c, sort displays a diagnostic message if the input records have any duplicates.

-y[*n*]   Restricts the amount of memory available for sorting to *n*K of memory (where a K of memory is enough to hold 1024 characters). If you omit *n*, sort chooses a reasonable maximum amount of memory for sorting, dependent upon system configuration. sort needs at least enough memory to hold five records simultaneously. If you try to request less, sort takes the amount it needs anyway. When the amount of data in the input files surpasses the amount of memory available, sort automatically does a polyphase merge (external sorting) algorithm that is, of necessity, much slower than internal sorting. Using -y can therefore improve sorting performance for medium to large input files.

-z*n*   Indicates that the longest input record (including the newline character) is *n* characters in length. By default, record length is limited to 400 characters.

The following options control the way sort compares records; this determines the order in which the records are sorted. If the command line contains one of these order options without an accompanying sorting key, the option affects all comparisons;

479

otherwise, it just affects the comparisons done on the associated sorting key. For more on sorting keys, see the *Sorting Keys* section.

-b   Skips any leading whitespace (blank or tab) in any field (or key specification) before making comparisons.

-d   Makes comparisons using *dictionary* ordering. sort only looks at upper- and lowercase letters and numbers (alphanumerics) when doing the comparison.

-f   Converts uppercase letters into lowercase letters for the purpose of the comparison.

-i   Ignores all non-ASCII and control characters for comparison purposes.

-M   Assumes the field contains a month name for comparison purposes. sort ignores any leading whitespace. If the field starts with the first three letters of a month name in upper- or lower-case, sort makes comparisons in month order. If a field is not a recognizable month name, it is considered to come before January.

-n   Assumes the field contains a number. sort skips any leading whitespace. The number can contain an optional leading + or - sign, and can have an integer and/or functional part, separated by a decimal point.

-r   Reverses the order of all comparisons: output is written from largest to smallest rather than smallest to largest.

Sorting Keys

By default, sort examines entire input records to determine ordering. By specifying *sorting keys,* you can tell sort to restrict its attention to one or more parts of each record.

On the sort command line, you specify a sorting key by telling where the key starts and/or ends in the input record. The start of a sorting key can be indicated with

```
-k m[.n][options]
```

where *m* and the optional *n* are positive integers. You can choose the `options` from the set `bdfiMnr` to specify the way comparisons are done for just that sorting key. If no `options` are specified for the key, the global ordering options are used.

The number *m* specifies which field in the input record contains the start of the sorting key. The first field is number 1, the next is 2, and so on. Fields are separated by the character given with the `-t` option; without `-t`, fields are separated by whitespace. The number *n* specifies which character in the *m*th field is the start of the sorting key. If you do not specify *n*, the sorting key starts at the first character of the *m*th field. In this form of the `-k` option, the key begins at the specified position and extends to the end of the line.

You can also specify an ending position for a key, with

`-k m[.n][options],p[.q][options]`

where *p* and *q* are positive integers, indicating that the sorting key ends with the *p*th character of the *q*th field. If you do not specify *q*, the sorting key ends at the last character of the *p*th field. If the end of a sorting key is not a valid position after the beginning key position, the sorting key extends to the end of the input record.

Multiple sort key positions can be specified by using several `-k` options. In this case, the second sorting key is only used for records where the first sorting keys are equal. The third sorting key is only used when the first two are equal, and so on. If all key positions compare equally, the entire record is used to determine ordering.

When you specify `-u` to determine the uniqueness of output records, `sort` only looks at the sorting keys, not the whole record. Therefore, records are considered to be duplicates if they have equal sorting keys, even if other fields are not identical. (Of course, if no sorting keys are specified, the whole record is considered to be the sorting key.)

Examples

Suppose an input file has lines consisting of the day of the month, whitespace, and the month, as in

```
30 December
23      MAY
25 June
10      June
```

You can sort this file into chronological order with

```
sort -k 2M -k 1n
```

Suppose you have two *dictionary* files (text files with one word per line and each file sorted in dictionary order). You can merge the two dictionaries with

```
sort -m -dfi dict1 dict2 >newdict
```

Diagnostics

Possible exit status values are

0   Successful completion. Also returned if you specify -c and the file is in correctly sorted order

1   Returned if you specify -c and the file is not correctly sorted. Also returned to indicate failure because of a nonunique key in a record if -u is specified, inability to open the output file, error in writing to the output file, inability to create a temporary file or temporary filename, or an error writing to the temporary file

2   Failure because of a missing key description after -k, more than one -o option, a missing *filename* after -o, a missing character after -t, more than one character after -t, a missing *number* with -y or -z, an *endpos* coming before a *startpos*, a badly formed sort key, an invalid command line option, too many key field positions specified, or insufficient memory

The following are some of the more likely error messages that can appear:

`Missing key definition`	You specified -k, but did not specify a key after -k definition after the -k.
`Non-unique key in record: ...`	With the -u and -c options, sort found a nonunique record.
`Not ordered properly at: ...`	With the -c option, sort found the input was not correctly sorted.
`Line too long - truncated`	An input line was longer than the default (400 characters) or the number specified with the -z option. sort truncated this line by discarding characters from the end of the line until it was short enough.

`No new-line at end` `of file`	sort adds a newline character to any file that doesn't already end in one.
`Insufficient memory` `for ...`	This error normally occurs when very large numbers are specified for -y or -z options and there is not enough memory available for sort to satisfy the request.
`Write error (no space)` `on output`	Some error occurred in writing the standard output. Barring write-protected diskettes and the like, this normally occurs when there is insufficient disk space to hold all of the intermediate data.
`Temporary file error` `(no space) for ...`	Insufficient space was available for a temporary file. Make sure that you have a directory named /tmp, and that this directory has space to create files. The directory for temporary files can be changed using the ROOTDIR and TMPDIR environment variables (see Appendix E, "POSIX.2 Utility Summary").
`Tempfile error on ...`	sort could not create the named temporary (intermediate) file. Make sure that you have a directory named /tmp, and that this directory has space to create files. The directory for temporary files can be changed using the ROOTDIR and TMPDIR environment variables; see Appendix E.
`Tempnam() error`	sort could not generate a name for a temporary working file. This should almost never happen.

Files

/tmp/stm*   Temporary files used for merging and -o option. The /tmp directory is located using the ROOTDIR environment variable. You can specify a different directory for temporary files using the TMPDIR environment variable. For further information, see Appendix E.

Portability

POSIX.2. X/Open Portability Guide. MKS Toolkit. Available on all UNIX systems, with only UNIX System V.2 or later having the full functionality described here.

Notes

Previous versions of sort used sorting keys of the form

+m.n[options] -p.q[options]

instead of the -k form. This form numbered the first fields of the record as 0, the next as 1, and so on. This old format is still supported, but the POSIX.2 standard regards it as obsolete. Therefore, you should use the -k format.

tail—Display the Last Lines of a File

Synopsis

tail [-f] [-bcklmn[±]number] [file]
tail [-f] [±number[bcklmn]] [file]

Description

When tail is called without options, it displays the last 10 lines of a file. This is useful for looking at the most recent entries in log files and any file where new information is added on the end.

Options

An argument of the form +*number* skips that number of lines, then displays the rest of the file. For example, +100 will print from line 101 to the end of the file.

An argument of the form -*number* prints that number of lines from the end of the file. For example, -20 prints the last 20 lines in the file.

Both +*number* and -*number* may be preceded or followed by b, c, k, l, m, or n, to specify units of blocks, characters, kilobytes, lines, megabytes, or lines respectively. The default unit is lines.

The -f or *follow* option monitors a file as it grows. After displaying the end of the file, tail sleeps for two seconds, then prints any new data at the end of the file. This is useful on UNIX, where you can run tail while another program writes to files; it is not useful on DOS, unless you have software like Microsoft Windows which lets you run several programs simultaneously.

Diagnostics

Possible exit status values are

0	Successful completion
1	Failure because of an unknown command line option, insufficient memory for buffering, a write error on the standard output, a badly formed line or character count, a missing number after an option, or an error reopening a file descriptor

Possible error messages include

Badly formed line/	In an option of the form +*number* or character count "*string*" -*number*, the *number* was not a valid number.
Re-opening file	-f was used to follow a file as it grew.
descriptor "*number*"	tail closed the file associated with the given file descriptor *number* then tried to open it two seconds later. At this point, tail found it could not reopen the file for reading, and therefore could not follow the file any longer.

Portability

POSIX.2. X/Open Portability Guide. All UNIX systems. MKS Toolkit.

See Also

`cat`, `head`, `pg`

tar—USTAR—Compatible Tape Archiver

Synopsis

```
tar -c[#sbfvwlzU] [blocksize] [archivefile] [-V volpat] [file ...] [-C pathname] [file ...]
tar -r[#sbfvwlzU] [blocksize] [archivefile] [-V volpat] [file ...] [-C pathname] [file ...]
tar -t[#sbfvzU] [blocksize] [archivefile] [-V volpat] [file ...]
tar -x[#sbfvwpmozU] [blocksize] [archivefile] [-V volpat] [file ...]
```

Description

`tar` manipulates archives. An archive is a single file which contains the complete contents of a set of other files; an archive preserves the directory hierarchy that contained the original files. The name `tar` was derived from *tape archiver;* however, you can use archives with any medium, including diskettes.

This version of the `tar` utility writes and reads the original `tar` format from UNIX systems as well as the USTAR format defined by the POSIX standard.

Options

The four forms of the command shown in the synopsis represent the main functions of `tar`.

Primary Options

You must specify one of these primary options as the first character of an option string.

-c   Creates an archive. This command writes each named file into a newly-created archive. Directories recursively include all components. If - appears in place of any file name, `tar` reads the standard input for a list of files one per line. This allows other commands to generate lists of files for tar to archive.

-r   Writes the named files to the end of the archive. It is possible to have more than one copy of a file in an archive using this method.

-t   Displays a table of contents. This displays the names of all the files in the archive, one per line. If you specify one or more files on the command line, tar prints only those file names. Under the verbose (-v) option, more information about each archive member is printed, in a format similar to that produced by ls -l.

-x   Extracts files from an archive. tar extracts each named file to a file of the same name. If you do not specify any files on the command line, tar extracts all files in the archive. This extraction restores all file system attributes as controlled by other options.

Secondary Options

Unlike other commands, you must give secondary options to tar as a single string; for example, you might say -tv, but cannot separate them as in -t -v. You may omit the leading dash - if you want. The only exceptions to the single string rule for secondary options to tar are -C and -v; see below for a full explanation of the secondary options.

-b   Sets the number of blocks used for tape archive read/write operations to *blocksize*. If you specify -b, you must specify a *blocksize* argument. Blocks are typically 512 bytes, although some tape drives support other sizes. When reading from the tape archive, tar automatically determines the blocking factor by trying to read the largest legal blocking factor and using the actual number read to be the blocksize. For UNIX compatibility, the largest valid value for *blocksize* is 20 blocks; in USTAR mode, it is 60 blocks. If -b comes before -f in the options string, the *blocksize* must come before the *filename*.

-C *pathname*   Is an unusual option because it is specified in the middle of your file list. When tar encounters a -C *pathname* option while archiving files, `tar` treats *pathname* as the current directory and treats all following entries in your file list (including another `-C`) as being relative to *pathname*.

`-f`   Uses the *archivefile* for the tape archive rather than the default device. If `-f` is used, the *archivefile* argument must be specified. If `-f` comes before `-b` in the options string, the *archivefile* must come before the *blocksize*. If *archivefile* is the character `-`, `tar` uses the standard input for reading and the standard output for writing archives.

`#s`   Sets the default archive filename to a specific tape unit number and density. On DOS, the default archive filename used by `tar` is `/dev/mt/0m`. This option is the least general way to override this default. For a more general method, see the `-f` option. The filename generated by this option has the form `/dev/mt/#s`. The `#` may be any digit between `0` and `7`, inclusive, to select the tape unit. The density selector `s` may be `l` (low), `m` (medium), or `h` (high). On DOS, the density is ignored and the drive's default density is used.

`-l`   Complains if all links are not resolved when adding files to the tape archive.

`-m`   Does not restore a file's modification time stamp when extracting it from an archive. By default, `tar` restores the time stamp from information contained in the archive.

`-o`   When extracting files, does not attempt to assign owner and group information to extracted files. Most operating systems will then assign your owner and group information by default.

`-p`   When extracting, preserves the three high-order file attribute bits, exactly as in the archive. DOS systems use these bits to indicate system, archive, and hidden attributes. On UNIX systems, they indicate the set-user-ID, set-group-ID, and saved-text attributes; to use `-p` on

these systems, you must have appropriate privileges. When -p is set, tar ignores the UMASK and restores the modes exactly as in the archive.
Note: On DOS, every extracted file has the archive attribute turned on.

-U   When creating a new tape archive with the -c option, forces tar to use the USTAR format. The default format used when creating a new archive is the original UNIX tar format. When you do not specify -c, tar determines whether or not the tape archive is in USTAR format by reading it, so the U option does not affect file extraction. tar displays an error message for a UNIX tar format file containing a bad filename; -U will suppress this message and still extract the data if the filename is acceptable in USTAR format.

-v   Displays each filename, along with the appropriate action key letter (a for add, x for extract) as it processes the archive. With the -t form of the command, this option gives more detail about each archive member being listed.

-V *volpat*   Provides automatic multivolume support. tar writes output to files, the names of which are formatted using *volpat*. Any occurrence of # in *volpat* is replaced by the current volume number. When you invoke tar with this option, it asks you to insert the appropriate disk and then type a carriage return before it proceeds with the operation. tar issues the same sort of message when a write error or read error occurs on the archive; the reasoning is that this kind of error means that tar has reached the end of the volume and should go on to a new one.

-w   Is used to confirm each operation, such as replacing or extracting. tar displays the operation and the file involved. You can then confirm whether or not you want the operation to take place. Typing an affirmative answer (one that begins with y or Y) tells tar to do the operation; anything else tells tar to go on to the next operation.

-z   Reads and/or writes the tape archive at 16 bits, by first passing through a compression algorithm compatible with that of the UNIX compress program.

Examples

The compression option provides a more efficient way of expressing

```
tar -cvf - directory | compress >archive
```

as the command line

```
tar -cvzf archive directory
```

To identify all files that have been changed in the last week (7 days), and to archive them to a file on diskette, you might type

```
find directory -mtime -7 | tar -cvf a:archive -
```

Diagnostics

Possible exit status values:

0   Successful completion

1   Failure due to any of the following: invalid option, invalid command line arguments, out of memory, compression error, failure on extraction, or failure on creation

Limits

Pathnames in the tape archive are normally restricted to a maximum length of 100 bytes. However, in USTAR mode, pathnames may be up to 255 bytes long.

Portability

X/OPEN Portability Guide. 4.2 BSD UNIX. MKS Toolkit.

The -U option is an extension to provide POSIX USTAR format compatibility. The -p option is a common extension on BSD UNIX systems which is not available on UNIX System V systems. These two options as well as the -C, -V, and -z options are extensions to the x/OPEN standard. The -u option specified in XPG is not currently supported.

Some features of the UNIX file system, such as links, have no analogs in the DOS file system.

Warning

Before performing a raw disk input/output operation on a given disk, you must first read a properly formatted disk of the same size in the same drive. For example, if you want to use a 1.44MB disk in drive A: for raw disk input, you first perform a command like ls on a different, properly formatted 1.44MB disk in that drive. Once this is done, place the disk that you want to use for raw disk input/output in the appropriate drive and issue the tar command that you want to use.

Notes

The file permission modes of UNIX systems are not the same as those of DOS. In particular, the archive, hidden, and system attributes of such a file mean something else on UNIX systems.

When extracting UNIX files on a DOS (FAT) file system, tar attempts to open each file with the original name. If a filename error occurs, tar checks the filename to see if more than one period appears in it. If so, tar removes all but the last period, then performs filename truncation to create a valid FAT filename (that is, it has no more than eight characters before the period and no more than 3 characters in the extension), and creates a new file with this truncated name. If no filename error occurs, the file is extracted under the new filename; otherwise, tar issues an error message and moves on to the next file to be extracted.

test—Test for Condition

Synopsis

```
test expression
[ expression ]
```

Description

`test` checks for various properties of files, strings, and integers. It produces no output (except error messages), but it returns the result of the test as the exit status. See the *Diagnostics* section for more information.

The command line is a Boolean expression. The simplest expression is a *string*; a string is considered true if the string is nonempty (that is, it contains one or more characters). More complex expressions are composed of operators and operands, each of which is surrounded by whitespace. Different operators take different numbers and types of operands. Operators that take a *file* operand will fail (without error) if the file does not exist. *expression* can be

-b *file*	True if the *file* is a block special file
-c *file*	True if the *file* is a character special file (for example, a device file)
-d *file*	True if the *file* is a directory
-e *file*	True if the *file* exists
-f *file*	True if the *file* is an ordinary file
-g *file*	True if the setgid attribute of the *file* is on; explaining this is beyond the scope of this book
-k *file*	True if the save text attribute under UNIX (or the system attribute under DOS) of the *file* is on
-L *file*	True if the *file* is a symbolic link
-n *string*	True if the length of *string* is non-zero
-p *file*	True if the *file* is a FIFO (named pipe)
-r *file*	True if the *file* is readable
-s *file*	True if the size of the *file* is non-zero
-t *fd*	True if the numeric file descriptor *fd* is open and associated with a terminal
-u *file*	True if the setuid attribute of the *file* is on; explaining this is beyond the scope of this book
-w *file*	True if the *file* is writeable

-x *file*	True if the *file* is executable
-z *string*	True if the length of the *string* is zero
-L *file*	True if *file* is a symbolic link
string	True if the string is not a null string
string=*string*	True if the strings are identical
string!=*string*	True if the strings are not identical
number -eq *number*	True if the numbers are equal. Within the KornShell (only), either *number* can be an arbitrary let arithmetic expression; the same applies for the other five numerical comparisons that follow
number -ge *number*	True if the first *number* is greater than or equal to the second
number -gt *number*	True if the first *number* is greater than the second
number -le *number*	True if the first *number* is less than or equal to the second
number -lt *number*	True if the first *number* is less than the second
number -ne *number*	True if the first *number* is not equal to the second
file1 -nt *file2*	True if *file1* is newer than *file2*
file1 -ot *file2*	True if *file1* is older than *file2*
file1 -ef *file2*	True if *file1* has the same device and inode number as *file2*
expr -a *expr*	Logical AND; true if both *exprs* are true
expr -o *expr*	Logical OR; true if either *expr* is true
! *expr*	Logical negation; true if *expr* is false
(*expr*)	True if *expr* is true; this is used for grouping other operations and expressions

The precedence of the operators in descending order is

    Unary operators

    Comparison operators

    Logical AND

    Logical OR

The second form of the test command

```
[ expression ]
```

is synonymous with the first.

Examples

The following command reports on whether the first positional parameter contains a directory or a file:

```
if [ -f $1 ]
then
     echo $1 is a file
elif [ -d $1 ]
then
     echo $1 is a directory
else
     echo $1 neither file nor directory
fi
```

This example illustrates the use of test and is not intended to be an efficient method.

Diagnostics

Possible exit status values are

0	The *expression* was true.
1	The *expression* was false.
2	The *expression* was badly formed.

Portability

POSIX.2. X/Open Portability Guide. All UNIX systems. MKS Toolkit. The following file attributes do not apply to the DOS file system: -b, -c, -g, -p, -u, -x, -L, and -ef.

See Also

find, let, ls, sh

Notes

test is built into the shell and is also implemented as a separate utility. In the KornShell, test can compare variables; however, if the variable is null, the expression may be invalid for test. For example,

```
NULL=
test $NULL = "so"
```

will not work, because the KornShell will expand this to

```
test = "so"
```

which is not a valid expression for test. You can get around this by adding some value to the front of both strings, as in

```
test x$NULL = x"so"
```

trap—Intercept Abnormal Conditions and Interrupts

Synopsis

```
trap ['handler'] [traptype ...]
```

Description

trap intercepts certain kinds of exception conditions. The command is built into the KornShell.

The *handler* argument is a list of one or more commands. Because it usually contains more than one word, it must be quoted to serve as a single argument. It is scanned when you issue the trap command. If an appropriate exception condition occurs, the shell scans the command list again and executes the commands. A missing argument or an argument of - (dash) resets the default trap condition. A null argument (' ') causes the trap condition to be ignored.

If the *traptype* argument is the word ERR, the shell invokes the trap *handler* upon any command having a non-zero exit status. This trap is not triggered inside functions.

If *traptype* is 0 or the word EXIT, the shell invokes the trap handler when the shell terminates. Within a function, the trap is invoked when the function exits.

Any other traptype argument should be a number corresponding to a signal number. On DOS, the valid signal numbers are 2 (SIGINT), 14 (SIGALRM), and 10 (SIGSTOP). SIGINT is sent by Ctrl-Break or Ctrl-C. SIGALRM is sent when the TMOUT variable expires. SIGSTOP is sent when a program run under the shell exits through a terminate-and-stay resident program. The words INT, ALRM, and STOP can be used instead of the signal numbers.

If a signal is being ignored at the time that you enter the shell, it continues to be ignored without regard to any traps.

If there are no arguments at all, trap prints a list of all the traps and their commands.

Examples

```
trap 'rm -f /tmp/xyz$$; exit' ERR EXIT
trap 'read REPLY?"ABORT??"
    case $REPLY in
    y)   exit 1
    esac'   2
```

On error or exit, this example deletes a temporary file created during command execution. Upon an interrupt signal (Ctrl-C under DOS), the example asks whether to abort and exits if the answer is y.

Diagnostics

Possible exit status values are

0	Successful completion
1	Failure due to an invalid signal name or *number*
2	Failure due to an invalid command line argument

Possible error messages include

"*name*" Not a valid trap name	You specified an unrecognized trap name. This error usually happens because of a typing mistake on the command line.

496

Portability

POSIX.2. X/Open Portability Guide. MKS Toolkit. A built-in function of the Bourne Shell and KornShell on UNIX.

See Also

`sh`

typeset—Assign Attributes and Values to Variables

Synopsis

```
typeset [±f[tux]] name ...
typeset [±lprtuxH] [±iLRZ[number]] [variable[=value] ...]
```

Description

If no options are specified, `typeset` displays a list of all variables and their attributes. `typeset` is built into the KornShell.

Options

When only arguments of the form *+option* are specified, `typeset` displays a list of the variables that have all the specified attributes set.

If all parameters are of the form *-option*, `typeset` displays a list of all the variables having all the specified attributes set, and also displays their values.

When you specify the `f` option, `typeset` applies to functions. Otherwise, it applies to variables. For functions, the only applicable options are the ones shown in the *Synopsis* section.

If the command line contains at least one *variable*, `typeset` changes the attributes of each *variable*. Parameters of the form *-option* turn on the associated attributes, and parameters of the form *+option* turn off the associated attributes. Parameters of the form *variable=value* turn on the associated attributes and also assign *value* to *variable*.

When a function invokes `typeset`, the shell creates a new instance of each *variable*. After the function terminates, the shell restores each *variable* to the value and attributes it had before the function was called.

Here is a summary of the possible attribute options:

-l   Converts uppercase characters to lowercase characters in any value assigned to a *variable*. If -u is currently turned on, this option turns it off.

-p   Writes output to the coprocess. This is not useful on DOS because DOS does not have coprocesses.

-r   Makes each *variable* read-only.

-t   Tags each *variable*. Tags are user-definable and have no meaning to the shell. For functions, this turns on the xtrace option. See the man set page for a discussion of xtrace.

-u   Converts lowercase characters to uppercase characters in any value assigned to a *variable*. If -l is currently turned on, this option turns it off.

            When used with -f, -u indicates that the functions named in the command line are not yet defined. The attributes specified by the typeset command are applied to the functions when they are defined.

-x   Sets each variable for automatic export. See the man page for export.

-H   Performs UNIX to host-name file mapping. On DOS, slashes are mapped to backslashes.

-i[*number*]   Marks each variable as having an integer value, thus making arithmetic faster. If *number* is given and it is non-zero, the output base of each *variable* is *number*.

The following options justify the values assigned to each variable within a field. The width of the field is number if it is defined and non-zero; otherwise, the width of *variable* is the width of the first value assigned to variable.

-L[*number*]   Left-justifies the values assigned to each *variable* by removing any leading blanks. If -z is turned on, leading zeros are also removed. Then blanks are added on the end or the end of the value is truncated as necessary. If -R is currently turned on, this option turns it off.

-R[*number*]   Right-justifies the values assigned to each *variable* by adding leading blanks or by truncating the end of the value as necessary. If `-L` is currently turned on, this option turns it off.

`-Z[number]`	Right-justifies values assigned to each `variable`. If the first nonblank character of value is a digit, leading zeros are used. Also see the `-L` option.

Diagnostics

Possible exit status values are

0	Successful completion
2	Failure due to an invalid command line argument

If the command is used to display the values of variables, the exit status value is the number of names that are invalid.

Possible error messages include

`Base number not in [2,36]`	You used the `-i` option to specify a base for an integer, but the base was not in the range 2 through 36. All bases must be in this range.
`name: Not a function`	You tried to declare the given `name` as a function, but the name already referred to something that was not a function (for example, a variable).
`Subscripts illegal with integers`	You tried to subscript a variable that was a simple integer. Subscripts can only be applied to array variables.

Portability

POSIX.2. MKS Toolkit. typeset is a built-in command of the KornShell on UNIX, but it is not a Bourne Shell command.

See Also

sh

unalias—Remove Aliases

Synopsis

```
unalias name ...
unalias -a
```

Description

unalias removes each alias *name*. It is built into the KornShell.

Options

The -a option removes all aliases.

Diagnostics

Possible exit status values are

0   Successful completion.

Otherwise, unalias returns the number of specified names that are not currently defined as aliases.

Portability

POSIX.2. MKS Toolkit. On UNIX, unalias is built into the KornShell but not the Bourne Shell.

See Also

alias, sh

unset—Remove Shell Variable or Function

Synopsis

```
unset [-fv] name...
```

Description

unset removes the value and attributes of each variable *name*. This command is built into the shell.

unset cannot remove names that have been set read-only.

Options

If you specify -f, unset removes the value and attributes of each function *name*.

Using the -v option is equivalent to calling unset with no options.

Diagnostics

Possible exit status values are

0	Successful completion.
1	Failure due to an invalid command line argument.

Otherwise, unset returns the number of specified names that are invalid, not currently set, or read-only.

Portability

POSIX.2. X/Open Portability Guide. MKS Toolkit. unset is a built-in command of the Bourne and Korn shells on UNIX System V.

See Also

sh

vi, ex—Display-Oriented Interactive Text Editor

Synopsis

```
vi [-eRsvx] [-c command] [-t tag] [-w size] [file ...]
vi [-eRsvx] [+command] [-t tag] [-w size] [file ...]
```

Conventions

Throughout this document the following symbols are used:

Ctrl-D	CTRL followed by a single letter indicates the control character transmitted by holding down the CTRL key and the letter key at the same time.
BACKSPACE	This indicates the real backspace key. On the PC, this has a left arrow on it. This may differ from the CTRL-H key.
ENTER	This indicates the ENTER key, which is labeled RETURN on some keyboards. This may differ in effect from the CTRL-M key.
ESC	This indicates the Escape key.
INTERRUPT	This indicates the break key; CTRL-C or CTRL-BREAK on the PC.
rightarrow	This indicates the right arrow key.
leftarrow	This indicates the left arrow key.
downarrow	This indicates the down arrow key.
uparrow	This indicates the up arrow key.

Description

There are two components to vi: a screen editor (Vi), and a line editor (Ex). Each has a different set of commands; you can invoke the line editor from within the screen editor and conversely, you can invoke the screen editor from within the line editor.

In the screen editor, you are in either *insert mode* or *command mode*. In command mode, every character you type is immediately interpreted as a command. In insert mode, every character you type is added to the text that you are editing.

502

There are two ways to start your session in Ex mode: you can invoke the command under the name ex; or you can invoke it under the name vi but specify the -e option. Similarly, there are two ways to start your session in Vi mode; you can invoke the command under the name vi (without specifying -e); or you can invoke it under the name ex but specify -v.

Vi and Ex work on text files. If a file contains the NUL character (value 0 or \0); it is turned into the value 0x7F. The newline character is interpreted as a line delimiter. Each line is limited to a maximum length of 1K bytes, including the newline. If any lines exceed that length, they are truncated at that length. If the last line in the file does not end in a newline, a newline is added. In all these abnormal cases, vi marks the file as modified and displays a message.

Options

vi accepts the following options:

-c command   Runs command before displaying any text on the screen. command is any Ex command. To specify multiple Ex commands, separate them with a vertical line character (¦) and enclose them in quotes. The quotes ensure that the shell does not interpret the ¦ as a pipe character. For example,

-c 'set all ¦ ver'

runs both the set all and ver commands prior to displaying text.

-e   Invokes ex.

-R   Sets the *read-only* variable, preventing the accidental overwriting of files. Any command that writes to a file requires the ! suffix.

-s   Turns on quiet mode, which tells the editor not to display file information messages, thus allowing Ex to be used as a filter.

-t tag   Lets you search for a tag in the same way that you use with the Ex tag command (described later).

-v   Puts the editor into Vi mode. With vi, its use is redundant.

-x	Prompts you for an encryption key. All files read and written are run through the crypt program using the key that you enter. The crypt program must be in the current search path.
-w size	Sets the option variable window to size. See the *Set Option Variables* section for more information.
+command	Is an obsolete version of the -c option.

Current Position Pointer

The *current position pointer* indicates a position in the text that is currently being edited (or has just been edited). In Ex mode, the current position pointer is just the line number of the line being edited. In Vi mode, the pointer gives this line number plus the position of the cursor within the line. The line indicated by the current position pointer is always on the screen.

Display Conventions

vi uses three display conventions that should be noted.

vi displays the input for search commands (/ and ?), Ex commands (:), and system commands (!) on the bottom line of the screen. Error and informational messages also appear on this line.

If the last line in the file is above the bottom of the screen, screen lines beyond the end of the file are displayed with a single ~ character in column one.

In certain infrequent circumstances (usually involving lines longer than the width of the screen), vi is unable to fill the display with complete lines. In this case, one or more screen lines are shown with a single @ character in column one.

These lines are not part of the file content and should be ignored.

Vi Command Summary

Vi commands may be divided into several categories.

- *Scrolling commands* adjust the position of text on the screen. The current position pointer only changes if the current line is scrolled off the screen. For example, CTRL-E scrolls the text on the screen up one line. The cursor remains pointing to the same text, unless that text is moved off the screen.

- *Movement commands* move the cursor in the file. For example, the character j moves the cursor down one line and the screen is scrolled only if necessary. There are two types of movement commands: *absolute* movements and *context-dependent* movements. An absolute movement moves the cursor, regardless of the nature of the surrounding text; for example, j always moves the cursor down one line. A context-dependent movement moves the cursor based on the nature of the text; for example, w moves the cursor to the beginning of the next word, so it must look at the text to determine where the next word begins.

- *Manipulation* commands let you change the text that is already in the file.

- *Text insertion* commands let you add new text to the existing text.

Vi scrolling and movement commands may be preceded by a decimal integer that serves as a *count*, as in

`[count] command`

count means different things with different commands. If you type *count*, it is not displayed anywhere on the screen.

Scrolling

CTRL-B	Scrolls text back a page (that is, a screen), less two lines. The cursor is placed on the bottom line of the screen. *count* specifies a number of pages to scroll. The default value for *count* is 1.
CTRL-D	Scrolls text onto the bottom of the screen. The current position pointer moves forward the same amount in the text, which means that the cursor stays in the same relative position on the screen. If *count* is given, the screen scrolls forward by the given number of lines; this

number is used for all future CTRL-D and CTRL-U commands (until a new *count* is given). The default scrolling
amount is half the screen.

CTRL-E

Scrolls a new line onto the bottom of the screen. The
current position pointer is not changed unless the
current line scrolls off the top of the screen; then the
pointer is set to the top line. If *count* is given, the screen
scrolls forward the given number of lines. The default
value for *count* is 1.

CTRL-F

Scrolls text forward a page (that is, a screen), less two
lines. The cursor is placed on the top line of the screen.
count specifies the number of pages to scroll. The default
value for *count* is 1.

CTRL-U

Scrolls text onto the top of the screen. The current
position pointer moves backward the same amount in
the text, which means that the cursor stays in the same
relative position on the screen. *count* operates as for
CTRL-D. The default scrolling amount is half the screen.

CTRL-Y

Scrolls a new line onto the top of the screen. The current
position pointer is not changed unless the current line
scrolls off the bottom of the screen; then the pointer is
set to the bottom line. If *count* is given, the screen scrolls
backward the given number of lines. The default value
for *count* is 1.

[n] z [m] type

Redraws the screen in a window of *m* lines. *type* determines the position of the current line. If *type* is the
newline character, the current line is placed at the top of
the window. If *type* is a period (.), the current line is
placed in the middle of the window. If *type* is a minus
sign (-), the current line is placed at the bottom of the
window. If *n* is given, the current position pointer is first
set to that absolute line number; then the screen is
positioned according to *type*. If you omit *n*, it defaults to
the current line. If you omit *m*, it defaults to window (see
Set Option Variables).

Absolute Movement

All the following movement commands except *m*, *0*, *^*, *`*, and *'* may be preceded by *count* to repeat the movement that many times.

G	Moves to the absolute line number specified as *count*. If *count* is zero or is not specified, the cursor is moved to the last line of the file.
	h
	leftarrow
	CTRL-H
BACKSPACE	Moves the cursor one position to the left.
	j
	downarrow
	CTRL-H
CTRL-J	
CTRL-N	Moves the cursor to the next line at the same column on the screen. Scroll the screen one line if needed.
	k
	uparrow
CTRL-P	Moves the cursor to the previous line at the same column on the screen. Scroll the screen up one line if needed.
	l
	rightarrow
SPACE	Moves the cursor one position to the right.
m	Records the current position pointer under a *mark name*. A mark name is a single lowercase letter, given immediately after the *m*. For example, the command *ma* records the current location of the current position pointer under the name *a*.
0 (Zero)	Moves the cursor to the first character of the current line.
+	
CTRL-M	Moves the cursor to the first nonblank character on the next line. The screen scrolls one line if needed.

507

-     Moves the cursor to the first nonspace character on the previous line. Scroll the screen up one line if needed.

¦   Moves the cursor to the column number specified as *count*. This is a screen column number, not a line offset. If *count* is greater than the length of the current line, vi moves the cursor to the last character on the line. If the column indicated is spanned by a tab, vi moves the cursor to the first character after the tab.

^   Moves the cursor to the first nonblank character of the current line.

$ Moves the cursor forward to the end of a line. *count* specifies the number of lines, including the current line, to move forward.

`     When followed by a mark name, ` moves the cursor to the position that has been associated with that name. The position is set by the *m* command. A grave character followed by another grave character moves the cursor to the *previous context*. The previous context is typically the last place where you made a change. More precisely, the previous context is set whenever you move the cursor in a nonrelative manner.

'   Is similar to the grave (`) character, except that the cursor is set to the first nonblank character on the marked line.

Movement By Context

vi defines a word in the following two ways:

- A sequence of letters, digits, and underscores delimited at both ends by: 1) characters that are not letters, digits, or underscores, 2) the beginning or end of a line, or 3) the end of the editing buffer.

- A sequence of characters other than letters, digits, underscores, or whitespace delimited at both ends by: 1) a letter, digit, underscore, whitespace, 2) the beginning or end of a line, or 3) the end of the editing buffer.

vi defines a *full word* as a sequence of nonblank characters delimited at both ends by blank characters (SPACE, TAB, NEWLINE) or by the beginning or end of a line or file.

B	Moves the cursor back to the first character of the current full word. If the cursor is already at the beginning of a full word, vi moves it to the first character of the preceding full word.
b	Moves the cursor back to the first character of the current word. If the cursor is already at the beginning of a word, vi moves it to the first character of the preceding word.
E	Moves the cursor forward to the end of the current full word. If the cursor is already at the end of a full word, vi moves it to the last character of the next full word.
e	Moves the cursor forward to the end of the current word. If the cursor is already at the end of a word, vi moves it to the last character of the next word.
Fc	Searches backward in the line for the single character *c* and positions the cursor on top of it. When *count* is given, the editor searches back for the *count*th such character.
fc	Searches forward in the line for the single character *c* and positions the cursor on top of it. When *count* is given, the editor searches for the *count*th such character.
H	Places the cursor on the first nonblank character of the top line of the screen. *count* specifies the number of lines from the top of the screen.
L	Places the cursor on the first nonblank character of the bottom line of the screen. *count* specifies the number of lines up from the bottom of the screen.
M	Places the cursor on the first nonblank character of the middle line of the screen.
N	Repeats previous / or ? command, but in the opposite direction.
n	Repeats previous / or ? command.
Tc	Searches backward in the line for the character *c* and positions the cursor after the character being sought. *count* searches backward for the *count*th matching character, and then positions the cursor after the character being sought.

509

tc   Searches forward in the line for the character *c* and positions the cursor on the preceding character. *count* searches forward for the *count*th matching character and positions the cursor on the preceding character.

W   Moves to the start of the next full word.

w   Moves to the start of the next word.

(Moves back to the beginning of the current sentence. A sentence is bounded by a period (.), exclamation mark (!), or question mark (?); followed by any number of closing double quotes, ("), closing single quotes ('), closing parentheses ()), or closing square brackets (]); followed by two spaces or the end of the line. Paragraph and section boundaries are also sentence boundaries; see *[[* and *{*.

)   Moves to the beginning of the next sentence. See *(* for the definition of a sentence.

{   Moves back to the beginning of a paragraph. A paragraph begins on a blank line, a section boundary (see *[[*) or a text formatter macro in the paragraphs variable.

}   Moves to the beginning of the next paragraph. See *{* for the definition of a paragraph.

[[Moves back to the beginning of a section. A section begins on lines starting with a formfeed (*CTRL-L*); starting with an open brace *{*; a text formatter macro in the sections variable; or begin or end of file.

]]   Moves to the beginning of the next section. See *[[* for the definition of a section.

%   Finds the balancing character to that under the cursor. The character should be one of the following characters:

[{ (< >) }]

;   Repeats the previous *F*, *f*, *T*, or *t* command.

,   Repeats the previous *F*, *f*, *T*, or *t* command in the opposite direction.

/regexp   Searches forward in the file for a line matching the regular expression *regexp* and positions the cursor at the first character of the matching string. When used with an operator to define a text range, the range begins with the character at the current cursor position and ends with the first character of the matching string. You can specify whole lines by following *regexp* with /+*n* or /-*n* where *n* is the offset from the matched line.

?regexp   Is similar to /, but searches backwards in the file.

CTRL-]   Uses the word after the cursor as a tag. See *tag* under *Ex Commands. Object.*

Object Manipulators

An object manipulator command works on a block of text. The command character is followed immediately by any kind of movement command. The object that is manipulated by the object manipulator command is the text from the current position pointer to wherever the movement command would leave the cursor.

For example, in *dL*, *d* is the object manipulator command to delete an object. It is followed by the movement command *L* that means move to the bottom line of the screen. The object manipulated by the command thus extends from the current line to the bottom line on the screen; these lines are deleted.

Normally an object extends up to, but not including, the position of the cursor after the move command; however, some movements work in a *line* mode; for example, *L* puts the cursor on the first nonblank character of the last line on the screen. If it is used in an object manipulation command, it includes the entire starting line and the entire ending line. Some other objects include the cursor position; for example, *d$* deletes up to and including the last character on a line; by itself the *$* would have placed the cursor on the final character. Repeating the command letter (or symbol) implies working on a line basis; thus *5dd* deletes five lines.

Objects that are deleted or otherwise manipulated have their original values placed in a *buffer*, an area of computer memory that can hold text. There are several ways this can be done.

- You can use a *named* buffer. Buffers are named with single lowercase letters. To place an object in a buffer, type a double quote " followed by the buffer name, followed by the object manipulator command, as in

"adL

This deletes text from the current line to the bottom line on the screen and puts the deleted text in buffer a. Normally, this sort of operation overwrites the current contents of the buffer; however, if you use the same form but specify the buffer name in uppercase, the object is appended to the current contents of the buffer. For example,

```
"AdL
```

deletes from the current line to the bottom line on the screen, and adds the deleted text to buffer a.

- If you are deleting material and delete at least one full line, vi uses buffers numbered 1 through 9. The first time a full line or more is deleted, the text is placed in buffer 1. The next time, the old contents of 1 are copied to 2, and the newly deleted text is put into 1. In the same way, deleted text continues to be *rippled* through the nine numbered buffers. When text is rippled out of buffer 9, it is gone for good.

- In all other cases, the object manipulated goes to the *unnamed* buffer. For example, the unnamed buffer is used if you delete less than a line of text. The unnamed buffer is like the other buffers, but doesn't have a name.

The following examples illustrate the use of buffers.

dL	Deletes text from current cursor position through to the bottom of the screen and places it into buffer 1; it also ripples numbered buffers.
"ad/fred/	Delete from current cursor position through to the next position containing (but not including) the string *fred*, and place the deleted text into buffer a.
dw	Deletes the current word and places it in an unnamed buffer.

The object manipulator commands are

c	Deletes the object and enters insert mode for text insertion after the current cursor position. If less than one line is changed, a dollar sign ($) is placed on the final character of the object and typing goes directly over top of the current object until the dollar sign ($) is reached. Additional text is inserted, and the existing text shifts to make room for the new text.
d	Deletes the object.

y	*yanks* the object to the appropriate buffer; the original object is not changed. This may be used to duplicate or copy objects.
<	Shifts the object left by the value of the variable shiftwidth. This operator always works on a line basis. This command replaces existing blanks and tabs at the beginning of the line with the minimum number of tabs and spaces required to create the new indent amount. *count* shifts *count* lines.
>	Shifts the object right by the value of the variable shiftwidth. This operator always works on a line basis. This command replaces existing blanks and tabs at the beginning of the line with the minimum number of tabs and spaces required to create the new indent amount. *count* shifts *count* lines.
!	Filters the object through an external command. After typing the object, the command line opens up for a system command which is parsed in the same manner as the Ex system command (`:!`). This operator then invokes the given command and sends the entire object on a line basis to that command. The object is then deleted and the output from the command replaces it. For example, `1G!Gsort` moves to the first line of the file; then takes all the text from the first line to the last line and runs it through the `sort` command.

Object Manipulator Abbreviations

To make things easier, `vi` supports the following shorthand commands. Each can be preceded by *count* and/or by a buffer name to save the manipulated text.

C	Changes to the end of the current line. This is equivalent to the `c$` command.
D	Deletes to the end of the current line. This is equivalent to the `d$` command.
S	Substitutes current line. This is equivalent to the `cc` command.
s	Substitutes current character. This is equivalent to the `cl` command.
X	Deletes the previous character. This is equivalent to the `dh` command.

x	Deletes current the character. This is equivalent to the *d1*.
Y	yanks current line. This is equivalent to the *yy* command.

Inserting Text

vi supports the following commands for inserting text:

A	Enters insert mode at end of line. This is equivalent to the *$a* command.
a	Enters insert mode after the current cursor position.
I	Enters insert mode before first nonblank character on line. This is equivalent to the *^i* command.
i	Enters insert mode before the current cursor position.
O	Opens up a new line before the current line and enters insert mode on it.
o	Opens up a new line after the current line and enters insert mode on it.
R	Replaces characters on the screen with characters typed up to the next ESC. Each character typed overlays a character on the screen. The newline character is an exception; it is simply inserted and no other character is replaced. While you are doing this, the screen may not correspond exactly to the contents of the file, due to tabs, and so on. The screen is properly updated when you leave insert mode.
r	Replaces the character under the cursor with the next character typed. When *count* is given, *count* characters following the cursor are all changed to the next character typed. If *count* is given and the newline character is the replacement character, *count* characters are deleted (as usual) and replaced with a single newline character, not *count* newlines.

Miscellaneous

J	Joins *count* lines together. If you do not specify *count* or *count* is less than 2, vi uses a *count* of 2, joining the current line and the next line. This command supplies appropriate spacing: one space

between words, two spaces after a period, and no spaces at all when the first character of the next line is a closing parenthesis (**)**). When a line ends with whitespace, vi retains the whitespace, does not add any further spaces, and then appends the next line.

P	Puts buffer contents before the cursor. This is also called a *paste* operation. If preceded by quote *buffername* (for example, "*b*), the contents of that buffer are used; otherwise the contents of the unnamed buffer are used. If the buffer was created in Ex mode, the contents of the buffer are inserted before the current line. If the buffer was created in Vi mode, the contents are inserted before the cursor. As a special case, if a paste operation is repeated with the period (.) command and it used a numbered buffer, the number of the buffer is incremented. Thus, "*1p*....., pastes in the contents of buffer 1 through buffer 6; in other words the last six things that were deleted are put back.
p	Is similar to P except that text is pasted after the cursor instead of before it.
Q	Switches to Ex mode. You leave Vi mode and the Ex prompt is shown on the bottom line of the screen.
U	Undoes all changes to current line. As soon as you move off a line or invoke an Ex command on the line, the original contents of the line are forgotten and U is not successful.
u	Undoes last change. If repeated, you undo the undo (that is, go back to what the text was before the undo). Some operations are treated as single changes; for example, everything done by a global G is undone with undo.
ZZ	Writes the file out, if changed, then exits. Equivalent to the Ex command *xit*.
.	Repeats the last command. Any command that changes the contents of the file may be repeated by this command. If you do not specify *count* with the . command, vi uses the *count* that was specified for the command being repeated.
~	Toggles the case of the character under the cursor and moves the cursor right by one. This command may be preceded by *count* to change the case of *count* characters.

&   Repeats the previous Ex substitute command using the current line as the target. Flags set by the previous command are ignored. Equivalent to the Ex command **&**.

:   Invokes an Ex command. The editor places the cursor on the bottom line of the screen and displays a colon (:) to prompt for input. You may then type an Ex command; when you press ESC or ENTER, the line you have entered is passed to Ex and run there.

@   Invokes a macro. When the next character is a letter from a through z, vi treats it as the name of a buffer. The contents of that buffer are treated as input typed to vi. The text of a macro may contain an @ calling another macro. A macro may call itself, provided it is invoked at the end of the macro (tail recursion). Such a macro runs forever or until an error occurs or the INTERRUPT key is pressed. A macro that invokes itself at the beginning (head recursion) loops until it runs out of memory. A vi error terminates all currently executing macros. All changes made during a macro call are treated as a unit and may be undone with a single *u* command.

CTRL-G   Displays the current pathname, current line number, total number of lines in the file, and the percentage of the way through the file. This is equivalent to invoking the Ex command file.

CTRL-L   Redraws the screen assuming another process has written on it. This should normally never happen unless a filter *!* command writes to the screen rather than the standard output.

CTRL-R   Redraws the screen, removing any deleted lines flagged with the @ convention.

CTRL-^   Switches to editing the alternate file (see write under *Ex Commands*). If you attempt this and you have not written out the file since you made the most recent change, vi does not switch to the alternate file.

Special Keys

Keys like the function keys and the cursor arrow keys do not correspond to particular characters. These keys can be programmed to be interpreted as any character sequence, using the Ex *map* and *map!* commands.

Insert Mode

The object manipulation command *c*, and the text insertion commands [*AaIiOoRr*] put Vi into INSERT mode. In this mode, most characters typed are inserted in the file. The following characters have special meaning.

CTRL-D	Decrements the *autoindent* for the current line by one level. This is only relevant if the variable *autoindent* is on. See the *Set Option Variables* section for more details.
CTRL-H	
BACKSPACE	Deletes the last typed character. The character is not removed from the screen; however it is no longer in your file. When you backspace over characters, new text overwrites the old ones. You are permitted to backspace to the start of the current line regardless of where you started to insert text. (This is not true of some other versions of Vi.)
CTRL-J	
CTRL-M	
ENTER	Ends the current line and starts a new one.
CTRL-Q	
CTRL-V	Inserts the next character typed as that character instead of using its special meaning. This is normally used to escape, say, the ESC character itself. It is impossible to escape *CTRL-J* or the null character in your line.
CTRL-T	Increments the *autoindent* for the current line by one level. This is only relevant if the variable autoindent is on.
CTRL-W	Deletes the word preceding the cursor and blanks. Even though the characters are not removed from the screen, they are no longer in your file.

CTRL-@

Alt-A   When this is the first character typed after entering insert mode, the previously typed insert mode contents are repeated; after this, you exit insert mode. Only up to the first 256 characters from the previous insertion are inserted. CTRL-@ is the keystroke that performs this operation on UNIX; however on DOS, this keystroke is not returned by the system. ALT-A must be used instead.

leftarrow   Backs over the last typed character. Characters typed are inserted before these characters are backed over.

CTRL-U   Deletes inserted line. The cursor is moved to the first character that was inserted on the current line. The characters are not removed from the screen; however they are no longer in your file. If you have backspaced past the point that you started inserting text, this deletes to the start of the current line. You can change the character that deletes an inserted line with the *linedelete* variable described in *Set Option Variables.*

ESC

INTERRUPT   Leaves insert mode.

Ex Command Mode

Ex commands may be typed if the program is invoked with the -e option or if the Q command is issued from Vi. A single Ex command may be issued from Vi using the : command.

An Ex command takes the general form

```
[address-list] [[command] [!] [parameters]]
```

Each part is optional and may be invalid for some commands. You may specify multiple commands on a line by separating them with a vertical line character (¦).

address-list   Commands may take zero, one, or two addresses. The address % is a short form to indicate the entire file. You may omit any or all of the addresses. In the command description in the *Ex Commands* section, the addresses shown are the addresses that the commands use by default.

Possible default addresses are

[. , .]   Indicates a two address line range defaulting to the current line.

[1,$]   Indicates a two address line range defaulting to the entire file.

[.+1]   Indicates a single address defaulting to the next line.

address   An address refers to a line in the text being edited. An address may be an expression involving the following forms:

.   The value of the current line indicator.

n   A line number indicating an absolute line in the file; the first line has absolute line number 1.

$ The last line in the file.

+[*n*]   *n* lines forward in the file. If you omit *n*, it defaults to 1.

-[*n*]   *n* lines backward in the file. If you omit *n*, it defaults to 1.

'*x*   The value of the mark *x*.

/*pat*/   Search for regular expression *pat* forward from the current line.

?*pat*?   Search for regular expression *pat* backwards from the current line.

Thus,

```
/pattern/+3
++
100
```

are three addresses: the first searches for a pattern and then goes three lines further; the second indicates two lines after the current line; and the third indicates the 100th line in the file.

command	The *command* is a word, which can be abbreviated. Characters shown in square brackets are optional. For example,

a[ppend]   Indicates that the *append* command can be abbreviated to simply *a*.

!   Some commands have a variant; this is usually toggled with an exclamation mark (!) immediately after the command.

parameters   Many Ex commands use parameters so that you can specify more information about the command. Common parameters include

buffer   Specifies one of the named areas for saving text. For more information, see the description of buffers in the *Object Manipulators* section of this man page.

count   Is a positive integer, specifying the number of lines to be affected by the command. If you do not *count*, it defaults to 1.

file   Is the pathname for a file. If *file* includes the % character, vi replaces that character with the pathname of the current file. If *file* includes the # character, vi replaces that character with the pathname of the alternate file. If you do not specify *file*, the default is the current file.

flags   Indicate actions to be taken after the command is run. It may consist of leading plus (+) and minus (-) signs to adjust the value of the current line indicator; followed by *p*, *1*, or # to display, list, or number a line.

Thus

```
.+5 delete 6==#
```

deletes starting five lines down from the current line; six lines are deleted; the current line indicator is set to the following line, then incremented by two; and that line is displayed with its line number.

Regular Expressions and Replacements

Many Ex commands use *regular expressions* when searching and replacing text. A regular expression (indicated by `pat` in the command descriptions) is used to match a set of characters. A replacement (indicated by `repl` in the command descriptions) describes what to put back in a line for the set of characters matched by the regular expression.

A regular expression consists of a string of normal characters that exactly match characters in a line. These may be intermixed with special characters (known as *metacharacters*) which allow matching in some special manner. Metacharacters may themselves be matched directly by preceding them with the backslash (\) character. If the variable magic (see the *Set Option Variables* section) is turned off, all but two of the metacharacters are disabled; in this case, the backslash character must precede them to allow their use as metacharacters. See Appendix B, "Regular Expression Summary," for examples.

Regular Expression Summary

^	Matches the start of a line. This is only a metacharacter if it is the first character in the expression.
$	Matches the end of a line. This is only a metacharacter if it is the last character in the expression.
.	Matches any single character.
*	Matches zero or more occurrences of the previous expression.
\<	Matches the empty string preceding the start of a word. A word is a series of alphanumeric or underscore characters preceded and followed by characters that are not alphanumeric or underscore.

\>
    Matches the empty string following the end of a word. A word is a series of alphanumeric or underscore characters preceded and followed by characters that are not alphanumeric or underscore.

[string]
    Matches any of the characters in the class of characters defined by *string*. For example, [aeiouy] matches any of the vowels. You can put a range of characters in a class by specifying the first and last characters of the range, with a dash (-) between them. For example, in ASCII [A-Za-z] matches any upper or lowercase letter. If the first character of a class is the caret (^), the class matches any character not specified inside the square brackets. Thus, in ASCII [a-z][^0-9] matches a single alphabetic character or the underscore, followed by any non-numeric character.

\(...\)
    May surround a set of characters in the pattern. See the discussion of the \n replacement pattern, which appears under *Replacement Pattern Summary,* to find the meaning of this construct. This is not affected by the setting of the variable magic (see the *Set Option Variables* section).

~
    Matches the replacement part of the last substitute command.

Replacement Pattern Summary

&
    Is replaced by the entire string of matched characters.

~
    Is replaced by the entire replacement pattern from the last substitute.

\n
    Is replaced by the string that matched the *n*th occurrence of a \(... \) in the regular expression. For example, consider

s/\([a-zA-Z]*\)our/\1or/

    The \1 represents the string that matched the regular expression \([a-zA-Z]*\). Thus the previous command might change the word *color* to color.

\u
    Turns the next character in the replacement to uppercase.

\l
    Turns the next character in the replacement to lowercase.

\U	Turns subsequent characters in the replacement to uppercase.
\L	Turns subsequent characters in the replacement to lowercase.
\E, \e	Turns off the effects of \U or \L.

Ex Commands

These commands can be entered as shown in Ex mode. In Vi mode, they must be preceded by the colon (:) character.

`ab[breviate] [word rhs]`	Indicates the word *word* is to be interpreted as an abbreviation for *rhs* (see previous definition of *word* in the section entitled *Movement By Context*). If you enter *word* surrounded by whitespace (or any characters that cannot be part of a word) in Vi Insert mode, it is automatically changed into *rhs*. If you do not specify any arguments for the *ab* command, it displays the abbreviations that are already defined.
`[.] a[ppend][!]`	Enters Ex Insert mode. Text is read and placed after the specified line. An input line consisting of one period (.) leaves Insert mode without inserting the period. If you specify an address of zero, text is inserted before the first line of the file. The current line indicator points to the last line typed.
	If an exclamation mark (!) is specified, the autoindent option is toggled during input. This command may not be invoked from Vi mode.

`ar[gs]`	Displays the current list of files being edited. The current file is shown enclosed by square brackets.
`cd[!] [path]`	Changes the current directory to *path*. If you omit *path*, *cd* sets the current working directory to the directory identified by the home variable. If *path* is a relative pathname *cd* searches for it using the directories specified in the cdpath variable. If path is - (the dash), then, *cd* changes to the previous working directory. If you have modified the buffer since the last write, vi displays a warning message. You can override this behavior by including the exclamation mark (!).
`[.,.] c[hange][!] [count]`	Deletes the line range given and then enters Insert mode. If an exclamation mark (!) is specified, autoindent is toggled during input. This command may not be invoked from Vi mode.
`chd[ir][!] [path]`	Is the same as *cd*.
`[.,.] co[py] addr [flags]`	Copies the line range given after *addr*. If *addr* is zero, the lines are inserted before the first line of the file. The current line indicator points to the last line of the inserted copied text.
`[.,.] d[elete] [buffer] [count] [flags]`	
	Deletes the specified line range. After deleting the line range, the current line indicator points to the line after the deleted range. A *buffer* may be specified as a letter

a-z; if so, deleted lines are saved in the buffer with that name. If an uppercase letter is specified for *buffer*, the lines are appended to the buffer of the corresponding lowercase name. If no buffer name is given, deleted lines go to the unnamed buffer.

```
e[dit] [!] [+line] [file]

ex [!] [+line] [file]
```

Begins a new editing session on a new file; the new file replaces the old file on the screen. Normally, this command is invalid if you have modified the contents of the current file without writing it back to the file. Specifying an exclamation mark (!) goes on to start a new session even if you have not saved the changes of the current session.

You can specify *line* as either a line number or as a string of the form */regexp* or *?regexp* where *regexp* is a regular expression. When *line* is a line number, the current line indicator is set to that position. When it has the form */regexp*, vi searches forward through the file for the first occurrence of *regexp* and sets the current line indicator to that line. *?regexp* is similar to */regexp*, except that vi searches through the file backwards. If you omit *line* and do not specify a *file*, the value of the current line indicator does not change; otherwise if a file is specified, the current line indicator is set to either the first or last line of the buffer, depending on whether the command was issued in Vi or Ex mode.

The *edit* command does not destroy buffers, so you can use the *yank* and *put* commands to move text between files.

f[ile] [file]

Changes the current filename to *file* and marks it [Not Edited]. If this file exists, it may not be overwritten without using the exclamation mark (!) variant of the *write* command. If no *file* is specified, the editor displays information about the current file.

[1,$] g[lobal] [!] /pat/ [commands]

Matches *pat* against every line in the given range. On lines which match, the *commands* are run. If the exclamation mark (!) variant is set, the *commands* are run on lines that do not match. This is the same as using the *v* command (described later in this section).

The *global* command and the *undo* command may not occur in the list of *commands*. A subsequent *undo* command undoes the effect of the entire *global* command. In Ex mode, multiple command lines may be entered by ending all but the last with backslash (\). Commands that would take input are permitted; the input is included in the command list, and the trailing period (.) may be omitted at the end of the list. For example,

```
g/rhino/a\
hippo
```

appends the single line hippo to each line containing rhino. The total length of a global command list is limited (see *Limits*).

You can use any nonalphabetic character to delimit *pat* instead of the slash (/).

[.] i[nsert][!]

Enters Ex Insert mode, reads text, and places it before the specified line; otherwise, this is identical to the *append* command. This command may not be entered from Vi mode.

[.,.+1] j[oin][!] [count] [flags]

Joins together the lines of text within the range. Unless an exclamation mark (!) is specified, all whitespace between adjacent joined lines is deleted. Two spaces are provided if the previous line ended in a period (.); zero spaces if the joined line begins with a closing parenthesis ()); and one space otherwise.

[.] k x

Is synonymous with the *mark* command.

[.,.] l[ist] [count] [flags]

Displays the line range in a visually unambiguous manner. This command displays tabs as ^I, and the end of lines as $. The only useful flag is #, for line numbering. The current line indicator points to the last line displayed.

map[!] [lhs rhs]

Defines macros for use in Vi. The *lhs* is a string of characters; whenever that string is typed exactly, vi behaves as if the string *rhs* had been typed. If *lhs* is more than one character long, none of the characters are echoed or acted upon until either a character is typed that isn't in the *lhs* (in which case all the characters up to that point in the *lhs* are run) or the last character of *lhs* is typed. If the variable remap is set, *rhs* itself may contain macros. If the flag ! is specified, the map applies within Vi Insert mode; otherwise it applies to command mode. A *map* command with no arguments lists all macros currently defined.

`[.] ma[rk] x`	Records the specified line as being marked with the single lowercase letter *x*. The line may then be addressed at any point as `'x`.
`[.,.] m[ove] addr [flags]`	Moves the specified line range after the *addr* given. If *addr* is zero, the text is moved to the start of the file. The current line indicator is set to the last line moved.
`n[ext][!] [+command] [file ...]`	Begins editing the next file in the file list (where the file list was either specified on the command line or in a previous *next* command). If the current file has been modified since the last write, Ex normally prevents you from leaving the current file; you can get around this by specifying an exclamation mark (!). If autowrite is set, the current file is written automatically and you go to the next file.

If a list of files is specified, they become the new file list. If necessary, expressions in this list are expanded; thus

```
next *.c
```

sets the file list to all the files in the current directory with names ending in .c (typically C source files).

`[.,.] nu[mber] [count] [flags]`

`[.,.] # [count] [flags]`

Displays the specified line range with leading line numbers. The current line indicator points to the last line displayed.

`[.] o[pen] [/pat/] [flags]`

Enters open mode, which is simply Vi mode with a variable length one line window. If a match is found for the regular expression *pat* in the specified line the cursor is placed at the start of the matching pattern.

You can use any nonalphabetic character to delimit *pat* instead of the slash (*/*).

`[.,.] p[rint] [count] [flags]`

Displays the specified line range. The current line indicator points to the last line displayed.

`[.] pu[t] [buffer]`

Pastes deleted or yanked lines back into the file after the given line. If no buffer name is given, the most recently changed buffer is used.

Since the *edit* command does not destroy buffers, you can use that command in conjunction with *put* and *yank* to move text between files.

q[*uit*][*!*]

Exits from Vi/Ex. If the current file has been modified, an exclamation mark (!) must be used or you cannot exit until you write the file.

[.] r[*ead*][*!*] [*file*]

Reads the contents of *file* and inserts them into the current file after the given line number. If the line number is 0, the contents of the given file are inserted at the beginning of the file being edited. If the current filename is not set, a *file* must be given, and it becomes the current filename; otherwise, if a *file* is given, it becomes the alternate filename. If the *file* begins with an exclamation mark (!), it is taken as a system command. The output from that system command is read in via a pipe after the given line number.

rew[*ind*][*!*]

Rewinds the file argument list back to the beginning and starts editing the first file in the list. If the current file has been modified, an exclamation mark (!) must be specified; otherwise, you cannot leave the current file until you have written it out. If autowrite is set, the current file is written out automatically if it needs to be.

se[*t*] [*parameter-list*]

Assigns or displays the values of option variables. If you do not specify a parameter list, *set* displays all the variables with values that have changed since the editing session started. If the parameter all is specified, Ex displays all variables and their values. You may use the parameter list to set or display each of many variable values. Each argument in the list is a variable name; if it is a Boolean variable, the value is set on or off, depending on whether the name is prefixed by no. Non-Boolean variables alone in an argument are a request to display their values. You may display a Boolean variable's value by appending a question mark (?) to the name. You can set numeric or string variables with

```
name=value
```

In a string variable, spaces must be preceded by a backslash. As an example,

```
set readonly? noautowrite
shell=/bin/sh
```

shows the value of the readonly flag, sets noautowrite, and sets the shell to /bin/sh.

```
set report report=5
```

shows the value of the report variable and then sets the value to 5. See section *Set Option Variables* for further details.

sh[ell]   Invokes a subshell. On DOS, this is normally command.com. The environment variable SHELL is used to find the name of the shell to run. On DOS, you normally return to the editor from command.com using the exit command.

so[urce] file	Runs editor commands from *file*. A file being run with *source* may contain *source* commands of its own.
st[op]	Suspends the editor session and returns to system level. For further information, see the description of the Vi command *CTRL-Z*.
[.,.] s[ubstitute] [/pat/repl/] [options] [count] [flags]	
	Searches each line in the line range for the regular expression *pat* and replaces matching strings with *repl*. Normally, Ex only replaces the first matching string in each line; if *options* contains *g* (global), all matching strings are changed. If *options* contains *c* (confirm), Ex first displays the line with caret (^) characters marking the *pat* matching location; you can then type y if you want Ex to go ahead with the substitution. *pat* cannot match over a line boundary; however in Ex mode, *repl* may contain a newline, escaped by a preceding backslash (\). See the section on regular expressions for full information on both *pat* and *repl*. If there is no *pat* and/or *repl*, Ex uses the most recently specified regular expression and/or replacement string. You can use any nonalphabetic character in place of the slash (/) to delimit *pat* and *repl*.
su[spend]	Is the same as *stop*.
[.,.] t addr [flags]	Is the same as the *copy* command.

`ta[g][!] tagname`

Looks up *tagname* in the files listed in the variable tags. If the tag name is found in a tags file, that file also contains the name of the file that contains the tag and a regular expression required within that file to locate that tag. If the given file is different from the one you are currently editing, Ex normally begins editing the new file; however, if you have modified the current file since the last time it was written out, Ex does not start editing a new file unless the *tag* command contains an exclamation mark (!). (If autowrite is on, the current file is automatically written out and the new file read in.) When the new file is read in, the regular expression from the tags file is invoked with the variable magic off (see the *Set Option Variables* section).

Tag names are typically used to locate C function definitions in C source files. The first step is to create a tags file using the ctags command. Once you do this, you can use the Ex *tag* command to look up a particular function definition and go directly to that definition in the file that contains it.

All characters in tag names are significant unless the variable *taglength* is non-zero; in this case, only the given number of characters are used in the comparison.

una[bbreviate] *lhs*	The abbreviation *lhs* previously created by *abbreviate* is deleted.
u[ndo]	Undoes the last change or set of changes that modified the buffer. Global changes and Vi macros are considered single changes that can be undone. A second *undo* undoes the *undo* restoring the previous state. The *edit* command may not be undone, because it cleans up the temporary file used to maintain undo information. You cannot *undo* operating system commands and commands that write output to the file system.
unm[ap][!] *lhs*	Deletes the map of *lhs*. If the flag !, this applies to the insert mode maps; otherwise it applies to the command mode maps.
[1,$] v /*pat*/ *commands*	Is the same as the *global* command with the ! flag; that is, a global for all nonmatching lines. You can use any nonalphabetic character to delimit *pat* instead of the slash (/).
ve[rsion]	Displays the current version information for Vi/Ex.
[.] vi[sual] [*type*] [*count*] [*flags*]	Enters Vi mode. If no *type* is specified, the current line is at the top of the screen. If *type* is caret (^), the bottom line of the screen is one window before the current line. If type is a minus sign, (-), the current line is at the bottom of the screen and if *type* is a period (.), the current line is in the middle of the screen.

You can use the *undo* command to undo all changes that occurred during the `vi` command.

`[1,$] w[rite][!] [>>] [file]` Writes the given range of lines to `file`. If two right angle brackets (`>>`) are included, the lines are appended to the file's current contents. If the current filename is not set, `file` must be given; this becomes the current filename; otherwise, `file` (if specified) becomes the alternate filename. If `file` begins with an exclamation mark (`!`), it is taken as a system command, `vi` writes the given range to the command through a pipe.

If a `file` is given, it must not already exist. The variable `readonly` must not be set. If a `file` is not given, the file must be *edited*; that is, it must be the same file as that read in. All these conditions may be overridden by using the flag `!`.

`[1,$] wn[!] [>>] [file]` Is similar to *write*, except that it begins editing the next file in the file list immediately afterwards (if the write is successful).

`[1,$] wq[!] [>>] [file]` Is similar to *write*, except that it exits the editor immediately afterwards (if the write is successful).

`[1,$] x[it][!] [file]` If you have modified the current file since the last write, performs a *write* command using the specified range and filename and terminates.

`[.,.] y[ank] [buffer] [count]`	Copies the given line range to the specified *buffer* (a letter from *a* through *z*). If a buffer is not specified, the unnamed buffer is used.
	Because the `edit` command does not destroy buffers, you can use that command in conjunction with *put* and *yank* to move text between files.
`[.+1]z [type] [count] [flags]`	Displays *count* lines. If no count is specified, Ex uses the current value of the scroll variable. The lines are displayed with the given line located according to the *type*. If *type* is a plus sign (+), the editor displays the given line and a screenful after that. If *type* is a period (.), the editor displays a screenful with the given line in the middle. If *type* is a minus sign (-), the editor displays a screenful with the given line at the end. If *type* is a caret (^), the editor displays the screenful before that and if *type* is an equals sign (=), the current line is centered on the screen with a line of hyphens displayed immediately before and after it. The current line indicator points to the last line displayed.
`[.,.] <[<...] [count] [flags]`	Shifts the line range by the value of the shiftwidth variable. If there are multiple left angle brackets (<), each one causes another shift. The current line indicator points to the last line of the range. If a *count* is specified, that many lines are shifted.

`[.,.] >[>...] [count] [flags]`	Shifts the line range right by the value of the shiftwidth variable. If there are multiple right angle brackets (>), each one causes another shift. The current line indicator points to the last line of the range. If a *count* is specified, that many lines are shifted.
`[range] ! command`	Submits *command* to be run by the command interpreter named by the shell variable. If a *range* is given, the *command* is invoked with the contents of that line range as input. The output from the *command* then replaces that line range. Thus

`1,$!sort`

sorts the entire contents of the file.

Substitutions are made in *command* before it is run. Any occurrences of an exclamation mark (!) are replaced by the previous *command* line, while occurrences of percentage (%) and hash mark (#) characters are replaced with the pathnames of the current and alternate files, respectively. If any such substitutions actually take place, the new command line is displayed before it is run.

If the file has been modified and the variable autowrite is on, the file is written before calling the command. If *autowrite* is off, a warning message is given.

`[$] =`	Displays the given line number. The current line indicator is not changed.

" *a line of text*   This is a comment.

[.,.] & [*options*] [*count*] [*flags*]   Repeats the last *substitute* com-
                                             mand. If any *options*, *count*, or
                                             flags are specified, they replace the
                                             corresponding items in the previous
                                             substitute command.

[.,.] ~ [*options*] [*count*] [*flags*]   Repeats the last *substitute* com-
                                             mand; however, the regular expres-
                                             sion that is used is the last regular
                                             expression; that is, if there has been
                                             a search, the search's regular
                                             expression is used. The simple
                                             substitute with no arguments, or
                                             the & command, uses the regular
                                             expression from the previous
                                             substitute. *substitute* with an
                                             empty regular expression uses the
                                             last regular expression, like ~. If any
                                             options, *count*, or *flags* are
                                             specified, they replace the corre-
                                             sponding items in the previous
                                             substitute command.

@ *buffer*   Executes each line in *buffer* as an
                                             Ex command. If you do not specify
                                             buffer or you specify a buffer
                                             named @, the last buffer executed is
                                             used.

CTRL-D   Displays the number of lines of text
                                             given by the scroll variable. Under
                                             DOS, the CTRL-D must be
                                             followed by ENTER The current
                                             line indicator points to the last line
                                             displayed.

Special Characters in Ex Commands

When an Ex command contains the percentage character (%), the character is replaced by the name of the current file. For example, if you are about to try out a macro and you are worried that the macro may damage the file, you could say

```
!cp % /tmp
```

to copy the current file to a safe holding place. As another example, a macro could use the percentage character (%) to refer to the current file.

When an Ex command contains the hash mark (#), the character is replaced by the name of the alternate file. The name of the alternate file may be set with the read command as described previously. Thus a command like

```
e #
```

tells Ex to edit the alternate file. Using an alternate file can be particularly convenient when you have two files that you want to edit *simultaneously*. The command just given lets you flip back and forth between the two files.

Option Variables

Option variables are set with the *set* command. For example,

```
set autowrite
```

sets the autowrite option. Options are turned off by putting no in front of the name in the *set* command, as in

```
set noautowrite
```

In the descriptions that follow, the minimal abbreviation of each option variable is shown after the comma.

autoindent, ai	When autoindent is on and you are entering text, the indentation of the current line is used for the new line. In Vi mode, you can change this default indentation by using the control keys CTRL-D (to shift left) and CTRL-T (to shift right). In Ex mode, a tab or spaces may be typed at the start of a line to increase the indent, or a CTRL-D may be typed at the start of the line to remove a level. Under DOS, the new indent is not seen immediately. ^CTRL-D temporarily removes the indent for the current

line. 0CTRL-D places the current line at a zero indent level, and the next line has this indent level as well.

The size of indent levels is defined by the variable shiftwidth. Based on this value and the value of tabstop, the editor generates the number of tabs and spaces needed to produce the required indent level.

The default is no autoindent.

autoprint, ap   When this option is set in Ex mode, the current line is displayed after the following commands: *copy*, *delete*, *join*, *move*, *substitute*, *undo*, &, ~, <, and >. Automatic displaying of lines does not take place inside *global* commands.

The default is autoprint.

autowrite, aw   When this option is on, the current file is automatically written out if it has been changed since it was last written and if you have run any of the following commands: *next*, *rewind*, *tag*, *CTRL-^* (Vi), and *CTRL-]* (Vi). Using an exclamation mark (!) with any of these commands stops the automatic write.

The default is noautowrite.

beautify, bf   When this option is on, the editor discards all nonprinting characters from text read in from files.

The default is nobeautify.

cdpath   Used by *cd* to find relative pathnames when changing directory. You must delimit entries with a semicolon (;). If the current directory is to be included in the search, it must be indicated by a dot (.). cdpath defaults to the contents of the CDPATH environment variable if it exists or to dot (.) if it does not.

directory, dir

The editor uses temporary files with unique names under the given directory. Any error on the temporary files is fatal.

The default is directory=/tmp.

edcompatible

When this option is on, the editor attempts to make *substitute* commands behave in a way that is compatible with the ed editor. The g and c options on the substitute commands are remembered and toggled by their occurrence. The r option uses the last regular expression rather than the last substitute regular expression. Percentage mark (%) as the entire pattern is equivalent to the previous pattern.

The default is noedcompatible.

errorbells, eb

When this option is on, vi precedes error messages with the alert character. When it is off, the editor warns you of an error by displaying a message using a standout mode of your terminal (such as inverse video).

The default is noerrorbells.

exrc

When this option is on, Ex and Vi access any .exrc (ex.rc on DOS) files in the current directory during initialization. If it is off, Ex and Vi ignore such files unless the current directory is the HOME directory.

The default is noexrc.

home

Used as the destination directory by *cd*. If no path is specified, home defaults to the contents of the HOME environment variable if it exists or to the vi startup directory if it does not.

ignorecase, ic

When this option is on, the case of letters is ignored when matching strings and regular expressions.

The default is noignorecase.

linedelete	On a UNIX system, Vi sets the line delete character automatically to the current terminal line delete character, as specified by the user. Under DOS, ESC is the line delete and is not setable. Because ESC is used by Vi for other purposes, the linedelete variable sets the line delete character that is used in Vi. The value is the numeric value of the line delete character. The default is 0x15, the ASCII value for *CTRL-U*. Another popular value is 0x18 for *CTRL-X*.
list	When this option is on, tabs are displayed as a caret mark (^) rather than being expanded with blanks, and the ends of lines are indicated with a dollar sign ($).

The default is nolist. |
| magic | When this option is off (nomagic), regular expression characters ^ \ and $ become the only ones with special meanings. All other regular expression metacharacters must be preceded by a backslash (\) to have their special meaning.

The default is magic. |
| maxbuffers | This is the number of K units (1024 bytes) of memory which is to be used for the editor buffers. These are allocated in units of 16K. The default is maxbuffers=512, but if that is not available on entry this is set to the number actually obtained. At least 32K is needed. This is in addition to the code and data space required by vi; this may be as much as 128K. Changing maxbuffers has no effect. |
| mesg | When this option is on, Ex allows others to use the write or talk commands to write to your terminal while you are in visual mode. The command

mesg n

overrides this option. |

The default value is mesg. This option has no effect on DOS and other systems not supporting mesg.

number, nu

When this option is on, line numbers are displayed to the left of the text being edited.

The default is nonumber.

paragraphs

This list of character pairs controls the movement between paragraphs in Vi mode. Lines beginning with a period (.) followed by any pair of characters in the list are paragraph boundaries (for example, .IP). Such lines are typically commands to text formatters like nroff or troff.

The default is paragraphs="IPLPPPQPP LIpplpipbp""

prompt

When this option is on, Ex command mode prompts with a colon (:). (No prompts are given if input is not being read from a terminal.)

The default is prompt.

pwd

This is a readonly variable. The value always refers to the current working directory, and can only be changed by the *cd* command.

quiet

When this option is on, vi does not display file information messages.

The default is set by the -s option.

readonly

When this option is on, vi does not let you write to the current file.

The default is based on the permissions of the current file. If you do not have write permission on this file, the default is readonly; otherwise the default is set by the -R option.

remap

If this option is on and a *map* macro is expanded, the expansion is re-examined to see if it too contains *map* macros.

The default is remap.

report
: The editor displays a message whenever you issue a command that affects more than this number of lines.

  The default is `report=5`.

restrict
: When this option is on, all filenames are restricted to the current directory. No subcommands may be called. This variable is automatically set if you invoke the editor with a command that starts with the letter r, as in `rvi`. Once the option is turned on, it cannot be turned off. The default is `norestrict`.

scroll
: This sets the number of lines to scroll for the *z* (Ex), and *CTRL-D* (Ex) commands.

  The default is the value of the variable window divided by two.

sections
: This list of character pairs controls the movement between sections in Vi mode. Lines beginning with a period (.) followed by any pair of characters in the list are section boundaries (for example, .SH). Such lines are typically commands to text formatters like `nroff` or `troff`.

  The default is `sections="SHNHH HU"`.

shell, sh
: This is the name of the command interpreter to be used for *!* commands and the *shell* command.

  The default value is taken from the SHELL environment variable. On DOS, if SHELL is not defined, the name of the command interpreter is taken from the COMSPEC environment variable.

shiftwidth, sw
: This sets the width of indent used by shift commands and autoindent.

  The default is `shiftwidth=8`.

showmatch, sm
: If this option is on and you type a closing parenthesis ()) or closing brace (}) in input mode, the cursor moves to the matching open parenthesis or brace. It stays there for about one second and then

544

moves back to where you were. This lets you note the relationship between opening and closing parentheses/braces.

The default is `noshowmatch`.

showmode
: When this option is on, `vi` displays an indicator in the bottom right-hand corner of the screen if you are in Insert/Open/Change/
Replace mode. If no indicator is displayed, you are in Command mode.

The default is `noshowmode`.

tabstop
: Tab stops for screen display in Vi mode are set to multiples of this number.

The default is `tabstop=8`.

taglength, tl
: If this variable is non-zero, tags are only compared for this number of characters.

The default is `taglength=0`.

tags
: The value of this variable should be a list of filenames separated by spaces. These are used by the *tag* Ex command and the *CTRL-]* Vi command. The files are typically created with the `ctags` program.

The default is `tags=tags`.

term
: The value of this variable is the terminal type. The `TERM` environment variable specifies this variable's default value. Under DOS, the variable provides information only. To specify a setting other than the one specified by the `TERM` environment variable, you need to set a value for `term` in the editor initialization file set in the `EXINIT` environment variable (for more information, see the *Editor Initialization* section).

terse
: If this option is on, messages are displayed in a very abbreviated form.

The default is `noterse`.

warn   When this option is on, commands with an exclamation mark (!) display a warning message if the current file has been modified. When off, no message is displayed.

The default is warn.

window   This variable gives the number of text lines available in Vi mode or the default number of lines to display for the z command.

The default is given by the -w option. If it is not specified with the -w option, its value defaults to the environment variable LINES or the value found in the terminfo database for TERM.

wrapmargin, wm   If this variable is non-zero in Vi insert mode, when a line reaches this number of characters from the right of the screen, the current word moves down to the next line automatically; you don't have to press Enter.

The default is wrapmargin=0.

wrapscan, ws   If this option is off, forward searches stop at the end of the file and backward searches stop at the beginning.

The default is wrapscan.

writeany, wa   If this option is off, the editor does not let a file marked [Not edited] overwrite an existing file.

The default is nowriteany.

Editor Initialization

Initialization code consists of one or more Ex commands that are run when the editor starts up. Initialization code may be obtained in several ways.

■ If there is an environment variable named EXINIT with a non-null value, it is assumed to hold initialization code. vi runs this code using an Ex *source* command.

- If EXINIT does not exist or has a null value, the editor attempts to find a file named .exrc (ex.rc on DOS) under your home directory. If you have an environment variable named HOME, the value of this variable is assumed to be the name of your home directory. If you have no HOME variable, the editor uses ROOTDIR as your home directory. vi runs the .exrc file using an Ex *source* command.

- If the EXINIT variable or the $HOME/.exrc ($HOME/ex.rc on DOS) file sets the option variable exrc and there is a file named .exrc (ex.rc on DOS) under the current directory, it is assumed to hold initialization code. vi runs this code using an Ex *source* command.

- vi executes any commands given by the -c or + options.

vi reads the .exrc file as if it were a sequence of keystrokes typed at the beginning of an Vi session. As a result, the contents of .exrc must be the same as the characters you would type if you were in Vi. In particular, if the input contains any unusual characters (for example, a carriage return) that you would normally precede with CTRL-V, there must be a CTRL-V in the .exrc file. When using vi to create .exrc, you must type CTRL-V CTRL-V to put a CTRL-V character into your initialization file, then *CTRL*-V followed by the special character. The .exrc file must show both *CTRL*-V and the special character.

Files

vi uses the following files and directories:

$ROOTDIR/tmp	Directory used for temporary files if neither TMPDIR nor TMP is defined
$ROOTDIR/tmp/vi[1nty]*nnnnn.mmm*	Temporary files
.exrc	Startup file (ex.rc on DOS)

Environment Variables

vi uses the following environment variables:

COLUMNS	Contains the number of columns between the left and right margins (see option variable wrapmargin). This is also used as the horizontal screen size.

COMSPEC	Contains the name of the command interpreter. On DOS, this must point to command.com if you want to use that command interpreter in any way.
ENV	Contains the pathname of a file containing MKS KornShell commands. When you invoke sh, it runs this file before doing anything else.
EXINIT	Contains a list of Vi commands to be run on editor startup. HOME contains the directory to be searched for the editor startup file.
LINES	Contains the number of lines in a *screenful* (see option vari-able windows). This is also used as the vertical screen size.
PATH	Contains a list of directories to be searched for the shell com-mand specified in the Ex commands read, write, and shell.
ROOTDIR	Contains MKS Toolkit's root directory on DOS.
SHELL	Contains the name of the command interpreter for use in !, shell, read, write and other Ex commands with an operand of the form !*string*. The default is the sh utility.
TERM	Contains the name of the terminal type.
TERMINFO	Contains the pathname of the terminfo database.
TMP	Contains the pathname that MKS Toolkit uses as the directory for temporary files if TMPDIR is not defined. TMPDIR takes prece-dence over TMP.
TMPDIR	Contains the pathname that MKS Toolkit uses as the directory for temporary files.

Diagnostics

Possible exit status values are

0	Successful completion.
1	Failure because of any of the following:

> Unknown option
> No such command from open/visual
> Missing *lhs*
> Missing filename
> System does not support job control

Write forms are *w* and *w>>*
Internal error: bad seek pointer
Internal error: Line out of range
Internal error: line too long
Non-zero address required on this command
No lines in the buffer
Nothing to undo
Cannot escape a newline in global from visual
Global command too long
Argument list too long
File is read only
No previous command to substitute for *!*
Command too long
No previous re or No previous regular expression
Buffers are 1–9, a–z
Line too long
System does not support job control
Digits required after =
Nothing in buffer
Missing *rhs*
Too many macros
Recursive map expansion
Nothing to repeat
Last repeatable command overflowed the repeat buffer
Bad tag
No tags file
No such tag in tags file
Negative address—first buffer line is 1
Not an editor command
Unimplemented Ex command
Wrong number of addresses for command
Mark requires following letter
Undefined mark referenced
Global within global not allowed
First address exceeds second
Cannot use open/visual unless open option is set
Regular expression \ must be followed by / or ?
No address allowed on this command
No more files to edit
No current filename

Extra characters at end of command
Not that many lines in buffer
Insufficient memory
Restricted environment
Command too long
Trailing address required
Destination cannot straddle source in *m* and *t*
No filename to substitute for %
No alternate filename to substitute for #
Filename too long
Too many filenames
Argument buffer overflow
Incomplete shell escape command
Regular expressions cannot be delimited by letters or digits
No previous scanning regular expression
No previous substitute to repeat
Cannot escape newlines into regular expressions
Missing *[*
Badly constructed regular expression
No remembered regular expression
Line overflow in substitute
Replacement pattern contains \d—cannot use in regular
expression
Replacement pattern too long
Regular expression too complicated
Cannot escape newline in visual
No such set option
String too long in option assignment

Portability

POSIX.2. X/OPEN Portability Guide. Most UNIX systems. MKS Toolkit.

Limits

Maximum number of lines: 65279 (64K - 256 - 1)

Longest command line: 256 bytes

Length of filenames: 128 bytes

Length of string options: 64 bytes

Length of remembered regular expressions: 256 bytes

Number of *map*, *map!* and *abbreviate* entries: 128 each

Number of saved keystrokes for . in Vi: 128

Length of the *lhs* of *map*, *map!* or *abbreviate*: No fixed limit. Limit is based on available memory

Maximum number of characters in a tag name: 30

Number of characters in a : escape from Vi: 256

Requires 128K of memory plus the set option maxbuffers K of auxiliary memory. On DOS, auxiliary memory is freed during *CTRL-Z*, *:stop*, *:!:w !*, *.,.!*, and *:r !* commands. During startup, maxbuffers is changed to reflect available memory; at least 32K is required.

Number of nested source files is 3.

See Also

sed

wc—Count of Lines, Words, and Bytes

Synopsis

```
wc [-lwc] [file ...]
```

Description

wc counts the number of lines, words, and bytes in text files. If you specify several files on the command line, wc produces counts for each file, plus totals for all files.

A word is considered to be a character or characters delimited by whitespace (spaces, tabs, and/or newline characters).

wc counts bytes, not characters. This is a change from previous versions of wc, and one that is dictated by the POSIX.2 draft standard. There are several ways the number of bytes can differ from the number of characters.

On DOS, the end of the line is usually marked with a pair of bytes (carriage return and linefeed). In earlier versions of wc, this counted as a single character; now it counts as two bytes.

If you have a file containing multibyte characters, the byte count will be higher than the character count. (Multibyte characters use more than one byte to represent a single character. They are needed in languages like Chinese, where there are so many characters you can't represent them all with a single byte.)

Options

The -c option only prints a byte count; -w only prints a word count and -l only prints a line count. The order of options can dictate the order in which counts are displayed. For example, -cwl displays the number of bytes, then the number of words, then the number of lines. If no options are specified, the default is -lwc: lines, then words, then bytes.

Diagnostics

Possible exit status values are

0	Successful completion.
1	Failure because of an invalid command line option, or inability to open the input file.

Portability

POSIX.2. X/Open Portability Guide. All UNIX systems. MKS Toolkit.

See Also

vi

whence—Tell How Shell Interprets Command Name

Synopsis

```
whence [-v] name ...
```

Description

whence tells how the shell would interpret each name if you used it as a command name. It tells you whether a name is a shell keyword, alias, function, built-in command, or executable file. For executable files, whence gives the full pathname.

Some UNIX systems have a similar command named which. The difference is that whence is built into the KornShell, while which is a separate command.

Options

-v gives a more verbose report.

Diagnostics

Possible exit status values are

0	Successful completion.
1	Failure due to an inability to find the command name .
2	Failure due to an invalid command line argument.

Portability

MKS Toolkit. On UNIX, whence is built into the KornShell, but is not in the Bourne Shell.

See Also

sh

REFERENCE

Appendix

BIBLIOGRAPHY

There are many UNIX books available for both the beginner and the advanced reader, and more books are published every day. The following titles are those I've found useful over the years. The list is certainly not exhaustive, but it should provide useful starting places for various topics.

Standards and Manuals

AT&T Inc. *UNIX System V Interface Definition.* 3rd ed. Englewood Cliffs: 1989.

Computer Systems Research Group, Computer Science Division, Department of Electrical Engineering and Computer Science, University of California. *UNIX User's Reference Manual (URM), 4.3 Berkeley Software Distribution.* Berkeley, California: 1986.

Institute of Electrical and Electronics Engineers. IEEE Standard, Portable Operating System Interface for Computer Environments, IEEE Std 1003.1-1988 [POSIX.1]. New York: 1988.

Institute of Electrical and Electronics Engineers. Information Technology-Portable Operating System Interfaces (POSIX)-Part 2: Shell and Utilities, P1003.2/D12. New York: July, 1992.

X/Open Company Ltd. *X/Open Portability Guide, XSI Commands and Utilities*. Englewood Cliffs: Prentice Hall, 1988.

General UNIX References

Bourne, S.R. *The UNIX System*. Reading: Addison-Wesley, 1983.

Kernighan, Brian W. and Rob Pike. *The UNIX Programming Environment*. Englewood Cliffs: Prentice Hall, 1984.

Kochan, Stephen G. and Patrick H. Wood. *Exploring the UNIX System*. Carmel, IN: Hayden Books, 1989.

Smith, Ben. *UNIX Step-by-Step*. Carmel, IN: Hayden Books, 1990.

Topham, Douglas. *The First Book of UNIX*. Carmel, IN: Sams Publishing, 1990.

Waite, Mitchell, Donald Martin, and Stephen Prata. *The Waite Group's UNIX Primer Plus*. Indianapolis: Sams Publishing, 1983.

MKS Documentation

Mortice Kern Systems Inc. *MKS Toolkit Reference Manual*. Waterloo, Ontario: 1993.

Mortice Kern Systems Inc. *MKS Toolkit User's Guide*. Waterloo, Ontario: 1991.

Mortice Kern Systems Inc. *MKS RCS Reference Manual*. Waterloo, Ontario: 1993.

Other References

Aho, Alfred V., Peter J. Weinberger, and Brian W. Kernighan. *The AWK Programming Language*. Reading: Addison-Wesley, 1987.

Bolsky, Morris I. and David G. Korn. *The KornShell Command and Programming Language.* Englewood Cliffs: Prentice Hall, 1989.

Hansen, August. *VI: The UNIX Screen Editor.* New York: Prentice Hall, 1986.

Holliker, William. *UNIX Shell Commands Quick Reference.* Carmel, IN: Que Corporation, 1990.

Kochan, Stephen C. and Patrick H. Wood. *UNIX Shell Programming.* Revised ed. Carmel, IN: Hayden Books, 1985.

Appendix

B

REGULAR EXPRESSION SUMMARY

This appendix provides a quick reference summary about regular expressions, which are first discussed in Chapter 5, "Popular Tools." The appendix provides a number of examples to clarify various points.

With a regular expression, you can search for strings in text files. No regular expression can match the newline character at the end of a line, so no regular expression can match strings that extend over more than one line.

Regular expressions may be made up of normal characters and/or special characters, sometimes called *metacharacters*. There are two types of regular expressions: basic and extended. These types differ only in the metacharacters they can contain.

vi and ed recognize basic regular expressions; all other UNIX commands recognize extended regular expressions. grep and sed recognize both basic and extended regular expressions, depending on the options used.

The basic regular expression metacharacters are

```
^  $  [ ]  \  \d  *  \+  \?  \{  \}  \( \)  \< \>
```

The extended regular expression metacharacters are

```
^  $  [  ]  \  \d  *  +  ?  {  }  ¦  (  )  \<  \>
```

The following list explains the meanings of these characters

A dot character matches any single character of the input line.

The ^ character does not match any character, but it represents the beginning of the input line. For example, ^A is a regular expression matching the letter at the beginning of a line. The character is only special at the beginning of a regular expression or after the (or ¦ characters.

The $ character does not match any character, but it represents the end of the input line. For example, $ is a regular expression matching the letter at the end of a line. The character is only special at the end of a regular expression, or before a) or ¦ character.

[abc] matches any one of the characters found between the [and] characters. If there is an _ sign in the expression as in [a_z] it stands for a range of characters; for example, [a_z] matches any lowercase character. If the first character after the [is a caret (^), the regular expression matches any character except the ones specified within the brackets. Other than this, regular expression metacharacters lose their special significance inside square brackets. To match a ^ character in this case, it must appear anywhere except as the first character inside the brackets. To match a], the] should appear as the first character inside the brackets. A - (dash) character loses its special significance if it is the first or last character of the class.

Within a character class expression (one made with square brackets), the following constructs may be used to represent sets of characters:

[:alpha:]	Any alphabetic character
[:lower:]	Any lowercase alphabetic character
[:upper:]	Any uppercase alphabetic character

`[:digit:]`	Any digit character
`[:alnum:]`	Any alphanumeric character (alphabetic or digit)
`[:space:]`	Any whitespace character (blank, horizontal tab, vertical tab)
`[:graph:]`	Any printable character except the blank character
`[:print:]`	Any printable character including the blank character
`[:punct:]`	Any printable character that is not whitespace or alphanumeric
`[:cntrl:]`	Any nonprintable character

\ is used to turn off the special meaning of metacharacters. For example, \. only matches a dot character. Note that \\ matches a literal \ character. Also note the special case of \d

\d is used to represent any single decimal digit (from 1 to 9). This pattern is equivalent to the string matching the *d*th expression enclosed within the () characters (or \(\) for some commands) found at an *earlier point* in the regular expression. Parenthesized expressions are numbered by counting (characters from the left.

Constructs of this form can be used in the replacement strings of substitution commands (such as the `:s` command in `vi`) to stand for constructs matched by parts of the regular expression. For example, in the following `vi` command,

`:s/\(.*\):\(.*\)/\2:\1/`

the \1 stands for everything matched by the first \(.*\), and the \2 stands for everything matched by the second. The result of the command is to swap everything before the : with everything after.

`re*` is a regular expression. `re` followed by * matches a string of zero or more strings that would match `re`. For example, `A*B` matches `AB`, `AAB`, `AAAB`, and so on. It also matches just `B` (zero occurrences of `A`).

With extended regular expressions, `re` followed by + matches a string of one or more strings that would match `re` With basic regular expressions, the principle is the same, except that you must write \+ instead of just +.

With extended regular expressions, re followed by ? matches a string of one or zero occurrences of strings that would match re. With basic regular expressions, the principle is the same except that you must write \? instead of just ?.

char{n}
char\{n\}

In this expression (and the ones to follow), *char* is a regular expression that stands for a single character (a literal character or a .). Such a regular expression followed by a number in braces stands for that number of repetitions of a character. For example, x{3} stands for xxx. With extended regular expressions, you just use normal brace characters; with basic regular expressions, you must put backslashes in front of the characters, as in x\{3\}. This principle applies to the following constructs as well.

char{min,}
char\{min,\}

When a single-character regular expression is followed by a number in braces, and the number is followed by a comma, it stands for at least that number of repetitions of a character. For example, x{3,} is an extended regular expression that stands for at least three repetitions of x; x\{3,\} is a basic regular expression meaning the same thing.

char{min,max}
char\{min,max\}

When a single-character regular expression is followed by a pair of numbers in braces, it stands for at least min repetitions and no more than max repetitions of a character. For example, x{3,7} is an extended regular expression that stands for three to seven repetitions of x; x\{3,7\} is a basic regular expression meaning the same thing.

re1¦re2

This expression matches either regular expression re1 or re2.

(re)
\(re\)

With this construct, you can group parts of regular expressions. In extended regular expressions, you use the normal parentheses characters; in basic regular expressions, you must put backslashes in front of the characters, as in \(and \).

| \\< | This matches the beginning of a word, where the beginning of a word is defined as the boundary between nonalphanumerics and alphanumerics (including the underscore character). This matches no characters, only the context. |
| \\> | This construct is analogous to the \\< notation except that it matches the end of a word. |

Several regular expressions can be concatenated to form a larger regular expression.

Examples

The following patterns are given as illustrations, along with plain language descriptions of what they match.

`abc`

matches any string containing the three letters abc in that order.

`a.c`

matches any string beginning with the letter a, followed by any character, followed by the letter c (for example, a!c).

`^.$`

matches any line containing exactly one character.

`a(b*¦c*)d`

matches any string beginning with a letter a followed by either zero or more of the letter b or zero or more of the letter c followed by the letter d. For example, this would match ad, abd, acd, abbd, accd, and so on.

`.* [a_z]+ .*`

matches any line containing a "word." In this case, a word consists of lowercase alphabetic characters delimited by at least one space on each side. For example, this would match the line abc def g.

```
(morty).*\1
(morty.*morty
```

The preceding expressions both match lines containing at least two occurrences of the string `morty`; for example `morty drove morty's car`.

`[[:space:][:alnum:]]`

matches any character that is either a whitespace character or alphanumeric.

For further examples of regular expressions, see the discussion of `grep` in Chapter 5, "Popular Tools."

Portability

The basic regular expressions are available on most UNIX systems. Extended regular expressions may not be. Systems compatible with POSIX.2 support the extended set.

Appendix

SUMMARY OF FILENAME GENERATION WITH GLOB CONSTRUCTS

A command-line argument containing glob constructs may be used anywhere that a pathname or list of pathnames is valid. The shell expands each such argument into a list of all existing pathnames that have the form corresponding to the pathname.

The following glob constructs are recognized by the KornShell:

?   Matches any single character in a file or directory name, except for a leading dot (.).

*   Matches zero or more characters, except for a leading dot (.), anywhere in a file or directory name.

[...]   Matches any single character given inside the brackets. Inside the brackets you can use ranges of characters. You specify a range by giving the first character in the range, a minus (-) sign, and the last character in the range. For example, [a-z] stands for the lowercase letters. If you want to have a literal minus sign as one of the characters in the brackets, put it first or last.

[!...]   Matches any single character not given inside the brackets. You can use ranges inside the brackets. For example, [!a-z] matches any character that is not a lowercase letter.

If an argument contains glob constructs and you do not want the shell to expand the constructs, enclose the argument in single or double quotation marks. For example, in

```
find /lu -name "*.exe" -print
```

the shell won't expand the * because the * is inside quotation marks. However, find will indeed list all files ending in .exe, as requested.

Appendix

COMMON ENVIRONMENT VARIABLES

When the KornShell executes a program, it gives the program a set of variables, called the program's environment. Each variable has a name and a value. These variables are called *environment variables*.

Note that a shell variable is only an environment variable if the variable is passed to the programs that the shell executes. This means that a shell variable is only an environment variable if it's marked for export. This situation is different from DOS, where all variables are environment variables because all variables are shared by all executing programs.

The following variables are used by several commands in the MKS Tools and are frequently used on true UNIX and UNIX look-alike systems:

COLUMNS
If you set this variable to a numeric value, various commands use its value as the width of the output device (measured in columns). Usually, the output device is a display screen, but you can also use COLUMNS to set up wider lines for line printers or typewriter terminals.

ENV
The value of this variable should be the name of a file of KornShell commands. When the KornShell is invoked, it executes the commands inside the file named by ENV before it does anything else. Thus your ENV file may contain definitions of aliases, shell functions, and so on, that can be used by shell scripts.

HOME
This variable is set during the log-in process. Its value is the name of your home directory. Your home directory is specified in the etc/passwd file (lu/etc/passwd) with MKS Tools, which also records such information as your log-in name and your password.

LINES
If you set this variable to a numeric value, various commands use its value as the number of lines available on the output device.

LOGNAME
This variable is set during the log-in process. Its value is your user name.

PATH
This variable is set to a default value by the log-in process. Normally, you would use your profile file to set your PATH. PATH lists the directories that the shell should search when it is looking for commands. On a true UNIX or UNIX look-alike, names in the PATH list are separated with colon (:) characters; with MKS Tools, names are separated with semicolon (;) characters. With MKS Tools, be sure to enclose the directory list in single or double quotation marks when you assign a value to PATH.

ROOTDIR
Because DOS has a multidevice file system, it's necessary to keep track of the standard root directory that holds information files (such as lu/etc). ROOTDIR contains a device name and possibly a directory where

all such files can be found. With the MKS Tools, ROOTDIR is always the name of the directory where you installed the MKS Tools package. By default, this is c:/lu. ROOTDIR is not needed on a true UNIX or UNIX look-alike system, because such systems have different ways of referring to devices.

SHELL
This variable should contain the full pathname of the shell you are using. With the MKS Tools, the default is c:/lu/bin/sh.exe.

TERM
This variable serves little purpose with the MKS Tools, but on a true UNIX or UNIX look-alike system, its value is a string that tells the type of terminal you are using. Various programs that interact with the terminal (such as vi) make use of TERM. Typically, these programs look up information about your type of terminal in a file called a termcapfile. *Termcap* stands for *terminal capability,* and the termcap file describes the special capabilities of various types of terminals, as well as any special keys or character sequences that such terminals use.

UNIX has the ability to interact with many different types of terminals from many different manufacturers. Historically, this has been one of UNIX's greatest strengths. However, UNIX terminal handling is a complicated subject and one that is outside the scope of this book.

TMPDIR
By default, MKS Tools commands store temporary files under $ROOTDIR/tmp. To use a different directory, set TMPDIR to the name of the directory you want to use. Some UNIX systems use TMP instead of TMPDIR; others use neither TMPDIR or TMP.

TZ
Commands that print times (and dates) use this variable to determine the time zone. On a true UNIX system, the TZ variable would be set in the global profile file so that all of the system's users will have the same time-zone setting.

Appendix

E

POSIX.2 Utility Summary

The following list gives capsule summaries of the utility commands required by the POSIX.2 standard (IEEE Std. 1003.2-1992). This list includes the commands that are built into the shell.

awk
: A report generator and prototyping language, awk has strong information retrieval and programming capabilities.

basename
: Obtains the basename component of a pathname. The input is a pathname. The output is that pathname without directory names and (optionally) without an extension either. Useful in scripts to strip suffixes like .c.

bc	Simple desk calculator utility.
break	Command to break out of a loop (for, while, until) in the shell programming language.
cat	Displays the contents of one or more files.
cd	Changes the current directory and/or disk.
chgrp	Changes the group ownership of one or more files.
chmod	Changes file characteristics. For example, chmod can change the permissions on a file.
chown	Changes the owner of one or more files.
cksum	Displays checksums and block counts for one or more files.
cmp	Compares two files on a binary basis. Can be used to report offsets of each difference.
colon	This command is just :. It always returns a true exit status, and it is used as a do-nothing operation in the shell programming language.
comm	Finds common lines in two files. The files are assumed to be sorted.
command	Executes a simple command.
continue	Skips to the next iteration of an until, while, or for loop in the shell programming language.
cp	Makes a copy of one or more files.
cut	Displays portions of input lines.
date	Displays the date and time in a large variety of formats. Can also be used to set the current date and time.
dd	Copies and possibly converts data into other formats, and handles disks directly.
diff	Compares two text files, and displays the differences between them.
dirname	Similar to basename, but returns the directory names from a pathname instead of the filename.

dot	Executes a file containing commands. The command is simply a . (dot).
echo	Prints its arguments.
ed	A text editor (line editor).
env	Displays all environment variables.
eval	Constructs a command by evaluating a string of expressions and concatenating the results.
exec	Executes a collection of commands, and opens, closes, and/or copies a group of file descriptors.
exit	Terminates a shell script and returns an exit status.
export	Sets the export attribute for variables and functions (determining which functions and/or variables will be passed on to processes that are invoked later on).
expr	Evaluates an expression and prints the result.
false	A utility that always returns a non-zero status value. It is called false because a non-zero status value is interpreted as a "false" answer to a true-or-false question.
find	Prints names of files that meet a certain set of criteria.
fold	Breaks up long lines into shorter lines. This is usually used when you want to display a file with lines that are too wide to fit on the terminal screen.
getconf	Obtains information about the POSIX configuration (such as the settings given to various options when the system was set up).
getopts	Analyzes command line options to a shell script.
grep	Reads a file and displays lines that contain a given pattern of characters.
head	Prints the first few lines of a file.
id	Displays the name of the current user and any group affiliations.
join	"Glues together" two sorted, textual, relational databases.

kill	Kills a running program or sends a signal to a process.
ln	Creates a link.
locale	Obtains locale-specific information (such as information on the native character set of the country where the UNIX system is running).
localedef	Specifies locale-specific information.
logger	Records a log message.
logname	Determines the log-in name of the user running the command.
lp	Sends data to a line printer.
ls	Sorts and lists the contents of a directory.
mailx	Utility for sending and reading electronic mail messages.
mkdir	Creates a new directory.
mkfifo	Creates a first-in, first-out special file (similar to a pipe, only it is given a name).
mv	Renames or moves files and/or directories.
nohup	Runs a job at a higher priority and makes sure that there is no hang-up (the job will not be delayed or put on hold).
od	Dumps a file in any of a number of selected formats (octal, hexadecimal, decimal, and so on).
paste	Concatenates the lines of one or more input files.
pathchk	Checks that a pathname is valid and/or portable to other POSIX systems.
pax	Reads and writes special archive files for data interchange or for file backup and restoration.
pr	Prepares and formats a text file for printing on a hard copy printer.
printf	Formats output according to a specified output description.
pwd	Displays the name of your current working directory.

read	Reads input from the terminal, possibly assigning the input values to shell variables.
readonly	Makes shell variables and functions read-only (which means that other processes can read their values but cannot change them).
return	Returns from a shell function or shell script, possibly specifying an exit status for the function or script.
rm	Deletes files.
rmdir	Deletes directories.
sed	A noninteractive text stream editor.
set	Sets shell options and assigns values to parameters.
sh	A shell (a command interpreter). This can be the Bourne Shell, the KornShell, or something else compatible with these shells. The sh command invokes a new copy of the shell.
shift	Used in manipulating arguments passed to a shell script or function.
sleep	Suspends execution for a specified amount of time. Primarily used in shell scripts.
sort	Sorts and/or merges data.
strip	Removes unneeded information from executable files (such as symbol tables and debugging information).
stty	Sets terminal options; in other words, this indicates how you want certain input sequences to be interpreted.
tail	Prints the last few lines of a file.
tee	Copies one input file to several output files (and also displays the input).
test	Determines whether a given condition is true. This is used primarily in shell scripts.
touch	Changes the file change date for a file.

`tr`	Translates input characters into other characters. Can be used for such jobs as converting from upper- to lowercase or encrypting data in a simple way.
`trap`	Sets up signal handlers for shell scripts.
`true`	Always returns a zero exit status (indicating "true" in true-or-false tests).
`tty`	Displays the terminal name.
`umask`	Sets default permissions for your files.
`uname`	Prints configuration-specific information, such as the host machine name, the operating system, the machine type, and so on.
`uniq`	Displays all the unique lines in a sorted file.
`unset`	Is the reverse of `set`. It discards values and attributes of shell variables and/or functions.
`wait`	Waits for a program to finish.
`wc`	Displays the number of lines, words, and characters in one or more files.
`xargs`	Constructs a command line and executes it.

The preceding list shows the commands that are part of the main body of the POSIX.2 standard. In addition, the POSIX.2 standard includes a User Portability Utilities Option. The User Portability Utilities Option includes various commands that are optional on a system that conforms with POSIX.2, for example, `vi`.

Appendix

F

KornShell Editing Features

The KornShell has built-in facilities for interactive command editing and filename generation that not only aid in entering new commands but also that you can use to modify and re-execute previous commands. This capability is distinct from that provided by the fc command, which passes previous command lines to a separate program for editing. The built-in facilities mimic the vi screen editor. You can enable the facilities with the command

```
set -o vi
```

and disable them with

```
set +o vi
```

Unlike full-screen editors, shell editing works through a one-line window, extending from the end of the prompt to the second to the last column. Multiline history entries are displayed with new-lines, represented as ^J.

The number of columns on the output device is obtained from the COLUMNS variable, if this variable is defined (see the man page for sh); otherwise, it is assumed to be 80. A command line that would extend into the extreme right column can be scrolled horizontally. If you try to move the cursor beyond the edge of the window, the line is scrolled to center the cursor in the window. The second to the last column will display a character indicating that you are only seeing part of the line: < indicates extra data off the left side of the screen; > indicates extra data off the right side of the screen; and * indicates extra data off both sides.

When the vi editing facilities have been enabled, the shell is initially in *Insert Mode* after each new prompt. Keyboard input is normally inserted at the current position in the current command line; the exceptions are the *action keys* described in the following list. (Note that in Insert Mode, the cursor arrow keys are ignored.)

Backspace, Ctrl-H	Delete the character to the left of the cursor.
Ctrl-Z	Terminate the shell (which can cause a log-out). On a UNIX system, you would use Ctrl-D instead.
Ctrl-W	Delete the word (a string delimited by whitespace) to the left of the cursor.
Ctrl-U, **Ctrl-X**	Delete the current line. Ctrl-U is MKS Tools only, not UNIX.
Ctrl-J, **Ctrl-M**, **Enter**	Execute the current line.
Esc	Switch from Insert Mode to Command Mode.
Ctrl-V	Take the next character literally; useful for entering any of the preceding characters as text.
\	Escape the following action key. If the next character is any of the preceding except Ctrl-J, Ctrl-M, or the Enter key, the \ is erased and the escaped character is entered literally; otherwise the \ is entered, and the next character is treated normally.

If you press the Esc key while you're in Insert Mode, the shell enters Command Mode, and keyboard input is interpreted as commands to reposition the cursor, scroll through the command history, delete or change text, or re-enter Insert Mode. In Command Mode, you will not see the commands you type, but you will see their results.

Many commands may be preceded by a number called a *count;* this tells the shell to execute the command that number of times. Except where otherwise noted, the count defaults to 1.

The following sections describe the available commands. Commands are grouped together according to their purposes. In all command descriptions, N is a number serving as the count and may be omitted. Also, c stands for any character.

Cursor-Movement Commands

These commands reposition the cursor in the command line. The commands only work in Command Mode; to get out of Insert Mode and into Command Mode, press Esc.

Nh, Nleftarrow	Move back N characters.
Nl, Nrightarrow	Move forward N characters.
0 (zero)	Move to the first character on the line.
^	Move to the first nonblank character on the line.
$	Move to the last character on the line.
Nw	Move to the beginning of the Nth next word (where a word is a string of alphanumerics, or a string of nonblank nonalphanumerics).
NW	Move to the beginning of the Nth next full-word (where a full-word is a string of nonblanks).
Nb	Move to the Nth previous beginning of the word.
NB	Move to the Nth previous beginning of the full-word.
Ne	Move to the Nth next end of the word.
NE	Move to the Nth next end of the full-word.
Nfc	Move to the Nth next character c.

NFc	Move to the Nth previous character c.
Ntc	Move to the character before the Nth next character c.
NTc	Move to the character after the Nth previous character c.
N;	Repeat the previous f, F, t, or T command.
N,	Repeat the previous f, F, t, or T command, but in the opposite direction.

Line Search

The following commands change to display a different command line.

Nj, N+, Ndownarrow	Display the Nth next command line from the command history. Using the down arrow key is MKS Tools-specific because UNIX doesn't know if a particular terminal will have arrow keys.
Nk, N-, Nuparrow	Display the Nth previous command line from the command history. Using the up arrow key is MKS Tools-specific.
NG	Display the command with history number N. If N is omitted, the shell displays the latest command (based on the vi G (go to) command).
N/stringEnter	Display the Nth command line, searching backward, that matches string. If string is omitted, the shell uses the previous search string.
N?stringEnter	Display the Nth command line, searching forward, that matches string. If string is omitted, the shell uses the previous search string.
Nn	Repeat the last string search (/ or ?) command.
NN	Repeat the last string search, but in the opposite direction.

Text Change

The following commands alter the text in the current command line. Some of these commands operate on a text block, defined by a cursor-movement command immediately following the text change command. The descriptions designate the cursor movement by M (for movement). The text block extends from the current cursor position to the new position determined by the movement command.

i	Enter Insert Mode, inserting text before the character under the cursor.
I	Insert before first nonblank on line (equivalent to ^i).
a	Move the cursor forward one character and enter Insert Mode, appending text after the character originally under the cursor.
A	Append to the end of the line (equivalent to $a).
NdM	Delete text block. If N is given, it is applied to the movement command M.
dd	Delete the entire command line.
D	Delete from the cursor to the end of the line (equivalent to d$).
Nx	Delete N characters to the right of the cursor (equivalent to Ndl).
NX	Delete N characters to the left of the cursor (equivalent to Ndh).
NcM	Change text block; deletes block of text and enters Insert Mode. If N is given, it is applied to the movement command M.
cc,S	Change the entire command line.
Ns	Change the next N characters, beginning at the cursor.
Np	Paste N copies of the last block deleted by a text-change command. Text will be placed immediately after the cursor position.

Np	Like Np, but text is placed immediately before the cursor position.
rc	Replace the single character under the cursor with the character c and advance the cursor one position.
R	Enter *Replace Mode,* a special case of Insert Mode in which each character entered overwrites that under the cursor and advances the cursor one position.
u	Undo the last text change to the current line. This is itself a text-change command, so pressing u a second time "undoes the undo."
U	Undo all changes to the current line.
N~	Switch the case of the next N characters, advancing the cursor over them. (Uppercase letters turn to lowercase and vice versa.)
N.	Repeat the last text change command. If N is given, it overrides the count originally given with the command.
N_	Append the Nth argument from the previous command line and enter Insert Mode. If N is not specified, the shell appends the last argument from the previous command line.
*	Replace the current word with the list of filenames that would match the word with a * appended. In the case of no match, the terminal will beep, and the word will not be changed. Otherwise, the cursor is positioned at the end of the list, and the shell enters Insert Mode.
\	Used to complete a pathname. If there is only one existing pathname that matches as much as you've typed, the shell completes the pathname and adds a space after the complete pathname. If there are several matching pathnames, the shell will expand what you've typed by adding all the characters that are common to all matching pathnames.
=	Lists all pathnames that match the current word.

Miscellaneous Commands

Ny M	yank text block. Does not alter the command line or cursor position, but makes the text block available to subsequent paste (p or P) commands. If N is given, it is applied to the movement command M.
yy	yank the entire command line.
Y	yank the rest of the line (equivalent to y$).
#	Insert a # at the beginning of the line and start a new command line immediately. Essentially, this turns the current line into a comment so that the line will be ignored.
Nv	Call the real vi editor to let you edit command N from the history file. If you omit N, you can edit the current line.
Ctrl-L	Redisplay the current line.
Ctrl-J, Ctrl-M, Enter	Execute the current line.

Warning

Selecting a previous history line for editing while at a secondary prompt (that is, while entering a subsequent line of a new multiline command) may yield unpredictable results.

Appendix

G

INSTALLING THE MKS TOOLS PACKAGE

This appendix describes the process of installing the MKS Tools on your DOS system. You can use any release of DOS from Version 3.1 up.

Space Requirements

The installation procedure will tell you how much space you need to have available on your hard disk in order to install the MKS Tools. If you do not have enough free space, you will have to clear some space for the software. To do this, back up some files you won't need for a while, delete those files from your hard disk, and then run the installation procedure again.

Choosing a Directory

Before you begin installing the software, you must decide where you want to store it. You must store it on a hard disk. If you only have one hard disk, this will be disk C:; otherwise, choose a hard disk that has sufficient space to hold the software.

Next you must decide on a directory in which to store the software. By default, the installation procedure stores the software in a directory named \lu. You are strongly advised to accept this default, unless you already have a directory named \lu that is being used for something else.

If \lu is already being used for something else, decide on another name for the directory (such as \lux, short for *Learning UNIX*). During the installation procedure, you'll be asked to enter the name that you have chosen. The installation procedure automatically creates the directory if it doesn't already exist.

If You Don't Use \lu

Many examples in this book assume that the MKS Tools are installed under the \lu directory. If you choose a different directory, remember your decision and adapt the examples accordingly. For example, if you choose to install the software under \lux and an example asks you to type

```
ls /lu
```

you should type

```
ls /lux
```

instead.

Running the Installation Procedure

(The following few instructions also may be found on the Installation page at the back of this book.)

Insert the MKS Tools diskette into drive A: or drive B:. If you use drive A:, enter the command

```
a:install
```

If you use drive B:, enter the command

```
b:install
```

The installation procedure displays a box asking Where do you want the Learning UNIX tools installed? At the bottom of the box, you'll see a line that already contains the name

```
c:/lu
```

which stands for the \lu directory on the C: disk. (This is your first taste of UNIX; UNIX uses the slash (/) in filenames, where DOS uses the backslash.) If you want to accept the preceding directory, press Enter. Otherwise, type the disk drive and directory name that you have chosen and press Enter.

Next, the installation displays a box asking What log-in name would you like to use? Your answer should be the name that you would like to use when interacting with the computer (such as jim or juanita). The name can be up to eight characters long and can contain letters or digits. You are advised to use lowercase letters, because UNIX traditionally uses lowercase whenever possible. When you've entered your chosen name, press Enter.

The installation procedure then begins copying files from the diskette to your hard disk. It does this using a command named tar (described in Chapter 5, "Popular Tools," of this book). Everything happens automatically, so you don't need to worry about how tar works right now; however, you'll see the word tar displayed on your screen while the copying takes place. (I thought you'd like to know what it means.)

When all the files have been copied from the disk(s), the installation procedure displays the message

```
Installation Completed Successfully
Press ENTER to Continue.
```

Press Enter, and the installation procedure will terminate.

Stopping Partway Through

If you find you must stop partway through the installation procedure for some reason, you can stop the installation by pressing Ctrl-C or Ctrl-Break. The procedure will display Interrupt? This question asks if you really want to cut the installation short. If you do, enter y for *yes;* if you don't, enter n for *no.* Press Enter when you have typed your answer.

Starting the MKS Tools

You can start the MKS Tools either from the DOS prompt or from within Microsoft Windows.

To start the MKS Tools from the DOS prompt, enter the following commands:

```
cd \lu
lu
```

(Always type the second command as lu, even if you choose a different directory to hold the software.)

To start the MKS Tools from within Microsoft Windows, open the Learning UNIX Program Group and double-click the Learning UNIX (with MKS Tools) icon.

The MKS Tools remind you what user name you chose during installation. You should use this name during the log-in procedure. For further information about logging in and using the MKS Tools, see Chapter 2, "Getting Started: Hello, World."

New Students

If a new student wants to start the *Learning UNIX* lessons, run the installation procedure as described previously. When the installation procedure asks for the directory where you want the UNIX tools installed, use the same directory used for the previous student. When the installation procedure asks for a user ID for the new student, enter an appropriate name; this name shouldn't be the same as any previous student's name.

Coexistence

If you install the lessons for a new student according to the procedures described in the previous section, previous students will find they can no longer log-in. The reason is that the installation procedure gets rid of the old user's password information in the passwd file.

If previous students want to be able to log-in to the MKS Tools after new students have been installed, follow these steps:

1. Before you install a new student, log-in to the MKS Tools and enter the command

   ```
   cp /lu/etc/passwd /lu/tmp
   ```

   This makes a copy of the old password file.

2. Install the new student, as described in the *Running the Installation Procedure* section in this appendix.

3. Log-in to the new student's account and issue the commands

   ```
   cat /lu/etc/passwd /lu/tmp/passwd >/lu/tmp/pass2
   cp /lu/tmp/pass2 /lu/etc/passwd
   rm /lu/tmp/passwd /lu/tmp/pass2
   ```

   These commands concatenate the old and new password files and copy the concatenation to the proper directory.

MKS Tools Versus the MKS Toolkit

The MKS Tools are a subset of the MKS Toolkit, a collection of more than 180 programs that simulate the look and feel of UNIX on a DOS, OS/2, or Windows NT system. The MKS Tools are only intended to be an educational aid; they are not intended to give you the capabilities of the full MKS Toolkit. The most important differences between MKS Tools software and the corresponding MKS Toolkit commands are

- The *Learning UNIX* version of vi can only write out a maximum of 100 lines of text. That limit is high enough that you should be able to experiment freely while you're using this book.

- Before you can execute any of the UNIX commands that come with this book, you must log-in to the MKS Tools program (named lu under the \lu directory). The real MKS Toolkit does not impose this restriction; you can use MKS Toolkit commands at any time that you could use any other DOS command. For example, you can execute MKS Toolkit commands in response to the usual DOS C> prompt; you don't have to log-in to use MKS Toolkit commands.

- The KornShell that comes with the MKS Tools will only execute other MKS Tools commands. For example, you can't execute spreadsheets or word processors while you are using the MKS Tools. With the real MKS Toolkit, the KornShell will execute any valid DOS program.

The following is a list of the commands that are provided in the MKS Toolkit:

alias	ar	asa	awk
awkc	awkl	banner	basename
bc	bdiff	break	c
cal	calendar	case	cat
cc	cd	chmod	cksum
clear	cmp	col	: (colon)
comm	command	compress	continue
cp	cpio	crypt	csplit
ctags	cut	date	dbz
dc	dd	deroff	dev
df	diff	diff3	diffh
dirname	. (dot)	du	echo
ed	egrep	env	eval
ex	exec	exit	expand
export	expr	false	fc
fg	fgrep	file	find
fmt	fold	for	function
functions	getconf	getopt	glob
grep	gres	hash	head
help	history	hostname	iconv
id	if-else	inews	init
injnews	integer	jobs	join
kill	lc	let	line
login	logname	look	ls
m4	mailx	make	makeq
man	mkdir	mksdiag	mksgroup
mksinfo	mksos	mksuucp	more
mt	mv	news	newsrun
nl	nm	nr	od
pack	passwd	paste	patch
pathchk	pax	pcat	pg
postnews	pr	print	printf
prof	ps	pwd	r
read	readonly	red	return
rev	rm	rmail	rmdir
rnews	rsh	sed	select
set	sh	shift	size

sleep	sort	spell	split
strings	strip	sum	switch
sync	tail	tar	tee
test	time	times	tklaunch
touch	tr	trap	true
tsort	tty	type	typeset
ulimit	unalias	uname	uncompress
unexpand	uniq	unpack	unset
unstrip	until	uucheck	uucico
uuclean	uuconfig	uucp	uudecode
uuencode	uulog	uuname	uustat
uutraf	uux	uuxqt	vdiff
vi	viw	wc	whence
which	while	who	xargs
zcat			

Many of these commands are explained in Appendix E, "POSIX.2 Utility Summary."

You Can Use Both!

It's possible to have both the MKS Tools and the MKS Toolkit installed on one DOS system. Because the MKS Tools work entirely within the /lu directory, they don't conflict with the MKS Toolkit, provided that the ROOTDIR for the full MKS Toolkit is not /lu.

Note, however, that the MKS Tools automatically change ROOTDIR to the directory where the MKS Tools are installed. Thus, when you quit using MKS Tools, ROOTDIR will be set for MKS Tools instead of MKS Toolkit. To use MKS Toolkit, you can either set ROOTDIR to the appropriate directory or just reboot the system.

GLOSSARY

These following terms are used and defined in this book. Terms shown in *italics* are also defined in this glossary.

Abbreviation. In vi, a *string* that stands for another string. Whenever you type an abbreviation, vi automatically converts it to the associated string.

Access Time. A *file characteristic* that tells the last time that a person or program *opened* a file.

Alias. A name that you associate with a *string* in the *KornShell*. When the KornShell sees an alias name used in a location where a *command* could begin, the shell replaces the name with its associated string. In other words, an alias stands for the first part of a command.

Append. To add text to the existing contents of a file. You can do this with the *redirection* construct >>. There is also a vi command that appends new text to the text being edited.

Archive. A file with contents that preserve the contents of many other files and *directories.* In this book, the tar *command* creates and manipulates archives. Some UNIX and UNIX look-alike systems offer other commands (such as pax, cpio) that can also manipulate archives.

Argument. See *Command-Line Argument.*

Arithmetic Expression. A sequence of arithmetic operations yielding a value.

Assignment. A *KornShell command* that gives a value to a *variable.*

Background Job. A program that is not a *foreground job.* See *Foreground Job* for details.

Backslash. The \ character. In the *KornShell,* the backslash is used as the default *escape character.*

Basename. The last part of a *pathname;* the part that remains when you remove all the directory names. For example, in dir1/dir2/file.c, the basename is file.c. Also see *Dirname.*

Binary. A method of representing numbers and other kinds of information using only the digits 0 and 1.

Binary File. On UNIX, any file that is not a *text file.*

Block. A unit for measuring the amount of disk space used by a file. Typically, UNIX blocks are 512 *bytes;* however, this size can be different on different UNIX systems.

Body of a Function. The *commands* inside the definition of a *shell function.* For example, in

```
function cdl
{
    cd $1
    ls -x
}
```

the body of the function consists of the cd and ls commands.

Built-In Alias. An *alias* that is automatically defined for you when you start the *KornShell.* For example, *history* is a built-in alias; it is an alias that you do not have to define yourself.

Built-In Command. A *command* that the *shell* can execute directly; the shell does not have to search for a file that contains the program. For example, set and alias are commands built into the *KornShell*. TYPE and DIR are commands built into DOS's COMMAND.COM *command interpreter*.

Byte. The amount of computer memory used to hold a single character (such as a letter or digit). Different types of computers can have different byte sizes, but the most common size, especially in personal computers, is eight bits.

Case-Sensitive. A description of any software that treats upper- and lowercase letters differently. For example, the UNIX file system is case-sensitive. Thus, the names FILE, file, and File are all different filenames and refer to different files. The opposite of case-sensitive software is case-insensitive or caseless software. For example, the DOS file system is case-insensitive; the names FILE, file, and File all refer to the same file.

Command. Any instruction to any piece of software. In this book, the most common type of command is an instruction to the *KornShell* to run a particular program. The standard programs on a system are sometimes called commands or utility commands.

Command Editing. The process of editing and re-executing a *command* entered previously. Command editing features are offered by the *KornShell*.

Command File. A file containing instructions to a program. In particular, a vi command file is a file containing the kind of vi instructions that normally begin with a colon (:). In the instructions contained by such a command file, the colon is omitted.

Command History. A list of all *commands* recently executed by the *KornShell*. This list is recorded in the *history file*.

Command Interpreter. A program that reads the *commands* that you type in, and then executes them. Also known as a *shell*.

Command Line. An instruction to the *shell*, consisting of a *command* name followed by *command line arguments*.

Command-Line Argument. A part of *command line*. Arguments provide information that tells a program what it should do. The most common command line arguments are *command line options* or *pathnames*. Command line arguments are separated from each other by *whitespace*.

Command-Line Option. A *command line argument* that changes the default behavior of a program. On a UNIX system, simple command line options consist of a minus sign character followed by a single letter or digit, as in `-x`. More sophisticated command line options may consist of a minus sign followed by a keyword, followed by a value, as in `-ctime 1`.

Command Mode. In a `vi` editing session, the editor is in Command Mode anytime it waits for you to enter a *command.* See also *Insert Mode.*

Command Prompt String. The *string* that the *KornShell* displays when it wants you to enter a new *command.* See also *Secondary Prompt String.*

Command Substitution. A feature of the *KornShell.* When a *command line* contains a construct of the form `$(command)`, the shell executes the given `command` and collects its *standard output.* The shell then puts the output in place of the original `$(command)` construct and executes the resulting command line.

COMMAND.COM. The standard *command interpreter* on a DOS system.

Comment. An English-language description of what a *shell script* or *shell function* does. In the *KornShell,* a comment begins with a number sign character (#) and goes to the end of the line.

Component. See *Pathname Component.*

Contextual Cursor Movement. In `vi`, a way of moving the *cursor* through text. Contextual cursor movement depends on the nature of the text itself. For example, the `w` command moves the cursor to the beginning of the next word in the text. To do this, `vi` must examine the text to find where the next word starts.

Control Character. Generally a character that is not one of the printable characters (letters, digits, or punctuation characters). Various types of software put control characters into files to convey a special meaning. For example, word processors use control characters to indicate formatting information.

Control Structures. In the *KornShell,* a group of special instructions that perform special processing. Examples include `if` constructs, `for` loops, `while` loops, and so on.

Current Directory. Roughly speaking, the *directory* you are "working in." Usually when you want to refer to a file, you must give the name of the directory that contains the file, the name of the directory that contains that directory, and so on. To reduce typing, you can designate any directory as your current directory. You can then refer directly to files and *subdirectories* in your current directory without specifying all the containing directories. You can change your current directory with the cd command and display the name of your current directory with the pwd command. The notation . refers to the current directory. See also *Pathname*.

Cursor. The marker on the display screen that shows where the next character you type will appear.

Default Options. With the *KornShell* and other software, the *options* that are in effect if you do not explicitly specify any options. For example, with vi, the default tab stops are set every eight columns on the display screen.

Device. Any piece of equipment that can give information to or receive information from your computer, such as a hard disk drive, a floppy disk drive, a video display terminal, a mouse, or a printer.

Device Driver. Software that looks after interactions between your computer and a particular *device*. For example, there will be a device driver for each line printer attached to your computer; this software will look after all interactions with that printer.

Device Files. A UNIX file associated with a *device*. The file looks like a normal disk file; however, if you perform I/O on the file, it has the effect of performing I/O on the device. For example, the file /dev/lp may be associated with the line printer, and if you write data to /dev/lp, the data will appear on the printer.

Directory. A construct for organizing computer files. If you picture files as folders that hold information, a directory is like a drawer that can hold several folders. Directories can also contain subdirectories, which can contain subdirectories of their own. When you want the computer to find a particular file, the computer has to know the name of the file, the name of the directory that contains the file, the name of the directory that contains this directory, and so on.

Dirname. The first parts of a *pathname;* the list of directory names. For example, in dir1/dir2/file.c, the dirname is dir1/dir2. See also *Basename*.

Encryption. The process of putting information into a specially coded form to keep the information secret. The reverse of encryption is decryption.

End-of-File. Something that indicates the end of the information that a file contains. This is often a special character. For example, the Ctrl-Z character is often used to mark end-of-file on DOS, and the Ctrl-D character is often used to mark end-of-file on UNIX. Another common approach is to record the number of *bytes* in the file, so that when a program has read that number of bytes, it knows it has reached the end of the file.

Environment. When using the *KornShell,* the collection of all features that can affect the execution of a *command.* This includes the current settings of all *shell options, shell functions, aliases, file descriptors,* and *variables.* Each executing program has its own environment.

Environment Variables. See *Variables.*

EOF. Short for *end-of-file.* Also commonly used as the name of a character or value signifying end-of-file.

Escape Character. A character used to "turn off" the special meanings of other characters. By default, UNIX software uses the *backslash* as its escape character. When you put the escape character in front of another character that has a special meaning (such as a *glob construct*), the escape character says that you want the second character to be taken literally instead of having its special meaning.

Executable. Able to be put into execution. An executable file is a file for which you have execute *permission* and which contains a program or *shell script* that the *KornShell* can execute.

Exit Code. The DOS terminology for a *status value.*

Expansion. To replace a special construct with its real meaning. For example, to expand an *alias,* the *KornShell* replaces the alias with the *string* associated with that alias. To expand a *variable,* the KornShell replaces the variable with its associated value.

Export. The act of one program passing information to another program. For example, when the *KornShell* exports a *variable* to another program, the KornShell passes the name and value of that variable to the program. If you want the KornShell to export a particular variable, you should mark that variable for export using the export command. As an alternative, you could use the command set -a to tell the shell to export all variables created in the future.

Field. A piece of data within a *record.* Usually, the fields of a record must be separated by special characters (such as blanks or commas).

File Characteristic. A piece of information about a file, such as the date and time that the file's contents were most recently changed.

File Descriptor. A number associated with an *open* file. Whenever a *process* wants to perform I/O on a particular file, the process identifies the file by specifying the file descriptor number. DOS sometimes uses the term *handle* for file descriptors. See also *Standard Input, Standard Output,* and *Standard Error.*

File Permissions. *File characteristics* that tell who can use a file and how those people can use it. There are three classes of permissions: owner permissions, which control use by the file's *owner;* group permissions, which control use by people in the file's *group;* and other permissions, which control use by everyone else. For each of these three classes there are three permission types: r permission lets you read a file, w permission lets you write to the file, and x permission lets you execute the file (as a program or *shell script*). These are often described in a *string* that gives owner, group, and other permissions in that order. For example, rwxr-xr-- stands for rwx permissions for the owner, rx for the group, and r for others.

File System. A collection of files and *directories* on a particular *device*. It is possible for a UNIX system to have several separate file systems. More loosely speaking, *file system* can refer to all the files and directories of a particular UNIX machine.

Filter. A general term for any program that reads in data from the standard input, "transforms" the data in some way, then writes out the result to the standard output. A simple example would be a program that reads in text, converts all letters to uppercase, and then writes out the result.

Folding. Displaying a long line of text by breaking it into several shorter lines on the display screen. For example, vi can fold a long line so you can read the line on the display screen; internally, however, vi keeps it as one long line instead of breaking it up into shorter lines.

Foreground Job. An executing program that can interact with the terminal. The opposite of a foreground job is a *background job,* a program that is running on its own and is shut off from interacting with the terminal. To start a program running in the background, put a & on the end of the command line that invokes the program. Background jobs are sometimes called *batch jobs.*

Glob Construct. A character or *string* that can be used in place of characters in a *pathname.* Each glob construct stands for a particular pattern of characters; for example, ? stands for any single character, while * stands for a string of zero or more characters. When the *KornShell* sees a pathname that contains a glob construct, the shell *expands* the construct into a list of all existing files with names that match the pattern given by the glob construct.

Group. A collection of users on a UNIX system. Groups are created by the UNIX system's administrators. Each group usually consists of a collection of people with something in common; for example, the administrators might set up a group for each project that a company is working on. A user can belong to any number of groups. One of these is designated the user's primary group, and the rest are considered secondary groups. Each group is identified by a name and a number.

Group Permissions. See *File Permissions*.

Handle. The DOS term for a *file descriptor*.

History File. A file used by the *KornShell* to record the commands most recently executed during this session. This file is always *open* while the shell is running. On UNIX systems, the history file is .sh_history under your home directory; with MKS Tools, the name is sh_histo.

Also, a file used by a revision control software package to record the history of changes made to another file.

Home Directory. A directory that usually serves as your personal directory when you use a UNIX system. When you first *log in,* your *current directory* will be your home directory. The name of your home directory is given by the HOME *variable.*

Initialization File. A file that contains instructions to be executed when a program starts up. For example, a vi initialization file contains instructions that should be executed when you start vi, before vi executes any instructions entered from the keyboard.

Insert Mode. In a vi editing session, the editor is in Insert Mode any time you are typing in text that is added to the text already shown on the screen. See also *Command Mode.*

Integer. A number that has no fractional part and no exponent. A whole number.

Interrupt. A signal that tells a program to stop what it's doing as soon as possible. UNIX systems often use the Ctrl-C or Del character to issue an interrupt. (Note: some programs can ignore interrupt signals.)

Kernel. The heart of an *operating system.* The kernel supplies services to all programs that execute under the operating system, and also keeps users and programs from interfering with each other. See also *Operating System.*

Kill. The action of manually terminating a *process.* On a UNIX system, this is commonly done with the kill command.

KornShell. A *command interpreter* developed on UNIX by David Korn. The KornShell is a descendant of the Bourne Shell, and accepts any input that the Bourne Shell accepts. The KornShell has many additional features that the Bourne Shell does not.

Line Editor. A type of *text editor* that takes input in a line-by-line mode. Editing commands appear on the screen as they are typed, and therefore interweave with any lines of text that are also on the screen. Contrast this with a *Screen Editor.*

Link. A name associated with a file. On a true UNIX system, a file can have more than one *pathname,* and therefore more than one link. Because this is not true on a DOS system, this book does not examine links in any detail.

Linking a Program. Combining several *object files* and/or *object libraries* to produce an *executable* program.

Log In. The process of identifying yourself to the system and proving you are who you say you are. To begin using a UNIX system, you must log in; unlike DOS systems, you can't just turn on the machine and start working.

Log Out. The process of telling the *shell* that you are finished working. This ends your *session.* With the *KornShell,* you log out by entering the `exit` command. "Log off" is another term for log out.

Loop. A *control structure* that repeats a set of *commands* until a given condition is met.

Makefile. A file that describes interdependencies between other files. Used in connection with the `make` command, which updates files to keep them in synch with each other. The makefile also shows the commands needed to update the files.

Man Page. A description of a *command* in a UNIX reference manual. For example, the `ls` man page describes the `ls` command.

Merging. Combining several files into a single file. You can do this with the UNIX `sort` command.

Metacharacter. A character that can have a special meaning in a *regular expression.* For example, $ is a metacharacter that stands for the end of a line.

Modification Time. A *file characteristic* that tells the last time that a person or program changed the characteristics of a file, particularly the *file permissions.*

Mount. To associate a *file system* with a *device.* You must mount a device before you can use it. For example, if you want to write to a file on a diskette on a UNIX system, someone must issue a `mount` command that associates the diskette with a directory in the normal file system. Writing to a file under that directory has the effect of writing to the corresponding file on the diskette. Some devices can be mounted automatically when the UNIX system starts up; this varies from system to system.

Multitasking. Executing several programs simultaneously.

Multiuser System. An *operating system* that can be used by several people simultaneously, and that provides security measures that let people protect their programs and data from other users.

Newline. A character or *string* that separates lines of text in a *text file.* On a keyboard, you generate a newline by pressing Enter.

Null String. A *string* that contains no characters. Often written " " or ' '.

Null Suffix. A file named *suffix* that contains no characters. For example, `file.` has a null suffix because it has a `.` and nothing afterward.

On UNIX, there's a difference between a file that has a null suffix and one that has no suffix at all. A file that has a null suffix has a `.` to show where the suffix begins, and no characters after the `.` (because the suffix is null). A file that has no suffix at all has no `.` in its name.

Object File. A file that contains all or part of a program, in a format that is close to the internal format used by the computing hardware. An object file is produced by compiling a *source file.*

Object Library. A file with contents that are constructed from several *object files.* Object files are put together into libraries, because some types of software work better with one large file than many small ones.

Opening a File. Asking the *kernel* to prepare a file for input or output. In order to open a file, a program must specify whether it wants to read the file, write to the file, or both. The kernel then checks to see if the program's user has appropriate *file permissions* on the file to perform such actions. If the file doesn't exist, the process of opening a file for writing creates the file. When the kernel opens a file, it assigns a *file descriptor* number to the file so that the program can identify the file in future actions.

Operating System. A collection of software that performs services for other programs and that enforces security measures to prevent programs and users from interfering with each other. An operating system can be divided into three parts:

- The *utilities,* commands for performing everyday operations, like copying or removing files

- The *shell,* which starts up the commands that the user wants to execute

- The *kernel,* which does the most basic work of the operating system, such as performing I/O. The kernel also supervises the programs and users who share the system.

Option. Something that controls or modifies the usual behavior of a program. See also *shell options* and *command line options.*

Owner of a File. Normally, the person who created the file.

Parameter. A symbol standing for an *argument.* In *shell scripts* and *shell functions,* the parameter $1 stands for the first argument, $2 stands for the second argument, and so on. These are called *positional parameters* because the numbers refer to positions in the argument list. There are also special parameters that stand for lists of arguments and other information.

Parent Directory. A *directory* that contains another directory. For example, if dir1 contains dir2, then dir1 is the parent directory of dir2. The notation .. refers to the parent directory of your *current directory.*

Pathname. A description of how to locate a desired file. An absolute pathname gives the full name of the file, beginning at the *root directory* and listing the sequence of directories that lead to the file. An absolute pathname always starts with a slash (/) character, signifying the root. Here are some examples of absolute pathnames:

```
/etc    # name of a directory directly under the root
/dir1/dir2    # name of a subdirectory
/dir1/dir2/file.ksh   # name of a file
```

A relative pathname describes how to find the file beginning at your *current directory.* You can identify a relative pathname because it does not start with a slash. Here are some examples of relative pathnames:

```
sonnet    # name of a file under current directory
testdir/sonnet # file under subdirectory of current directory
../sonnet # file under parent of current directory
```

Pathname Component. Part of a *pathname,* giving the name of a directory or file. For example, in /dir1/dir2/file.suf, the components are / (standing for the root), dir1, dir2, and file.suf. Components are separated by slash (/) characters. See also *Basename* and *Dirname.*

Pattern. Another name for a *regular expression.*

Pattern-Matching. The process of searching for *strings* of characters that conform to the pattern of characters specified by a *regular expression.*

Permissions. See *File Permissions.*

Pipe. A communication mechanism between two *processes* that connects an output *file descriptor* in one process to an input *file descriptor* in the other. Most commonly, the *standard output* of one process is connected to the *standard input* of the other.

Pipeline. A sequence of two or more *processes* connected by *pipes*. The *standard output* of each process becomes the *standard input* of the next process in the sequence. In the *KornShell*, a pipeline is written as

```
command ¦ command ¦ command ¦ ...
```

Placeholder. In the synopsis of a *command line* and in *command arguments,* a symbol that stands for a value. For example, in the command line synopsis

```
banner [-c char] [-f fontfile] [-w n] [text ...]
```

`char`, `fontfile`, `n`, and `text` are all placeholders. When you type in a real `banner` command, you replace these placeholders with real values. For example, you would replace the `text` placeholder with the actual text that you want `banner` to display.

Portable Character Set. The set of characters that are guaranteed to be valid for filenames in any system conforming to the *POSIX* standards. The set includes the 26 upper- and lowercase letters used by the English language, the 10 digits, the underscore (_), the dash (-), and the dot (.).

Porting. Taking a program that works on one computing system and making whatever changes are necessary to get it to work on another.

Positional Parameter. See *Parameter.*

POSIX. The umbrella name for a family of standards developed by the Institute of Electrical and Electronics Engineers. These standards describe the features and behavior of UNIX-like *operating systems.*

Process. A program that is currently executing. A process includes the memory that the program occupies, the files it has open, the program's *environment,* and any other attributes specific to a running program.

Process ID. A number that serves to distinguish one *process* from another. The *kernel* assigns each process a unique *process ID* when that process begins executing. On a standard UNIX system, the `ps` command lets you determine the process ID of a particular process.

Profile File. An *initialization file* for the *KornShell.* A file containing KornShell *commands,* intended to be executed whenever the KornShell starts up. Typically, people use profile files to set *options,* define *aliases,* define *shell functions,* and in general, to do any work needed to set up their shell sessions. On a true UNIX system, profile files are named `.profile`; with the MKS Tools, profile files are named `profile.ksh`.

Rapid Prototyping. The process of creating a prototype version of a program as quickly as possible. The program may be considered a prototype because it has not been optimized for efficiency or because it only does a part of the work that a finished program should do. For example, suppose a program is going to interact with the user by displaying menus; you might make a prototype that only displays menus, without doing any other work. This prototype makes it easier to experiment with the appearance of the menus and to ask the users if they like what they see. Producing a prototype very early in the program design process often helps the programmers detect problems and correct them before they've invested a lot of work in an unsatisfactory approach.

Read-Only File. A file that you can read but not write to. Typically, you make a file read-only if you don't want to overwrite the current contents by accident.

Record. For the purposes of sort, a line in a *text file* that is broken into one or more *fields*.

Redirection. Typically, the process of sending the *standard output* of a program to a file instead of the display screen, or of reading the *standard input* of a program from a file instead of the keyboard. More precisely, redirection is the process of changing the association of files and *file descriptors* before running a program. In particular, >file redirects the standard output to file, while <file redirects the standard input from file.

Regular Expression. A *string* describing a pattern of characters. Special characters (called *metacharacters*) within the regular expression can specify additional criteria for the pattern of characters.

Return Value. Another name for a *status value*.

Reverse Video. Displaying dark characters on a light background.

Root. Short for *root directory*.

Root Directory. The main *directory* in a UNIX file system. All other directories and files are contained in the root directory or in subdirectories of the root directory.

Screen Editor. A *text editor* that shows the text you are editing, not the commands that you enter in order to edit it. Contrast this with *Line Editor*.

Script. A file containing instructions for a piece of software. For example, a *shell script* contains instructions for a *shell* (such as the *KornShell*); a sed script contains instructions for sed.

Search Path. A list of directories that a *command interpreter* should search in order to find commands that you want to run. On UNIX, your search path is given by the value of the PATH variable.

Search Rules. Another name for your *search path*.

Secondary Prompt String. The *string* that the *KornShell* displays when it wants you to enter another line of a multiline *command* (such as an if construct). Also see the *Command Prompt String* entry.

Session. A period of interaction with a piece of software. For example, a vi session lasts from the time you start vi to the time you quit. A *shell* session lasts from the time you start the shell (for example, at *log in*) to the time you quit using the shell (for example, at *log out*).

Shell. A program that reads your *commands* and executes them. Also called a *command interpreter*. See also *Operating System*.

Shell Function. A *shell command* made up of several other commands, comparable to a subprogram in a programming language. To define a function, you specify a set of commands to make up the function and a name for the function. You can then use the function name as if it were a command name. When a command line starts with the function name, the shell will execute all the commands that make up that function.

Shell Option. An *option* that controls the behavior of a *shell*. The *KornShell* has several options that let you change its usual behavior. For example, set -x tells the shell to display each command before the command is executed, showing all the *expansions* performed in the *command line*.

Shell Script. A *script* containing input for a *shell*.

Sorting Key. A description of a *field* or collection of fields in a record. The sort command uses sorting keys to specify how records are to be sorted. The sorting key tells which pieces of information are to be used in sorting and what sorting order is to be used. A sort command can have several sorting keys.

Source File. A text file containing instructions written in a programming language such as C or Pascal. A compiler program translates the contents of a source file into a form closer to the internal machine language used by the hardware, and writes this translated information into an *object file*.

Standard Error. The usual name for *file descriptor* 2 (two). By convention, programs write diagnostics and error messages to this descriptor. Usually, the descriptor refers to the display screen, but this can be changed by *redirection.* This descriptor is separate from the *standard output,* so that error diagnostics are still seen when the standard output is redirected.

Standard Input. The usual name for *file descriptor* 0 (zero). By convention, programs read input from this descriptor. Usually, the descriptor refers to the keyboard, but this can be changed by *redirection.*

Standard Output. The usual name for *file descriptor* 1 (one). By convention, programs write output to this descriptor. The descriptor usually refers to the display screen, but this can be changed by *redirection.*

Status Value. An *integer* that a program uses to indicate whether or not it was successful. When a program is invoked by the shell, the shell receives the program's status value when the program finishes execution. *Shell scripts* and *shell functions* can also produce status values when they finish execution, by using the return statement. Status values are also called *return values, exit status values,* or *exit codes.*

Stream. A "route" by which input travels to a program and/or output travels from a program. For example, if a program wants to write to a particular file, the program asks the kernel to *open* an output stream to that file. Each open stream in a program has its own *file descriptor.*

Stream Editor. A *text editor* that does not interact with the user. The user specifies a set of commands or a *command file* on the editor's command line, and the editor simply executes those commands on all specified files.

String. Any sequence of characters, as in abc. Strings are often enclosed in single or double quotation marks.

Subdirectory. A *directory* contained by another directory. The *root directory* is the only directory that is not a subdirectory.

Subshell. A *shell* that was started by another program (usually by another shell).

Suffix. The final part of a file's *basename.* Also called a filename extension. For example, in /dir/file.c, the suffix is .c. The DOS file system treats suffixes as special parts of filenames. The UNIX file system does not offer any special treatment; on UNIX, users simply use suffixes as a convenient naming convention.

Superuser. A *userid* on UNIX systems, used for system administration tasks. The kernel allows the superuser to access any file, regardless of the permissions on that file, and to control all executing programs. The user number of the superuser is zero, and the user name is often root.

SVID. Short for **S**ystem **V** **I**nterface **D**efinition. A standard developed by AT&T to describe UNIX systems.

Temporary File. A file that a program creates while it is doing work, then deletes when the file is no longer necessary. For example, the sort command can create temporary files to hold partly sorted data; when sort finishes sorting the data, it gets rid of all the temporary files created during the sorting process. UNIX systems usually have a *directory* named /tmp where programs can store their temporary files. The MKS Tools use a directory named /lu/tmp for temporary files.

Termcap File. A file describing the capabilities of many different kinds of terminals. Commands like vi consult the termcap file to determine any special characters that might be used when interacting with your terminal.

Text Editor. A program that lets you create and modify *text files*. See also *Line Editor, Screen Editor,* and *Stream Editor.*

Text File. A file that contains readable text. Text files are broken into lines of text. Usually, these lines only contain "printable" characters: letters, digits, and punctuation characters. Contrast this with *binary files,* which often contain *control characters.*

UNIX. An operating system developed by AT&T Bell Labs.

Userid. A way of identifying a particular computer user. On UNIX, there are two types of userids: a user number (which is used internally to distinguish one user from another) and a user name (also known as a log-in name). Whenever you have to identify yourself to the computer (for example during *log in*), you enter your user name.

Utility. A standard command or program that accompanies an operating system. For example, every UNIX system has a cp command; cp is a standard utility program.

Variable. A name with an associated value. Variables are used to store information. When they are *exported* to other programs, they can pass the stored information on to those programs. The variables that the *shell* exports to another program are called the *environment variables* of that program.

Whitespace. A sequence of one or more spaces or horizontal tab characters. Whitespace is used to separate *arguments* on a *command line.*

Wildcard Construct. Another name for a *glob construct.*

Working Directory. Another name for your *current directory.*

X/Open. An international standard specifying requirements for UNIX-like *operating systems.*

Index

Symbols

A

D

E

F

G

J–K

L

M

N

Add to Your Sams Library Today with the Best Books for Programming, Operating Systems, and New Technologies

The easiest way to order is to pick up the phone and call

1-800-428-5331

between 9:00 a.m. and 5:00 p.m. EST.

For faster service please have your credit card available.

ISBN	Quantity	Description of Item	Unit Cost	Total Cost
0-672-30402-3		UNIX Unleashed (book/CD-ROM)	$39.95	
0-672-30464-3		Teach Yourself UNIX in a Week	$24.95	
0-672-30448-1		Teach Yourself C in 21 Days, Bestseller Edition	$24.95	
0-672-30339-6		Programming in ANSI C, Revised Edition	$29.95	
0-672-30194-6		The Waite Group's UNIX System V Primer, Second Edition	$29.95	
0-672-30373-6		On the Cutting Edge of Technology	$22.95	
0-672-30341-8		Absolute Beginner's Guide to C	$16.95	
0-672-30286-1		C Programmer's Guide to Serial Communications, Second Edition	$39.95	
0-672-30269-1		Absolute Beginner's Guide to Programming	$19.95	
0-672-22715-0		UNIX Applications Programming	$29.95	
0-672-30200-4		C++ Programming 101	$29.95	
		Shipping and Handling: See information below.		
		TOTAL		

❏ 3 ½" Disk

❏ 5 ¼" Disk

Shipping and Handling: $4.00 for the first book, and $1.75 for each additional book. Floppy disk: add $1.75 for shipping and handling. If you need to have it NOW, we can ship product to you in 24 hours for an additional charge of approximately $18.00, and you will receive your item overnight or in two days. Overseas shipping and handling adds $2.00 per book and $8.00 for up to three disks. Prices subject to change. Call for availability and pricing information on latest editions.

201 W. 103rd Street, Indianapolis, Indiana 46290

1-800-428-5331 — Orders   1-800-835-3202 — FAX   1-800-858-7674 — Customer Service

Book ISBN 0-672-30457-0

What's on the Disk

The disk contains MKS Tools, a collection of educational programs that simulate the UNIX environment under DOS, OS/2, or Windows NT.

Installing the Disk

Insert the disk in your floppy disk drive and follow these steps to install the software. You'll need at least one megabyte of free space on your hard drive.

1. Form the DOS prompt, change to the drive that contains the installation disk. For example, if the disk is in drive B:, type B: and press Enter.

2. Type INSTALL.

This will install all the files to a directory called C:\LU on your hard drive. For more information on the files, read Appendix G, "Installing the MKS Tools Package."

You must be using at least a 286 microprocessor and DOS Version 3.1 or greater to be able to use the MKS Tools software package.